THE EARLY BIBLICAL PERIOD

BENJAMIN MAZAR

THE EARLY BIBLICAL PERIOD
Historical Studies

Edited by
Shmuel Aḥituv and Baruch A. Levine

Israel Exploration Society
Jerusalem

This volume was published with the assistance of
The Dorot Foundation, New York, U.S.A.

ISBN 965-221-005-6

Editors: Shmuel Aḥituv and Baruch A. Levine
Assistant Editor: Janet Amitai
Copy Editor: Robert Amoils
Translators: Ruth and Elisheva Rigbi
Maps: Avraham Pladot

Typesetting and Printing: Ben-Zvi Printing Enterprises Ltd., Jerusalem
Plates: Tafsar, Jerusalem

The original place of publication of articles in this volume which have previously appeared in English is stated in the first footnote of the relevant articles.

Contents

Foreword

On the occasion of Prof. Mazar's 80th birthday, it is only appropriate to publish a collection of articles intended to illustrate the special brand of research which he pioneered and to which he devoted his academic career. All the articles in this volume are revised versions of previously published studies, the first of which appeared in 1945. Already in 1938, Benjamin Maisler (Mazar), in his publication *The History of Eretz-Israel* 1 (Hebrew), established the study of the Land of Israel and its early history, especially during the biblical period, as a scholarly discipline. He introduced a new interdisciplinary dimension to this field. His was a method of research which effected a synthesis between the history, archaeology, and historical-geography of the land. The data gleaned from the newly developing field of archaeology were always taken into consideration. Not only was the biblical text analyzed, but the epigraphic sources of the ancient Near East were also evaluated.

We hope that this volume of essays — some of which have not previously appeared in English — will serve to epitomize the progress made in studying the ancient history of Eretz-Israel during the past half century. In spite of the abundance of new evidence, Prof. Mazar's studies continue to be of great value, because they raise the basic questions and identify the central issues.

The movement known as *Wissenschaft des Judentums* was founded in the early 19th century with the aim of encompassing the entire history of the Jewish people, including the biblical period. The efforts of this ambitious research program, however, in reality tended to concentrate on post-biblical Judaism to the neglect of the earlier phases of Israelite-Jewish history. It was only in the early decades of this century, after the establishment of The Hebrew University of Jerusalem, that a group of scholars began to address the full potential of *Wissenschaft*. One of their leaders was Benjamin Mazar. Imbued with the progress achieved by such luminaries as W.F. Albright and Albrecht Alt, and stimulated by the reality of living on the soil of biblical Israel, the love of which pervades his very being, he mounted an intense intellectual effort aimed at recovering Israel's ancient past.

The wide range of inquiry characteristic of Prof. Mazar is also reflected in the articles comprising this volume. His study of the Middle Bronze Age in Canaan focuses on the material culture and ethnographic character of Canaan prior to the Israelite Settlement over a period of 700 years, in which many of the great biblical cities were established. The question of how the Israelite Settlement of Canaan actually occurred absorbs the energies of many archaeologists and historians. In an essay on the early Israelite Settlement in the hill country, Prof. Mazar relates to this problem.

In the study on the Book of Genesis, the biblical literary traditions are addressed in an attempt to identify the *Sitz-im-Leben* of the patriarchal narratives, so that this basic source might be better appreciated. Combining the insight of historical-geopraphy and ethnography with his keen sensistivity to literary composition and language, Prof. Mazar argues that the primary versions of the patriarchal narratives took shape in the early monarchic period.

The transition from tribal confederation to monarchy is highlighted in a study of David' military élite, those thirty-some heroes who fought at David's side supporting his rise to kingship. Further information on the establishment of social institutions at the beginning of the monarchy is revealed in the article on King David's scribe.

Three articles in this volume are clear examples of Prof. Mazar's historical-geographic outlook. The study on Lebo-hamath and the northern border of Canaan finally determined that this northern demarcation was an inheritance from the Egyptian province of Canaan in the 13th century B.C.E. Another article is devoted to the inheritance of the tribe of Dan. The Bible already indicated that the Danites did not succeed in expanding their original lot between Zorah and Eshtaol and were forced to seek territories in the north. Prof. Mazar illustrates that the description of the inheritance of Dan in the Book of Joshua dates from the time of Solomon. And in the third historical-geographic study, Prof. Mazar succeeds in awarding the petty but persistent kingdoms of the Golan, Geshur and Maachah, a real, if admittedly, minor place in ancient Near Eastern history.

The United Monarchy collapsed towards the end of the 10th century B.C.E. after the death of Solomon. It was not long before Pharaoh Shishak mounted an assault on the Land of Israel. Benjamin Mazar has succeeded in presenting the method by which the fragmentary Egyptian inscription recording Shishak's conquest should be read, and in so doing, presents us with a new picture of the campaign which conforms with the archaeological data and the biblical narrative.

Ancient epigraphy has always drawn the attention of Prof. Mazar, who realized its indispensability to the historian. By subjecting the Samaria Ostraca to careful study, he was able to date them to the reign of Jehoahaz, King of Israel. They were recorded at the end of the 9th century B.C.E. when the Arameans had been weakened by the power of the Assyrian ruler, Adadnirari III.

The high degree of continuity from earliest times to the period of the Second Temple and after is thus revealed by the method of Mazar's historical inquiry. In no article is this better demonstrated than in his discussion of Beth-sheʿarim, Gaba and Haroseth of the Peoples in historical perspective.

The peoples who occupied Eretz-Israel in the early biblical period — the Canaanites, Phoenicians, Philistines, Israelites and Arameans — were always of primary interest to Prof. Mazar, as evidenced by several of the essays in this volume. The language, religions, and military and political institutions of these peoples were viewed by him as influencing factors in the history of Israel in biblical times. The evolution of the Hebrew-Phoenician alphabet is also discussed from this point of view.

As some of the articles in this volume are revisions of studies previously published in English, we have not introduced conformity in the quotations taken from Bible translations.

Finally, we would like to express our appreciation to Joseph Aviram without whose encouragement and help we would not have been able to begin the work on this volume.

Jerusalem, July 1986

Shmuel Aḥituv
Baruch A. Levine

The Middle Bronze Age in Canaan

One of the longest and most obscure eras in the history and culture of Canaan was the Middle Bronze Age. Not without reason, the opinions of scholars have been divided on its nature and character, on its beginning and end and on its break-down into periods and phases; even up to this very day it is one of the most controversial topics in historical and archaeological research. Moreover, in the evaluation of the biblical tradition and the tracing of its historical kernel, there is much dispute over the theory that the beginnings of Hebrew history in the cycle of Patriarchal narratives in Genesis reflect a particular phase of this age, at least to some degree.

As archaeological research progresses it becomes more evident that the term "Middle Bronze Age", first introduced by Albright, is suitable for application to the whole era (including the so-called Early Bronze IV period) embracing the last quarter of the third millennium and approximately the first 450 years of the second millennium B.C.E. It is customary to divide this long era into periods, each of which is typified by specific and essentially divergent characteristics resulting from cultural and historical evolution, the causes of which can be learned from cuneiform sources, from Egyptian documents and, especially, from comparative archaeological material.

The beginning of the Middle Bronze Age dates from the downfall of the rich and highly developed Early Bronze Age civilization and its urban centres throughout the country. This was probably the result of the momentous upheavals throughout the western Fertile Crescent in the 23rd century B.C.E. The campaigns of the kings of Akkad, Sargon the Great and Narām-sin, to northern Syria and of the kings of the 6th Egyptian Dynasty to Palestine — which brought in their wake devastation of cities, oppression of the population and the uprooting of multitudes of people who were carried away captive from

* This study is a revised version of the article which appeared in *IEJ* 18 (1968), 65–97.

their homelands — certainly must have brought about the collapse of the political structure and the economic decline of these lands.[1] They were left open to incursions from Asia Minor and invasions by nomadic hordes who roamed the Syrian Desert and prowled along the border of the Fertile Crescent. Apparently, these were mainly the Amurrū ("Westerners") of the Akkadian sources (in Sumerian MAR.TU), nomadic and semi-nomadic tribes which grew in strength under the Akkadian dynasty.[2] The great-grandson of Sargon, Šar-kali-šarri, was forced to oppose them in battle at Basar (Jebel el-Bishri) in the middle Euphrates region, so as to prevent their mass penetration into Mesopotamia. These events in Hither Asia are probably closely connected with the weakening of the political regime in Egypt at the end of the Old Kingdom and its collapse in the Intermediate period, at which time Egypt was also subject to nomadic incursions from the east.[3]

1 For treatment of the documents from the Akkad Dynasty, see H. Hirsch, *AfO* 20 (1963), 1ff. For summaries, see G.J. Gadd, *CAH* 1, Part 2 (1971), 424ff.; and A. Malamat, *AS* (in honour of B. Landsberger) 16 (1965), 365ff. On the military campaigns of Pepi I, founder of the 6th Egyptian Dynasty, against the *ʿ3mw* in Canaan, we have an important testimony in the inscription of Uni describing the destruction of towns, the pillage of farms and the carrying away of prisoners to Egypt (*ANET*, 227–228). A 6th Dynasty date may also be given to the relief in the tomb of Anti at Deshasheh depicting the conquest of a fortified city; the accompanying inscription mentions the names of West Semitic cities conquered in Asia [W.M.F. Petrie, *Deshasheh* (1889), Pl. IV; see also W. Helck, *Die Beziehungen Aegyptens zu Vorderasien* (1962), 18ff.], and concerning the date, see H. Kees, *WZKM* 54 (1960), 99. Byblos developed commercial ties with Egypt as late as the reign of Pepi II, the last king of the 6th Dynasty (beginning of the 22nd century B.C.E.); these connections were broken at the beginning of the First Intermediate period and not renewed, apparently, until the reign of Mentuḥotep II.

2 On the Amurrū, cf. *Enc. Miq*. s.v. "ʾEmori"; D.O. Edzard, *Die zweite 'Zwischenzeit' Babyloniens* (1957), *passim*; S. Moscati: *I Predecessori d'Israele* (1956), 75ff.; J. Lewy, *HUCA* 32 (1961), 31ff. The origin of the term is apparently from a word meaning "west", which would indicate that the Land of Amurrū (MAR.TU) was the "western region", i.e. the territory between the Euphrates and the Mediterranean coast; the "Amorites" (Amurrū) were therefore the "Westerners", i.e. the population of Syria and the Syrian Desert in its broadest sense. The Amurrū (MAR.TU) appear in ancient cuneiform sources as foreigners without status in the local community; the implicaton here is that they were mainly Semitic nomads from the expanses west of the Euphrates, whose penetration into Mesopotamia endangered the sedentary population. See G. Buccellati, *The Amorites of the Ur III Period* (1966), *passim*; J. Bottero, *CAH* 1, Part 2, 562–563. For a description of the god Amurru who lived outside civilized society, cf. J.-R. Kupper, *Memoires de l'Academie Royale de Belgique, Classe de Lettres* 55, I (1961).

3 Cf. G. Posener, *CAH* 1, Part 2, 532ff. One may perhaps suggest that this wave of nomadic tribes came up against the military and political power of the kingdom of Akkad, guarding the gateways to Mesopotamia, and therefore its energy was diverted more forcefully to the lands of the western branch of the Fertile Crescent, from which it finally reached the Delta. Nevertheless, it is probable that even under the Akkadian Dynasty, and apparently also prior to it, many of them penetrated into Mesopotamia and became assimilated into its population.

I

In excavations and archaeological surveys, the Middle Bronze Age I (MB I),[4] which Illife and Kenyon have called the Intermediate Early Bronze–Middle Bronze period (EB–MB),[5] has emerged as a long chapter in the history of Canaan and adjacent regions. The society and culture of that era were dominated by nomads and semi-nomads, although on the Phoenician coast (e.g. Byblos) and in northern and central Syria [e.g. Tell Mardīkh and Hamath on the Orontes (period J)], some important settlements existed. The typical features of this age were the abundance and variety of individual burials (usually in shaft tombs and tumuli), often not in association with any permanent settlement, and a lack of homogeneity in the material culture of the various regions, mainly in the earlier stages. The latter found prominent expression in funerary typology and in ceramics; the pottery is strongly affected by influences which the successive waves of immigrants apparently brought from the north. Another new factor was the wide distribution of copper implements, especially weapons. These were probably the products of families of craftsmen who roamed across the entire Levant; their peregrinations may have taken them as far as the major metal-producing centres of Anatolia.[6]

4 See in particular W.F. Albright, *The Archaeology of Palesti* (1960), 3ff.; *idem*, *BASOR* 168 (1962), 36ff.; Ruth Amiran, *IEJ* 10 (1960), 104ff.; *idem*, *Ancient Pottery of the Holy Land* (1969), 78ff.; G.E. Wright, in *The Bible and the Ancient Near East* (G.E. Wright, ed.) (1961), 86ff. Concerning the problems related to Syria in this period, see C.F.A. Schaeffer, *Stratigaphie comparée et chronologie de l'Asie occidentale* (1948), *passim*; R.J. and L.J. Braidwood, *Excavations in the Plain of Antioch* 1 (1960), *passim*; and a review of the latter by Miriam Tadmor, *IEJ* 14 (1964), 264ff.

5 Cf. Kathleen M. Kenyon, *Excavations at Jericho* 1 (1960), 180ff.; *idem*, *CAH* 1, Part 2, 567ff. The term "Intermediate Bronze Age" was suggested by H.R. Smith.

6 Ruth Amiran distinguishes three "families" in the ceramic culture of this period (A, B and C). Albright seems to be correct in his opinion [*BASOR* 168 (1962), 37ff.] that "family A", the most widespread type in the mainly unfortified settlements such as Jericho, Beth-yeraḥ, Tell Beit Mirsim (levels H–I), Lachish and the Negeb settlements — which included the caliciform vessels, a type reflecting strong northern influence — is the latest and was in use till the end of the period. However, we still do not have sufficient data to divide MB I into phases such as MB IA (families B and C) and MB 1B (family A). In this regard, cf. Miriam Tadmor, *IEJ* 14 (1964), 267ff. An interesting problem relates to the highly developed copper industry on the coast, in particular at Byblos and Ugarit, and in the settlements of the Amuq (I–J) in MB I; cf. Kathleen Kenyon, *CAH* 1, Part 2, 583ff. It must be assumed that by this time copper was already being brought not only from Anatolia but also from Cyprus. Concerning the beginning of commerce between Cyprus and Canaan in the Middle Bronze Age, cf. Ruth Amiran, *EI* 5 (1959), 25ff. (Hebrew); H.J. Catling, *Cypriot Bronze Work in the Mycenaean World* (1964); *idem*, *CAH* 1, Part 2, 813. Concerning the ethnic background of the craftsmen, we have no evidence and many conjectures have been put forth about the origin of the immigrants who brought the metal industry and apparently a new cultural tradition with them; cf. P.W. Lapp, *The Dhahr Mirzbaneh Tombs* (1966), 97ff., and M. Kochavi, *The Settlements of the Negev in the Middle Bronze Age I* (Ph.D. diss., The Hebrew University of Jerusalem, 1967), Ch. 12 (Hebrew).

It would appear that transition to permanent settlement was slow, beginning with the establishment of unwalled villages by semi-nomads in the main regions of agriculture and pasturage on both sides of the Jordan River. With the passage of time, however, it gained momentum and took in more extensive areas outside the sown area until it reached the border of the wilderness. Most astonishing is the dense network of semi-nomadic settlements in the Negeb highlands during the later stage of MB I, surveyed and studied by Glueck and others.[7] It is possible to see in this phenomenon a consequence of the ceaseless wanderings by tribal groups and their struggles for control over the sources of sustenance. This movement produced an overflow of land-hungry people who spilled over from the agricultural regions into frontier districts. Settling in the arid regions, they tried to support themselves by sporadic agriculture, pastoral activity, hunting and manufacture of copper implements.

There is probably a cause-and-effect relationship between the complete destruction of these semi-nomadic settlements in the Negeb and Transjordan and their reversion to nomadic control, and the events which befell the ancient Near East in general in the second half of the 21st century B.C.E.: the reorganization of the Egyptian kingdom beginning with the reign of Mentuḥotep II of the 11th Dynasty (ca. 2060–2010B.C.E.), and the renewal of its political and economic activity towards the east;[8] the decline of the kingdom of Sumer and Akkad (the Third Dynasty of Ur), whose influence reached the Mediterranean coast (Byblos) at the peak of its prosperity; and, above all, the renewed migration of nomadic tribes, which left its stamp on Hither Asia and heralded a slow transition to a new period in the history and culture of the country, the Middle Bronze Age II.

7 See the surveys of Nelson Glueck in *BASOR*, beginning with 131 (1953) [bibliography in 152 (1958), 18, n. 1]. Cf. *idem*, *Rivers in the Desert* (1959), 60ff.; *idem*, *BASOR* 179 (1966), 6ff.; Y. Aharoni. *The Land of the Bible* (1966), 126–127. An instructive example of the MB I settlements in the Negeb is the site on Har Yeruham excavated by M. Kochavi [*IEJ* 13 (1963), 141ff.). Two distinct strata were distinguished here; the oldest level bore witness to settlers who brought with them the technical skills of building and pottery production and who supported themselves mainly by pastoral and seasonal agriculture, while the later stratum consisted of a camp occupied by nomadic shepherds and copper workers who lived in tents and built corrals for their flocks. Concerning the problems related to the settlements of this period in Transjordan, see in particular W.F. Albright, *BASOR* 95 (1944), 2ff.; and more recently (with reference to Bāb edh-Dhraᶜ) Lapp, *Dhahr Mirzbaneh Tombs* (see note 6), 94ff.

8 The political policy of Mentuḥotep not only found expression in military campaigns but also in the strengthening of the Egyptian defence line as a barrier facing nomadic tribes from the east, the renewed utilization of the mines in Sinai, and apparently also a renewal of the ties with the Lebanese coast [cf. G. Posener, *CAH* 1, Part 2, 535; W.A. Ward, *Orientalia* NS 30 (1961), 23ff.]. It seems most likely that Byblos renewed its commerce with Egypt after the break in relations with the kingdom of Ur in the reign of Šu-sin (2036–2027 B.C.E., according to the "middle" chronology). Concerning contacts between Ur and Byblos, see A. Malamat, *AS* 16 (1965), 373, n. 43; *idem*, *Western Galilee and the Coast of Galilee* (1965), 87ff. (Hebrew); J. Bottero, *CAH* 1, Part 2, 562ff.

II

In beginning the discussion of the earliest phase of the MB II, it is proper to emphasize that this period was marked by a complicated process of continued upheavals, entailing the occupation and subsequent urbanization of Canaan. It was coupled with the expansion of nomadic and semi-nomadic tribes speaking various West Semitic dialects,[9] whom Akkadian scribes continued to designate by the traditional and general term "Amurrū". Their inclusion within Mesopotamia in the 21st century B.C.E. is witnessed by documents from the reigns of the last kings of the Third Dynasty at Ur, Šu-sin and Ibbi-sin.[10] It culminated in their penetration deep into Mesopotamia and the establishment of "Amorite" kingdoms. One of these, the Old Babylonian kingdom founded by Sumuabum at the beginning of the 19th century B.C.E., reached the height of its power in the reign of Ḫammurapi (first half of the 18th century B.C.E.).[11]

An abundance of Akkadian texts, including the vast hoard of documents from the royal archives at Mari,[12] informs us about the personal names of the Amorites, their tribal and social organization, and their settlement in Mesopotamia. They included people who had already been assimilated into the Sumero-Akkadian culture and had formed a ruling class with drive and initiative in the political and cultural spheres. Others continued to follow a nomadic or semi-nomadic way of life and preserved their traditional, patriarchal tribal order. Moreover, from the Akkadian documents one may deduce that the

9 Cf. J.-R. Kupper, *Les nomades en Mesopotamie au temps des rois de Mari* (1957), *passim*; I.J. Gelb, *JCS* 15 (1961), 27ff.

10 Concerning the wall which was termed *muriq Tidnim* ("He who keeps [the tribes of] Tidnum at a distance"), which Šu-sin built against the invaders in the north-west of Babylon, and the wars of Šu-sin and Ibbi-sin with the Amurrū, cf. B. Maisler (Mazar), *Untersuchungen zur alten Geschichte Syriens und Palästinas* (1930), 17f.; C.J. Gadd. *CAH* 1, Part 2, 611ff.; W.W. Hallo, *JCS* 18 (1964), 74; A.L. Oppenheim, *Ancient Mesopotamia* (1964), 119. It is certainly no coincidence that similar fortifications ("the Wall of the Ruler") were erected by Amenemḥet I (1991–1962 B.C.E.), founder of the 12th Dynasty, on Egypt's eastern border. As recounted in the tale of Sinuhe, these fortifications were intended "to oppose the *ʿ3mw* and to crush the Sand-Crossers", also mentioned in the prophecy of Neferti.

11 In the present state of research, we prefer the "middle chronology" system adopted by Sidney Smith, as against the "high" chronology of Landsberger and Goetze, on the one hand, or the "low" system of Albright and Cornelius, on the other, even though the first is not without its difficulties. For a treatment of the whole complex problem, see, among others, S. Smith, *Alalakh and Chronology* (1940); W.F. Albright, *BASOR* 99 (1945), 9ff.; 144 (1956), 26ff.; 146 (1957), 26ff.; B. Landsberger, *JCS* 11 (1954), 31ff., 106ff.; V. F. Cornelius, *AfO* 17 (1956), 294ff.; A. Goetze, *BASOR* 146 (1957), 20ff.; *idem*, *JCS* 11 (1957), 53ff.; H. Lewy, *Melanges Isidore Lévy* (1955), 241ff.; M.B. Rowton, *JNES* 17 (1958), 97ff.; *idem*, *CAH* 1, Part 1 (1970) 193ff.; H. Tadmor, in B. Mazar (ed.), *The World History of the Jewish People*, 2: *Patriarchs* (1970), 63ff.

12 Cf. A. Malamat, *Enc. Miq.*, s.v. "Mari", and the bibliography listed there; F.M. Tocci, *La Siria nell'eta di Mari* (1960).

strong ties — ethnic, economic and religious — between the West Semitic elements in Mesopotamia and the people with whom they had ethnic affinities in the western Fertile Crescent did not cease. This fact serves to explain various phenomena, such as the similarity between personal, tribal and divine names of the West Semites in Mesopotamia and those in Canaan and Syria. These West Semitic tribes must certainly have played an important role in the international caravan trade, since they were in command of the principal lines of communication, as well as of the desert trails leading from Mesopotamia to Syria and thence on to Canaan and Egypt.[13]

From Egyptian sources we learn that during the 12th Dynasty (1991–1786 B.C.E.) political and economic ties between Egypt and the western Fertile Crescent gradually became stronger, reaching their peak in the later phase of that period. Another conclusion to be derived from Egyptian documents is that the social life of Canaan consisted of an interaction between the tribal-patriarchal order observed by the nomads and semi-nomads (who were still making their influence felt on the populace), and the system of city-state government which had begun to develop slowly under the 12th Dynasty, particularly in regions of permanent agriculture and at important strategic points along major trade routes and on the sea coast.[14]

13 Cf. the detailed treatment by W.F. Albright, *BASOR* 163 (1961), 38ff. Concerning the principal routes, see W.W. Hallo, *JCS* 17 (1964), 57ff.; and with regard to means of transport, see A. Dajani, *ADAJ* 8/9 (1964), 56ff. In this connection one should note the famous wall painting in the tomb of Khnum-ḥotep at Beni Hasan (ca. 1890 B.C.E.) depicting a caravan coming to Egypt with merchandise, implements [Albright, *Archaeology of Palestine* (see note 4), 207f.], weapons [Y. Yadin, *The Art of Warfare in Biblical Lands* 1, (1963), 59f.] and even a lyre for entertainment. The accompanying inscription explains that these are *ʿ3mw* bringing eye-paint to Egypt from the Land of the Šutu [concerning the reading, cf. *RHJE* 1 (1947), 60]. The entourage was headed by a certain Abišar who bore the title *ḥq3 ḫ3st* ("ruler of a foreign land"). The Šutu tribes (cf. Num 24:17, where the "sons of Seth" appear as a synonym of Moab) are referred to in the Execration Texts and are known to us from cuneiform sources (beginning in the reign of Rīm-sin of Larsa and especially in the Mari documents) as nomadic tribes in the region of the Euphrates, in the Syrian Desert and in the kingdom of Qaṭna in central Syria. Cf. Mazar, *Canaan and Israel*; J.-R. Kupper, *RA* 55 (1961), 197ff. One should also note that one Mari document speaks of the wanderings of the "sons of Iamin" from the Euphrates region to Yamḫad, Qaṭna and Amurru in north and central Syria. Cf. Kupper, *Les nomades en Mesopotamie* (note 9), 49, 179.

14 Very illuminating from this standpoint is the Sinuhe story from the reign of Senusert I, which shows that in the 20th century B.C.E. a patriarchal-tribal order was still in vogue in the Land of Retenu. The tale describes an influential ruler in Upper Retenu who maintained diplomatic relationships with the Egyptian court; it depicts a highly developed agriculture in the territory where Sinuhe had settled (*ʿi33*), apparently the Yarmuk region, to which Egyptian emissaries also came; cf. Mazar, *Canaan and Israel*, 20. Byblos is also mentioned in this tale as a well-known maritime city. The fact should be stressed that at various sites in Israel (Tell el-ʿAjjul, Gezer, Lachish, Beth-shean), scarabs of Senusert I have been discovered, while in Ugarit a pectoral bearing the cartouche of the same pharaoh was also found [Schaeffer, *Stratigaphie comparée et chronologie* (see note 4), 25; W.A Ward; *Orientalia* 30 (1961), 38ff.). On the other hand, scarabs such as these remained in use over long periods and thus far-reaching conclusions should not be drawn from

Nevertheless, it is important to note that in spite of the great progress in archaeological research in Israel and the data available from Egypt, the beginning and the growth of the MB IIA culture, which is clearly distinguished from the culture of the previous period, remain an enigma. It is particularly characterized by an ever-increasing process of urbanization, first and foremost in the coastal region and its adjacent districts, a strengthening of political and economic ties with 12th Dynasty Egypt, and development of extensive commercial relations both by sea and by land.[15] Various discoveries, especially the Montet jar and its rich artifacts from Byblos (probably from about 2000 B.C.E.) and the eṭ-Ṭōd treasure found in the foundations of a temple of Amenemḥet II (1929–1895 B.C.E.), most of the contents of which apparently derive from one of the maritime centres on the Syrian coast,[16] witness not only a great advance in craftsmanship and commerce, but also connections with Mesopotamia and the Minoan cultural sphere in the 20th century B.C.E. Thus, it is probable that the process of building fortified cities on sites which had previously known only open villages had already begun, particularly at strategic points on important highway junctions. An instructive example of this is the fortress city of level XIIIA at Megiddo, built on the ruins of the open village of level XIIIB.[17]

them. A special problem arises from the stele of Nesumont from the 24th year of Amenemḥet I, which alludes to a military campaign against the *ʿ3mw* and to the destruction of their fortresses; cf. G. Posener, *CAH* 1, Part 2, 539f.

15 W.F. Albright [*BASOR* 176 (1962), 49ff., and in R.W. Ehrich (ed.), *Chronologies in Old World Archaeology* (1965), 54ff.] is now inclined to lower the dates of MB IIA approximately in the 18th century B.C.E., that is, later than what he had formerly suggested (1850–1750 B.C.E.). This determination is based on his latest system, but in view of various archaeological and historical data presently available, we find this difficult to accept.

16 The treasure contains luxury items (especially silver bowls of Minoan type), ornaments, bars of silver and gold, and lapis lazuli, including cylinder seals of various periods — prior to the Old Babylonian period — some of them bearing cuneiform inscriptions. Cf. F. Bisson de la Roque et al., *Le Trésor de Tod* (1953). Concerning the problems associated with this collection, see H. Kantor, in Ehrich, *Chronologies* (note 15), 11f. On the Montet jar from Byblos and its contents, see O. Tufnell and W.A. Ward, *Syria* 43 (1966), 165ff., according to whom the jar should be dated between 2130 and 2040 B.C.E.

17 A complicated problem arises from levels XV–XIII at Megiddo and the dates of the temples at that site. Cf. Kathleen M. Kenyon *EI* 5 (1959), 51ff.* Dame Kenyon assigned level XV, including the three temples in the sacred area, to MB I. On the other hand, I. Dunayevsky and A. Kempinski have proposed — with good stratigraphical reason — that these temples be assigned to the Early Bronze Age. The only evidence to indicate that there was an MB I settlement, apparently semi-nomadic, at this spot is ceramic and not architectural. Level XIVA dates to the beginning of MB IIA when an unwalled settlement had sprung up around the temenos which contained a chapel (in place of the other temple, No. 4040) and a "high place" [4009 — G. Loud, *Megiddo* (1948), Figs. 189f., 396]. This settlement continued to exist during the subsequent period (level XIIIB). Especially important for chronology is the double-eyed axehead from MB IIA [found on the northern wall of chapel 4040 and belonging to level XIVA; cf. Y. Yadin, *Warfare in Biblical Lands* (note 13), 168], and particularly the finds discovered on "high place" 4009, including a

However, the development of the towns in Canaan and the intensification of direct Egyptian influence in Western Asia, both political and cultural, found their fullest expression only in the reign of Senusert III (1878–1843 B.C.E.), a time when the imperialistic aspirations of Egypt had become the dominant factor in the region. From this standpoint the sphinxes and statuettes of Egyptian kings and officials, which have been found in sites along the Via Maris [Megiddo, Gezer, Beth-Eglaim (Tell el-ʿAjjul)] and on the Syrian coast (Ugarit, Byblos, Beirut), and even in the interior of Syria (Qaṭna) and more distant regions, are most illuminating.[18] The statuette of Tuthḥotep, a high-ranking official in the service of Amenemḥet II and Senusert III, and also the fragments of other Egyptian objects found at Megiddo, provide evidence that that city served as an Egyptian stronghold in the middle and in the second half of the 19th century B.C.E. The remains discovered in stratum XII were apparently those of this fortress.[19] It is also probable that Senusert III and his successors dominated a number of fortified towns along the major highway and on the coast. From this standpoint, the Egyptian artifacts discovered at Tell el-ʿAjjul and at Gezer, and especially in the great maritime centres of Ugarit and Byblos, are instructive. It would seem that Abi-šemu and Yapaʿ-šemu-abi, two rulers of Byblos, whose richly furnished tombs have been discovered in the royal cemetery of that harbour city, were actually vassals of both Amenemḥet III and IV.[20] To this we may add the testimony of Khu-

double-headed Minoan axe and a "lamp" of a type common in the Nahariya temple from MB II (cf. *Megiddo* 2, Pl. 16: 8–16, 18 and 21; also Pl. 182: 7 — as pointed out to me by A. Kempinski). It seems probable, therefore, that during the course of MB IIA (perhaps during the reign of Amenemḥet II) the settlements had developed from undefended towns to cities surrounded by walls with "offsets and insets" (level XIIIA in area BB; cf. *Megiddo* 2, Fig. 397), cities in which many houses were built around the sacred area, which continued to preserve the sacred tradition of a chapel and a "high place". Concerning the later phase of MB IIA (level XII), see below.

18 Cf. W.A Ward, *Orientalia* 30 (1961), 129ff. The earliest of these is apparently that of the daughter of Amenemḥet II discovered at Qaṭna. Cf. du Mesnil du Buisson, *Syria* 9 (1928), Pl. XII. A contemporary Egyptian statuette was discovered at Jiʿarā, a site on one of the secondary routes leading from Megiddo to the Sharon; cf. R. Giveon, *Yediot* 27 (1963), 293ff. (Hebrew).

19 Cf. G. Loud, *Megiddo 2: Seasons of 1935–39* (1948), Pls. 265f.; J.A. Wilson, *AJSL* 58 (1941), 225ff. According to the inscription from his tomb in Deir el-Barsha, Tuthḥotep played an official administrative role with regard to the import of cattle from Retenu (cf. G. Posener, *CAH* 1, Part 2, 544f.). The finds at Megiddo include the scarab of an Egyptian official found in level XII; cf. G. Loud, *Megiddo* 2, Pl. 149:32; see also C. Watzinger, *Tell el-Mutesellim* 2 (1929), 13.

20 Concerning the royal cemetery in general, and the tombs of Abi-šemu (II) and Yapi-šemu-abi (I?) in particular, see P. Montet, *Byblos et l'Égypt* (1939), 143ff.; M. Dunand, *Fouilles de Byblos* 1 (1939), 197ff.; and W.F. Albright, *BASOR* 176 (1964), 38ff.; 179 (1965), 38ff. A major problem is raised by the Egyptian inscriptions from Byblos discovered by Dunand and published by P. Montet [*Kemi* 17 (1964), 61ff.], from which we learn about another king from Byblos named Abi-šemu and his sons Yapaʿ-šemu-abi and *ʿkr* (or *ʿk3i*, "Egla"?). Montet is undecided on their date, while Albright suggests bringing them down to the end of the 18th century B.C.E. and identifying Abi-šemu with the king known as Abi in two inscriptions in Tomb XI. But in view of the finds in Tomb XI,

sebek's inscription concerning the military campaign of Senusert III against the *ʿ3mw* in Retenu and his conquest of the hill country around Shechem, probably with the aim of expanding the sphere of Egyptian political influence in the regions along the Via Maris.[21]

An illuminating picture may be derived from the earliest Execration Texts, which can be dated to the end of the period under discussion. At that time Egyptian political influence was beginning to decline, although Egypt still remained in control of Byblos and the key points along the coastal plain.[22] In the list of countries and cities in Canaan and on the Syrian coast which the Egyptians viewed as rebels and belligerent foes, very few Canaanite city-states mentioned can be identified with certainty: Ashkelon, Jerusalem and Rehob (*ʿ3ḥbw*).[23] It is logical to assume that in MB IIA these towns were fortified

and on the basis of the names of the rulers, one must assume that Abi-šemu and his son Yapaʿ-šemu-abi lived before Abi-šemu, the father of Yapi-šemu-abi and that they were contemporary with Senusert III. Another, albeit less likely, possibility is that they lived during the period between Yapi-šemu-abi and Yakin-el. The first assumption requires the following order for the kings of Byblos:

Abi-šemu I (Ab) — Tomb VIII?	Reign of Senusert III (and
Yapaʿ-šemu-abi — Tomb XI	Amenemḥet III)
Abi-šemu II — Tomb II	Reign of Amenemḥet III and IV
Yapi-šemu-abi — Tomb I	
Yakin-el — ?	Reign of Seḥetepibre II

Cf. also K.A. Kitchen, *Orientalia* 36 (1967), 39 ff.

21 Cf. J.E. Peet, *The Stela of Sebek-khu* (1914); J.A. Wilson, in *ANET*, 230. The inscription speaks of a district called Shechem (*skm3m*, written in a manner similar to that of the Execration Texts), probably a political entity of which the centre was evidently the city Shechem; compare *māt Šakmi*, "the land of Shechem" in EA 289:21ff.; "Mount Shechem" in Papyrus Anastasi I; and also the title of Shechem son of Hamor, "prince of the land" (*nᵉśī haʾareṣ* — Gen 34:2). To this period one may date the oldest fortress at Shechem (called "Temenos 2" by the excavators), which was surrounded by outer wall D (on the north-west) and by wall 900 (on the south-east), which separated the fortress from the residential quarters of the city; G.E. Wright, *Shechem* (1965), Fig. 63, 110ff.; 237, n. 3; and also S.H. Horn, *Jaarberict 'Ex Oriente Lux'* 18 (1965), 299. The collection of weapons, including a double-eyed axehead discovered at Shechem [cf. C. Watzinger, *Denkmäler Palästinas* 2 (1933), Pls. 24–25], must certainly be from this same period.

22 Cf K. Sethe, *Die Ächtung feindicher Fürsten, Völker...* (1926). It is generally accepted that this earlier group is from the mid-19th century B.C.E. or, what is more likely, from the second half of this century. Cf. W. F. Albright, *BASOR* 81 (1941), 16ff.; *idem*, in G.E. Wright (ed.), *The Bible and the Ancient Near East* (1961), 233; G. Posener, *CAH* 1, Part 2, 543; A. Alt, *Kleine Schriften* (1959), 59ff.; Mazar, *Canaan and Israel*, 42. Concerning a collection of Execration Texts of the type discovered at Mirgissa in Nubia, cf. S.J. Vercoutter, *Kush* 12 (1964), 61; and G. Posener, *Syria* 43 (1966), 277ff. In disagreement with the majority of scholars, W.F. Edgerson [*JAOS* 50 (1940), 492] proposed to date them to the 13th Dynasty. Cf. also W.A. Ward, *Orientalia* NS 30 (1961), 141ff. It seems to us that various historical and archaeological factors require that the early collection of Execration Texts be dated to the end of the 12th Dynasty, perhaps to the reigns of Amenemḥet III and IV. In any case it is clear that between it and the later group (see below), which I am inclined to date to the reign of Neferḥotep (third quarter of the 18th century B.C.E.), there was a considerable lapse of time.

23 Concerning *ʾs3n* in the two groups and its identification with Beth-shean, see Mazar, *Cities and Districts*, 217. For an opposing view, see S. Yeivin, in *The Beth-shean Valley* (1962), 21–22(Hebrew).

city-states. But during the time of the earlier Execration Texts, it is almost certain that the process of urbanization had not reached great proportions, especially in the regions far removed from the coast and the major highways.[24] Furthermore, an interesting fact emerges from these documents: the number of rulers in the city-states and ethnic-political units was not fixed (sometimes being three or even four), with only one at ʿIrqata and two each at Rehob and Jerusalem. This would indicate that, even in the settled areas, the tribal-patriarchal order remained in force and that the city-state regime with a single ruler typical of MB IIB had not yet completely crystallized.

III

At same the time, archaeological research indicates that the period under discussion witnessed a great cultural development, particularly in its later phase. This progress is deeply felt at Byblos, where the prevailing conditions favoured extensive maritime commerce as well as trade with cities along the major trade routes, especially those serving as Egyptian strongholds. Thus, the fortifications at Megiddo and Gezer testify to well-planned construction and great technical ability.[25] The same holds true for smaller sites, such as Tell Beit Mirsim in the Shephelah (levels F and G) and Tel Poleg and Tel Zeror in the Sharon plain,[26] as well as Shechem and Jerusalem in the mountains. The Megiddo excavations show that from the reign of Senusert III to the period of the 13th Dynasty it was an important fortified town (stratum XII), outstanding not only for its mighty wall (twice as thick as that of the previous settlement, in level XIIIA) and well-fortified gate with an indirect entry, but also for its great palace erected on the western side of the temenos, around which stood very large buildings.

24 It is possible to assume that the important fortified towns along the main lines of communication (e.g. Megiddo and Gezer) do not appear in the lists of hostile cities and groups because they were strongholds of Egyptian rule. Cf. Mazar, *Canaan and Israel*, 45. With regard to Byblos, see also G. Posener, *CAH* 1, Part 2, 548.

25 Cf. G. Loud, *Megiddo* 2, 6ff., 84ff., Figs. 378, 397–398; and also the survey by S. and E. Yeivin, in J. Liver (ed.), *The Military History of the Land of Israel in Biblical Times* (1964), 370ff. (Hebrew). The suggestion of I. Dunayevsky and A. Kempinski is probably correct: the latest stage of MB IIA is represented at Megiddo by level XII in area BB and by level XIII in area AA, while level XII in area AA (Loud, *Megiddo* 2, Fig. 378) really belongs to the beginning of MB IIB, so that the latter should be redesignated as level XIB. With regard to Gezer, it is important to note the results of the trial excavations carried out there [W.G. Dever, *BA* 30 (1967), 55f.], which have provided some confirmation for the conclusions reached by Macalister [*Excavations at Gezer* (1912), 311ff., 339ff.], that in this period Gezer was a fortified town, probably an Egyptian stronghold.

26 Concerning Tell Beit Mirsim, see W.F. Albright, *AASOR* 17 (1938), 17ff. For the discoveries at Tel Poleg and Tel Zeror, see *RB* 72 (1965), 548ff.; M. Kochavi and K. Ohata, *Tel Zeror* (1966), 28.

Information about the sacred areas in this country has been derived from the excavations at Byblos, Megiddo and Nahariya, and apparently also at Gezer (the "High Place"). It seems likely that the tradition of a temenos, containing a chapel or small temple and an unroofed "high place" surrounded by an enclosure wall, was generally preserved from the beginning of the Middle Bronze Age down to the end of MB IIB; except that during this particular period — in the second half of the 19th century B.C.E. — attention was already being paid to the erection of an elaborate entryway and service quarters. The practice of setting up stelae in the "high place" area had by now become common and votive objects were being placed there in abundance.[27]

No less worthy of attention is the perfection in the ceramic industry during MB IIA, which bears witness to an upsurge in cultural development. It is characterized by advances in technique: the extensive use of the potter's wheel, the attractive shapes of the vessels (including the carinated bowls) and the excellent wheel-combing, red slip, high burnishing and beautifully coloured ornamentation.[28]

Most notable are the vessels with painted decorations resembling a style prevalent in the Khabur region, especially at Chagar Bazar (evidently ancient Ašnakum), where it began during the reign of Šamši-adad I, King of Assyria.[29] Decorated vessels of this type have been found only in a few sites in Israel — Geba-shemen (Tell ʿAmr), Aphek in the Sharon (Ras el-ʿAin) and Gezer — and even these only in tombs; similar decorations also appear on vessels in a few places in the north, such as Byblos and Qaṭna. These vessels have aroused a great deal of interest. The historical background of this style is as yet controversial, but most likely it was closely connected with the painted and decorated pottery which developed in northern Syria and the adjacent regions of Anatolia. It is not impossible that its origin was in northern Syria, and that from there it spread first to the south and then to the Khabur region, where it was applied to local forms.[30]

Another ceramic type worthy of attention is the Tell el-Yehudiyeh ware, which had already begun to appear late in this period. However, its exten-

27 G. Loud, *Megiddo* 2, 90, Figs. 206–207; M. Dunand. *Fouilles de Byblos* 2 (1958), Fig. 767; *idem, Atlas* (1950), Pl. XXIII. For the temple at Nahariya, see M. Dothan, in *Western Galilee and the Coast of Galilee* (1965), 63ff. (Hebrew); *idem*, *IEJ* 6 (1956), 14ff.

28 Cf. in particular Amiran, *Ancient Pottery* (note 4), 80ff.; Kathleen M. Kenyon, *Archaeology in the Holy Land* (2nd. ed., 1965), 162ff. Concerning the pottery of Beth-eglaim (Tell el-ʿAjjul), see O. Tufnell, *Bulletin of the University of London Institute of Archaeology* 3 (1962), 1ff.

29 Cf. the survey of the excavations at Chagar Bazar by M.E.L. Mallowan [*Iraq* 3 (1936); 4 (1937); 9 (1947)].

30 Cf. Amiran, *Ancient Pottery* (note 4), 113ff.; A.L. Perkins, in Ehrlich, *Chronologies* (note 15), 50f.; in particular, see the detailed discussion by B. Hrouda, *Die bemalte Keramik des 2. Jahrtausends in Nord-Mesopotamien und Nordsyrien* (1957), and O. Tufnell and W.A. Ward, *Syria* 43 (1966), 165ff.

Ceramic vessels with painted decoration resembling a style prevalent in the Khabur region [Ruth Amiran, *Ancient Pottery of the Holy Land* (1969), Fig. 35]

sive dissemination — particularly of the pear-shaped juglets, black or dark brown in colour with a peculiar dotted pattern filled with white — took place in MB IIB.[31] The form of the juglet and its use as a container for perfume provide the basis for the conjecture that the source of these "Tell el-Yehudiyeh" vessels was actually in the Jordan Valley and the adjacent regions (one of the principal centres for production of expensive perfumes).[32] From there they were distributed via commercial land and sea routes to Ugarit and Cyprus, on the one hand, and Upper Egypt and Nubia, on the other. The appearance of this type in Canaanite pottery in MB IIA is certainly not without historical and cultural significance.

But with this we have already reached the beginning of a new development in Syria and Canaan which heralds the dawn of another period: the Middle Bronze Age IIB.

31 Cf. in particular Ruth Amiran, *IEJ* 7 (1957), 93ff.

32 It was not without cause that perfumes and ointments brought renown to the Plain of Jericho and particularly to the Plains of Moab and other districts of the Jordan Valley along the eastern bank of the river which were reckoned with the Land of Gilead (Gen 37:25 etc.). It is not impossible that this was the most important source of income of the inhabitants of that heavily populated district; cf. also Mazar, *Canaan and Israel*, 35f. It is noteworthy that in groups I–V of the Jericho Tombs, which are mostly from MB IIB, there is an abundance of perfume juglets including many of the "Tell el-Yehudiyeh" type. One may perhaps interpret the two black burnished juglets from Tomb K-III [which date to MB IIA; cf. Kathleen M. Kenyon, *Excavations at Jericho* 2 (1965), 203f., Fig. 93] as the prototype of the "Tell el-Yehudiyeh" ware. By way of conjecture, the ornamentation might be considered an attempt to represent the flora from which the perfume was derived.

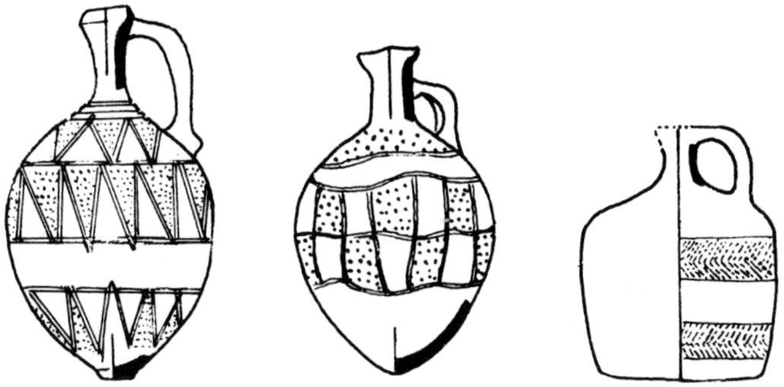

Tell el-Yehudiyeh ware [Ruth Amiran, *Ancient Pottery of the Holy Land* (1969), Fig. 36]

IV

The last quarter of the 19th century B.C.E. was characterized by an increase in the strength of the West Semitic dynasties and competition between them for hegemony in Mesopotamia and northern and central Syria. These competitors were Yamḫad in northern Syria and Mari on the Euphrates. In a foundation inscription from the Shamash temple at Mari, Yaḫdun-lim son of Yagid-lim, founder of the dynasty, boasts of a military campaign to the Mediterranean coast in order to fell trees in the Lebanon and to impose his authority on the coastal towns. Sometime after this the West Semitic ruler of Assyria, Šamši-adad I son of Ilu-kabkabu, began the consolidation and expansion of his powerful kingdom in Mesopotamia. Šamši-adad also conducted a campaign of conquest in Syria and set up a victory stele in the Land of Laban (Mount Lebanon) on the coast.[33]

During this period events occurred which determined the fate of Syria and Canaan for many generations to come. Šamši-adad gained control of Mari and appointed his son, Yasmaḫ-adad, as his viceroy there (1795 B.C.E.). Qaṭna in central Syria, whose ruler Išḫi-adad acknowledged the hegemony of Assyria, became an important city-state.[34] During his reign, commercial activity was also renewed at Kanis and other Assyrian colonies (*kārū*) in Anatolia, particularly at Ḫattuša.[35] As a consequence of these events in the political and economic spheres, the ties between the West Semitic kingdoms in the Fertile Cres-

33 Cf. in detail A. Malamat, *AS* 16 (1965), 370ff.; J.-R. Kupper, *CAH* 2, Part 7 (1973), 1ff.

34 One of several indications in this regard is the fact that Šamši-adad stationed a garrison at Qaṭna and married his son, Yasmaḫ-adad, to the daughter of Isḫi-adad, King of Qaṭna. Cf. J.-R. Kupper, *CAH* 2, Part 7 (1973), 21ff.

35 Note in particular K. Balkan, *Observations on the Chronological Problems of the Kārum Kanish* (1955), 43ff.; H. Otten, *MDOG* 89 (1956), 68ff.

cent were strengthened and commerce grew between Mesopotamia on the one hand, and Anatolia, Syria, Canaan and the Mediterranean coast, on the other. Furthermore, the Akkadian language was adopted as the commercial and diplomatic *lingua franca* and, above all, there came about an extensive urbanization, i.e. the rapid growth of urban centres throughout the Levant. These developments are evidenced by the Mari documents from the reign of Šamši-adad I and the period immediately following his death (1780 B.C.E.), when rivalry between the various West Semitic kingdoms over the political and economic hegemony was renewed with even greater intensity. This competition was particularly keen after the return to power of Zimri-lim son of Yaḫdun-lim, at Mari (1772 B.C.E.), with the aid of his ally and father-in-law Yarim-lim, King of Yamḫad. It continued until the conquest of Mari by Ḫammurapi, King of Babylon (1760 B.C.E.).

An interesting picture of the political fragmentation that prevailed before Ḫammurapi may be derived from a letter sent by one of Zimri-lim's officials:

> There is no king strong by himself; ten or fifteen kings follow Ḫammurapi of Babylon; about the same number follow Rim-sin from Larsa; likewise after Ibalpiel of Ešnunna; likewise after Amutpiel of Qaṭna; twenty kings follow Yarim-lim of Yamḫad.[36]

During the reign of Zimri-lim, Yamḫad and Qaṭna were probably the strongest kingdoms in Syria, and the allies of Yarim-lim and Amutpiel included many rulers of royal cities and smaller states. From the Mari documents and other contemporary sources, we know of two other countries south of Qaṭna: Amurru, a large territory destined to play an important role in the political affairs of a later era,[37] and Āpum, the Damascus region, through which passed the main caravan routes from Mesopotamia and from Syria to the Land of Canaan.[38] However, special prominence was without doubt enjoyed by Hazor, mentioned several times along with Yamḫad and Qaṭna as an independent city-state. It had established diplomatic and commercial ties with Mari and Babylon probably during the last years of Zimri-lim's reign.[39] At the same time commerce flourished between Mari and the two great maritime cities Ugarit and Byblos.[40]

36 Cf. G. Dossin, *Syria* 19 (1938), 117; J.M. Munn-Rankin, *Iraq* 18 (1956), 68ff.

37 Particularly striking is the fact that in one Mari document, Amurru is alluded to as a horse-producing country; B. Landsberger, *JCS* 8 (1954), 56; I.J. Gelb, *JCS* 15 (1961), 41ff.

38 Concerning Āpum, cf. W.F. Albright, *BASOR* 33 (1941), 30ff.

39 Cf. especially A. Malamat, *JBL* 89 (1960), 12ff. During the reign of Zimri-lim a certain Ibni-adad reigned at Hazor; this is probably the West Semitic name Yabnî-hadad in its Akkadian form. For the name Ishme-ilam, inscribed in cuneiform on the shoulder of a jar discovered at Hazor, see A. Malamat and P. Artzi, in Y. Yadin et al., *Hazor* 2 (1960), 116–117.

40 Cf. Tocci, *La Siria nell'eta di Mari* (note 13), *passim*.

To this picture we must add the important fact that Egypt had declined as a political force in Asia. This process seems to have begun during the conquest of Šamši-adad I and the spread of his influence westward. From the time of the accession of the 13th Dynasty (1786 B.C.E.), Egypt had become weak internally and its status in Canaan and on the Syrian coast had become more and more shaky. Among the causes for this were the multitudes of West Semites migrating from Canaan and the frontier to the Delta region, and the arrival of an increasing number of mercenaries and slaves in Egypt[41] — an unceasing movement which reached major proportions at the end of the 18th century B.C.E., at which time West Semitic tribes gained control of Lower Egypt. The chieftains of these tribes were denoted by the Egyptians by the title *ḥq3 ḫ3swt*, "ruler of foreign lands". It is worthwhile to recall that the sources stress the Asiatic origin of some of the Egyptian rulers of the 13th Dynasty and even their predecessors.[42] Concommitantly, there is no doubt that under certain political conditions some of them were able to restore to Egypt a measure of relative influence in Canaan and on the Syrian coast. One of these rulers, Seḥetepibre II (ca. 1770 B.C.E.), still held sway over Byblos as evidenced by a cylinder seal on which the ruler of Byblos, Yakin-ilu, is described as his servant (i.e. vassal). From the middle through the third quarter of the 18th century B.C.E., Neferḥotep I undoubtedly enjoyed a strong position as indicated by a bas-relief in which he is depicted with the local ruler, ʾEntin, seated before him in obedience.[43] ʾEntin is almost certainly identical with Yantin-ḫammu (Yantin-ʿammu), the ruler of Byblos, who sent a vessel of gold to Zimri-lim, King of Mari.[44]

With this period we may also associate the later group of Execration

41 For this problem, see W.F. Albright, *JAOS* 74 (1955), 222ff.

42 W.C. Hayes, *CAH* 2, Part 1 (1973), 47–48.

43 Cf. Dunand, *Fouilles de Byblos* (note 20), Pl. XXX. Concerning Neferḥotep I, cf. W.C. Hayes, *CAH* 2, Part 1 (1973), 51ff.

44 This identification was proposed by W.F. Albright, *BASOR* 77 (1940), 27; 99 (1945), 9ff.; he thus indirectly established a synchronism between Babylon and Egypt which created some chronological difficulties. Yantin-ʿammu ruled at Byblos during the reign of Zimri-lim at Mari and Ḫammurapi at Babylon, and when Neferḥotep I ascended the throne in Egypt [according to Albright and others, ca. 1740 B.C.E., and according to Säve-Söderbergh, *JEA* 37 (1951), 54, ca. 1750 B.C.E.], Yantin-ʿammu transferred his allegiance to this pharoah, perhaps as a consequence of the developments in Syria during the reign of Samsu-iluna, Ḫammurapi's successor. In connection with this synchronism, Albright's conjecture is interesting: Yantin-ʿammu was the son of Yakin-ilu, a contemporary of Seḥetepibre II (1770 B.C.E.), a view based on the attempt to reconstruct the inscription and to read his father's name as *y-k-n* (a shortened form of Yakin-ilu[m]; cf. W.F. Albright, *BASOR* 99 (1945), 11; 176 (1962), 39ff. The important status of Yantin-ʿammu on the Syrian coast is also evidenced by a fragment of an alabaster vessel and scarabs bearing his name and title ("ruler of Byblos", and also "ruler of the rulers"). One of these scarabs was found at Qalʿat er-Rūs, 25 km south of Ugarit.

Texts,[45] which differs from the earlier in several respects. These texts, written on clay figurines in the form of kneeling foreign captives, include a long list of districts and city-states in the Land of Canaan, southern Syria and on the Syrian coast; that is, in the territories to the west and south of the kingdom of Qaṭna. Above all, the later Execration Texts are different in the type of political system they reflect: in each of the city-states or principalities there was usually only one ruler; in a few rare instances, the heads of ethnic groups are mentioned (particularly from the frontier areas), or an urban aristocracy is sometimes hinted at.

In everything pertaining to the West Semitic kingdoms in Syria and Mesopotamia the general picture is, therefore, the same as that derived from the Mari archives. It is worthy of note that the overwhelming majority of the names of the kings are derived from the West Semitic onomasticon also known to us in the documents from Chagar Bazar, Mari and Alalakh (level VII).[46] Likewise, it should be stressed that among the theophoric names in the earlier Execration Texts the divine name Hadad is not found at all, while in the later group, it appears frequently as an element in various combinations. The origin of this phenomenon dates from the period when the West Semitic kingdoms were flourishing, i.e. it goes back to the end of the 19th century B.C.E. It was then that the West Semitic storm-god, Haddu (Hadad — identical to the Akkadian Adad), whose cult was centred at Aleppo, the capital of Yamḫad, assumed a position of prime importance in the Semitic pantheon. His name consequently began to serve as an element in many compound personal appellations.[47]

The later Execration Texts bear witness to the considerable progress which had taken place in the urbanization of Canaan and adjacent regions, as well as the rise of governmental centres, in the 18th century B.C.E. Besides a number

45 Cf. G. Posener, *Princes et pays d'Asie et de Nubie* (1940); Mazar, *Canaan and Israel*, 20ff. and the bibliography cited there, 21, n. 30; G. Posener, *CAH* 1, Part 2, 557; Helck, *Die Beziehungen Aegyptens* (see note 1), 49ff.

46 Cf., among others, A. Goetze, *JSS* 4 (1959), 144f.; I.J. Gelb, *JCS* 15 (1961), 33ff.; and H.B. Huffmon; *Amorite Personal Names in the Mari Texts* (1965).

47 Concerning the deity Hadad and his cult centre at Aleppo, cf. H. Klengel, *JCS* 19 (1965), 88f. It is certainly no coincidence that Šamši-adad I and his two sons bear names which include the element Adad (= Hadad). Compare the names of Išḫi-adad from Qaṭna, Ibni-adad (the Akkadian form of the West Semitic name Yabnî-hadad) from Hazor, ʿIbšddw from Shechem and those of five other rulers mentioned in the later Execration Texts. The name of the ruler of *ʾs3n* (Beth-shean?), i.e. *Nqmwpʿi*, is also illuminating; it is identical with the name of the founder of the dynasty at Yamḫad spelled Niqmepuḫ in syllabic cuneiform (and *nqmpʿ* in Ugaritic script). It is not impossible that Aleppo, the capital of the mighty kingdom of Yamḫad and the home of the magnificent temple to Hadad, had exercised special political, economic and religious influence not only over the adjacent regions in north Syria and Mesopotamia, but also in the whole Levant; this influence may have increased during the 18th century B.C.E.

One of the Execration Texts written on a clay figurine (18th century B.C.E.) (Institut Royal du Patrimoine artistique, Brussels)

of districts and names of cities for which the identification is doubtful, or whose parallels in other sources are lacking, we find a long list of well-known urban centres on the Phoenician coast, in southern Syria (south of the kingdom of Qaṭna), in the Land of Canaan and in northern Transjordan. The sites within the boundaries of Canaan include, among others: Ijon, Laish, Hazor, ʿAkko, Achshaph, Mishal, Aphek, Shamʿūna (Simonias), Piḥilum (Pella), Ashtaroth and Shechem,[48] as well as Rehob, Jerusalem and Ashkelon, which also appear in the earlier Execration Texts; the majority of these places were also city-states in the Late Bronze Age.

The historical and cultural situation in the country is reflected in the abundant archaeological evidence from MB IIB pertaining to every phase of life. First and foremost, we are presented with an astonishing picture of vigorous development in the construction of political centres and fortified towns throughout the land. In several regions — particularly in the valleys, on the coast and in the Shephelah — these were of great density. At various places in Syria and Canaan, both on sites long occupied and on those that had not previously been settled, mighty ramparts, topped by brick walls, and various types of *terre pisée* ramps on the slopes of tells, are typical for this period. One may assume that during the reign of Šamši-adad I all the West Semitic kingdoms had begun to adopt this method of defence. There may be some connection between the great profusion of this type of fortification and the adoption of the battering ram and siege tower, inasmuch as we have specific testimony to both in the Mari documents.[49]

It is illuminating that the discoveries from MB IIB at Carchemish, Qaṭna and Hazor (all major political centres in Syria and Canaan mentioned in the Mari texts) reveal an essentially identical picture: a large urban centre with an upper city on the area of the tell proper, including the ruler's fortified palace, and an extensive lower city, rectangular in shape. The lower city was attached to the upper fortress and protected by mighty ramparts. The excavations at Hazor are most informative on this point.[50] One may say confidently that the lower city with its strong fortifications was founded in an early stage of MB IIB, perhaps one generation before Hazor reached the degree of political and economic prosperity evidenced by the Mari texts (from the end of Zimri-lim's reign, ca. 1765–1760 B.C.E.). It is not impossible that Hazor had

48 Cf. especially Mazar, *Canaan and Israel*, 20.

49 Cf. Y. Yadin, *BASOR* 137 (1955), 23ff. (who includes a list of the sites where fortifications of this type have been found). In recent years ramparts of *terre pisée* have been found in additional tells, such as Tel Nagila, Jaffa, Achzib, etc., and even at Khirbet el-ʿOrme (biblical Arumah) south-west of Shechem.

50 Cf. Y. Yadin et al., *Hazor* 1 (1958), 1–3, 74–75.

Tel Hazor; an aerial photograph from the north [Y. Yadin, *Hazor* 1 (1958), Frontispiece]

already been built in the days of Šamši-adad I when Qaṭna rose to the status of a major political centre in Syria (1795–1785 B.C.E.).[51]

To this age one may also assign the establishment of towns surrounded by ramps of *terre pisée*, such as those mentioned together with Hazor in the later Execration Texts: Laish (Tell el-Qāḍi), Achshaph (apparently Tell Keisan), Rehob (Tell eṣ-Ṣarem) and Shechem (Tell Balāṭah). A good example of this type is at Tell eṣ-Ṣaliḥīyeh about 15 km east of Damascus where this type of fortification was discovered with the remains of a brick wall on top.[52] This city was probably an important centre in the land of Āpum, known from the Mari

51 As mentioned above, this was also the time of decline in the 12th Dynasty (1786 B.C.E.). It must be assumed that about one generation passed before the construction of the fortifications was completed and until Hazor had reached the high level of prosperity in the reign of Ibni-adad (Yabnî-hadad) witnessed to by the Mari documents [concerning Hazor in the Mari texts, cf. A. Malamat, *JBL* 89 (1960), 1ff.]. It is worthy of note that in the earlier Execration Texts Hazor is not mentioned at all; this corresponds to the fact that in the lower city comparatively few remains from MB IIA have been found. As for the later Execration Texts, the ruler of Hazor bears the name *Gṯ3i* [Posener, *d'Asie et de Nubie* (see note 45), E 15], probably one of the successors of Ibni-adad, and perhaps the founder of a new dynasty at this major centre.

52 Cf. H.H. Von der Osten, *Svenska Syrienexpeditionen, 1952/3 I, Tell eṣ-Ṣaliḥiye* (1956). For the rampart at Khan Sheikūn, cf. du Mesnil du Buisson, *Syria* 13 (1932), 171ff.

archives and perhaps the foremost city of northern Āpum referred to in the Execration Texts. There can be no doubt that this defence system was in vogue for a long time — until the second half of the 17th century B.C.E.[53]

Furthermore, an illuminating picture has emerged from an attempt to clarify the stratigraphy of Megiddo. It has become quite clear that the fortifications of MB IIB were constructed in two phases, XIB and XIA. Both are typified by a sloping rampart and a gate of the direct-entry type, instead of the previous indirect type. In this period the large palace to the east of the sacred area was also erected. In the temenos itself on the other hand, only minor changes were made, such as the scrapping of the gateway with its angular opening on the north, and the erection of many stelae on the "high place" to the south of the chapel.[54]

From all that has been said above, one may conclude that at the beginning of MB IIB (early 18th century B.C.E.), urbanization was steadily on the increase, commensurate with the development of government by a single ruler in each fortified town. Political and economic ties became increasingly stronger between these local rulers and the West Semitic kings reigning over Syria and

53 Three occupation levels were apparently associated with the rampart at Tell eṣ-Ṣaliḥiyeh: XIIB, XIIA and XI. As for Shechem, Wright is of the opinion that the rampart and supporting wall C are to be associated with temenoi 4–5; cf. Wright, *Shechem* (note 21), 62ff. However, it seems more likely that the rampart was constructed at the time of temenos 3, when wall D ceased to serve within the defences of the city and many changes were taking place in the structure of the citadel (*ibid.*, Fig. 64). Further, it would seem that this rampart, and likewise the citadel wall N. 900, which divided the citadel from the city, were added in levels 3–5 (*ibid.*, Figs. 64, 66 and 70). Should it prove that MB IIB pottery was already present in phase 2 (*ibid.*, 230, 237, n. 3), there will be some basis for assuming that the rampart was built during the second quarter of the 18th century B.C.E. The rampart at Jericho, which has not yet been sufficiently clarified as to its construction, is of great importance [cf. Kenyon, *Archaeology in the Holy Land* (note 28), 177ff]. It may be assumed that it was erected during an early phase of MB IIB at a time when Jericho was an important fortified town, though in the preceding period it had apparently been an unwalled settlement. In view of the abundant material discovered in the cemeteries and published so thoroughly in the report [Kathleen M. Kenyon, *Excavations of Jericho* 1 (1960); 2 (1965)], it is possible to assume with a great degree of certainty that the five tomb groups from MB II (I–V) with their rich assemblage of artifacts, including many Egyptian scarabs from the 13th–15th Dynasties and "Syrian" cylinder seals from the 18th–17th centuries B.C.E., belong essentially to MB IIB, and are contemporary with the rampart, which resembles those at Hazor and other sites mentioned above. The *terre pisée* fortification at Tell Beit Mirsim was assigned by Albright to two occupation levels (E1 and E2), while the rampart at Tel Nagila probably has two or three related strata [cf. Ruth Amiran and A. Eitan, *Yediot* 28 (1964), 196 (Hebrew)].

54 Cf. G. Loud, *Megiddo* 2, Figs. 206–207. Analysis of the stratigraphic situation at Megiddo by I. Dunayevsky and A. Kempinski led to the conclusion that the level in area AA which the Chicago Chicago excavators designated as XII (*ibid.*, Fig. 378:2) is in fact the earliest stage of level XI, since the level in that same area, which they called XI (*ibid.*, Fig. 379), is the latest phase of that stratum, and since these two phases in area AA parallel stratum XI in area BB (*ibid.*, Fig. 399). The transition from stratum XII to stratum XI apparently took place in the second half of the 18th century B.C.E.

Mesopotamia. In every cultural sphere strong northern influence is felt, including the early dissemination of the Akkadian language, written in cuneiform, along with Old Babylonian cylinder seals. In contrast, the political influence of Egypt was weakened towards the end of the 12th Dynasty, even though during the 13th Dynasty its contacts with the Land of Canaan and the Phoenician coast continued, especially at Byblos.

It is important to note that in the Mari documents Egypt is never mentioned at all. Of course, from time to time during the reigns of strong monarchs such as Neferḥotep I, its influence was strengthened, but in general Egypt is characterized during the 18th century B.C.E. by the disintegration of its central authority and an unceasing influx of multitudes of West Semites into the land of the Nile. Already at the beginning of the 13th Dynasty foreign rulers had risen to power, while by the end of the 18th century B.C.E. the West Semitic element in Egypt had gained decisive proportions. Thus, a new chapter was opened in Egyptian history, viz. the "Hyksos" age. This term, which was used by Manetho, is certainly derived from the Egyptian designation *ḥq3 ḫ3swt* ("ruler of foreign lands"), which served to denote rulers of the Asian countries during the Middle Kingdom. In the Second Intermediate period it came to be applied also to the foreign rulers in Egypt. It is not our intention here to discuss the many problems associated with the Hyksos era in Egypt. We shall confine ourselves to several observations directly pertaining to the history of the Land of Canaan and its culture in that period.[55]

From the standpoint of chronology, special significance is attached to the "Stele of the Year 400" of Ramesses II discovered at Ṣan el-Ḥagar. The text on this stele describes the coming to Tanis of Seti I, father of Ramesses II, in the capacity of vizir for Haremheb in order to celebrate a festival commemorating the 400th anniversary of the inauguration of the Seth cult in that place.[56] This date (ca. 1730 B.C.E.) must indicate the founding of Hyksos rule at Tanis, and this same event is most likely alluded to in the Bible (Num 13:22). From the meagre data, one may deduce with some degree of certainty that, during the early phase of this particular period, Lower Egypt was under the control of West Semitic rulers such as ʿAnat-har and Yaʿqub-har, and perhaps also *Ššy* and *Bbnm*, whose sphere of authority was relatively limited. To this period may be attributed the giant camps at Tell el-Yehudiyeh and

55 Among the extensive literature on the Hyksos, the following are especially worthy of note: R. M. Engberg, *The Hyksos Reconsidered* (1939); H. Stock, *Studien zur Geschichte und Archäologie der 13. bis 17. Dynastien Ägyptens* (1942); H.E. Winlock, *The Rise and Fall of the Middle Kingdom in Thebes* (1947); F. Säve-Söderbergh, *JEA* 37 (1951), 53ff.; Alt, *Kleine Schriften* (see note 22), 49ff.; Helck, *Die Beziehungen Aegyptens* (see note 1), 92ff.; W.C. Hayes, *CAH* 2, Part 1, 54 ff. (and the bibliography cited there on pp. 726–728); and J. Van Seters, *The Hyksos: A New Investigation* (1966).

56 Cf. W.C. Hayes, *CAH* 2, Part 1, 50, and H. Goedicke, *Chronique d'Égypte* 41 (1966), 23ff.

Heliopolis, fortified with mighty ramparts of *terre pisée* similar to the type discussed above.[57]

We have no evidence concerning the degree to which the events taking place in Egypt affected the political and economic situation in the Land of Canaan and Syria. One may assume that the immigrants who succeeded in gaining a foothold in the land of the Nile and establishing their principalities there maintained strong ties with the population of their homeland, since they were closely related to one another ethnically. They must have cooperated with them — to an even greater degree than under the 13th Dynasty — in the economic exploitation of Egypt. This found expression in the unceasing stream of Egyptian products that flowed into Canaan during MB IIB, as is evidenced by the richly furnished tombs discovered at Jericho and other sites. It is possible that the wealth of Egypt reached Canaan not only by way of reciprocal trade but also was brought by the marauding bands that were raiding and plundering the Nile valley.

In this period, the Land of Canaan enjoyed economic prosperity accompanying vigorous progress in urbanization. Improved craftsmanship is clearly demonstrated by the pottery repertoire which attained new heights in technique and in the adoption of foreign influences, especially from Syria. It would seem that political events towards the end of the 18th century and the beginning of the 17th century B.C.E. brought tremendous upheavals and the partial destruction of various cities, including even the decline of Byblos as a centre of maritime commerce with Egypt.[58] It is also noteworthy that at this time Yamḫad was achieving a very strong position: Abbael, son of Ḫammurapi II, King of Yamḫad (a contemporary of his namesake at Babylon), established his younger brother Yarim-lim on the royal throne of Alalakh, the principal city of the land of the Orontes. In his reign and those of his successors, Alalakh

57 Published by F. Petrie, *Hyksos and Israelite Cities* (1906), 3ff., Pl. IV. For the conjecture by H. Ricke [*ZA* 71 (1935), 270ff.; 72 (1936), 79], cf. Y. Yadin, *BASOR* 137 (1955), 25, n. 20. But see G.E.R. Wright, *ZDPV* 84 (1968), 1–17.

58 To this period one may assign the transition from level E2 to level E1 at Tell Beit Mirsim, the destruction of temenos 4 at Shechem, and also partial destructions that took place in MB IIA at other sites in Israel. With regard to Byblos, it seems that the important harbour city, which in the reigns of the successors to Neferḥotep I was still under Egyptian control [concerning the cylinder seal of Ḥasrūrum, a contemporary of Si-ḥatḥor, cf. H. Goedicke, *MDAIK* 19 (1963), 1ff.; W.F. Albright, *BASOR* 176 (1962), 44f.], had declined towards the end of the 18th century B.C.E., which fact is striking in the temples and royal tombs. See Ora Negbi and S. Moskowitz, *BASOR* 184 (1966), 21ff. (and also Albright's remarks, *ibid*., 26ff., in which he expresses a different opinion). This harmonizes with the testimony of the "Lamentations of Ipu-wer" on the cessation of maritime contacts between Egypt and Byblos. It is noteworthy that J. Van Seters, *JEA* 50 (1964), 13ff. [and following him W.F. Albright, *BASOR* 179 (1965), 40f.] assigns this literary source to the beginning of the Hyksos period. Now one may conjecture that this development at Byblos was a result of the declining power of Egypt and perhaps it was influenced by some occurrence associated with the expansion of the kingdom of Yamḫad, an event which remains entirely obscure.

became a prosperous city-state, albeit subservient to the king of Yamḫad (Alalakh level VII).[59] From the royal archive at Alalakh and the testimony of Ḫattušili I, King of Ḫatti, we learn of the independence enjoyed by "the great kingdom" of Aleppo until the military campaigns of Ḫattušili, and about the great influence that it exercised on political and economic life in Syria.[60]

On the other hand, it is still impossible to delineate the connection between this development in northern Syria and the rise of the 15th "Hyksos" Dynasty at Memphis in Egypt in the first quarter of the 17th century (ca. 1685 B.C.E.). According to Manetho, its founder was Salitis, during whose reign and those of his successors the "Hyksos" kingdom gained in strength and territory. There are many conjectures about Salitis and the other kings of the 15th Dynasty,[61] but the fact remains that only two kings listed by Manetho can be identified with any degree of certainty: Iannes, who is evidently none other than Ḫyān, and Apophis who can be identified, it would seem, with ʿAuserre ʿApopi (I). It is especially striking that during the reign of Ḫyān (who apparently ruled in the last third of the 17th century B.C.E.)[62] the foreign ruling

59 Alalakh was fortified in the contemporary style, that is, with a surrounding rampart of *terre pisée*, while the gate had a broad and straight entryway with piers on either side narrowing its central axis down to little more than the width of a chariot. Typical of this period are both the great palace (in which the royal archive was discovered) and the temple beside it. Concerning level VII at Alalakh, cf. L. Woolley, *Alalakh — An Account of the Excavations at Tell Atchana 1937–1949* (1955); *idem*, *A Forgotten Kingdom* (1953), 66ff. For the chronology of the kings of Yamḫad, cf. M.B. Rowton, *CAH* 1, Part 1 (1970), 210f.

60 Worthy of special attention is the date on one of the documents, relating to an important event that took place during the reign of Ammitaqum, King of Alalakh, and Yarim-lim, King of Yamḫad: "The year in which Yarim-lim defeated Qaṭna". Cf. D.J. Wiseman, in D. Winton Thomas, *Archaeology and OT Study* (1967), 121. It is surely no coincidence that from the end of the 18th century (or the beginning of the 17th century B.C.E.) there was a ruling dynasty at Ugarit consisting of kings with names typical of the contemporary royal family at Yamḫad. In this regard, note a cylinder seal of Old Babylonian style mentioning a king of Ugarit called Yaqarum son of Niqmaddu [J. Nougayrol, *Palais royal d'Ugarit* 3 (1955), xli; C.F.A. Schaeffer, *Ugaritica* 3 (1956), 66ff.]. And compare the remarks above on the spread of the Hadad cult.

61 Cf. W.C. Hayes, *CAH* 2, Part 1, 19ff. It is difficult to accept Hayes' suggestion that the name Salitis represents a corrupt form of the name of the Hyksos king *śrk* (*ślk*). Cf. A.H. Gardiner, *Egypt of the Pharaohs* (1961), 158ff. W.F. Albright [*BASOR* 146 (1957), 30f.] considers the possibility of identifying Salitis with Zālūt/di, a leader of the *Ummān manda* who was, according to a Boghazköy text, an ally of the king of Aleppo in his war against the king of Ḫatti [H. Otten, *MDOG* 86 (1953), 60]. But the Hittite king referred to is none other than Ḫattušili I, and between these two there is a considerable time gap. Furthermore, there is no evidence for the assumption that the kings of the 15th Dynasty were of Indo-Iranian origin, although their ethnic identification does raise many problems.

62 Various dates have been proposed for the years of Ḫyān's reign: W.F. Albright [*BASOR* 99 (1945), 17] suggests that he reigned from 1605 to 1580 B.C.E.; W. Helck [*MDAIK* 17 (1961), 110; cf. also P. Aström, *Remarks on Middle Minoan Chronology* (1963), 147] is of the opinion that he reigned in ca. 1600 B.C.E., while Winlock [*The Middle Kingdom in Thebes* (see note 55), 99] moves him back to 1644–1604 B.C.E. In view of the fact that Ḫyān preceded Apophis I (at least according to

caste made its influence felt in the cultural life of Egypt; it even succeeded in expanding its political and economic power in very great measure both in Egypt and outside of it. The decline of the kingdom of Yamḫad during the reign of Ḫattušili I may have assisted in this development. Concerning Egypt's extensive international relations during this period, one finds evidence in the luxury items bearing the name of Ḫyān that have been unearthed in places as far removed as Babylon, Knossos and Hattusa.[63] Against this background it becomes understandable why in the last phase of Alalakh VII — on the eve of the city's destruction by Ḫattušili I — there was an abundance of artifacts in the Syro-Egyptian style (in particular, seals).[64] The situation finds further intensive expression in the dissemination of many Egyptian cultural objects in mounds in Eretz-Israel.

V

In the third quarter of the 17th century B.C.E. the political position of the West Semitic kingdoms in Hither Asia began to deteriorate; the heavy pressure exerted by non-Semitic peoples from the east and north became steadily stronger. Foremost among these were the Hurrians and the Kassites. From the Mari period on, the Hurrians had gradually spread across northern Mesopotamia and the territory north of Yamḫad; by the middle of the 17th century B.C.E. they had already become a formidable military and political force.[65] Kassite incursions, apparently from the north, into the Babylonian kingdom had begun as early as the reign of Samsu-iluna, son of Ḫammurapi, and with each passing generation their influence gained in momentum. Another important force was the Hittite kingdom which rose to the status of a great power under Ḫattušili I (third quarter of the 17th century B.C.E.) who invaded the Hurrian kingdom and Yamḫad, and conquered Alalakh.[66] His successor, Muršili I, followed in his footsteps and destroyed Yamḫad, "the great kingdom" of Aleppo. Muršili even succeeded in bringing an end to the West Semitic

Manetho), who reigned for some forty years, until the rise of Kamose (cf. W.C. Hayes, *CAH* 2, Part 1, 63ff.), it can be deduced that he lived in the last third of the 17th century B.C.E.

63 Cf. H. Stock, *MDOG* 94 (1963), 73ff. The obsidian vessel bearing Ḫyān's name may have reached Ḫattuša along with the booty that Muršili I took at Aleppo. Concerning the scarabs of Ḫyān from Gezer and Tell eṣ-Ṣāfi, cf. R. Giveon, *JEA* 51 (1965), 202ff.

64 Cf. in particular H. Kantor, *JNES* 15 (1956), 158ff.; W.F. Albright, *BASOR* 146 (1957), 29f.

65 Cf. E.A. Speiser, *Cahiers d'histoire mondiale* I, 2 (1953), 311ff.; I.J. Gelb, *Hurrians and Subarians* (1944), *passim*; R.T. O'Callaghan, *Aram Naharaim* (1948), 37ff.; J.-R. Kupper, *CAH* 2, Part 1 (1973), 24ff., 38ff.; H. Schmökel, *Geschichte des alten Vorderasiens* (1957), 154ff.; J. Laesse, *People of Ancient Assyria* (1963), 150ff.

66 For the campaigns of Ḫattušili and Muršili, cf. O. R. Gurney, *CAH* 2, Part 1, 243ff.

kingdom of Ḫana (which also had a Kassite substratum) on the middle Euphrates, as well as to the West Semitic dynasty of Babylon (ca. 1595 B.C.E.).[67]

As a consequence of these events a complete change was effected in the ethnic and political geography of the ancient Near East. After the collapse of the West Semitic kingdoms, the Kassites overran southern Mesopotamia and established a strong kingdom which endured for a considerable period of time. By this time the process of invasion of northern Mesopotamia and northern Syria by Hurrian elements had probably reached its peak, along with their penetration into middle and southern Syria and also Canaan. In these events a considerable role was evidently played by Indo-Iranians whose earliest appearance in the historical arena of the Fertile Crescent is apparently heralded by allusions to the hordes of *manda* (*Ummān manda*) led by Zālūt/di. They were allied with the Hurrians and the kingdom of Yamḫad in their war against Ḫattušili I. They seem also to be referred to in connection with the war of Ammiṣadūqa, King of Babylon, against the *manda*.[68]

At this time no political or military force was able to repulse the Hittite armies or to halt the waves of foreign invaders storming into Syria. It seems likely that during the long reign of Apophis I, who succeeded Ḫyān, Hyksos control in Egypt gradually declined. Radical convulsions in Western Asia and the disintegration of the political and social order in Egypt itself led to the downfall of the foreign rule and the rise of the 17th Dynasty in Thebes. Seqenenre II, and especially his son Kamose, not only threw off the yoke of the monarchs at Tanis, but also succeeded in maintaining active hostilities against them. This resurgence culminated in the conquest of Avaris by Aḥmose, founder of the 18th Dynasty (ca. 1560 B.C.E.). Thus was opened a new chapter in Egyptian history, viz. the era of the New Kingdom.[69] Probably with the levelling off of the influx of peoples, political life in northern Mesopotamia began to crystallize, a process which culminated in the establishment of the Hurrian-Indo-Iranian kingdom of Mitanni, perhaps by Sutarna the son of Kirta (in the middle of the 16th century B.C.E.).

67 Concerning the developments and the chronological problems, cf. *ibid*.; M.B. Rowton, *CAH* 1, Part 1, 233.

68 With regard to this problem, cf. H. Otten, *MDOG* 86 (1953), 59ff.; B. Landsberger, *JCS* 8 (1954), 58; W.F. Albright, *BASOR* 146 (1957), 31; and also O'Callaghan, *Aram Naharaim* (see note 65), 56ff.; J. Nougayrol, *RA* 44 (1950), 12ff.

69 On the uncertainty of development at this time in Egypt, cf. W.C. Hayes, *CAH* 2, Part 1, 64ff. On chronological problem, cf. Helck, *Die Beziehungen Aegyptens* (see note 1), 97ff.; W.F. Albright, *BASOR* 176 (1964), 44; and J. von Beckerath. *Untersuchungen zur politischen Geschichte der 2. Zwischenzeit in Ägypten* (1964), 218ff. Helck, Albright, Nims [*Thebes of the Pharaohs* (1965), 199, n. 2], and others adopt the "low" chronology for the kings of the 18th Dynasty, about which we can be somewhat sceptical. Cf. M.B. Rowton, *CAH* 1, Ch. VI; Tadmor, in *History of the Jewish People* (see note 11), 84ff.; E. Hornung, *Untersuchungen zur Chronologie und Geschichte des Neuen Reiches* (1964).

As a result of this historical development, peoples of different origin, language and culture began to settle down in Syria and Canaan. The Hurrians and the Indo-Iranian elements accompanying them, with additional immigrants from Anatolia, overpowered the West Semitic population in the great majority of the territories in Syria and Canaan;[70] and they became a ruling caste whose strength lay in its command of the battle chariot and the strongly fortified cities. It did not matter at first that the conquering class gradually succumbed to the influences of the local inhabitants and was assimilated by them. This military nobility, which in later sources bore the Indo-Iranian title of *maryannū*,[71] became the basic element in the new military-political order. The *maryannū* maintained their semi-feudal regime for many generations over an ethnically and socially fragmented population, in spite of what had occurred in the political arena and in the social life of Hither Asia.

VI

The stirring events that took place in the second half of the 17th century and the beginning of the 16th century B.C.E. left their imprint upon the cultural life of all of Mesopotamia and Syria. At sites excavated in Eretz-Israel, this particular period is well represented by the destruction of cities and their revival, as well as by notable changes in many aspects of life. Archaeologists have come to the conclusion that the culture of the country permits the distinguishing of two sub-periods, MB IIB and MB IIC,[72] although they have not clarified sufficiently the historical background to this distinction. In fact the MB IIC period is still a problematic topic in the archaeology of Eretz-Israel, though there is no longer doubt that this transitional stage from the Middle to the Late Bronze Age was a most important chapter in the history of the country. Among the innovations appearing in MB IIC, the most noteworthy is the system of fortification which replaced the *terre pisée* ram-

70 It would seem that the Phoenician coast was less affected by the decisive upheaval and the influx of foreign ethnic elements than was the interior; cf. Mazar, *Cities and Districts*, 251. This was also the case, and even more so, in the desert regions and the frontier areas bordering on them, where tribes of West Semitic nomads and semi-nomads continued to wander.

71 Cf. R.T. O'Callaghan, *JKF* 1 (1951), 309ff. Though the *maryannū* are mentioned for the first time in Egyptian documents and in the epigraphic material from Alalakh (level IV) dating from the 15th century B.C.E., there is little doubt that this class became crystallized in Syria and Eretz-Israel long before that, even though the lack of documents from the 16th century B.C.E. prevents us from tracing the beginning of its establishment.

72 Cf. Albright, *Archaeology of Palestine* (see note 4), 84. Albright later [*BASOR* 176 (1964), 44] proposed that the dates of MB IIC be lowered (level D at Tell Beit Mirsim) to ca. 1575–1500 B.C.E. in accordance with his new chronology, in which "all stratified deposits of MB should be re-dated"; cf. above, note 69.

parts: massive walls of large, unhewn stones arranged in straight courses, the level top of which served as the base for a mud-brick upper structure. Particularly illuminating is the mighty "Cyclopean wall" (A) of Shechem, contemporary with "Temenos 6", which was preserved to a height of 10 m,[73] and also the sloping rampart of level D at Tell Beit Mirsim, which was of a similar nature.[74] The origin of this method of defence was apparently in eastern Anatolia.[75]

The "Cyclopean" walls found at sites such as Bethel, Beth-zur, Beth-shemesh (level V) and Lachish (levels VIII–VII)[76] show that in MB IIC there was a great upsurge in the construction of large fortresses in the hill country and the Shephelah. There is practically no doubt that these works were connected with the semi-feudal regime that brought to power the new ethnic elements in the country. An important detail in those fortifications was the strong gate with a straight entryway through a covered passage. The roof of the passage was supported by piers, three on each side, which narrowed it down to the width required for the passage of a chariot, thereby forming three successive gates. This type of gate, which had apparently come into use already in the 17th century (Alalakh VII), became the standard for the fortified towns of Canaan. It is a verification that horses and the battle chariot were used by the military aristocracy.[77]

Another important innovation which came into use in Canaan during MB IIC was the fortified temple or — as we have suggested calling it — the "migdal"-temple.[78] The most instructive example of this type is that discovered in the citadel at Shechem, a solid, rectangular building with a single long hall within its very thick walls. In front of the building was a fortified gate protected by two towers and entered from a spacious courtyard. On the basis of stratigraphic investigations, one may deduce with certainty that the building was erected in MB IIC (Temenos 6), which makes it contemporary with the "Cyclopean wall".[79] The temple uncovered in Area BB at Megiddo (2048),

73 Cf. Wright, *Shechem* (see note 21), 57ff., Figs. 13 and 20.

74 Cf. W.F. Albright, *AASOR* 17 (1938), 27ff.

75 Cf. M. I. Maksimova, *JNES* 10 (1951), 77; Y. Yadin, *BASOR* 137 (1955), 26; Albright, *Archaeology of Palestine* (see note 4), 88f. This type of fortification may have been adopted during the reign of Hattušili I, later becoming more widespread.

76 Concerning the fortifications of Beth-zur, cf. R.W. Funk, *BASOR* 150 (1958), 10–12; and for Lachish, cf. O. Tufnell, *Lachish 4: The Bronze Age* (1958), 48.

77 Yadin, *Warfare in Biblical Lands* (see note 13), 68–69. The Egyptians were already using the battle chariot in the reign of Kamose; cf. M. Hammand, *Chronique d'Égypte* 30 (1955), 207; L. Habachi, *ASAE* 53 (1955), 195ff.

78 B. Mazar, *Enc. Miq.* 4, 635–636.

79 Concerning the earliest phase of the temple discovered at Shechem, cf. L.E. Toombs and G.E. Wright, *BASOR* 161 (1961), 32ff.; Wright, *Shechem* (see note 21), 87ff., Fig. 41.

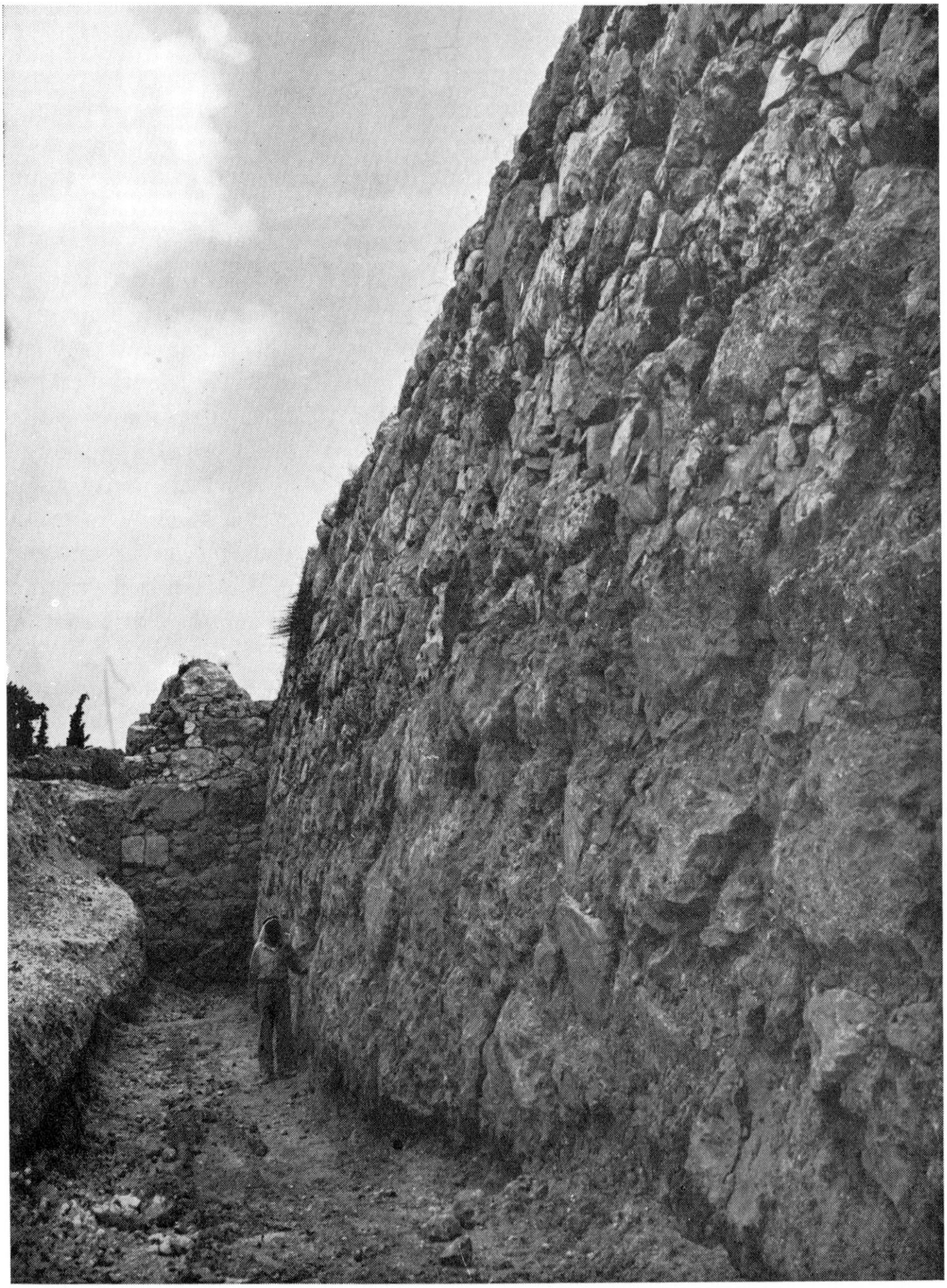

The MB IIC Cyclopean wall at Shechem

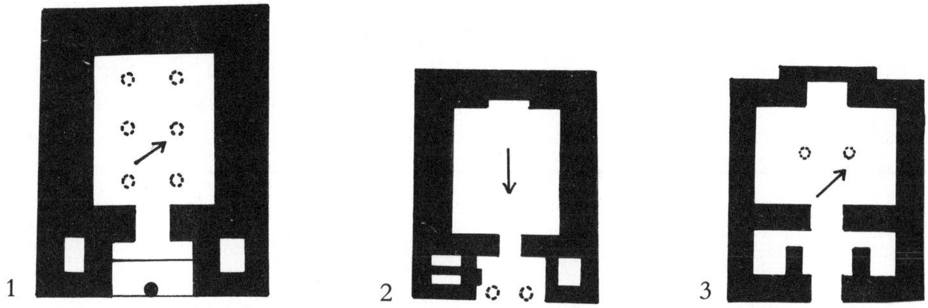

Plans of MB IIC "migdal-temples": 1) Shechem (Temenos 6); 2) Megiddo (2048); and 3) Hazor (stratum XVI in the Upper City)

which was also erected in the MB IIC (level X),[80] is very similar. Equally noteworthy are two rows of pillars supporting the roof of the central hall, and also the niche in the back wall, opposite the entryway, where the statue of the deity once stood. But the special feature of these two buildings was the existence of one or more additional storeys, access to which was gained by a flight of stairs within one of the towers. It is also important that both of the temples continued to exist throughout the entire Late Bronze Age (it is possible to discern various stages of repair in both of them) and that they were destroyed at the end of the 12th century B.C.E. The rather dilapidated temple at Shechem, which represented its last phase of existence, may have been none other than the "temple of Baal-berith" mentioned in the story of Abimelech.[81]

The temple discovered in level 3 in area H of the lower city at Hazor (MB IIC; stratum XVI in the upper city) resembles in plan and style both the Shechem and Megiddo temples, except that it does not have a long hall but rather a broadroom. Its later development is also different from that of the other two temples, and it would seem that it had already been destroyed by the end of the 13th century B.C.E.[82] From these observations one may conclude that this type of temple came into vogue in Eretz-Israel during MB IIC — probably at the beginning of the invasion by foreign ethnic

80 Loud, *Megiddo* (see note 54), Figs. 402–404. In an examination carried out by I. Dunayevsky at Megiddo, Wright's conjecture was verified, viz. that the earliest phase of the temple there was contemporary with Temple Ia at Shechem. The investigation proved that the temple was erected on a fill and that it belongs to level X (and not level VIII as suggested by the Chicago expedition) and that it was contemporary with other buildings to the west of the sacred area (5033, etc.) in the same level (*ibid*., Fig. 40). Cf. also Claire Epstein, *IEJ* 15, 204ff.

81 Wright, *Shechem* (see note 21), 123ff.

82 Cf. Y. Yadin, *EAEHL* 2 (1976) 482ff.; *idem*, in Winton Thomas, *Archaeology and OT Study* (see note 60), 230.

elements from the north and the establishment of new fortified towns over the ruins of previous cities[83] — and that it continued to function until the conquest of the land by the Israelites. It is not impossible that the incense stands discovered in the later temples of Beth-shean, in the form of a building of several stories with large windows in the walls, represent a sort of model of the temple towers of this type.[84]

The developments which took place in cultural life also found expression in the palaces and houses of the nobility that have been uncovered at various sites such as those at Tell el-ʿAjjul (palace 1), Megiddo (stratum X) and Tell Beit Mirsim (stratum D). A good example is the spacious, patrician home of the courtyard-house type (*Hofhaus*) which came to light in level D at Tell Beit Mirsim.[85] Testimony to the political and social regime which prevailed in the land at this time may be found in the striking contrast between the solid, spacious buildings of the ruling caste and the inferior dwellings of the lower classes, a difference much more marked at this time than in the previous era.[86]

In the ceramic industry interesting changes also took place. The highly developed tradition from the preceding period continued, of course, but there was a general decline in the quality of the vessels and in the artistic ability displayed. At this time new pottery types came into use which had originated in the north. To the MB IIC period one may assign the beginning of the appearance of the "chocolate-on-white" ware with its special quality and unique artistic style.[87] The importing of decorated wares was also begun; some vessels resemble the earliest "Nuzi ware" (levels VI–IV at Alalakh),[88] as evidenced by the sherds found in level 3 of the lower city at Hazor.[89]

A special problem relates to the dating of the first importation of Cypriot pottery (White Slip I and Base Ring I wares), which gradually increased during LB I, and the significance of this phenomenon in the historical and cultural development of Canaan in the 16th century B.C.E.[90]

83 The view that the royal temple of level VII at Alalakh [Woolley, *Alalakh* (see note 59), Fig. 35] is the prototype of these temples is only a conjecture.

84 Cf. B. Mazar, *Enc. Miq.* 4, 635.

85 Cf. W.F. Albright, *AASOR* 17 (1938), 35ff.

86 *Ibid.*; Wright, in *The Bible and the Ancient Near East* (G.E. Wright, ed.) (see note 4), 90.

87 This term was proposed by F. Petrie, *Ancient Gaza* 1 (1931), 10. Cf. Amiran, *Ancient Pottery* (see note 4), 158ff., Pl. 49; and also *idem*, *BASOR* 169 (1963), 51, 60.

88 The material was published by Woolley, *Alalakh* (see note 59), Pls. XCIII–XCIV.

89 Cf. Y. Yadin et al., *Hazor III–IV. Plates* (1961), Pl. CCCX, especially no. 4, and Pl. CCLX, no. 3.

90 For the beginning of the imports from Cyprus probably towards the end of the Middle Bronze Age, cf. W.F. Albright, *AASOR* 12 (1932), 25ff.; J.R. Stewart, *BASOR* 138 (1955), 47ff.; Wright, *Shechem* (see note 4), 91, 109; Amiran, *Ancient Pottery* (see note 4), 172ff. Concerning the first appearance of bichrome ware, so typical of the earliest phase of the Late Bronze Age, cf. Claire Epstein, *Palestinian Bichrome Ware* (1966).

We will not discuss here other outstanding phenomena in the Canaanite culture of MB IIC, such as in glyptic art, but will refer only briefly to one point: the beginning of alphabetic writing. Albright's convincing demonstration that the tablets bearing alphabetical script from Serābīt el-Khādem in Sinai belong to the first half of the 15th century B.C.E.,[91] placed the study of earlier alphabetic inscriptions which had been discovered in Canaan on a firm chronological base. Now, with the increase in number of known texts which are designated by the inclusive term "proto-Canaanite", it is possible to trace, with less uncertainty, the continuous development of this script into its various forms in the Late Bronze Age and the beginning of the Iron Age. At this time and up to the 11th century B.C.E., when the cursive script written from right to left began to crystallize and the number of signs diminished, it gradually became more linear although its direction had not been fixed.[92] This was, of course, the prototype of the classic Phoenician-Hebrew alphabet.[93]

When trying to trace the beginning of the pictographic alphabet we meet with the surprising phenomenon that up to now there have been discovered in Eretz-Israel only three inscriptions which may be associated with the period preceding the proto-Canaanite texts of the Late Bronze Age: the plaque from Shechem,[94] the dagger from Lachish[95] and the sherd from Gezer.[96] The second is written in a vertical column while the other two are horizontal. Their signs have a more archaic style than the "proto-Sinaitic" script and the letters on the prism from Lachish from the 15th century B.C.E. Although these three inscriptions have a great deal in common, it is neither possible to decipher them nor to definitely assign them to a West Semitic language. As to their date, one may conjecture that the plaque from Shechem

91 W.F. Albright, *BASOR* 110 (1948), 6ff.; F.M. Cross, *BASOR* 134 (1954), 15ff.; and later W.F. Albright, *HTS* 22 (1966), 1ff.; F.M. Cross, *EI* 8 (1967), 8ff.*

92 The square "seal" from Lachish [Tufnell, *Lachish 4* (see note 76), Pl. 38:295], which has the name of Amenḥotep II on one side and a representation of the god Seth on the other, with an accompanying inscription in a style similar to the proto-Sinaitic script, must be assigned to the last quarter of the 15th century B.C.E.; cf. F.M. Cross, *HTR* 55 (1962), 239. To the inscriptions from the 15th century B.C.E., an interesting example may be added from Tel Nagila [Ruth Amiran and A. Eitan, *Yediot* 28 (1964), 198, Pl. 18:5 (Hebrew)].

93 Cf. in this volume, "The Philistines and the Rise of Israel and Tyre", pp. 63–82, n. 15.

94 Fr. Bohl, *ZDPV* 61 (1938), 1ff.; B. Mazar, *JPOS* 18 (1938), 281ff.; *idem*, *Yediot* 6 (1938), 42ff.; 7 (1940), 90ff. (Hebrew); and especially P. Kahana, *Yediot* 12 (1946), 30ff. (Hebrew).

95 Cf. Tufnell, *Lachish 4* (see note 76), *Plates*, 22:15, 42:2; *Text*, 128.

96 Concerning the three inscriptions referred to here, cf. S. Yeivin, in *History of the Jewish People* (see note 11), 26f. In Yeivin's opinion the inscriptions are from the 18th–17th centuries B.C.E. The conjecture that the graffiti from Kahūn [F. Petrie, *Ancient Egypt* 6 (1921), 1ff.] are from the 12th Dynasty seems to me to be implausible. Cf. also I.J. Gelb, *A Study of Writing* (1952), 122ff.; and G.R. Driver, *Semitic Writing* (rev ed, 1954), 94ff.

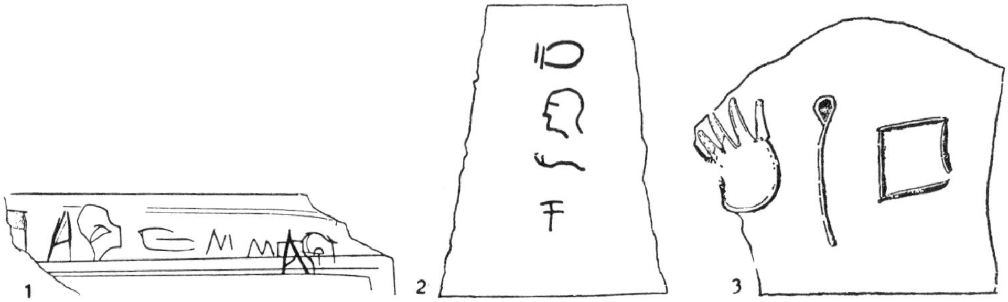

Three inscriptions dating to the Middle Bronze Age: 1) the plaque from Shechem; 2) the dagger from Lachish; and 3) the sherd from Gezer (*Enc. Miq.*)

is from MB IIC, apparently from the end of that period, since stylistically it has a close affinity with the stele fragment discovered in level D at Tell Beit Mirsim.[97] It is worthy of note that the figure depicted on it, probably a deity wrapped in a cloak, testifies to the influence of a style prevalent in north Syria.[98] To approximately the same age one may assign the dagger found in Tomb 1502 at Lachish, along with pottery from the latest stage of MB II.[99] In any case, the scanty material available enables us to establish with some degree of certainty that the beginning of the proto-Canaanite script belongs to MB IIC. This material also makes it possible to reconstruct to some extent the continuous development of the alphabetic script from ca. 1600 B.C.E. without notable gaps.

One may summarize by saying that the "Canaanite" culture of the Late Bronze Age, which lasted for a considerable time and attained many notable achievements in every sphere of life, both material and spiritual, began to rise in MB IIC. The MB IIC was a brief but very eventful and momentous period in which the Land of Canaan became a settling-ground for peoples of varied origin and culture. These gained control over the autochthonous West Semitic populations and became amalgamated with them in the course of time. From the conquering caste a class of chariot nobility had already arisen as rulers of the fortified cities; it was they who determined the special

97 Cf. W.F. Albright, *AASOR* 17 (1938), 42f., Pls. 21a, 22.

98 Cf. P. Kahana, *Yediot* 12 (1946), 35ff. (Hebrew). In the opinion of Albright [*BASOR* 173 (1964), 51, and *The Proto-Sinaitic Inscriptions and Their Decipherment* (1966), 10f.], the relief from Shechem is from the 15th century B.C.E.

99 Cf. Tufnell, *Lachish 4* (see note 76), *Text*, chart on pp. 60–61.Starkey had suggested that the sword was from ca. 1600 B.C.E., while Albright [*The Proto-Sinaitic Inscriptions* (see note 98), 10] places it in the first part of the 16th century B.C.E. Tufnell, on the other hand, dates the whole assemblage of artifacts in Tomb 1502 to the 17th century B.C.E. [*Lachish 4* (see note 76), 254].

character of the social and political order in Canaan during the period of Egyptian rule in the 15th–13th centuries B.C.E.

We have tried to deal here with a series of fundamental problems connected with the history and culture of the Land of Canaan in the Middle Bronze Age, basing ourselves on both literary and archaeological material. It has not been possible to actually solve any of the familiar riddles, much less to produce a complete picture of the historical and cultural development during these several centuries. However, the progress of research and interpretation of the documents, the clarification of the stratigraphical situation at various sites, and the recovery of comparative material, all force us to re-examine formerly accepted archaeological and historical conclusions and to strive for a deeper understanding of the factors which determined the fate of Canaan and its neighbours.[100]

100 I wish to thank my former student, Dr. A. Kempinski, for several references and helpful observations.

A COMPARATIVE CHRONOLOGICAL CHART OF THE MIDDLE BRONZE AGE

Eretz-Israel	*Mesopotamia*	*South Anatolia North Syria*	*Byblos*	*Megiddo*	*Hazor*	*Shechem*	*Tell Beit Mir-sim*	*Egypt*	*Date* B.C.E.
MB I	End of Akkad dynasty Ur III	EB III ʿAmūq I–J Hamath J	(Pepi II) Ib-dadi	Unforti-fied settle-ment	XVIII (Upper City)		I H	End 6th Dynasty First Inter-mediate period	2200 to 2000
MB IIA	Isin-Larsa period	MB I–II (Kārum Kaniš IV–II)	Abi-šemu I — Yapa-šemu-abi — Abi-šemu II — Yapi-šemu-abi	XIVA XIIIB XIIIA XII ↓	Tomb in Upper City	Temenos 1 Temenos 2	G F	12th Dynasty	2000 to 1800
MB IIB	Old Babylonian period (Šamši-adad to Ammiṣadūqa)	MB III Kaniš I Alalakh VII	Yakin-ilu — Yantin-ʿammu — Ḥasrurum	XI B XIA	Lower City 4; XVII (Upper City)	Temenos 3 Temenos 4 Temenos 5	E1 E2	13th-16th Dynasties (Second Intermediate period)	1800 to 1630
MB IIC*	End of Old Babylonian period, beginning of Kassite period	MB IV Alalakh VI		X	Lower City 3; XVI (Upper City)	Temenos 6 (temple tower 1a)	D	15th-17th Dynasties (Second Intermediate period, beginning 18th Dynasty)	1630 to 1550

* Intermediate phase from Middle Bronze Age to Late Bronze Age.

The Early Israelite Settlement in the Hill Country

When we come to examine the history of the settlement of the Israelite tribes in the mountainous region west of the Jordan, particular attention should be given to the implication of the excavations and archaeological surveys carried out over the years. It now appears with a fair degree of certainty that in the last stage of the Late Bronze Age (14th–13th centuries B.C.E.) there were only a few fortified towns and some scattered undefended hamlets on the ridge of the mountains, where since earliest times the main north-south highway followed the line of the watershed. The towns are mainly those familiar from biblical sources: Shechem, Luz-Bethel, Jerusalem, Hebron-Kiriath-arba, and Debir-Kiriath-sepher (probably to be identified with Kh. Rabūd, south of Hebron).[1]

No doubt these towns served both as foci for the caravan trade and as political centres, where various crafts and small-scale agriculture were also practised. The population of the hill country (that is, "the hill country of Israel", Josh 11:16) consisted mostly of nomadic and semi-nomadic tribes, tent-dwellers whose main livelihood depended on pasture for their livestock. Their way of life is reflected in the sagas of the Patriarchs in Genesis, according to which the places where the Fathers of the Israelite nation dwelt or sojourned were in the hill country of Judah, Ephraim, and Gilead, and also in the wide expanses of the Negeb. Sometimes they pitched their tents near sacred oaks and altars, as well as in the vicinity of ancestral tombs.[2] In this

* This study is a revised version of the article which appeared in *BASOR* 241 (1981), 75–85.

1 M. Kochavi, *Tel Aviv* 1 (1974), 1ff.

2 Y. Kaufmann, *Toledot HaEmunah HaIsra'elit (History of the Religion of Israel)* 2 (1954), 126ff. (Hebrew); R. de Vaux, *Ancient Israel, Its Life and Institutions* (1961), 289ff.; M. Haran, *Temples and Temple Service in Ancient Israel* (1978), 48ff.; on the historical background of the patriarchal sagas in Genesis, see in this volume, "The Historical Background of the Book of Genesis", pp. 49–62.

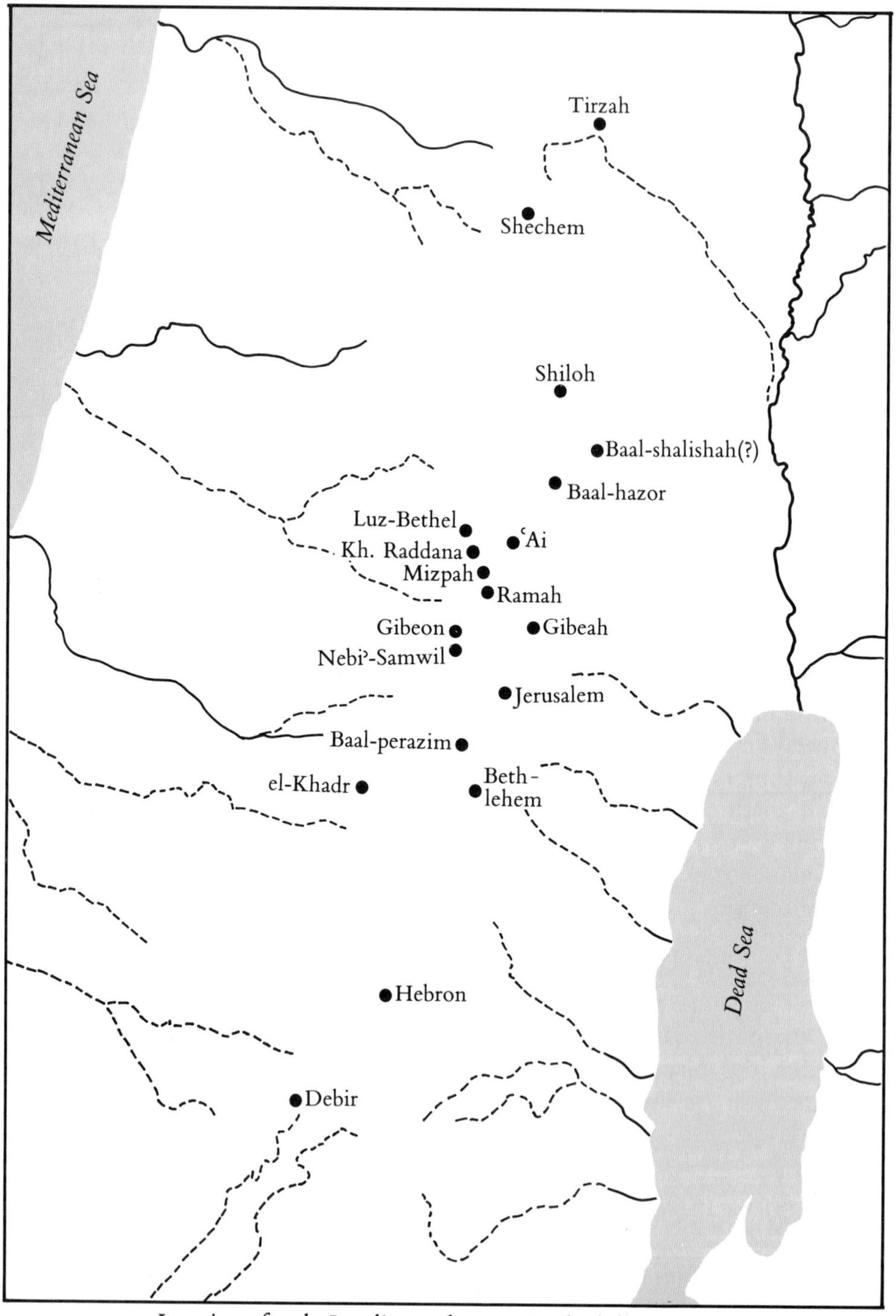

Location of early Israelite settlements in the hill country

connection, the Egyptian "Satirical Letter" (Papyrus Anastasi I), from the second half of the 13th century B.C.E., is of special interest. The author of this document gives an instructive account of prosperous life in the coastal towns, in the valleys, and in the north of Eretz-Israel. At the same time, he notes the dangers posed for travellers by the Shosu bands, while mentioning only incidentally the hill country in the centre of Canaan, which he calls the "mountain of Shechem".[3] He also refers to a nomadic group designated as *ʾiśr*, probably to be identified with the tribe of Asher, which according to obscure biblical passages settled first in the southern hill country of Ephraim.[4]

Excavations and soundings carried out in early Iron Age settlements in the hill country, such as Shechem, ʿAi, Bethel, Kh. Raddana near Ramalla, Gibeon, and elsewhere reveal a picture of a relatively well-developed material culture. Some of these settlements were fortified, and their houses show evidence of planning and even of technological achievement equal to the best standards then current in the country. Especially characteristic are pillared houses with three or four rooms.[5] Other features of these dwellings are the numerous round grain silos and cisterns for storing rainwater installed in almost every house, features that must have played an important role in the development of the settlements. The pottery of the period is plain and utilitarian, typical of that found in all areas of Israelite settlement.[6] Especially distinctive are the "collared-rim" pithos, the cooking pot with elongated triangular or "adze" rim and loop handles, and the heavy bowl with disk or ring base.[7] Callaway's excavations at Kh. Raddana uncovered a deposit of metal tools, a fragment of an early alphabetic inscription on a jar handle (early 12th century B.C.E.?), as well as a fragment of a cultic krater, unique in Eretz-Israel, which may have Anatolian connections.[8] Up to the present, no traces of the Late

3 *ANET*, 477f.

4 A.H. Gardiner, *Ancient Egyptian Onomastica* 1 (1947), 191*ff.; S. Yeivin, *The Israelite Conquest of Canaan* (1971), 31f.; R. de Vaux, *Histoire ancienne d'Israël* 2: *La periode des Juges* (1973), 99.

5 Y. Shiloh, *IEJ* 20 (1970), 180ff.; *idem*, *EI* 11 (1973), 277ff. (Hebrew); A. Kempinski and V. Fritz, *Tel Aviv* 4 (1977), 136ff.

6 See J. Callaway's reports on the excavations at ʿAi, *BASOR* 196 (1969), 5ff.; 198 (1970), 19ff.; *idem*, *EAEHL* 1, 44ff.; cf. also his article in *JBL* 87 (1968), 312ff.

7 This pottery, especially the collared-rim jar, was first recognized as characteristic of the Israelite Settlement (12th century B.C.E.) by W.F. Albright [*Excavations and Results at Tell el-Fūl (Gibeah of Saul) = AASOR* 4 (1924), 10; *idem*, *The Archaeology of Palestine* (rev ed, 1960), 118], and following him Y. Aharoni [*The Settlement of the Israelite Tribes in Upper Galilee* (1957), 21ff. (Hebrew)] and others. M.M. Ibrahim [in P.R.S. Moorey and P.J. Parr (eds.), *Archaeology in the Levant: Essays for Kathleen Kenyon* (1978), 117–126] has shown that collared-rim jars were in widespread use also in Transjordan (especially in Saḥab). In his opinion, therefore, it is doubtful whether they can be attributed to any particular ethnic group.

8 J.A. Callaway and R.E. Cooley, *BASOR* 201 (1971), 9ff.; F.M. Cross and D.N. Freedman, *ibid.*, 19ff.; A. Kempinski, *Biblical Archaeology Review* 5 (1979), 43–45.

Bronze Age have been found at Gibeon (el-Jib), though tombs of the Middle and Late Bronze Ages have been discovered nearby.[9] The early Iron Age village is represented by part of an enclosing wall on the edge of the mound and by a water system that was fed by water from a spring outside the town.[10]

The settlement of the Israelite tribes in the hill country appears from the first to have been governed by their sense of national-religious destiny and by their way of life as stock breeders who ranged with their herds over Canaan and Transjordan. It was only gradually that the early Israelites adapted to the conditions of a settled life, to living in permanent villages, and to direct contact with their non-Israelite neighbours whose influence made itself felt in the establishment of their settlements and in their gradual transition to an economy based mainly on agriculture. The Israelite tribes and associated groups contracted alliances with these neighbours on the one hand, but they also fought them fiercely to secure life and property, for the right to settle surplus populations, in order to make subject the autochthonous inhabitants or absorb them into the Israelite tribal framework, and eventually to attain political supremacy.[11] These events are reflected in many biblical sources — especially in early episodes embedded in the historiographic works, as well as in the national poetry and in fragments of memories scattered in the genealogies. Instances are the mention of the bloody clash between the inhabitants of Gath[12] and the tribe of Ephraim, "whom the men of Gath who were born in the land slew, because they came down to raid their cattle" (1 Chr 7:21); or the account of how the heads of Benjamin in Aijalon "put to flight the inhabitants of Gath" (1 Chr 8:13).

Who were these peoples in the hill country at the time of the Israelite Settlement? Three ethnic groups played the most important role as neighbours

9 J.B. Pritchard, *The Bronze Age Cemetery at Gibeon* (1963); R. Gonen, *Burial in Canaan in the Late Bronze Age* (Ph.D. diss., The Hebrew University of Jerusalem, 1979), 85–87 (Hebrew).

10 J.B. Pritchard, *The Water System of Gibeon* (1961); *idem*, *Gibeon, Where the Sun Stood Still* (1962), 55ff., 158ff.

11 In recent decades different and even contradictory methods of study and research concerning the process of the Israelite conquest and settlement have been developed, especially by Alt and Noth, Albright, Yeivin, and Kaufmann, and more recently Mendenhall and others. These methods are based on differing approaches to biblical sources and on original solutions of historical, archaeological, and sociological problems. Cf. the summaries of the subject in Y. Aharoni, *The Land of the Bible* (2d ed, 1979), 191ff.; M. Weippert, *The Settlement of the Israelite Tribes in Palestine* (1971); R. de Vaux, *Histoire ancienne d'Israël. Des origines a l'installation en Canaan* (1971), 443ff.; and J.M. Miller, in J.H. Hayes and J.M. Miller (eds.), *Israelite and Judaean History* (1977), 213ff.

12 For Gath-Gittaim and its identification with Rās Abu Ḥamid, see B. Mazar, *IEJ* 4 (1954), 227ff. Some fragmentary sources which merit notice testify that Amorite towns in the area of the Aijalon Valley continued to exist, "but the hand of the house of Joseph prevailed and they became tributaries" (Judg 1:35), whereas the Danites, who were attached to the house of Joseph, settled in the region of Eshtaol-Zorah, where they were "forced by the Amorites into the mountains, for they would not suffer them to come down to the valley" (Judg 1:34, cf. also Judg 18:12 and 1 Sam 7:14).

of the tribes of Israel until the crystallization of the Monarchy. They are: (1) the Hivites in Shechem and in the four neighbouring cities of Beeroth, Chephirah, Baalath-Kiriath-jearim, and Gibeon, which "was a great city, like one of the royal cities" (Josh 10:2); (2) the Hittites in Hebron and, according to Judg 1:22–26, also in Luz-Bethel; and (3) the Jebusites in the Jerusalem region, who most probably were related to the Hittites.

These groups differed from each other both ethnically and in their descent either from the Amorites, a term used in the historiographic sources as a general name for the non-Israelite population, and especially the autochthonous inhabitants of the hill country, or from the Canaanites, a name generally applied to the population of the Egyptian province of Canaan.[13] It should be noted that the Hivites stand out as an alien element and even as new settlers in the hill country. Their origin, as Judg 3:3 and Josh 11:3 indicate, should be sought in the area of Mount Hermon, Mount Lebanon, and the Beqaᶜ "as far as Lebo-hamath",[14] that is, in the border region between the Hittite and Egyptian empires in the 13th century B.C.E. From there they spread to the Canaanite cities (2 Sam 24:4) and to Shechem and to Gibeon and its vicinity, north-west of Jerusalem in the hill country. It should be recalled that in the folk tale recounted in Josh 9 the Hivites-Gibeonites told the Israelites encamped at Gilgal that "we have come from a far country, so now make a covenant with us" (v. 6), and they said to Joshua "from a very far country your servants have come" (v. 9). The story goes on to tell, however, that after the covenant had been made the deception came to light, and the congregation discovered "that they were their neighbours and that they dwelt among them" (v. 16). For this reason they were employed to cut wood and to carry water for the congregation and for the altar of Yahweh, the latter perhaps referring to the great *bāmāh* that the Israelites set up at Gibeon, which served as a cult place until the time of Solomon.[15]

As for Hivite Shechem, it should be remembered that in the story of Abimelech (Judg 9), which has its counterpart in the folk tale about Dinah (Gen 34), the rulers of the town were "the men of Hamor the father of Shechem" (Judg 9:28). Hamor is the name of the noble family (and its

13 B. Maisler (Mazar), *Untersuchungen zur alten Geschichte und Ethnographie Syriens und Palästinas* (1930), and de Vaux, *La periode des Juges* (see note 4), 123ff.; for a summary of the subject, see T. Ishida, *Biblica* 60 (1979), 465ff. and selected bibliography there.

14 Mazar, *Untersuchungen zur alten Geschichte* (see note 13), 75; Weippert, *Israelite Tribes in Palestine* (see note 11), 36, n. 103.

15 Possibly the great *bāmāh* at Gibeon, a site sacred to the Israelites in the Hivite-Gibeonite region, should be placed at Nebiʾ Samwīl, a high hill towering over el-Jib [cf. de Vaux, *Des origines a l'installation en Canaan* (see note 11), 573, n. 4]. A parallel situation can be seen at the holy site of Gibeath/Kiriath-jearim (Deir el-ᶜAzhar), which dominates the Hivite town of Kiriath Baal (Baalath)-Kiriath-jearim (Abu-Ghosh) (cf. *Enc. Miq*. 7, s.v. "Kiriath-jearim").

"father") who headed the "lords of Shechem", that is, the ruling class who entered a covenant with Gideon and his family, the Manassite clan of Abiezer. This covenant found expression in the sanctuary or "house" of El-berith/Baal-berith (i.e., the God of the covenant) in Beth-millo, which is probably synonymous with the "Tower" of Shechem, the citadel where the lords of Shechem resided.[16] Of particular interest is the opening of the story in Gen 34, where Shechem is called "the son of Hamor the Hivite, the chief of the land (*nᵉśīʾ hāʾāreṣ*)" (v. 2), indicating that Hamor, the "father" of the noble Shechemite family, was a Hivite bearing the honorific title "prince of the land", that is, the Land of Shechem. Both stories are based on a common tradition reflected in the record of the relations between the Israelites and their Hivite neighbours, the inhabitants of Shechem: the covenant between the two peoples and its violation caused by complex quarrels, culminating in the annihilation of the Hivite nobility and the destruction of the city and its sanctuary. Eventually, in the beginning of the Monarchic period, an Israelite town, the Levite town of Shechem in the hill country of Ephraim, arose on the ruins of the Hivite city.

The Hittites were found mainly in Hebron, where the ruling class before the Calebite conquest was called by the Israelites *ʿam hāʾāreṣ*, "the people of the land, the children of Heth". Ephron son of Zohar the Hittite, who owned the field and the cave of Machpelah "which was before Mamre", was a member of this class. He sat "among the Hittites at the gate of the city", and there he sold to Abraham the field and cave of Machpelah as a burying place for "four hundred shekels of silver according to the weights current among the merchants" (Gen 23). Abraham the Hebrew was "a stranger and sojourner" among them (v. 4); during their wanderings he and his descendants sojourned at the Oaks of Mamre (cf. Gen 35:27). According to a tradition associated with the time of the Calebite settlement, Sheshai, Ahiman, and Talmai, "the descendants of Anak", were the heads of the noble families of Hebron in the pre-Israelite period (Num 13:22; Josh 15:14), and they may well have been Hittite noblemen.

The central role played by the Hivites and Hittites in the non-Israelite population of the hill country is further indicated by sources such as Gen 36:2ff. The short account in Judg 1:22–26 concerning the conquest of Luz-Bethel by the Joseph clans poses a particular problem. According to this story, the man who delivered the city to the House of Joseph migrated with his family to the land of the Hittites and built there a city that he called Luz, after the town he had left, and "that is its name to this day". It is reasonable to assume

16 G.E. Wright, *Shechem: Biography of a Biblical City* (1965), 95ff.; W.G. Dever, *BASOR* 216 (1974), 31ff.; and Mazar, *Canaan and Israel*, 147–148.

that Luz is the town Lawazantiya (with the common Anatolian suffix *-antiya*) in the land of Kizzuwatna, in Hittite Anatolia, often mentioned in the Boghazköy texts.[17] In any event, this story shows that a bond of origin and kinship existed between the inhabitants of Canaanite Luz before it became Israelite Bethel at the time of the Settlement, and the city of Luz in Hittite Anatolia.

The Jebusites (Jebus) were the inhabitants of Jerusalem and its neighbourhood in the 12th–11th centuries B.C.E. and until David's reign. Their capital was called by the Israelites the "Stronghold of Zion", or "Jebus ... the city of foreigners, who do not belong to the people of Israel" (Judg 19:11–12).Jebus undoubtedly refers to one of the ethnic groups that, like the Hivites, migrated from a distant country, probably the land of the Hittites, and settled in Jerusalem. This event may perhaps have taken place after the destruction of "Canaanite" Jerusalem by Judah, an enigmatic episode mentioned in Judg 1:8. The kinship of the Jebusites with the Hittites (the general name for the peoples of the neo-Hittite empire) is underlined by Ezekiel's words addressed to Jerusalem: "Your origin and your birth are of the land of the Canaanites; your father was an Amorite, and your mother a Hittite" (Ezek 16:3); and "Your mother was a Hittite and your father an Amorite" (v. 45). However, it should be remembered that Uriah the Hittite, one of David's heroes, was a permanent inhabitant of Jerusalem (2 Sam 11:8ff.). Furthermore, the valley south of ancient Jerusalem is called the "Valley of the Son (Sons) of Hinnom", reminiscent of the land of *Hnm* in Lebanon, at the southern end of the neo-Hittite empire.[18] It can reasonably be conjectured that the family that gave its name to the valley reached Jerusalem from *Hnm*, within the boundaries of Hittite rule in southern Syria.

Especially instructive is the title of the head of the Jebusite noble family, Arawnah, Awarnah, or the Awarnah, the Jebusite owner of the threshing floor that David purchased for a price and where he built an altar to Yahweh (2 Sam 24:18–25).The meaning of the Horite word *eweri* (with the suffix *-ne*), which was also taken over in Hittite, is "lord" and certainly also "feudal lord".[19] It is noteworthy that David purchased the threshing floor from Araunah the Jebusite for the full price in perpetuity, just as Jacob bought the plot

17 Cf. Mazar, *Cities and Districts*, 25, n. 19; for this town, see J.J. Garstang and O.R. Gurney, *The Geography of the Hittite Empire* (1959), 52ff.

18 A scene showing the felling of trees in Lebanon for Sethos I at the town of *qdr* in the land of *hnm* is depicted in the great hypostyle hall at Karnak; *ANET*, 254f.; Mazar, *Cities and Districts*, 25, n. 19.

19 For a detailed treatment, see Mazar, *Canaan and Israel*, 219–220; cf. C.H. Gordon, *Ugaritic Textbook* (1965), Glossary N. 116. Yadin's suggestion should be mentioned here, namely that the affair of the lame and the blind in the story of the conquest of the Jebusite stronghold of Zion (2 Sam 5:7–9) is a magic act, which recalls a similar incantation of the Hittite army in a text from Boghazkoy; cf. Y. Yadin (Sukenik), in *World Congress of Jewish Studies, 1947* (1952), 222ff. (Hebrew).

of land in Shechem from the sons of Hamor, "father" of Shechem (Gen 33:19; Josh 24:32), and Abraham bought the field of Machpelah from Ephron the Hittite in Hebron. Perhaps it can be suggested that the title "chief of the land" (*nᵉśīʾ hāʾāreṣ*) borne by Hamor the Hivite, the "father" of Shechem, has a meaning similar or identical to Arawnah (Awarnah, the Awarnah), indicating that Hamor was the lord of Hivite Shechem, just as Araunah was the feudal lord of Jebusite Jerusalem. On the other hand, when Ephron the Hittite called Abraham "prince of God (*nᵉśīʾ ʾelohīm*) among us" (Gen 23:6), this may well have been a rhetorical title, perhaps an abstraction of the concept "prince of the land" (*nᵉśīʾ hāʾāreṣ*), by which Ephron wished to honour a famous Hebrew "stranger and sojourner" who dwelt frequently at the Oaks of Mamre and who sought peaceful relations and an alliance with the Hittite lords of Hebron.

It must be emphasized that nothing is known of a monarchic system in any of the ethnic territorial groups of the Hivites, Hittites, and Jebusites who remained as enclaves among the Israelite tribes.[20] Only late sources, like Josh 10 and 12:7–24, mention the "kings" of Hebron, Debir, ʿAi, Bethel, etc., "all the kings who were beyond the Jordan in the hill country and in the lowlands" (Josh 9:1), according to a schema acceptable to the Israelite historiographers in the latter days of the Monarchy. The political system in all the above-mentioned cities actually was based on a ruling aristocracy, known to us by inclusive terms such as the "lords of Shechem", the "people of the land" at Hebron, or the "elders" at Gibeon. Through their leaders — the Hivite "prince of the land" in Shechem or the Jebusite Arawnah in Jerusalem — they entered into treaty relationships with the Israelites, intermarried with them, and continued to be absorbed by them. This process was accompanied by syncretistic practices recorded in the historical sources (Judg 3, 5, etc.).

In the light of the foregoing, it can be assumed that all the ethnic groups discussed — the Hittites, Hivites, and Jebusites — reached the hill country of Canaan, which was sparsely settled and economically backward, from the Hittite provinces in Syria and Anatolia at the time of the catastrophe that overtook the Hittite empire. This tremendous upheaval happened during the transitional period between the 13th and 12th centuries B.C.E., when the Hittite empire broke up during the reigns of its last kings, Arnuwanda III and Shuppiluliuma II. There is a cause-and-effect relationship between this historic development and the massive migratory movement of the "Sea Peoples" in the Aegean Basin and along the Anatolian coast, which was fraught with momentous consequences.

20 This phenomenon is also found in border areas, and especially in Geshur and Maachah in the Golan, where a monarchial regime apparently was established in the second half of the 11th century B.C.E.; cf. in this volume, "Geshur and Maachah", pp.113–125.

The "Sea Peoples" ravaged the Hittite provinces in Syria and even threatened the very existence of the Egyptian empire. Our main documentary source for these events is the description of the assault of the five "Sea Peoples" in the inscriptions of the 5th and 8th regnal years of Ramesses III in the temple of Amon at Medinet Habu.[21] The complete destruction of the flourishing harbour town of Ugarit also serves as striking evidence of the catastrophe that overtook the Hittite empire and its vassal states. However, the migratory tide of the "Sea Peoples" was not the only decisive factor in the decline and disintegration of the Hittite empire and the widespread population shifts within its borders. This process was certainly accelerated by the pressure of the population groups invading from the north and by the power struggle with Assyria on the east, but first and foremost by the breakdown of the political and social system and the collapse of the economy within the empire. This was accompanied by famines and epidemics (and, according to some opinions, by earthquakes and climatic changes), and by the mass migration of uprooted population groups into Egyptian lands.[22]

The "Sea Peoples", made up of various ethnic groups and tribes including the Philistines, the Shikal (*Ṯkr*), and the Danuna, invaded the coastal areas of Canaan down to the very south and settled there in towns or in encampments, either on their own initiative or as captives or mercenaries under the protection of Egyptian rule. Together with this influx of the "Sea Peoples" came a host of refugees and immigrants consisting of various ethnic groups, including Hittites, Jebusites, and Hivites, as well as Girgeshites and Perizzites,[23] who had abandoned their homelands in Syria and Anatolia and settled mainly in sparsely populated areas in the hill country. They seized power in the few existing cities, some of which they destroyed and rebuilt, and established new settlements on the major highways. In this fashion, mountainous areas in Canaan became a refuge for immigrants from the Hittite kingdom at the time of the catastrophe that took place there. Among them must have been merchants (especially in Shechem), artisans, and farmers (cf. Judg 9:27), and perhaps also military men (see below). At the time when the Egyptians were still sufficient-

21 W.F. Edgerton and J.A. Wilson, *Historical Records of Ramses III* (1936); *ANET*, 262f.

22 W. Helck, H. Otten and K. Bittel, *Geschichte des 13. und 12. Jahr. v. Chr., Jahresbericht des Instituts für Vorgeschichte* (1976); H. Tadmor, in F.M. Cross (ed.), *Symposia: Celebrating the Seventy-fifth Anniversary of the Founding of the American Schools of Oriental Research* (1979), 1ff.; and on the decline of the Mycenean civilization, see W.H. Stieling, *BA* 43 (1980), 7ff.

23 Cf. *Enc. Miq*. 2, s.v. "Girgeshi"; *ibid*. 6, s.v. "Perizzi". For Karkiša in Hittite Anatolia, see *RLA* 5, 446ff. It is not in vain that the Israelite historiographer so frequently describes Canaan before the Israelite conquest as the country of the seven nations — Amorites, Hittites, Girgeshites, Perizzites, Hivites, Jebusites and Canaanites — who dwell in large fortified cities and have houses full of fine goods and rock-cut cisterns. This, at least, was the way the people during the Monarchy saw their distant past; cf. T. Ishida, *Biblica* 60 (1979), 463ff.

ly powerful to retain their hold on the coastal areas, their political and military strength in the interior of the country was completely spent. They could not check the influx of immigrants from Syria, and they certainly could not contend with the Israelites and their kinfolk who entered the country with increasing thrust from Transjordan as well as from the Negeb,[24] and who were to determine the fate of the country for generations to come.

Some of these peoples survived within the borders of Israel until the days of the United Monarchy. The members of the Hivite clan Hamor were slain in Shechem, but it may well be that remnants of the population were assimilated as a "family" into the tribe of Manasseh. This is the Shechem known to us as a "family" territory already in the Samaria Ostraca of the 8th century B.C.E. Many of the Hivites in Gibeon were slain by Saul "in his zeal for the people of Israel and Judah" (2 Sam 21:2–6). The Jebusite "stronghold of Zion" was conquered by David early in his reign, while Joab "repaired the rest of the city" (1 Chr 11:8; cf. also Josh 15:63, Judg 1:21). At the same time, we find non-Israelite military men in Saul's and David's service, including captains and "heroes" (*śarīm* and *gibborīm*). These came mainly from the Hivite cities Beeroth, Kiriath-jearim, and Gibeon, as well as from Jebusite-Hittite Jerusalem.[25] It is possible that the arrowheads of the 11th century B.C.E. that were found at el-Khadr near Bethlehem, each bearing the inscription in alphabetic script *ḥṣ ʿbdlbʾt*, "Arrow of the servant of the Lioness", may indicate the existence of a professional guild of archers (known from an administrative Ugaritic text). Perhaps these were the bowmen led by Saul's "Benjaminite kinsmen" (1 Chr 12:2).[26] Of special interest is the story about the two sons of Rimmon, Saul's captains, who were Beerothites, "for Beeroth was also reckoned to Benjamin" (2 Sam 4:2). The author's intention must surely have been that they were Beerothites of Hivite extraction who were assimilated by Benjamin and served the Israelite royal house. After the sons of Rimmon had slain Eshbaal, and David had them put to death in retribution, "the Beerothites fled to Gittaim, where they have lived ever since" (v. 3). This Gittaim seems to be the Gath-rimmon (the estate of the Rimmon family) in the territory of Dan.[27]

As for the Israelite tribes settling in the hill country — and especially the large national units of the Joseph and Judah tribes — they adjusted to condi-

24 W.F. Albright, *BASOR* 163 (1961), 36ff.; and the critical notes of E.A. Speiser, *BASOR* 164 (1961), 23ff.

25 Mazar, *Canaan and Israel*, 198, n. 59–60; 210–211.

26 J.T. Milik and F.M. Cross, *BASOR* 134 (1954), 5ff.; Mazar, *Canaan and Israel*, 186. It should be recalled that not only Uriah the Hittite, but also Abimelech the Hittite (1 Sam 26:6), was one of David's mighty men, although the latter's name does not appear in the list of these heroes.

27 Cf. in this volume, "The Military Elite of King David", pp. 83–103, n. 61. For the meaning of the name Gath, see M. Heltzer, *Journal of Northwest Semitic Languages* 9 (1979), 31ff.

tions in their new surroundings through a complex and eventful process of gaining a foothold in the vicinity of non-Israelite cities, clearing the forests (Josh 17:15–18),and breaking virgin soil for agriculture. Archaeological excavations and surveys[28] have revealed a situation that corresponds to or approximates the historical-cultural fabric reflected in reliable sources from the pre-Monarchic period preserved in the Bible. These discoveries unfold before our eyes an illuminating picture of widespread settlement, of increasing adaptation to conditions in the hill country, and of growing sophistication in utilizing its economic resources. At the same time, this period is characterized by wars and clashes with the Israelite's neighbours and with invaders, as well as by conflicts among the tribes themselves, which sometimes resulted in the destruction of settlements and the migration of the settlers to other places and regions. Undoubtedly, this was a dynamic process accompanied by vigorous development and by the creation of a dense settlement pattern, as revealed in archaeological surveys. This change, which can be traced also in the hill country of Transjordan and of Upper Galilee as well as in the Negeb,[29] reached its peak in the days of the United Monarchy.

The new settlements were generally established on previously uninhabited sites and only a few arose on the ruins of destroyed cities [mainly Shechem, Tirzah(?)-Tell el-Farʿah (N), Shiloh, Luz-Bethel, and Hebron] or on the remains of Early Bronze Age settlements (ʿAi, Mizpah-Tell en-Nasbeh). They were usually of a lower standard than the non-Israelite cities; their character is consistent with the life-style of clans and families living on their lands. Some of them were modestly fortified; others were undefended villages or temporary dwellings, forts, or watchtowers for defence. In the permanent settlements that continued to exist there appeared a type of house with three or (more frequently) four rooms, which became very common in Israel and among its neighbours (see above). Among the pottery, too, characteristic vessels make their appearance from the beginning of Settlement onward. A few iron implements begin to appear, together with the traditional copper ones, and their spread in Israel may perhaps be attributed to migrants from Hittite lands. Furthermore, the first signs of the introduction of the alphabetic script in Israel can be discerned.[30]

28 See the articles on Bethel, Gibeah, ʿAi, Mizpah (Tell en-Nasbeh), Shiloh, Shechem, and Tell el-Farʿah (N) in *EAEHL*. For surveys, see especially M. Kochavi (ed.), *Judea, Samaria and the Golan, An Archaeological Survey 1967/8* (1972), 20–21, 153–155, 169–199 (Hebrew); R. Bach, *ZDPV* 74 (1958), 41ff.; E.F. Campbell, *BASOR* 190 (1968), 19ff.

29 Aharoni, *The Land of the Bible* (see note 11), 217ff., and N. Glueck, *The Other Side of the Jordan* (1940), *passim*.

30 F.M. Cross in *Symposia* (see note 22), 97ff.; A. Demsky, *Tel Aviv* 4 (1977), 14ff.

Many of the events and the authentic patterns of daily life and of socio-religious practices of the settlers are reflected in the historiographic fabric of the monumental literary creation that took shape in Israel in the course of many generations. At the same time it is clear that in addition to the various national, tribal, and family traditions — "things which we have heard and known, that our fathers have told us" (Ps 78:3), literary or prose compositions, fragments of chronicles, epic poems and folk tales that have been preserved in the biblical sources — special significance should be attached to the early genealogies. These genealogical lists, as well as the names of ancestral heads of clans and families and their settlements and territories, are often authentic and factual material for the study of the conquest and settlement of the Israelite tribes. They contribute a great deal to our understanding of the settlers' society and of clans and families and of their adherence to ancestral traditions and attachment to their holy sites.[31]

Numerous new settlements have names like Geder, Gederah, Gederoth, Gederothaim (with the locative *-aim*) and Gedor (also a Phoenician term); Hazer, Hazor, Hazerim, Hezron; Atarah, Ataroth[32]; and Mezad, Mezudah, Mizpah, Zephat, Bezer, Chesalon — all of which describe various kinds of settlements and strongholds. Similarly, names like Ramah, Ramoth, Ramathaim, Gebaᶜ (which also serves as a Canaanite term), Gibeah, and Gibeon refer to the topographical character of the settlement. Terms like Migron, Naweh, Naioth, and Goren signify places of grazing and crafts within the settlement, while Kedesh (also a Canaanite term), Gilgal, and Elon indicate sanctified sites. It is not surprising that several of these place names are found in combination with another designation, usually that of a tribe, clan, or a family in Israel. Many are the toponyms whose first component is a common West Semitic element, such as *bayit, qiryah, migdal, gat*(estate).

Especially instructive is the term "land", meaning the territory of an Israelite family or a non-Israelite territorial unit. Saul looks for his father's asses in the land of Shalishah, the land of Shaalim, the land of Benjamin, and the land of Zuph. On the evidence of the genealogical lists of Asher (1 Chr 7:31–40), the land of Shalishah and the land of Shual were the territories of the early Asherite families Shalishah and Shual (vv. 36–37), and evidently Baal-

31 For place names in Eretz-Israel in the biblical period, see W. Borée, *Die Alten Ortsnamen Palästinas* (2d ed, 1968); A.F. Rainey, *BASOR* 231 (1978), 1ff.

32 For the term *ḥṣr*, see S.E. Loewenstamm, *Enc. Miq.* 3, 273–274; A. Malamat, *Yediot* 27 (1963), 180ff. (Hebrew). As for Ataroth (Ataroth of the Archites, Atroth-Shophan, Atroth-Beth-joab, etc.), it seems that this name was given to encampments enclosed by a circular fence (no doubt from the word *ᶜatarah*, "diadem"). The origin of names like Geder, Gedor, is indicated by the verses "we will build sheepfolds (*gdrwt ṣʾn*) for our cattle and cities for our little ones ... and our little ones shall dwell in the fenced cities" (Num 32:16–17). All these designations serve as names of settlements, as well as of clans and families.

shalishah served as a centre (probably cultic) of the Shalishah family in the land of Ephraim (2 Kgs 4:42).[33] Similarly, Baal-hazor (2 Sam 13:23) must be the cult centre of the village of Hazor in Ephraim.[34] In the land of Yemini (Benjamin) such a site existed at Gibeah, which is Gibeath Benjamin, "the hill of Benjamin". On the hilltop stood the *bāmāh* of the tribe (originally the clan) of Benjamin, and therefore it was called Gibeath ʾElōhīm.[35] As for the land of Zuph, its central settlement was at Ramah, also called Ramathaim-zophim, home of the prophet Samuel, who belonged to the Zuph family (1 Sam 1:1). The *bāmāh* of the family was situated on the summit of the promontory implied in the name Ramah[36] (1 Sam 9:11–14,18, 19, 25).

In the light of the foregoing, it seems reasonable to assume that Baal-perazim near Bethlehem, David's birthplace, is none other than the cult centre of the widely ramified family whose "father" was Perez, according to tradition Judah's eldest son, and to which David son of Jesse belonged (cf. the genealogy of Perez in Ruth 4:18–22). Perhaps this is the site of the cult assembly of the people of Bethlehem and the other members of the clan to which David hastened from Gibeath of Saul, "for there is a yearly sacrifice there for all the family" (1 Sam 20:6).[37] Significantly, the first bloody clash between David and the Philistines, after he had been annointed king over Israel, took place in Baal-perazim near Bethlehem and in the vicinity of the Valley of Rephaim, where the Philistines were encamped: "And David came to Baal-perazim, and David defeated them there, and he said: 'Yahweh has broken through my enemies before me like a bursting flood'; therefore the name of that place is called Baal-perazim" (2 Sam 5:20; 2 Chr 14:11). It is to this event that the verses in 2 Sam 23:13–14 refer: "And a troop of Philistines was encamped in the Valley of Rephaim. And David was then in the stronghold [apparently the stronghold of Zion, that is the City of David], and the garrison of the Philistines was then at Bethlehem". This event was deeply engraved upon the national memory and is referred to by Isaiah: "For Yahweh will rise up as on Mount Perazim" (28:21).

33 Z. Kallai, *Enc. Miq.* 7, 716. The identification of Baal-shalishah with the important site of Khirbet el-Marjame (near ʿAin eṣ-Ṣamiyeh), in the south-eastern hill country of Ephraim, seems likely; cf. A. Mazar, *IEJ* 26 (1976), 138. Late Bronze Age and Early Iron Age remains have been uncovered at this site.

34 The identification of Baal-hazor with Jebel el-ʿAṣūr is generally accepted. The site lies 9 km north-west of Bethel and is the highest peak in the hill country of Ephraim (more than 1003 m above sea level). Abel proposed to read in 1 Macc 9:15 ʾΑξώρου ὄρους [*RB* 33 (1924), 386; *GP* 1, 372]. For the phrase "Baal-hazor, which is near Ephraim" (2 Sam 13:23), see de Vaux, *La periode de Juges* (note 4), 591; H. Seebach, *VT* 14 (1964), 497ff.

35 On Gibeath ʾElohīm, see Mazar, *Cities and Districts*, 80ff., and the suggestion by J.M. Miller, *VT* 25 (1975), 145ff.

36 Z. Kallai, *Enc. Miq*. 7, 374–375.

37 See the discussion of A. Malamat, *JAOS* 88 (1968), 173, n. 29.

Amihai Mazar has suggested that Baal-perazim should be identified with the site in Giloh (a suburb of modern Jerusalem), on the top of the ridge between the Valley of Rephaim and Beit Jalla (830 m above sea level), which he investigated. During three seasons of excavations he uncovered a hamlet from the Iron I period.[38] Several factors support this identification: the site's proximity to Bethlehem and its command over the Valley of Rephaim; its lofty situation confirmed by its mention in Isaiah's prophecy (Mount Perazim); and the equation of Baal-perazim with Mount Perazim, just as Baal-hazor is Mount Hazor. The remains uncovered at the site complete the picture.

It is a reasonable assumption that "Baal", as an epithet meaning "Lord", and its substitution for Yahweh in Israelite theophoric titles of the pre-Monarchic period and of the days of Saul and David, was usual both in geographic terms — especially those of family cult places such as Baal-shalishah, Baal-hazor, and Baal-perazim — and in personal names such as Eshbaal,[39] Mephibaal, Meribaal, and Aḥibaal.[40] Its replacement by a term of derision in personal names such as Ishbosheth, Mephibosheth, or Ahithophel in historiographic sources, is similarly the result of the historical development that began in the first half of the 9th century B.C.E. with the establishment and spread in Israel of the worship of the Tyrian Baal under the Omrite dynasty, and its suppression in the reign of Jehu with the rise of the national-religious movement initiated by Elijah and continued by the "faithful of Israel".[41]

38 A. Mazar, *Qadmoniot* 13 (1980), 34ff. (Hebrew).

39 The first component of the name is *yeš/□eš*, and the second is *baʿal* or *Yahu* (1 Sam 14:49; Septuagint Lag. = Ιεσσιου). Cf. Mazar, *Canaan and Israel*, 191, n. 18; 210, n. 47; and in this volume, "The Military Elite of King David", p. 91, n. 20.

40 Interchanges in theophoric names, such as Ahibaal-Ahijahu, or Beeliada (1 Chr 14:7, David's son)-Eliada (2 Sam 5:16), were widespread in the early part of the Israelite Monarchy, when the national-religious spirit was strong.

41 Cf. O. Eissfeldt, *Kleine Schriften* 1 (1962), 1ff.; F.M. Cross, *Canaanite Myth and Hebrew Epic* (1973), 190ff.; B. Mazar, *EI* 14, 39ff. (Hebrew).

The Historical Background of the Book of Genesis

In our generation, research on the Book of Genesis has progressed significantly due to the abundance of epigraphic documents and archaeological evidence which have shed new light on many phenomena relating to cultural life in the ancient Near East in general, and in Canaan in particular, during the second and early part of the first millennium B.C.E. Numerous studies and commentaries have treated in detail the diverse problems pertaining to the literary sources of Genesis and their affinity to neighbouring cultures — in language and literary form, in political, social, legal, and religious background, and with regard to Israelite origins. I make reference particularly to the study of Genesis by Ephraim A. Speiser, which appeared only a few months before the passing of this esteemed scholar.[1]

In contrast to most scholarly opinion, which continues to subscribe to the viewpoint of the Documentary Hypothesis with its many ramifications, positing that the Book of Genesis was compiled from the sources J, E, and P by means of a complex process of editorial activity, various scholars have attempted to develop their own theories concerning the character, sources, and mode of composition of the Book of Genesis within the framework of the Old Testament.[2] Thus, the late Umberto Cassuto regarded it as a single, unified composition, created according to a pre-determined plan, the sources of which were traditions of various origin and character culled and selected from the store of those prevalent in ancient Israel.[3]

* This study is a revised version of the article published *JNES* 28 (1969), 73–83.

1 E.A. Speiser, *Genesis* (1964).

2 See O. Eissfeldt, *Einleitung in das Alte Testament* (3d ed, 1964), 205ff., where there is a detailed bibliography.

3 U.D Cassuto, *A Commentary on the Book of Genesis* 1: *From Adam to Noah* (1961); 2: *From Noah to*

Views are no less divided with respect to the dating of various sources of Genesis, assessing the patriarchal sagas as a historic source, the degree of their reliability, and their importance for research on the emergence of the Israelite people.

Genesis reveals itself to us as a monumental historiographic composition, the product of rich and variegated material collected, combined, arranged, and worked into one harmonious tract, with the purpose of portraying both the beginnings of mankind and the origins of Israel in the spirit of the monotheistic concept, and with a didactic aim. That pure religious notion, expressed in the belief in the one God of Israel, who is also the sole God ruling over the hidden recesses of creation, who had revealed Himself to the fathers of the nation by His various epithets, as well as by His explicit name, and had promised to their seed the whole land from the Euphrates to the River of Egypt — that notion corresponds precisely to the national and religious spirit which surged within the Israelite people during the period of the United Monarchy and the extension of its borders far beyond the limits of the Israelite settlement. It is within reason that Genesis was given its original written form during the time when the Davidic empire was being established, and that the additions and supplements of later authors were only intended to help bridge the time gap for contemporary readers, and had no decisive effect on its contents or its overall character.

This dating is indicated, in particular, by the poetic utterances inserted in the partriarchal accounts, including the blessing of Jacob, which stresses Judah's ascendancy over the other Israelite tribes, and the blessing of Isaac (as well as Noah's curse on Canaan) aimed to justify Israelite hegemony in Canaan and among nearby neighbours. Also attributable to this period is Gen 14, in which a two-fold objective is prominent: (1) to substantiate the claim to the land on both sides of the Jordan, from El-paran, which apparently is none other than Elath, all the way to the region lying north of Damascus, on the basis of the father of the nation having acquired it by virtue of his victory over external enemies; (2) to mention Abraham's relationship to Melchizedek, King of Salem, and a priest of ʾEl-ʾElyōn, who had blessed him and received from him "a tenth of everything". The words of the poet in Ps 110 may well testify that with the conquest of Jerusalem by David that genealogical tradition which had linked the rulers of the city to Melchizedek — and with it the claim to the city

Abraham (1964); *idem*, *La Questione della Genesi* (1934). On the viewpoint of the Scandinavian school, see H.S. Nyberg, *Oral Tradition* (1954); and of the German school, M. Noth, *Überlieferungsgeschichte des Pentateuchs* (1948); G. von Rad, *Die Theologie der geschichtlichen Überlieferungen Israels* (1957). On Y. Kaufmann's system, see his monumental *Toledot HaEmunah HaIsraʾelit* (History of the Religion of Israel) 2 (1954) (Hebrew). There is an abridged translation by M. Greenberg, *The Religion of Israel* (1960). Cf. also G. Fohrer, *Introduction to the Old Testament* (1970), 103ff.

— was transferred to the House of David. It is within reason that what is written in Gen 14 is only a link in a chain of traditions then being forged in the new capital, including the traditions about Jerusalem as a site holy to ʾEl-ʾElyōn ("Jahweh the Most High, creator of heaven and earth" of Gen 14: 22); about the "binding of Isaac" on a mountain in the land of Moriah where Abraham built an altar, naming the place "the Lord appears" (Hebrew: *yeraʾeh*; Gen 22:14); and about the building of an altar by David on the threshing floor of Arawnah, the Jebusite, at the very sanctified spot on Mount Moriah "where He appeared to David" (Hebrew: *nirʾah*; 2 Chr 3:1), and where Solomon erected the Temple.[4] It is in place to mention the anachronisms in Gen 14, such as Ashteroth-karnaim (Ashteroth in the region of Karnaim), and Hazazon-tamar (Hazazon in the region of Tamar), Dan, and "the valley of the king" (cf. 2 Sam 18:18). Even the divine epithet "ʾEl-ʾElyōn, creator of heaven and earth" apparently cannot be dated much earlier than 1000 B.C.E.[5]

Moreover, the narrative in Gen 14 fits in organically with that of the sacrifice-covenant in Gen 15, which reflects the political aspirations of David's and Solomon's time ("To your descendants I give this land, from the river of Egypt to the great river, the river Euphrates"), and the promise of mastery over the Canaanite peoples, including the Kenites and the Kenizzites, who up to the time of David still comprised separate ethnic entities in Judah.

Another fact meriting attention is that during the period of the United Monarchy the fixed, articulated, Phoenician-Hebrew alphabetical script became the accepted, widespread script in the Land of Israel, and made possible the lively literary activity in the royal court and the priestly circles of Jerusalem. This creativity was manifested in various literary genres, in poetry and in prose, encompassing historiographic works, epic, religious and didactic poetry, and wisdom literature, which drew their inspiration both from Israelite traditions and from Mesopotamian, Canaanite-Phoenician, and Egyptian sources. It was not idly said of Solomon: "The wisdom of Solomon exceeded that of all of the peoples of the East, and all of the wisdom of Egypt," which means that wisdom literature, in different forms and of various origins, was known in Israel and was particularly current in the royal court in Jerusalem.[6] It is, then,

4 See U.D. Cassuto, *Biblical and Oriental Studies* 1: *Bible* (1973), 71ff.; B. Mazar, in the anthology *Judah and Jerusalem* (1957), 27ff. (Hebrew).

5 On ʾEl ʾElyōn, creator of heaven and earth, see F.M. Cross, *HTR* 60/4 (1964), 241ff. It is worth noting that outside of the biblical sources the appellation (ʾEl) ʾElyon is mentioned in the theogony of Sanchunyaton and in the Sefire inscription (אל ועלין, A10), but is not known from epigraphic sources from the second millennium B.C.E. Cf. R. Rendtorff, *Fourth World Congress of Jewish Studies* 1 (1967), 167ff.

6 See A. Alt, *Kleine Schriften* 2 (1953), 90ff. With regard to the circulation of the Mesopotamian literary works, it is worth mentioning that sections of the Gilgamesh Epic in various versions from the 14th and 13th centuries B.C.E. have been discovered in Megiddo and in Ugarit, and, in Hittite and Hurrian translations, also in Boghazköy.

in place to assume that at the time of the composition of Genesis, whose chief purpose was in the nature of: "Give ear, O my people, to my teaching; incline your ears to the words of my mouth ... which we have heard, and we know them; our ancestors have recounted them to us" (Ps 78:1–2), the authors of Genesis had recourse not only to the national traditions then current but to various literary works, including Mesopotamian and Canaanite mythological and epic works. Some of these were embedded in the Book, especially in the primeval history, after having undergone thorough literary reformation (though there are cases of different versions of the same story having been retained), in the spirit of Israelite monotheism, and in conformity to the historiographic conception which assigns great importance to genealogies in the history of mankind generally, and in Israelite history particularly.[7]

One may, apparently, also count among these the resemblance to ancient epics, such as that of Nimrod, incorporated into the Table of Nations. According to Speiser, this story is based on the exploits of Tukulti-Ninurta I, King of Assyria at the end of the 13th century B.C.E.[8] In like fashion, the account of the expedition of Chedorlaomer, King of Elam, and his allies, including Amraphel, King of Shinar, and Tidal, King of Goyim, which apparently resembles a variety of ancient epics, is also incorporated into the tale of Abraham's exploits in Gen 14. Although it is not possible to prove the identification of Chedorlaomer with the Elamite king, Kudur-Naḫūnde I, as has been suggested by Albright, it is certainly worth mentioning that the exploits of the latter had achieved notoriety and were related in later generations as well.[9] In any event, the practice of incorporating sections of epics or their semblance

7 Complex problems have arisen in connection with the first chapters of Genesis, among them the accounts of the Creation, the Garden of Eden, and the Tower of Babel, and the degree to which they were influenced, directly or indirectly, by the Mesopotamian and Canaanite epics [cf. C. Westerman, *Genesis* 1/1 (1966)]; see also the detailed discussions in Speiser's exegesis of Genesis, on the one hand, and, on the other hand, W.G. Lambert's criticism of the views current among scholars [*JThS* 16/2 (1965), 287ff.]. Speiser's opinion [*Orientalia* 34 (1956), 317ff.] that the story of the Tower of Babel had its source in the Babylonian *Enūma eliš*, is quite instructive; but Lambert dates this literary work not before the 11th century B.C.E. It is conceivable that the Mesopotamian poems, in common with other mythological and epic works, came to Israel not only through the intermediation of the Canaanite culture, but indirectly as well, via travellers in caravans who traversed the trade routes — and that they were included in the general term "the wisdom of all the people of the east" (1 Kgs 4:30). With respect to the problem of genealogy, see W. Dufy, *The Tribal Historical Theory on the Origin of the Hebrew People* (1944), and J. Liver, *Enc. Miq*. 3, s.v. *yaḥas*. Concerning the exaggerated importance attributed to genealogy lists already at the time of the "Amoritic" kingdom of Babylonia (Ḫammurapi's dynasty), we can now learn a great deal from an extremely interesting document from the time of Ammiṣadūqa. See J.J. Finkelstein, *JCS* 20 (1966), 95ff.

8 See E.A. Speiser, *EI* 5 (1959), 32ff.*; on the exploits of Tukulti-Ninurta I, see also E. Weidner, *AfO* 20 (1963), 113ff.

9 See W.F. Albright, *BASOR* 88 (1942), 33ff.; 163 (1961), 53, n. 76.

into historical narrative, and even into royal annals, was not unfamiliar to the ancients.[10]

The fundamental problem before us is the extent to which we can ascertain the delimitations in time of the way of life reflected in the series of patriarchal narratives, clarifying the historical context relevant to the political and ethnic picture which is portrayed in them. It seems to me that many contemporary scholars have gone too far in their recurring attempts to discover in the Akkadian sources, such as the Mari documents from the 18th century B.C.E., the Nuzi tablets from the 15th and 14th centuries, and even in the Egyptian sources from the Middle Kingdom, corroboration of the antiquity of the patriarchal stories, or at least of the antiquity of the traditions embedded in them. These scholars see in the sources monumental testimony to the existence of the "patriarchal period" as an actual, chronologically defined, historical era.[11] This is the case with the regard to the overall picture as reflected by the archaeological excavations and surveys at sites of the Middle Bronze Age, and particularly MB I in the Negeb.[12] There is certainly room for thought on and reconsideration of the conflicting views as to the dating of the "patriarchal period" to the first, second, and third quarters of the second millennium B.C.E.

Though it is undoubtedly true that the Israelites retained vague memories of the common origin and destiny of the tribes in the remote past, and traditions about the names and genealogies of their forefathers, of their origin in Mesopotamia and their connections with the "sons" of Nahor,[13] of their migration to Canaan and of their descent to Egypt, a penetrating analysis of the sagas recorded in Genesis does not permit us to consider them as a faithful representation of the actual history of the Patriarchs and their exploits. Nor can we consider them to be ancient sources from which we may reconstruct,

10 See A.L. Oppenheim, *Ancient Mesopotamia* (1964), 150f., 362; and H.G. Güterbock, *JCS* 18 (1964), 1ff.

11 The increasing number of epigraphic sources of the second millennium B.C.E. (particularly from Mari, Ugarit, Alalakh, and Boghazköy) put to a severe test the entire theoretical framework dealing with Hebrew origins and with the traditions contained in the Book of Genesis and their evaluation as a historical source. This raises the question as to what degree the parallelism in ancient social and legal forms, in customs and in motifs, can validly serve as a basis for establishing a chronology of the stories about the Patriarchs of the Hebrew nation, not to speak of the credibility of the events described therein. The various opinions, which are often contradictory, and even undergo changes from time to time, have found expression in books on biblical history, entries in encyclopaedias, and numerous scholarly papers. See *inter alia* C.H. Gordon, *The World of the Old Testament* (2d ed, 1960), 113ff.; *idem, Biblical and Other Studies* (1963), 3ff.; W.F. Albright, *BASOR* 163 (1961), 36ff.; M. Noth, *Die Ursprünge des alten Israel im Lichte neuer Quellen* (1961); R. de Vaux, in J.Ph. Hyatt (ed.), *The Bible in Modern Scholarship* (1965); S. Yeivin, *RSO* 38 (1963), 277ff.

12 See N. Glueck, *Rivers in the Desert* (1959), *passim*; W.F. Albright, *BASOR* 163 (1961); and against their theory, M. Kochavi's "The Settlement of the Negev in the Middle Bronze I Age" (Ph.D. diss., The Hebrew University of Jerusalem, 1967), 232ff. (Hebrew).

13 See B. Mazar, *Zion* 11 (1946), 1ff. (Hebrew).

to any significant extent, the stages of the Israelite emergence against the background of general history, dwelling on the processes and developments relating to the lives of the Patriarchs over the generations, till the time of the formation of the "amphictyony" of the twelve tribes of Israel.

In my view, it is much more within reason that the way of life and the ethnic and socio-political picture reflected in the patriarchal accounts generally correspond to the end of the period of the Judges and the beginning of the Monarchy. That is to say: the *Sitz-im-Leben* of these narratives, part of which are certainly based on folk legends from the time of the Israelite occupation of Canaan, derives principally from a period preceding by only a generation or two that during which the great historiographic work was given its original written form. This hypothesis is supported by certain data which can be interpreted only against the background of their historical period.

We must first give our attention to what are customarily termed "anachronisms", which run like a scarlet thread through the tableau of the patriarchal sagas, and which are also to be found in the first chapters of Genesis, such as the important role assigned to the Philistines and the Arameans, two nations which entered the arena of history in the 12th century B.C.E.

Particularly instructive are the stories about the Patriarchs in the Negeb, in Beer-sheba and in the region west of it, i.e. Gerar, which was an integral part of the Philistine country. In the ancient sources of Chronicles, Gerar, lying on the periphery of the area settled by Judah and its sub-groups, is described as a broad, open country, excelling in good pasture land, containing relatively few permanent settlements, being inhabited by various semi-nomadic tribes (1 Chr 4:39f.; 2 Chr 14:13–14). In Gen 10:19, on the other hand, Gerar is placed in the western Negeb, the southernmost region of the Land of Canaan. The same is true of the stories about Abraham and Isaac, who are pictured to us as "great men", living as semi-nomads in the region of Beer-sheba, and from there migrating, especially in times of drought, to Philistine Gerar. By virtue of their treaty with Abimelek, King of the Philistines, they would reside there under his protection, grazing their flocks and even engaging in seasonal agriculture (Gen 26:12). At times disputes broke out between them and the Philistines over wells, and occasionally they moved southward with their flocks to the expanses of the Negeb, reaching Kadesh-barnea and Beer-lahai-roi on the road to Shur. When there was a severe drought, they went down as far as the Nile Delta with Pharaoh's consent.[14]

14 From various sources relating to the Middle and Late Kingdoms, and particularly from the story in Papyrus Anastasi VI [R.A. Caminos, *Late Egyptian Miscellanies* (1954), 293ff.] about permission being granted to nomads from Edom to enter the Delta regions under similar circumstances (ca. 1200 B.C.E.), it may be assumed that this was a prevalent custom, not confined to any particular period.

The way of life and conditions of settlement reflected in these narratives do not differ from those existing in the days when David and his men resided in the western Negeb, in the territory and under the protection of Achish, King of the Philistines, whose capital was Gath; and they correspond very well to all that the archaeological surveys have revealed concerning the unwalled settlements of the semi-nomads of the 11th century B.C.E. in that region.[15]

One may find in the tales about Abraham, Isaac, and Abimelek transparent allusions to the relations between the Judeans and their sub-groups in the Negeb and the Philistine kingdom during the last quarter of the 11th century B.C.E. It is, therefore, not surprising that Achish is called by the name Abimelek in the title verse of Ps 34: "To David, when he feigned madness before Abimelek, so that he drove him out, and he departed". There is no need to alter the text, or to assign to it a later date.

It is not by chance, therefore, that the author of the Book of Samuel was careful to distinguish between the Cherethite Negeb and the Negeb of Judah and its sub-groups (1 Sam 30:14), which parallels the distinction in the same passage between the Land of the Philistines and the Land of Judah (v. 16). This also explains the fact that the narrative in Genesis recognizes a king of the Philistines, accompanied by his general, his "councillor" (Hebrew: *mereʿēhu*) and his slaves. What is here reflected is a monarchial regime, apparently established in Philistia at the time when the league of the five Philistine *śeranīm* became obsolete, during the third quarter of the 11th century B.C.E. A corresponding system existed contemporaneously in the Israelite kingdom (cf. 2 Sam 3:8).

As to the Arameans and the appellations of the Aramean countries — Aram Naharaim and Padan Aram — we have no convincing evidence for their appearance on the stage of history before the end of the 12th century B.C.E. Tiglath-Pileser I was the first Assyrian king who fought against the Aḫlamē-Arameans, i.e. the nomadic Arameans in the broad area between the middle Euphrates and Mount Sirion.[16] In the course of the 11th century B.C.E.

15 About the unwalled settlements in this region, see R. Gofna, *Yediot* 28 (1964), 236ff. (Hebrew); *idem*, *ʿAtiqot* 3 (1966), 44ff. (Hebrew). On the basis of the pottery, they may be dated to the second half of the 11th century and the beginning of the 10th century B.C.E.

16 The various attempts to prove that the Arameans appeared earlier [see A. Dupont Sommer, *VT* 1 (1953), 40ff.; M.F. Unger, *Israel and the Aramaeans of Damascus* (1957), 39; S. Moscati, *JSS* 4 (1959), 303ff.] have been fruitless, and no conclusive proof of this view has been found in the cuneiform sources; see also N. Schneider, *Biblica* 30 (1949), 109ff.; J.C.S. Gibson, *JNES* 20 (1961), 229ff. This is also the case in regard to the "proto-Aramean" language of the Western Semites in Mesopotamia [Noth, *Die Ursprünge des alten Israel* (see note 11)]; see also D.O. Edzard, *ZA*, N.F. 22 (1964), 142ff. To approximately this same period of time may be dated the initial appearance of the nomadic Chaldeans (Gen 25:22; Job 1:17). This is the source of the combination "Ur-of-the-Chaldees", which indicates that the Chaldeans resided in Ur. The land of the Chaldeans (^{māt}*Kaldū*) at the southern

they gained a foothold in the Euphrates crescent and in the adjoining areas in Mesopotamia. This background explains the description of the life of the semi-nomadic Arameans of Padan Aram, whose principal occupation was still herding. So, too, we can well understand the fact that in the genealogical lists Aram appears as the younger branch in the "amphictyony" of the tribes of Nahor (Gen 22:21), and that in the popular legend, Laban the Aramean is accorded an honoured position among his people, whose central area of settlement was Harran in Aram Naharaim, spreading from there to eastern Transjordan.[17]

The historic course of events during the second half, and more particularly the end, of the 11th century B.C.E. is reflected here. On this background we can understand the reference in Genesis to the name Gilead, explaining it as being derived from the Hebrew *gal'ed*, "mound of witness" (in Aramaic: *yegar śahadūthā*), which describes the treaty concluded between Laban the Aramean and Jacob, the eponymus of the Israelite tribes, in Mizpah, in the region of Mount Gilead, which determined the territorial boundaries of the two nations (Gen 31:45–54). What we have, in fact, is an enlightening portrayal of the relationship between Aram and Israel before the beginning of David's war against the kingdom of Aram Zobah and its allies in Transjordan.

Mentions of Moab and Ammon, the nations of the eastern border region, who are genealogically linked to Lot, are also fitted into the political and ethnic picture, as are the tales and poems alluding to Edom's subservience to Israel in the days of David's reign. Against this background are comprehensible also the lists of the kings of Edom "before a king ruled in Israel" (Gen 36: 31–39).

No less oriented to this period are the references to Ishmael, described as the father of a great nation, genealogically associated with Abraham and Hagar. The Ishmaelites were tribes of nomads, tent dwellers and camel riders, whose religious centre was Beer-lahai-roi on the road to Shur, a site associated with the traditions about Isaac. Certainly we cannot assign to the appearance of the Ishmaelites on the border region of Eretz-Israel a date earlier than the 11th century B.C.E. In the course of their tremendous expansion, they dispossessed the Midianites, who had preceded them in the border regions and in the nearby desert areas, and absorbed them into their midst, which explains the relationship between the Midianites and the Ishmaelites in Genesis and in the Book

extremity of Mesopotamia is known to us from the first half of the 9th century B.C.E. See also H.W.F. Saggs, *Iraq* 22 (1960), 200ff. It is now evident that the Aramaeans' appearance on the stage of history was earlier. The name "the Aramu" is mentioned in the topographical list of Amenḥotep III from Kom el-Hetan; cf. S. Aḥituv, *Canaanite Toponyms in Ancient Egyptian Documents* (1984), 66.

17 See in this volume, "The Aramean Empire and Its Relations with Israel," pp. 151–172.

of Judges.[18] The merging of their tribes became a most important factor in the operation of the desert caravan trade: "And they dwelt from Havilah by Shur, which is close to Egypt, all the way to Asshur. They made raids against all their kinsmen" (Gen 25:18). This geographical definition reminds us, by the way, of the area within which the desert nomads operated in the days of Saul: "from Havilah by Shur, which is close to Egypt" (1 Sam 15:7).

There is certainly a connection between the description of Ishmael as "a wild colt of a man, his hand against everyone, and everyone's hand against him, and in the face of all of his kin he shall camp" (Gen 16:12) and the tradition preserved in 1 Chr 5, concerning the tremendous pressure exerted by the Hagarites against the borders of the Israelite settlement in Transjordan during the reign of Saul. This is particularly so as they are described as tent dwellers and camel, donkey, and sheep owners, the tribes of Jetur and Naphish (whose names also appear in the genealogy of Ishmael in Gen 25:15) being ascribed to them. At the end of the 11th century B.C.E. the Hagarites began to be pushed out of their positions by the Israelites on the one side and the Arameans on the other, and to become absorbed by associations of other tribes who replaced them both in the border region of the country and in the desert areas which surround it from the east and the south.

The over-all ehtnographic picture described above is, then, similar in many details to that which is presented in Ps 83, one of the earliest psalms, which can be assigned to the end of the period of the Judges, in any event to a time prior to the westward expansion of the Arameans:

> For they have taken counsel together, against you they form a pact, the tents of [*ʾōhole*, but cf. the variant reading *ʾelōhē*, "the gods of", in the scroll from Masada] Edom and the Ishmaelites, Moab and the Hagarites, Gebal and Ammon, and Amalek, Philistia with the residents of Tyre; even Assyria is joined with them. They have become an arm of the Sons of Lot.[19]

The ethnographic situation in Canaan itself, as depicted in Genesis, can also be explained against the background of this same period. In the Table of Nations, which underwent a number of transformations in the course of the

18 See Mazar, *Canaan and Israel*, 15; J. Liver, *Enc. Miq*. 3, s.v. "Ishmaʾel". It is worth stressing that, contrary to the stories about the Patriarchs, the imprint of desert life is manifest in the stories about Hagar and Ishmael. It is significant that the Hagarites and the Ishmaelites are depicted as possessing camels, which began to be used by nomads, it would seem, during the 12th and 11th centuries B.C.E. Concerning this problem, see W.F. Albright, *Archaeology and the Religion of Israel* (1942), 96ff.; R. Waltz, *ZDMG* (1951), 28ff.; (1954), 45ff. See also, W.F. Albright, in *Alt Festschrift* (1953), 1ff., about Sheba, Dedan, and Havilah. On the Ishmaelites, cf. I. Ephaʿl, *The Ancient Arabs* (1982), 231ff.

19 See B. Mazar, *Yediot* 4 (1937), 47ff. (Hebrew), and S. Feigin, *Misitre heʿavar* (Secrets of the Past) (1943), 31ff. (Hebrew). At present I tend to date this psalm to the time of Samuel.

generations, Canaan appears as one of the "sons" of Ham, which is a general designation for the Egyptian empire and its spheres of influence; there is room for the view that the territorial and political scheme upon which the list of the sons of Ham is based is the product of a conception originating in the period of the 19th and 20th Dynasties. In this list, Canaan is the eponym of the Phoenician city-states, of Hittite Hamath, which, according to archaeological excavations at the site, was founded in the 12th century B.C.E., and of the ethnic elements which survived in Eretz-Israel until the period of the Israelite Monarchy. Sidon is considered "the first-born son" of Canaan by virtue of this city's pre-eminence in Phoenicia during the 11th century. Even after Tyre rose to prominence, southern Phoenicians were still called "Sidonians". On the other hand, the Philistines are classified within the territorial framework of Egypt (Gen 10:14 should be read "and Caphtorim, whence came out the Philistines"), not only because of the settlements of the Sea Peoples ("Caphtorim") in Lower Egypt at the time of the 20th and 21st Dynasties, but also because of the restoration of pharaonic rule over the Philistine coast during the time of David, apparently during the reign of Pharaoh Siamon.[20]

Particularly enlightening is the fact that in Genesis the ancestors of the Israelites are called Hebrews, especially when the author wishes to characterize their origin. Thus, in Gen 14, it is Abram the Hebrew (*ʿibrī*) who dwells among the Amorites in Hebron, and, in the Joseph stories, Joseph is variously described by the Egyptians as "a Hebrew man", "a Hebrew youth", and "a Hebrew slave", and he testifies concerning himself that "I was kidnapped from the land of the Hebrews" (Gen 11:15), i.e. the Land of Israel. In like manner, the contrast between the Egyptians and Israelites is stressed by writing: "for Egyptians could not eat bread with the Hebrews".

There have been various attempts to explain the meaning of the term "Hebrew" (*ʿibrī*) and its possible relation to the *Ḫapiru* of Akkadian sources and the *ʿApiru* of the Egyptian texts.[21] From the standpoint of our subject, it should be stressed that the use of this appellation in Genesis, Exodus, and 1 Samuel is pronouncedly identical. Particularly worthy of attention are passages such as: "and be as Philistine men; lest you become servile to the Hebrews, just as they once served you", or "No skilled craftsmen could be found in Israel, for the Philistines said: Lest the Hebrews fashion swords or javelins", and the words of the Philistine commanders concerning David and his band: "Who are these Hebrews? And Achish replied to the Philistine commanders:

20 See A. Malamat, *BA* 21 (1958), 99f.; and in this volume, "The Philistines and the Rise of Israel and Tyre", pp. 63–82.

21 See especially J. Boterro, *Le problème des Habiru* (1954); M. Greenberg, *The Hap/biru* (1955); J. Lewy, *HUCA* 28 (1957), 1ff.; W.F. Albright, *BASOR* 163 (1961), 36ff.; J.C.S. Gibson, *JNES* 20 (1961), 234ff.; N.A. van Uchelen, *Abraham de Hebreeër* (1964).

'Is that not David, a royal officer of Saul, king of Israel?'" In all of these passages, as in 1 Sam 13:7 (and even in 1 Sam 14:21) the references can only be to the Israelites and the minor nationalities associated with them. It is self-evident that the use of the ethnic appellation "Hebrew", especially when applied to the Israelites in their relations with foreign peoples such as the Egyptians, the Philistines, or the Canaanites, was accepted practice at the end of the period of the Judges and that of the Monarchy. On the other hand, its relation to the designation *Ḫapiru* (*ʿApiru*) of the external second millennium B.C.E. sources, which refers to a social class, remains, for the time, unsolved. It is significant that Shem, the eponymous ancestor of the Israelites and related ethnic groups (Gen 9:26–27),[22] appears in the Table of Nations as the ancestor of all the Hebrews (Gen 10:21), and primarily of Abraham and his family (cf. Gen 11:10–26).

I will confine myself to a few remarks on the migrations of the Patriarchs in the Land of Israel and their relationship to sacred sites. It appears reasonable to me that the Genesis narrative corresponds, generally speaking, to the chronological context of the end of the period of the Judges and the beginning of the Monarchy, when memories and echoes of events and exploits from the period of the Settlement of the Israelite tribes in the land were still fresh, and when various traditions about their ancestors, their lives, and their ties with the sacred sites were still current. It should be noted that most of the sites mentioned as the places where the Patriarchs sojourned, or as stopping-off spots in their migrations, are located within the area of the principal Israelite Settlement, i.e. Judah, Mount Ephraim, and Gilead. The vast majority of them are known as the locations of shrines and cultic celebrations during the period of the Judges and the beginning of the Monarchy, and several of them as important centres of the Israelite tribes as well.

Even the ever-recurring motif that the Patriarchs pitched their tents near sacred terebinths (Hebrew: *ʾelōnīm*) in the proximity of cities, erecting altars and *maṣṣebōth*, and binding themselves by treaty and protective arrangements to the inhabitants of the cities, has its parallels in the period of the Judges. Thus, in the story of Heber the Kenite (one of the descendants of Hobab, the father-in-law of Moses), who dwelled in Arad, he pitched his tents "all the way to Elon-bezaanaim" (Judg 4:11), undoubtedly a sacred site in the area of Naphtali, entering into a protective treaty with the king of Hazor.[23] In a number of stories we discover transparent allusions to temples, as in the words Jacob uttered at Bethel: "... and this stone that I have set up as a pillar shall be

22 Cf. Speiser, *Genesis* (see note 1), 62f.

23 See B. Mazar, *JNES* 24 (1965), 300ff. Concerning shrines in general in Genesis, see R. de Vaux, *Ancient Israel* (1961), 289ff.; Kaufmann, *Toledot HaEmunah HaIsraʾelit* (see note 3), 126ff.; W.A. Irwin, *RB* (1965), 161ff.

God's abode, and of all that you may grant to me, I will always set aside a tenth for you", certainly referring to the house of God in Bethel, known from the time of Samuel (1 Sam 10:3) and from the tale of the concubine in Gibeah (Judg 20:18). The story of Jacob's "pilgrimage" to Bethel (Gen 35; cf. 1 Sam 10:3) also seems reasonable against the background of the end of the period of Judges and the beginning of the Monarchy.[24] It is also instructive that the altar between Bethel and ʿAi is mentioned, since in the light of the excavations at the latter site, present-day et-Tell, it becomes quite certain that an Israelite settlement existed there in the 12th and 11th centuries B.C.E., at the very time that Bethel attained a high degree of growth, while the ʿAi of the Bronze Age was already laid waste in the third quarter of the third millennium B.C.E.[25]

As regards Hebron and its sacred sites — the terebinth of Mamre and the field of Machpelah before Mamre — one cannot escape the conclusion that there is a causal relation between the great importance which Genesis attaches to this locality and the rise of Hebron to the status of a royal city and cultic centre at the beginning of David's reign. It was there that David was crowned king over all Israel "before the Lord", and there resided one of the most important priestly clans that performed cultic service. It is not by chance that Hebron and Shechem are numbered among the "cities of asylum" and the "cities of the priests and the Levites" during the period of the United Monarchy.[26] Moreover, as in Hebron, the central city of Judah, so in Shechem, the centre of Mount Ephraim, various traditions and folk legends concerning the past of these cities were woven into epics about events in the days of the original Settlement of the Israelite tribes and their sub-groups, and their relations with the autochthonous inhabitants, and bound together with matters pertaining to the sacred sites and to the burial places there, associated with imposing personalities of the remote past. It is possible that stories such as that of Shechem, the son of Hamor, and Dinah, in Gen 34 (cf. Gen 48:22) are nothing but reflections of the events described in the tale about Abimelek in Judg 9: the abrogation of the treaty which existed between the Israelites and the rulers of Shechem, the annihilation of the clan of the sons of Hamor, and the devastation of the foreign-populated city of Shechem.[27]

24 See A. Alt, *Kleine Schriften* 1 (1953), 79ff.

25 Conclusions drawn from the excavations conducted at et-Tell in 1933–1935 [J. Marquet-Krause, *Les fouilles de Ay (et-Tell)* (1949)] have in general been confirmed by the excavation season of 1964 [J.A. Callaway, *BASOR* 178 (1965), 231ff.]. Cf. also *EAEHL* 1 (1975), 36ff.

26 About the cities of the priests and the Levites, and their dating to the time of the United Monarchy, see W.F. Albright, *L. Ginzberg Jubilee Volume* (1949), 49ff.; B. Mazar, *VT Suppl.* 7 (1960), 193ff.; and about the cities of asylum, see M. Greenberg, *JBL* 78 (1959), 125ff.

27 The view that the historic event reflected in the story of Genesis 34 took place during MB II has been set forth in G.E. Wright's *Shechem* (1965), which includes a detailed review of the excavations at Shechem; see also E. Nielsen, *Shechem, a Traditio-historical Investigation* (1955). It stands to reason,

It is certainly not a coincidence that it is precisely with respect to each of the three major centres, Hebron, Shechem and Jerusalem, that traditions were preserved concerning the permanent purchase of sites from their foreign owners, with payment in silver currency: the field of Machpelah and the burial cave in it, acquired by Abraham from his Hittite allies (Gen 23); the section of the field in Shechem, where Jacob erected an altar and where Joseph's grave is located, bought by Jacob from the Hivite sons of Hamor (Gen 33:19; Josh 24:32); the threshing floor of Arawnah the Jebusite, purchased by David from the Jebusite ruler of Jerusalem (2 Sam 24:24).

With respect to the story of Joseph, without embarking on a clarification of the complex of problems involved, I will confine myself to asserting that the current hypothesis, according to which it is based on a historic event during the Hyksos period, or at the time of El-Amarna, is unacceptable. The character of the account, its tendency (Joseph's pre-eminent position among his brothers, the transfer of the primogeniture from Menasseh to Ephraim, Machir being mentioned as Menasseh's son, the prominent role played by Judah, etc.) and the numerous "anachronisms" (the Egyptian names, the Ishmaelites, the land of the Hebrews, the land of Ramesses) are such as to make us think that the traditions and motifs joined together in this single tableau were interwoven and developed on Mount Ephraim and were given their sophisticated novelistic literary form no earlier than the beginning of the Monarchy.[28]

In conclusion, I will make the further observation that the incorporation of the story of Judah and Tamar (Gen 38) into the series of narratives about the forefathers of the nation certainly has special significance. This chapter reflects not only a current tradition regarding the matter of the settlement of the tribe of Judah, its relations with the Canaanite population in the Shephelah, its branching out into clans, and their subsequent diffusion. It also serves as a kind of background to the history of David's family and its genealogical relation to Perez, son of Judah (as in the Book of Ruth). It is, then, joined with an entire complex of transparent allusions, in narrative and in poetry, about the origin and deeds of David, stressing the unique importance of the tribe of Judah, even in relation to the House of Joseph, to whom the deeply rooted Israelite historical traditions had assigned a position of centrality in the tribal organization.

in my opinion, that the historic kernel was swallowed up by the popular tale, and was accompanied by folkloristic motifs after having been included in the Jacob-cycle of traditions. As regards the roles played by Simeon and Levi in this tale, the source is apparently a motif that was prevalent during the time of the United Monarchy, i.e. that Judah's ascent to grandeur and his position at the head of the tribes were the result of the sins committed by his three elder brothers (Gen 49:3ff.).

28 On the Joseph stories, see J.M.A. Janssen, *Ex Oriente Lux*, 14 (1956), 63ff.; J. Vergote, *Joseph en Egypte* (1959), and D.B. Redford, *A Study of the Biblical Story of Joseph* (1970).

This conception, fundamental to the Book of Genesis, found an expression in the words of a later historiographer:

> And the sons of Reuben, the first-born of Israel — although he was the first-born son, since he violated his father's bed, his right of primogeniture was transferred to the sons of [in the Septuagint: "his son"] Joseph, son of Israel; and he [Reuben] was not in the line of primogeniture. For Judah became the mighty one among his brothers and a prince over him, but the birthright belongs to Joseph (1 Chr 5:1–2).

The author of Ps 78 summarizes his survey of history by emphasizing, with painstaking care, the ascendancy of Judah over Joseph: "for the Lord despised the tent of Joseph, and preferred not the tribe of Ephraim. He chose rather the tribe of Judah, Mt. Zion which he loves.... He has chosen David, his servant" (vv. 67–71).[29]

29 It is also worth mentioning that as a result of archaeological discoveries and critical study of their sources and traditions, similar problems have arisen concerning the historic background of the Iliad and the Odyssey and the events depicted in them (particularly the Trojan War). See the detailed discussions in A.J.B. Wace and F.H. Stubbings, *A Companion to Homer* (1962); D.L. Page, *History and the Homeric Iliad* (1963); R.C. Jebb, *A Companion to Greek Studies* (1963), 117ff.; M.I. Finley et al., *JHSt* 84 (1964); G.S. Kirk, *CAH* 2, Part 2 (1975), 820ff.; as well as de Vaux, *Ancient Israel* (see note 23), 29, n. 30.

The Philistines and the Rise of Israel and Tyre

One of the most remarkable chapters in the history of the eastern Mediterranean is the transition from the second to the first millennium B.C.E. The succession of events during this period determined for all time the destiny of Eretz-Israel and Syria. It was then that three Semitic peoples entered the arena of history, each of them becoming capable of establishing a national state and developing a unique culture. These three peoples were the Israelites, the Arameans and the Phoenicians.

To understand this phenomenon we must first note that it was during the 12th century B.C.E. that the great empires which had controlled the Near East for centuries, crumbled and fell. Simultaneously great shifts of populations occurred. The movement of the Sea Peoples on the shores of the Mediterranean and its islands, and of the Semitic nomadic tribes on the periphery of the Fertile Crescent, altered the ethnic and cultural configuration of the ancient Near East.

At the beginning of the 12th century B.C.E., the Hittite empire was shattered into fragments under the pressure of invading peoples. It was succeeded by small neo-Hittite kingdoms in northern Syria, while in eastern and southern Syria Aramean nomads were tempted to penetrate into the region and gained control over vast areas.

As for Egypt, its rule in Canaan had already begun to disintegrate by the end of the 13th century B.C.E. It was only thanks to the decisive sea and land victory won at the beginning of the 12th century by Pharaoh Ramesses III over the Sea Peoples, including the Philistines who had invaded the coast of

* This study is a revised version of the article which appeared in *The Israel Academy of Sciences and Humanities, Proceedings* 1/7 (1964), 1–22.

Canaan, that Egypt was still able to maintain its hold on the coastal areas and its control of the trade routes in Canaan. About the middle of the 12th century B.C.E., Egyptian domination declined and ceased entirely. The tenuous control during the twilight period of Egyptian rule had been based essentially on a corps of professional soldiers and on troops garrisoned in fortresses. The latter absorbed increasing numbers of mercenaries and captives of war from among the Sherden, the Philistines and the other Sea Peoples. In the course of time, the Philistine chiefs — the *śeranîm* of the biblical tradition — merely took over control and established their own principalities on the coast. The Philistines and other Sea Peoples also established new settlements in the coastal region, and amidst the subjugated population a ruling class emerged out of this alien minority.

Philistine prisoners depicted in the reliefs of Ramesses III's temple at Medinet Habu

At the same time, in the interior of Canaan on both sides of the Jordan, a loose confederation of Israelite tribes had already succeeded in becoming rooted and taking possession of large areas. This was a lengthy and complicated process of settlement characterized by the growth of a relatively dense population in the hill country and the lowlands, and the dispersion of surplus population in peripheral areas. Simultaneously, there was a persistent struggle with the neighbours as well as with invaders from the desert, and strife with Canaanite city-states which survived in various regions, especially on the coast and in the Jezreel Valley. Some of the Israelite tribes now established themselves firmly in the hill country, and constituted the dominant strain of the agricultural population in Ephraim and Judah.

During this period Assyria, under Tiglath-Pileser I, was the only kingdom in Mesopotamia that successfully regained power. Tiglath-Pileser fought fierce battles against the Arameans on the Euphrates and in the Syrian Desert, in an attempt to contain their forceful expansion. In his expeditions to the west, he reached the Mediterranean and imposed his rule on the main Phoenician cities. But the empire of Tiglath-Pileser was short-lived. It declined with his death in 1078 B.C.E., and did not rise again for several generations.

These conditions presented a challenge to the Phoenicians on the coast north of the Carmel, who had freed themselves from the yoke of Egypt, and to the Philistines, who had already seized key positions on the southern coast. Either one or the other had the opportunity to become the dominant maritime power in the eastern Mediterranean, inheriting the role long held by Egypt in the Canaanite coastal area, and by the Myceneans in the sea trade.

The first sources relating to the Sea Peoples and especially the Philistines date to the 11th century B.C.E. The Egyptian onomasticon of Amenope, apparently from the beginning of that century,[1] provides us with information concerning three Sea Peoples on Canaanite soil: the Sherden, the Sikala (*Tkr*) and the Philistines. Three cities are mentioned: Gaza, Ashkelon and Ashdod, which occupied an important position both in political affairs and in sea and land trade.

Authentic data of great value are to be found in the official report of Wen-amon, a priest in the temple of Amon at Karnak in the second quarter of the 11th century B.C.E. He had been sent to Byblos in Phoenicia to secure cedarwood for the ceremonial barge of Amon,[2] and we learn from his report, which is a mine of information not yet fully explored by scholars, that Smendes (Nesubanebded), the ruler of Tanis, had strong commercial ties with Byblos. Zekar-Baʿal, the prince of Byblos, says to Wen-amon: "Are there not twenty *mnš*-ships in my harbour which are in *ḫubûr* with Nesubanebded?" Zekar-Baʿal is referring to large ships (called *mnš*), which set out on the high seas. This is proof of a strong commercial alliance which had a very ancient tradition.

The *ḫubûr* mentioned here certainly refers to powerful commercial organizations, headed by the rulers themselves, with the collaboration of a mercantile aristocracy, known as *kinʿanû* according to an inscription of Amenḥotep II and

1 A. Gardiner, *Ancient Egyptian Onomastica* 1 (1947), 24ff.; A. Alt, *Kleine Schriften* 1 (1953), 231ff.
2 J.A. Wilson, in *ANET*, 25ff.; M.A. Коростовцев, *Пумешесмьие Ун-Амуна ь Библ* (1960); see W.F. Albright, in *Studies Presented to D.M. Robinson* (1951), 223ff.

as *k*ᵉ*na*ᶜ*nîm* according to the Bible, i.e. traders, merchants; cf. Isa 23:8: "Tyre, the crowning city, whose merchants are princes (*śarîm*), whose *k*ᵉ*na*ᶜ*nîm* are the honourable of the earth". This was the noble caste of a thalassocracy, engaged in ship-building, owners of storehouses and workshops. It was they who developed international trade and the various industries involved in it. The formation of such mercantile organizations was of great importance in the political and economic spheres. The *ḫubûr* was also the organization characteristic of the relations between Tyre, Israel and Judah during the 10th and 9th centuries B.C.E. It is significant that in the Bible we find the root *ḥbr* used in this sense (2 Chr 20:35–36), as well as the parallelism *ḥabbâr* = *k*ᵉ*na*ᶜ*anî*, "merchant" (Job 40:30).[3]

Another interesting fact in Wen-amon's report is his mention by name of four rulers of coastal cities lying between Egypt and Phoenicia. One of them was Badar, the prince of Dor, the port city of the Sikala in the Sharon. The other three bear the non-Semitic names of Warta, Makmura and Warkatara, which may be Anatolian or Aegean.[4]

Wen-amon is apparently referring to the princes of the three principal cities of the Philistines, Ashdod, Ashkelon and Gaza, which were known for their importance both in sea and land trade. These coastal cities were sovereign at that time and controlled the sea routes between Egypt and Phoenicia. This is particularly evident from what Wen-amon says concerning Badar. This prince had under his control both merchantmen and warships, and it was in his power to dispatch a navy of eleven warships to Byblos for the purpose of detaining Wen-amon. It should also be mentioned that the funds which Wen-amon brought with him from Egypt were in part tolls for Warta and Makmura, as well as for Badar.

In addition to mentioning the rulers of the Philistine and Sikalite cities, Wen-amon also speaks of three Phoenician cities: Byblos, Sidon and Tyre. Byblos, as we have noted, played an important role in the trade with Egypt. As to Sidon, it was certainly the main political and commercial centre of southern Phoenicia. Tiglath-Pileser I, during his expedition to the Mediterranean, imposed his rule on three Phoenician city-states — Arwad in the north, Byblos in central Phoenicia, and Sidon in the south. It is significant that both the Bible and the Homeric poems note the unique status enjoyed by Sidon. The name "Sidonians" in fact became equivalent to Canaanites or Phoenicians, and it is not accidental that Sidon is referred to as the firstborn son of Canaan in the list of the nations (Gen 10:15). Moreover, there are a number of

3 On *ḫubûr*, see B. Mazar (Maisler), *BASOR* 102 (1946), 9ff.; W.F. Albright, *The Bible and the Ancient Near East, Essays in Honor of W.F. Albright* (1961), 389, n. 80 (henceforth *BANE*).

4 *Ibid*., 359, n. 79, compares them to south-west Anatolian names.

references in the Bible which suggest Sidonian incursions and clashes between the Sidonians and the Israelites (Josh 13:6; Judg 10:12; 18:7–8, 28).[5]

Zekar-Baʿal, the prince of Byblos, makes an interesting statement: "As to this Sidon, the other [town] which you have passed, are there not fifty *baru*-ships which are in *ḫubûr* with Warkatara [or Warkatala], and which are drawn up to his house?" Zekar-Baʿal is here referring to the *ḫubûr* of Sidon with Warkatara, based on a fleet of small ships (Ugaritic; *baru*, Septuagint B: Βαρις)[6] belonging to this Philistine ruler. This passage even possibly points to an overlord-vassal relationship between Warkatara (or Warkatala) and the city-state of Sidon.

We are confronted with the following question: Over which of the three Philistine principalities did Warkatara rule? A conjectural answer would be that he was the lord of Ashkelon.

Ashkelon occupied a preferred position among the Philistine capitals by virtue of its convenient harbour and its ancient tradition of excellence in crafts and industry. Evidence of this excellence is the famous temple of the god Ptaḥ, the Great Prince of Ashkelon, mentioned in the 12th century B.C.E. ivory plaques uncovered in Megiddo.[7] This god was the Egyptian equivalent of the Canaanite deity Kôšâr (Χουσώρ in the Phoenician cosmogony) — *Kṯr-w-ḫss* of Ugaritic mythology — and of the Greek craftsman-god Hephaistos.[8] Early Hebrew poetry also alludes to the special importance of Ashkelon: "Tell it not in Gath, nor announce it in the bazaars of Ashkelon" (אל תבשרו בחוצות אשקלון — 2 Sam 1:20). Alongside of Gath in the Shephelah, which was the seat of the Philistine monarchy in the time of Saul and David, the verse mentions Ashkelon as representative of Philistia.

Note also that in the list of cities in Josh 15, only Ashkelon, of all the Philistine cities, is not included in the territory of Judah. Another important passage is the gloss in Zeph 2:5–7, in which כנען ארץ פלשתים, "the merchantry of Philistia", is interchangeable with Ashkelon. Moreover, from Sennacherib's inscription we learn that the district of Jaffa still belonged to Ashkelon in the 8th century B.C.E., a fact which demonstrates the extent of Ashkelon's maritime expansion along the coast of Eretz-Israel. It should also be noted that Ashkelon and its connections with southern Anatolia play an important part

5 On this problem, see the author's book, *Untersuchungen zur alten Geschichte Syriens und Palästinas* (1930), 67ff.; the problem should be reviewed.

6 On this kind of ship, see Cl. Schaeffer, *Ugaritica* 4 (1962), 138f., and on shipping in general, R.D. Barnett, *Antiquity* 32 (1958), 220ff.

7 G. Loud, *Megiddo Ivories* (1939), 12f., Pl. 63; Wilson, in *ANET*, 263; see also Alt, *Kleine Schriften* (note 1), 219f., 225, and W. Helck, *Die Beziehungen Aegyptens zu Vorderasien im 3. und 2. Jahrtausend v. Chr.* (1962), 480.

8 Cf. H.L. Ginsberg, *Orientalia* 9 (1940), 39ff.; J. Leibovitch, *EI* 4 (1956), 64f. (Hebrew); cf. J. Lewy, *IEJ* 5 (1955), 145ff.

in early Greek legends.[9] No less interesting is the ancient tradition preserved by the historian Justin, that the Sidonians rebuilt Tyre after a defeat at the hands of the ruler of the Ashkelonites. This event is said to have occurred "one year before the destruction of Troy".[10] The tradition evidently alludes to the important role which Ashkelon played in the history of the Sidonians before the rise of Tyre.[11]

It is therefore reasonable to assume, even from this sparse and varied evidence, that the powerful merchant-prince Warkatara was the ruler of Ashkelon, and that in the 11th century B.C.E. Ashkelon had a *ḫubûr* with Sidon, based on the strong political and commercial position of the former.

This interpretation of the situation on the eastern shores of the Mediterranean finds corroboration both in archaeological finds and in biblical sources. We will not concern ourselves here with the particular features which distinguished the eclectic Philistine culture nor with the process of its crystallization, diffusion and gradual assimilation into Canaanite culture during the 12th and 11th centuries B.C.E. We shall merely note that the distinctive Philistine painted pottery found in Cisjordan, especially on its southern coast, as well as the early Philistine tombs in the Egyptian garrison cities, such as Beth-shean in the north, Lachish in the Shephelah, and Sharuhen (Tell el-Farʿah) in the south, containing anthropoid coffins with characteristic weapons and other finds, reflects the original Aegean background of the Philistines, with the addition of Canaanite, Cypriot and Egyptian elements.[12] Along with this tangible evidence, we must take note of other Philistine contributions to the culture of Eretz-Israel, such as the introduction of a particular type of fortification — the so-called casemate walls — known in Anatolia and Cyprus as early as the Late Bronze Age,[13] and of a previously

9 R.A.S. Macalister, *The Philistines, Their History and Civilization* (1914), 94ff.; A.R. Burn, *Minoans, Philistines and Greeks* (1930), 151ff.

10 Justin XVIII, 3, 5; it is possible that he quotes the historian Timaeus of the 4th century B.C.E.

11 The commonly held opinion [Ed. Meyer, *Geschichte des Altertums* 2 (1953), 79ff.; O. Eissfeldt, *Philister und Phönizier* (1936), 25] is untenable; it assumes that this source refers to the invasion of the coasts of Canaan by the Sea Peoples, including the Philistines, in the 12th century B.C.E. Undoubtedly, the historical core of the tradition should be sought in the allusion to the king of the Ashkelonites who defeated Sidon, indicating that Ashkelon rose to the status of a maritime power that successfully fought the Phoenician metropolis. As for the traditional date for the foundation of Tyre, also mentioned by Josephus, no particular significance should be attached to it.

12 See T. Dothan, *EI* 5 (1958), 55ff. (Hebrew); *idem*, *Antiquity and Survival* 2 (1957), 151ff.; *idem*, *The Philistines and Their Material Culture* (1982).

13 The earliest fortress with a casemate wall in Israel was uncovered at Gibeah; it dates from the second half of the 11th century B.C.E. (see below note 20). The origin of this type of fortification must be sought in the Hittite kingdom, where we find characteristic examples at Ḫattuša (Boghazköy), Mersin and Carchemish [cf. W.F. Albright, *AASOR* 21–22(1943), §7]. The Late Bronze Age fortress uncovered at Nitovikla in Cyprus also appears to have a casemate wall protected by a glacis, but

unknown type of private building, namely the rectangular three-room house, as well as the development of metallurgy, and especially the use of iron.[14]

It is also apparent that there was progress in the evolution of the Canaanite consonantal alphabetic script during the period of the *pax Philistaea*. I should say that at this time right-to-left horizontal writing and the reduction of the number of consonants to twenty-two became standard, perhaps as a result of the adaptation of the Canaanite script to the needs of non-Semitic peoples who settled in Eretz-Israel and adopted Canaanite as their language, but could not pronounce the distinctive Semitic phonetics.

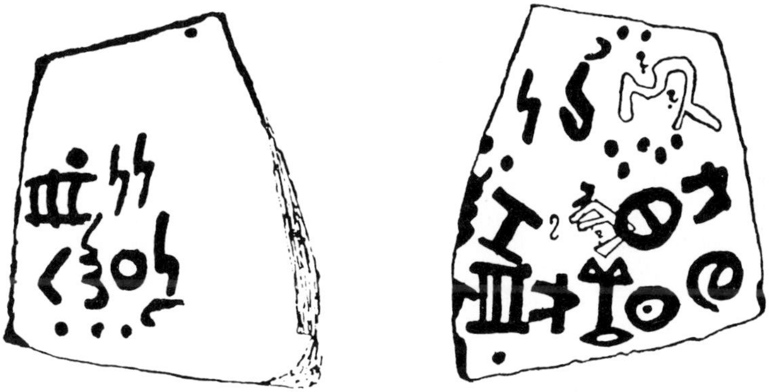

1

2

3

Inscriptions from 12th–11th centuries B.C.E.: 1) the Beth-shemesh ostracon; 2) a seal from the Ayalon Valley; 3) a fragment from Rehob (Tell eṣ-Ṣarem) near Beth-shean

its plan is not sufficiently clear [*Swedish Cyprus Expedition* 1 (1934), 374, Plan XV]; cf. also S. Marinatos, *Crete and Mycene* (1960), 163, Fig. 26 (Tiryns).

14 The problem of the appearance and diffusion of iron in Israel and neighbouring countries has not yet been elucidated. The origin of the iron-working industry should be sought first and foremost in Anatolia, where iron was a state monopoly in the Late Bronze Age. From there this metal found its way in small quantities — mainly in the form of valuable objects — also to Greece, Cyprus

Administrative, commercial and military needs may have stimulated the use and diffusion of this simplified script in Philistia and in the Israelite regions dominated by the Philistines. As yet only sparse evidence of this has been uncovered; it includes the Beth-shemesh ostracon, the fragment from Rehob (Tell eṣ-Ṣarem) near Beth-shean, the inscriptions on the arrow-heads from el-Khadr near Bethlehem, and a seal from the Ayalon Valley — all of them written in the 11th century B.C.E. However, the data are sufficient for us to assume that this script, which is the direct progenitor of the classical Phoenician-Hebrew script of the 10th century B.C.E., was used in the 11th century in that part of western Eretz-Israel which was under Philistine domination.[15]

An instructive example of a coastal city founded and inhabited by the Philistines is Tell Qasile on the northern shore of the Yarkon River in the area that is now Tel Aviv, which was excavated in 1948–1950 and in 1956.[16] This

and Egypt. A few iron objects were found in Philistine tombs at Tell el-Farʿah (Sharuhen) and in strata of the 12th–11th centuries B.C.E. at Megiddo and other sites; see W.F. Petrie, *Beth Pelet* 1 (1930), 8f., 12; P.L.O. Guy, *Megiddo Tombs* (1938), 162f. However, iron seems to have been introduced into common use — alongside copper — only later in the 11th century, apparently as a result of the development of commercial relations with the Anatolian coast (the mines in the Lebanon may also have begun to be exploited at that time). Its wide distribution in the eastern Mediterranean does not begin to play a prominent economic role till the 10th century B.C.E. On the problem as a whole, see G.A. Wainwright, *Antiquity* 10 (1936), 5ff.; G.E. Wright, *AJA* 43 (1939), 458ff.; V.R. d'A. Desborough, *Protogeometric Pottery* (1952), 308ff.; *idem*, *The Last Mycenaeans and Their Successors* (1964), 25f.; Ch. G. Starr, *The Origins of Greek Civilization* (1961), 87; H.L. Lorimer, *Homer and the Monuments* (1950), 111ff.; Helck, *Die Beziehungen Aegyptens* (see note 7), 410.

15 On this epigraphic material, see F.M. Cross, *BASOR* 134 (1954), 15ff.; 168 (1962), 12ff., and references there. I shall confine myself here to a few remarks, without discussing the problem in detail. The Beth-shemesh ostracon appears to belong to the early 11th century B.C.E. [according to Albright, *BANE* (see note 3), 358, n. 67 — about 1100 B.C.E.], and the inscriptions on the el-Khadr arrow-heads to the second half of the 11th century B.C.E. [according to F.M. Cross and J.T. Milik, *BASOR* 134 (1954), 15 — about 1100 B.C.E., but see B. Mazar, *VT* 13 (1963), 312]. Thus only a short interval separates these inscriptions from those on the Ruweisah arrow-head and from that of Aḥiram. The alphabetic inscriptions of the 11th century B.C.E. found in Israel are characterized by the linear cursive form of the letters (although they are not yet stabilized), and by the reduction of their number to twenty-two as a result of the disappearance of the differences between the specifically Semitic sounds. On the other hand, in the alphabetic scripts of the Late Bronze Age — the Proto-Sinaitic, the Canaanite, from which the South Arabic alphabet developed, and the Proto-Byblian script [cf. M. Martin, *Orientalia* 31 (1962), 250ff., 330ff.] — the transition from the pictorial to the linear is evident. They are characterized, like the Ugaritic cuneiform script, by the number of signs representing sounds peculiar to Semitic languages, and as a rule the direction of writing is not fixed. It should also be noted that in the 13th century B.C.E. a new phenomenon begins to make itself felt in Ugaritic script, namely mirror writing and probably a certain reduction in the number of signs through the merging of the sounds *ṯ* and *š*, *ḥ* and *ḫ*. This seems to be elucidated on the basis of a new document, which has not yet been published; cf. Ch. Virolleaud, *Comptes Rendus, Académie des Inscriptions* (12 Febr. 1958); *idem*, *AfO* 19 (1960), 194; C.H. Gordon, *Ugaritic Textbook* (1963), 16; see also M.F. Martin, *RSO* 37 (1962), 175ff.

16 On the new excavation at Tell Qasile, cf. A. Mazar, *Excavations at Tell Qasile 1. Qedem* 12 (1980); *idem*, *Excavations at Tell Qasile 2. Qedem* 20 (1985).

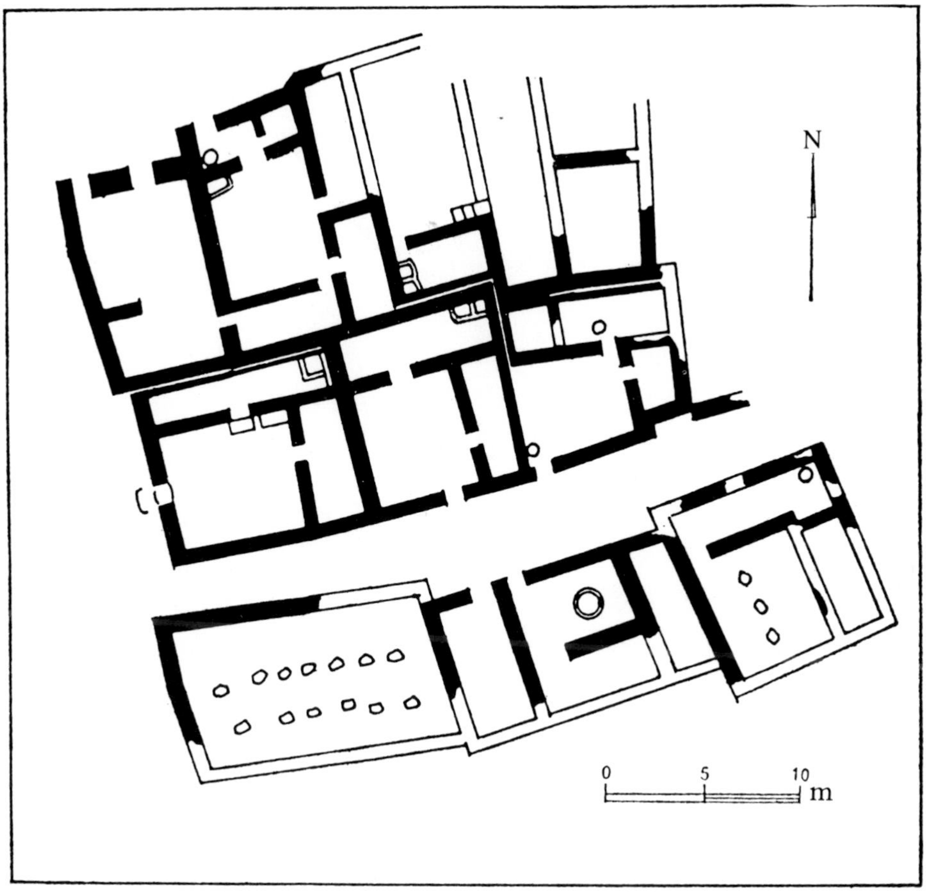

Plan of the quarter in the south of Tell Qasile X (ca. 1000 B.C.E.)

fortified city was built in the 12th century B.C.E. (stratum XI) and flourished as a centre of maritime trade with Egypt, Phoenicia, and Cyprus in the second half of the 11th and the early 10th centuries (stratum X).[17] This last period coincided with the time of the flowering of Philistine rule and commerce. Tell Qasile was destroyed by David, like another city under Philistine control, Megiddo (stratum VIA).[18]

17 Cf. the preliminary report in *IEJ* 1 (1951), 61–76, 125–140, 194–218. Dame Kenyon's statement "in no case do the Philistines seem to have founded new cities" [*Archaeology in the Holy Land* (1960), 225] has no foundation. The settlement in Tell Qasile was established by the Philistines and remained Philistine until the early 10th century B.C.E., and there are also other instances of settlements founded by the Philistines in the early Iron Age.

18 G. Loud, *Megiddo* 2 (1948), 33ff.; for the dating of stratum VIA, cf. B. Mazar, *BASOR* 124 (1951), 21f.; G.E. Wright, *BASOR* 155 (1959), 13f. The brick public building (No. 2072) appears to have

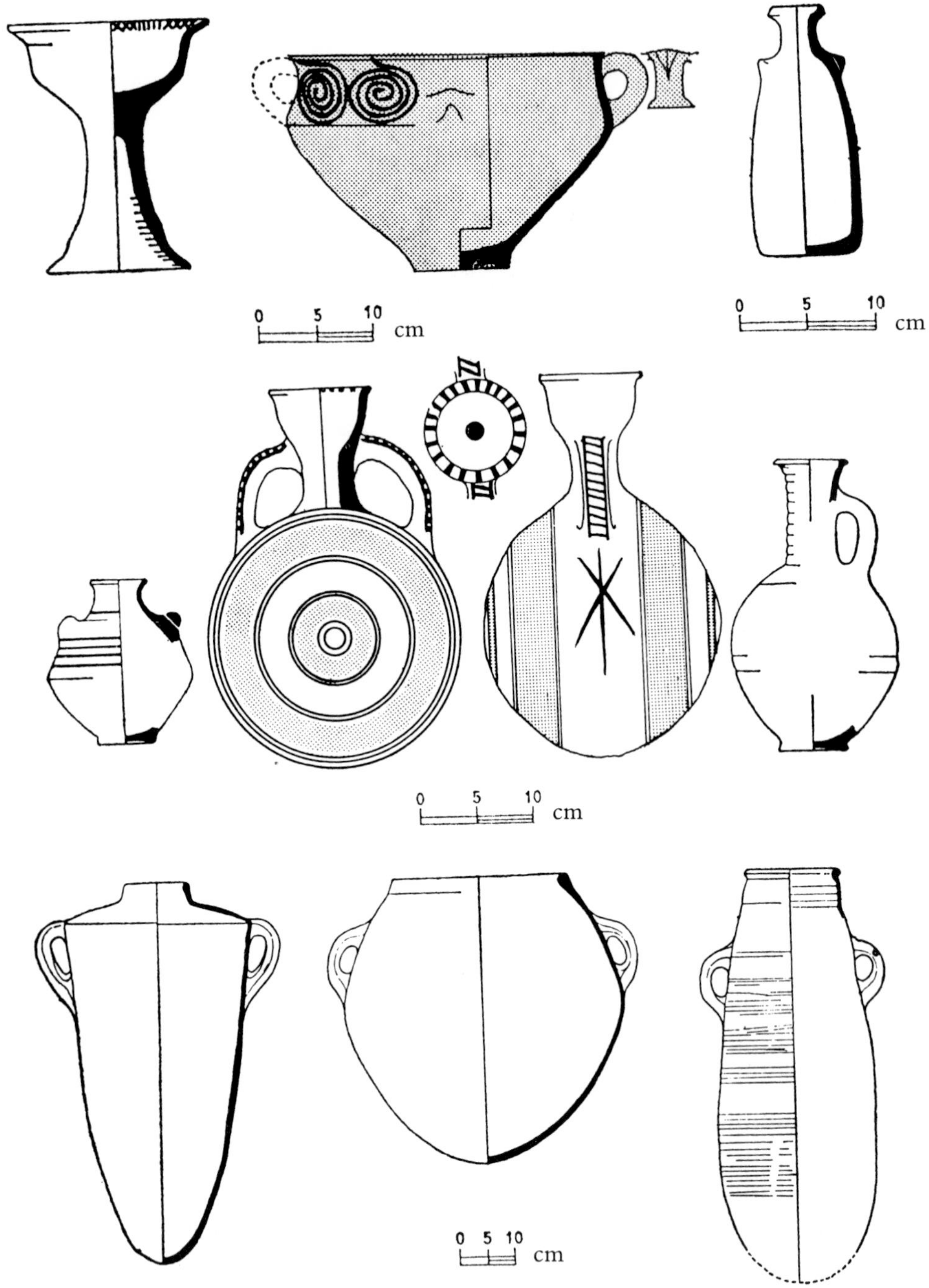

Pottery from Tell Qasile X (ca. 1000 B.C.E.)

Against this background we can appreciate the detailed data preserved in the Bible concerning the Philistines during the 11th century B.C.E. The picture is consistently one of the gradual spread of Philistine rule over large areas of western Eretz-Israel, inhabited by Israelite tribes and the remnant of the Canaanite population.

The main objective of the Philistines in extending the area of their domination was apparently not so much the exploitation of the subjugated farmers, as control over the vital overland communication routes, following the control they had already gained over the sea-lanes. In this respect the Philistines continued the Pharaonic policy of the preceding period. Nor did they differ from the Egyptians in the way they ruled the population.

In the course of time two more Philistine city-states, Gath and Ekron in the Shephelah, were added to the three original cities, and a confederation of five principalities was established. As a result of the Philistine victory over the Israelite tribes at Eben-ezer (near Aphek in the Sharon Valley) about the middle of the 11th century B.C.E., the road into the interior of the mountains of Ephraim was opened to them and their domination of the Via Maris made secure.

We have some instructive data concerning the methods employed by the Philistines in order to retain control over occupied areas. They posted governors (נציבים) and garrisons (מצבים) in strongholds located at strategic points and on the main roads. When an uprising occurred, the *mašḥit*, a mobile professional military unit, which included chariotry, was dispatched to aid the garrisons. The sources at our disposal indicate the superiority of the Philistines over both Israelites and Canaanites in respect of military organization and the quality of their weapons. Thus the Philistines were in a position to gain control over large areas and impose levies and taxes on the subjugated population. They could even mobilize auxiliary units from the native population (the *ʿibrîm* in 1 Sam 14:21). In addition, at least at the end of the 11th century B.C.E., the Philistines made all metallurgy of bronze and iron their monopoly, centred in the Philistine craft guilds. This was an additional means of economic subjugation (1 Sam 13:19–21).[19]

served as the residence of the Philistine governor. It is similar in plan (as far as it can be determined from the remains) — a quadrilateral courtyard with rows of rooms on two sides — to the private houses of stratum X at Tell Qasile, but it is much larger than them.

19 The development of metallurgy is illustrated by the excavations at Beth-shemesh (stratum III), Tell Qasile (XI–X) and Tel Gamma (Yurza); cf. E. Grant and G.E. Wright, *Ain Shems Excavations* 5 (1939), 56ff.; B. Mazar, *IEJ* 1 (1951), 75; W.F. Petrie, *Gerar* (1928), Pls, VII, IX. The Philistine smiths were apparently organized into guilds similar to these at Ugarit in the Late Bronze Age and in Judah during the Monarchy. For the problem as a whole, see I. Mendelsohn, *BASOR* 30 (1940), 17ff.; R. de Vaux, *Les institutions de l'Ancien Testament* I (1958), 119ff.; C.H. Gordon, in *Studies Presented to Hetty Goldman* (1956), 136ff.

Nevertheless, Philistine rule did not last very long; it crumbled quickly as soon as resistance arose in Israel. This movement was essentially part of the Israelite tribes' larger goal of liberation from the alien yoke and unification and political organization. It was aided by certain weaknesses in Philistine administration. Far removed from their home bases near the coast and surrounded by an inimical populace, the Philistines did not have the power to enforce their tyrannical rule over the hill country and were unable to make efficient use of their war chariots in the hour of need.

The historiographic sources in the Bible tell us that Samuel, the last of the Israelite charismatic judges, achieved a victory over the Philistines near Mizpah in the southern mountains of Ephraim (1 Sam 7:7–11). The subsequent proclamation of the Benjaminite Saul as king of Israel was a challenge which led to the unification of the Israelite tribes and to the establishment of national sovereignty based on a standing army including professional archers (1 Chr 8: 40; 12:2). The conquest of the Philistine fortress at Gibeah brought an end to Philistine domination in the territory of Benjamin. This stronghold, with its casemate walls and corner towers, was apparently built by the Philistines to serve as an administrative and military centre. After destroying it, Saul rebuilt it on the same plan, with some improvements, and made it his capital.[20] The war shifted from the mountains to the Shephelah, where the fringe of the Israelite area of settlement faced Philistia itself.

The Philistines then attempted to turn the tide by means of a tactical manouevre. They attacked Israel from their bases on the Via Maris in the Jezreel Valley. This assault ended in Saul's downfall and death on Mount Gilboa, and in the strengthening of Megiddo and Beth-shean, the Philistine bases in the Jezreel Valley. Apparently the Philistines also employed the ancient tactic of *divide et impera* by supporting David as lord of Judah against the House of Saul in Israel. These political and military ploys, however, missed their mark. David became king of all Israel, solidified the state Saul had founded, reunited the Israelite tribes, and annexed groups and the population of conquered areas under a stable centralized regime. This was strong enough to make Israel one of the important factors in the political life of western Asia, and Jerusalem, the new capital, the political, national and religious centre of Israel. David and his successor Solomon gave Israel a position which had far-reaching consequences for the historical development of the eastern Med-

20 On the fortress at Gibeah, see W.F. Albright, *BASOR* 52 (1933), 6ff.; R.L. Cleveland, *AASOR* 34–35 (1960), 10ff. Only a tower and part of the wall have been preserved from this fortress, so that it is difficult to determine its plan with certainty. According to Albright, it was built by Saul and rebuilt by him (or his son). It appears very likely, however, that it was erected by the Philistines as a residence for the Philistine governor (1 Sam 10:5; 13:3), cf. B. Mazar, *Yediot* 10 (1943), 73ff. (Hebrew); A. Alt, *PJb* 30 (1934), 8f. Cf. *Enc. Miq.* 2, s.v. "Gibeah"; P. Lapp, *BA* 28 (1965), 2ff.

iterranean and Syria. For the span of two generations Israel enjoyed a great measure of political success and economic prosperity. As for the fate of the Philistines, we learn from biblical sources that David defeated them in a number of battles in the northern Shephelah and opened the road to the Sharon and the Jezreel Valley. He gained control over large sectors of the Via Maris and the coastal plain; the cities he captured included Dor, Megiddo and Beth-shean. He succeeded in breaking Philistine military, political and economic power by annexing areas they had formerly controlled. However, he was not powerful enough to conquer great Philistine cities on the southern coast.

It would appear that as a result of Israel's spectacular rise to power, Egypt during the 21st Dynasty began to aspire to re-establish Egyptian rule over Philistia. We find allusions to this in biblical sources and on a fragmentary Egyptian relief of Pharaoh Siamon from Tanis. In particular, we learn from the story of Pharaoh's conquest of Gezer (1 Kgs 9:16–17) that Philistia, up to Gezer in the north, was under Egyptian control at the beginning of Solomon's reign. This is confirmed by an analysis of the list of towns conquered by Pharaoh Shishak. In this list, Gezer, the fortified Israelite town facing Philistia, comes immediately after Gaza, the starting point of Shishak's campaign, while other Philistine cities are not mentioned at all, indicating that at that time they were already under Egyptian suzerainty.[21]

When in the early 10th century B.C.E. the Philistines declined as a political and economic factor in the eastern Mediterranean, their sea power was inherited to a limited extent by Egypt and Israel, and to an ever increasing degree by the Phoenicians. Tyre, once a city kingdom but a dependent of Sidon since the 12th century B.C.E., now found the propitious moment to obtain independence and to establish a strong and far-flung sea empire. Of especial importance to us is the cause and effect relationship between the rise of Israel and the ascendancy of Tyre, the new capital of the Sidonians, the "trader of peoples even unto many islands" (Ezek 27:3). We cannot establish with certainty the date of Tyre's liberation from the control of Sidon and its subsequent emergence as an independent state, but this event could not have taken place much before the year 1000 B.C.E. Josephus Flavius, drawing his information from Menander of Ephesus and Dios, mentions Abibaal, father of Hiram I of Tyre; it may be conjectured that he was the founder of the dynasty which brought prosperity to Tyre (*Contra Apionem*, I, 18; *Ant.* V, 8, 4). It would seem that Abibaal knew how to capitalize on the rise of Israel and the decline of Philistia, and how to make use of the opportunity to impose the domination of Tyre upon southern Phoenicia and the sea-routes in the eastern Mediterranean.

21 J. Goldwasser, *Yediot* 14 (1948), 82ff. (Hebrew); in this volume, "Pharaoh Shishak's Campaign to the Land of Israel", pp. 139–150; A. Malamat, *The Kingdoms of Israel and Judah* (1961), 37f. (Hebrew); *idem*, *JNES* 22 (1963), 10ff.

It was, however, Hiram, his son, who brought greatness to Tyre as a commercial empire. Menander states that Hiram waged war against a Tyrian colony which had ceased to pay taxes, and that he subdued it by force. Its name is preserved only in an unclear form, and we cannot ascertain exactly whether it was Utica in North Africa, as proposed by Gutschmit, or, as seems more likely, Kition in Cyprus, Phoenician Kitti and biblical אי כתים, a reading proposed by Albright.[22] It is reasonable to assume that this colony was founded by Hiram's father, Abibaal. Another trading post established by the Tyrians at the very beginning of the 10th century B.C.E. was, in my opinion, Zalmona, the port city of Tell Abu Hawam north of Haifa. This city (stratum IVB) was built on the ruins of an earlier settlement dating to the Late Bronze Age, which may have been destroyed by the Sea Peoples. The new settlement on this site provides us with a useful example of a port which in the early stages of Tyrian power served the Phoenician cities in their trade with Israel and Egypt. The archaeological discoveries in this city bear witness to its extensive cultural relations.[23]

Menander and Dios tell us that Hiram carried out grandiose building projects in Tyre and turned it into a splendid metropolis. This reflects the rise of Tyre to greatness as a mercantile empire and as the first *amplificator mundi*.

The tradition of Tyre's greatness is prominent in classical literature, where it is called the "mother" of the Phoenician colonies in the Mediterranean. Similarly, on late Phoenician coins it is termed the "mother" of the Sidonians. This tradition corresponds to what is known from biblical sources. The Bible speaks of Tyre's unique position as a commercial and maritime power, as well as of its strong ties with Israel. These ties had already begun in the days of David, reached their peak during the reign of Solomon who concluded an alliance with Hiram, were renewed by the dynasty of Omri, and endured so long that Amos was still able to call them a "covenant of brothers" (ברית אחים — Am 1:9).

The turbulent events during the transitional period from the second to the first millennium B.C.E. help to explain the rise of Tyre. With the downfall of the Philistine principalities as a competitive power and the subsequent decline of their ally Sidon which was dependent upon them, great potentialities presented themselves to Tyre, the nearest Phoenician neighbour of Israel. Tyre entered into a *ḫubûr* with the rising kingdom of David and Solomon and

22 Albright, *BANE* (see note 3), 361, n. 101. On the excavations at Kition, see V. Karageorghis, *Report of the Department of Antiquities, Cyprus* (1963), and references there.

23 See the report by R.W. Hamilton, *QDAP* 4 (1935), 8ff., and the discussion of the chronology of stratum IVB by B. Mazar, *BASOR* 124 (1951), 21f.; G.W. van Beek, *BASOR* 138 (1955), 38, n. 15; G.E. Wright, *BANE* (see note 3), 95ff. Two richly equipped Phoenician cist-tombs discovered by M. Prausnitz at Achzib (ez-Zib) may be contemporary with Tell Abu Hawam IVB.

probably also with Egypt (cf. the relations between Byblos and Egypt), and established trading posts along the coast.

This cooperation opened the way for a new chapter in the history of international trade, which now encompassed not only the Near East and the nearby Aegean, but also new areas of maritime trade and colonization along the entire length of the Mediterranean, its shores and its islands, as far as Nora in Sardinia, Utica in North Africa and Gādara-Gades in Spain beyond Gibraltar.[24] From the Red Sea Phoenician-Israelite merchants made their way to southern Arabia, East Africa and, it has even been suggested, to India.[25] The kingdom of Israel now had the unique opportunity to serve as a bridge between the Mediterranean and the shores of the Red Sea. Moreover, the "King's Highway", the main route leading from Damascus through Transjordan to Elath and Arabia, was already under the control of David and Solomon.

A distinct cultural advance was made possible by the relative security which was imposed by the supremacy of Tyre and Israel and prevented invasions or incursions, and by the peaceful political and commercial relations with Egypt and the neo-Hittite kingdoms in Syria. Art and architecture, metal, wood and ivory working, and the purple-garment industry flourished, and agriculture and the exploitation of copper and iron mines reached new levels of development. Great progress was made in the construction of ships, especially of the seagoing "merchantmen of Tarshish", and in the foundation of harbours and trading posts. At the same time, the attractive Phoenician pottery came into widespread use, especially the black-on-red and the burnished bichrome wares.[26] We have the testimony of the Bible: "For the king [Solomon] had at sea a navy of Tarshish with the navy of Hiram. Once in three years came the

24 See D. Harden, *The Phoenicians* (1962), 57ff., and especially Albright, *BANE* (note 3), 343f., who disagrees with the various attempts [including R. Carpenter, *AJA* 62 (1958), 38ff.] to lower the date of Phoenician colonization in the west. Cf. Meyer, *Geschichte des Altertums* (see note 11), 77ff.; A. Garcia y Bellido, *Fenicios y Cartaginese en Occidente* (1942); *idem*, *Historia Mundi* 2 (1954), 328ff. It appears that the Phoenicians were able to reach these distant shores because they made use of the experience accumulated since Mycenean times; this seems likely in view of the abundant archaeological evidence attesting to the spread of Mycenean civilization to southern Italy and Sicily [L. B. Brea, *Sicily* (1957), 125ff., 169f., etc.; W. Taylour, *Mycenaean Pottery in Italy and Adjacent Areas* (1958)] and even further westwards, to the islands of the Tyrrhenian Sea.

25 We have no evidence about Ophir, with the exception of the fact that gold, almug wood and ivory were brought from there in ships to Elath. Ophir is generally thought to have been in East Africa or South Arabia. Barnett attempted to return, with new arguments, to Josephus' theory (Ant. VIII, 6, 4) that Ophir was situated in India, and to identify it with Supara near Bombay; see R.D. Barnett, *A Catalogue of the Nimrud Ivories* (1957), 59f., 168. For the present, however, we have no clear evidence to confirm such a far-reaching theory.

26 See J. Birmingham, *AJA* 67 (1963), 15ff. and references there. From the 10th century B.C.E. onwards the south-eastern part of Cyprus shows strong influence from the Phoenician coast, as well as connections westwards, especially with Sardinia.

The Phoenician inscription from Nora in Sardinia

navy of Tarshish, bringing gold and silver, ivory, and apes and peacocks" (1 Kgs 10:22).

An eclectic cosmopolitan culture, a sort of Phoenician *koine,* evolved. The Phoenician language, written in the fully standardized and stabilized cursive script consisting of twenty-two consonants (e.g. the Byblos inscriptions and the Gezer calendar from the 10th century B.C.E.), now became prominent in the eastern Mediterranean and within the periphery of Phoenician economic and colonial activity, and was used as a sort of *lingua franca* in commercial negotiations. We have clear evidence of this in the Phoenician inscriptions of the 9th century B.C.E. which have been uncovered in Sardinia and in Cyprus,[27]

27 On these inscriptions, see W.F. Albright, *BASOR* 83 (1941), 14ff. After examining the Phoenician inscriptions from Sardinia in the museum at Cagliari in August 1962, the author suggests that, from a palaeographic point of view, they should be dated to the 9th century B.C.E.

The inscription of Yehimelek, King of Byblos (mid-10th century B.C.E.)
[M. Dunand, *Fouilles de Byblos, Atlas* 1 (1937), Pl. 31]

and in the adoption by the Greeks and Phrygians of the cursive Phoenician script, probably at the end of the same century.[28]

This revolutionary development in Phoenicia apparently achieved striking expression in the sphere of religion as well. For in the first half of the 10th century B.C.E. the principal deity of the Phoenician pantheon appears for the first time under the name of Baᶜal Šamêm, the lord of the heavens. The earliest reference to him occurs in the inscription of Yehimelek, King of Byblos, a contemporary of Hiram and Solomon in the middle of the 10th century B.C.E.[29] This monumental inscription is dedicated to the erection of a temple to this god and his consort, the Lady of Byblos. Only incidentally does it mention repairs to the temples of other gods. Dios and Menander are apparently referring to the temple of Baᶜal Šamêm when they speak of the temple of Olympic Zeus at Tyre. They describe it as situated on a small island, which Hiram joined to the main island of Tyre. Distinct from this temple was that of Heracles, the Greek equivalent of Melqart (Melcarth), the national god of the Tyrians, which was restored by Hiram.[30] An interesting mention of Baᶜal Šamêm has been preserved in the fragments of Philo Byblius, who quotes various details of Phoenician mythology from the book of Sanchunyaton, an early Phoenician priest. According to Philo, this deity is identical with the

28 Or in the early 8th century B.C.E. at the latest. See detailed treatment in L.H. Jeffery, *The Local Scripts of Archaic Greece* (1961), 12ff.

29 Cf. in this volume, "The Phoenician Inscriptions from Byblos", pp. 231–247; W.F. Albright, *JAOS* 67 (1947), 157ff. It appears that Yehimelek was the father of Abibaal (the contemporary of Shishak I) and of Elibaal (the contemporary of Osorkon I), and hence Yehimelek must be placed in the time of Solomon.

30 Josephus, *Contra Apionem*, I, 18.

sun-god, the only god of the heavens; his name is *Baalsamen*, the lord of the heavens in Phoenician, called by the Greeks Zeus.[31]

From the treaty of Esarhaddon with Baᶜal, King of Tyre, we learn that Baᶜal Šamêm (*Ba-al-sa-me-me*) was a cosmic deity, particularly of the sea and of storms at sea, and the patron of shipping. Melqart, the god of Tyre, and Ešmûn, the god of Sidon, on the other hand, appear in this document as distinctly chthonic deities with disruptive powers.[32] It is for this reason that Baᶜal Šamêm was held in awe by Phoenician seamen, either under this name or under one of his other appellations. Little wonder that in a period of great maritime development, of flourishing international trade and negotiations which encompassed *orbis terrarum*, Baᶜal Šamêm should have assumed a cosmopolitan character.

On this basis, it is readily understandable why Solomon, a contemporary of Hiram and Yehimelek, built the temple in Jerusalem to Yahweh according to a Phoenician plan and with the help of Tyrian artisans, and why the deity worshipped in this temple appropriated some characteristics of Baᶜal Šamêm. This theological conception is presumably expressed in the dedicatory address of Solomon in 1 Kgs 8:23–53, which is basically authentic.[33] This is probably the meaning of the verse concerning the stranger in Solomon's prayer:

> Moreover, concerning a stranger, that is not of thy people Israel, but cometh out of a far country for thy name's sake. For they shall hear of thy great name ... when he shall come and pray towards this house. *Hear thou in heaven thy dwelling*, and do according to all that the stranger calleth to thee for, that all people of the earth may know thy name to fear thee, as do thy people Israel; and that they may know that this house, which I have built, is called by thy name.

It is no wonder that in the Book of Jonah, the God of Israel appears as the God who creates winds and tempests at sea. He is worshipped not only by the Israelites but also by gentile sailors and he is called the God of the heavens (אלהי השמים; Jonah 1:9). The cult of the lord of heavens, the cosmic and universal god of the Phoenician sea-power, who assimilated characteristics of

31 See O. Eissfeldt, *Ras Schamra und Sanchunjaton* (1939), 86.

32 R. Borger, *Die Inschriften Asarhaddons, Königs von Assyrien* (1956), 107ff.

33 On this chapter, see *inter alia* J.A. Montgomery, *The Books of Kings* (ICC, 1951), 185ff., and especially Y. Kaufmann, *Toledot HaEmunah HaIsra'elit* (*History of the Religion of Israel*) 2 (1954), 206ff., 361ff. (Hebrew); Kaufmann is certainly correct in saying: "...this prayer also serves as an expression of the ancient universalism which *antedates* literary prophecy"; he rightly stresses its antiquity. On the background, see also A.S. Kapelrud, *Orientalia* 32 (1963), 56ff. It seems likely that the ornaments and the paraphernalia of the Temple at Jerusalem [Jachin and Boaz, the *Kîyōr*, the Sea, the Cherubim, etc.; cf. W.F. Albright, *Archaeology and the Religion of Israel* (1942), 142ff.], in which the cosmic symbolism evolved in Phoenicia found expression, were created under the direct influence of the temple of Baᶜal Šamêm at Tyre.

the Canaanite El, the father of the gods, and of Yam, the god of the seas, as well as of the storm-god Hadad and the solar deity — this cult spread from Tyre and the cities of the Phoenician seaboard not only among the other Phoenicians, but especially among the Arameans and the other peoples of Syria. It assumed many forms and the name "Lord of Heavens" was applied to the chief gods to such an extent that we find the god of the ruling dynasty of Hamath in about 800 B.C.E. was called Baʿal Šamên.[34] It is possible that Jezebel's Baʿal in the Book of Kings is not Melqart, the god of Tyre, but as Eissfeldt has proposed, Baʿal Šamêm.[35]

The paramount position of Tyre, the capital of the Sidonian trade and sea empire, finds expression in the traditions and epics of the Phoenicians as they are preserved in classical literature and in the Bible. Especially worthy of note is the Tyrian poem, fragments of which Ezekiel wove into his prophecy on the destruction of Tyre (Ezek 26–28): "the renowned city, which was strong in the sea, she and her inhabitants, which cause their terror to be on all that haunt it." We may assume that when he dwelt in Tel Abib on the River Chebar, Ezekiel learned this poem from the inhabitants of Bīt Ṣurraia, a colony of Tyrian exiles in the neighbourhood of Nippur on the Chebar.[36] It was apparently composed in the 10th–9th centuries B.C.E., at the time of Tyre's greatness. It is not accidental that it attributes metaphorically to the prince of Tyre thoughts and phrases taken from the Phoenician mythos and from the traditions about the exalted position of Tyre:

> Because your heart is proud, and you have said: I am El, I sit on the divine throne in the midst of the seas (Ezek 28:2).
>
> O Tyre, you have said: I am perfect in beauty. Your borders are in the midst of the seas, your builders have perfected your beauty (*ibid*. 27:3–4).
>
> You were the signet of perfection, full of wisdom and perfect in beauty. You were in Eden, the garden of God (*ibid*. 28:12).

34 On the Sakur stele, see M. Noth, *ZDPV* 52 (1929), 124ff.; *Enc. Miq*. 3, s.v. "Hamath".

35 O. Eissfeldt, *ZAW* 57 (1939), 1ff. Baʿal Šamêm appears to have been worshipped especially on mountain tops. It is possible that Baʿal Hammon [the Baʿal of Mount Amanus?; cf. Eissfeldt, *Ras Schamra und Sanchunjaton* (see note 31), 36ff.] worshipped in the western Mediterranean (where he was identified with Zeus or Saturn-Kronos, and where he had his renowned sanctuary at Jebel Bū-Qurnein overlooking Carthage in Africa) and Baʿal Lebanon, the god whom the agent of Hiram II worshipped in Carthage in Cyprus, were only epithets of Baʿal Šamêm. This is the case also with respect to the Tyrian place of worship on Mount Carmel (Ὄρος ἱερὸν Διός of Pseudo-Scylax). On the spread of the worship of Baʿal Šamêm in the Phoenician world, see Meyer, *Geschichte des Altertums* (note 11), 159, n. 2. Baʿal Šamêm also heads the list of the great gods in the Karatepe inscription (B, 18). Cf. M. Avi-Yonah, *IEJ* 2 (1952), 118ff.; R. de Vaux, *RB* 63 (1956), 116ff.; O. Eissfeldt, *Der Gott Karmel* (1954); E. Brickermann, *Der Gott der Makabaer* (1953), 90ff. — on Baʿal Šamêm, the Olympian Zeus in the Hellenistic period.

36 Mentioned in neo-Babylonian inscriptions; see *RLA* 2, 52.

> With the abundance of your wealth and your merchandise you enriched the kings of the earth (*ibid.* 27:33).

One of these kings was, of course, the king of Israel, the closest neighbour and ally of Tyre, who supplied the capital of the trade empire with agricultural commodities;[37] he was Tyre's partner in commerce with Arabia and Ophir; and protected the caravan routes leading to Egypt, Syria and the shores of the Red Sea.

It is noteworthy that even in a much later period we find reminiscences of the greatness of the Phoenician nation and civilization. Pomponius Mela (I, 12) writes in the 1st century C.E.: "The Phoenicians were a clever race, who prospered in peace and war. They excelled in writing and literature and in other arts, in seamanship, in naval warfare, and in ruling an empire".

37 Ezek 27:17: "Judah and the land of Israel they were thy merchants; they gave wheat of Minnith [cf. Judg 11:33] and pannag(?) and honey and oil and balm as your exchange commodities". Incidentally, this verse furnishes proof that the source dates back to the time of the kingdoms of Israel and Judah. Cf. H. J. von Dijk, *Ezekiel's Prophecy on Tyre* (1968).

The Military Élite of King David

The complex military and administrative system, introduced by King David, included a unit known as "the heroes" (*haggibborim*). The historiographic sources of the Bible reveal that this élite group played an instrumental, even decisive role in establishing the military organization and political power structure, which made it possible for the twelve tribes of Israel to become a unified nation under a stable and centralized government. The first book of Chronicles (ch. 11) provides a list of the "heroes", which is essentially identical to a parallel list in 2 Sam 23. It is noteworthy that the introduction to the list in 1 Chr (11:10) states that David's chief warriors "strongly supported him in his kingdom, together with all Israel, to make him king".

The military and civil services were set up by Saul and David according to a very old, pre-monarchic local system. Foreign patterns became apparent only later, in order to meet the changing needs of the expanding and developing United Monarchy of Israel.[1] This is evident from the fact that during the reigns of Saul, Ishbaal, and David, the highest position after the king was that of the chief military commander. This is also typical of the Canaanite, Philistine, and Aramean systems of government.[2] As regards the institution of the military élite, the Bible indicates that the number thirty also had deep roots in pre-monarchic tradition; there are several references to thirty companions, henchmen, or even sons, surrounding charismatic figures or tribal leaders.[3] The Bible provides few explicit details on the origins, evolution, or

1 For details see below.

2 Judg 4:7; Gen 21:22; 2 Sam 2:16, etc. (and also "captain of the Lord's host" in Josh 5:14).

3 See Judg 14:11; 1 Sam 9:22. The view expressed by K. Elliger, *PJb* 31 (1935), 62f., that the number thirty is evidence of Egyptian influence is groundless. He rests his case on an inscription from Thebes that mentions a company of thirty in the train of Ramesses II. Actually the source in question refers to the thirty judges representing the three royal cities of Thebes, Memphis and Heliopolis, ten from

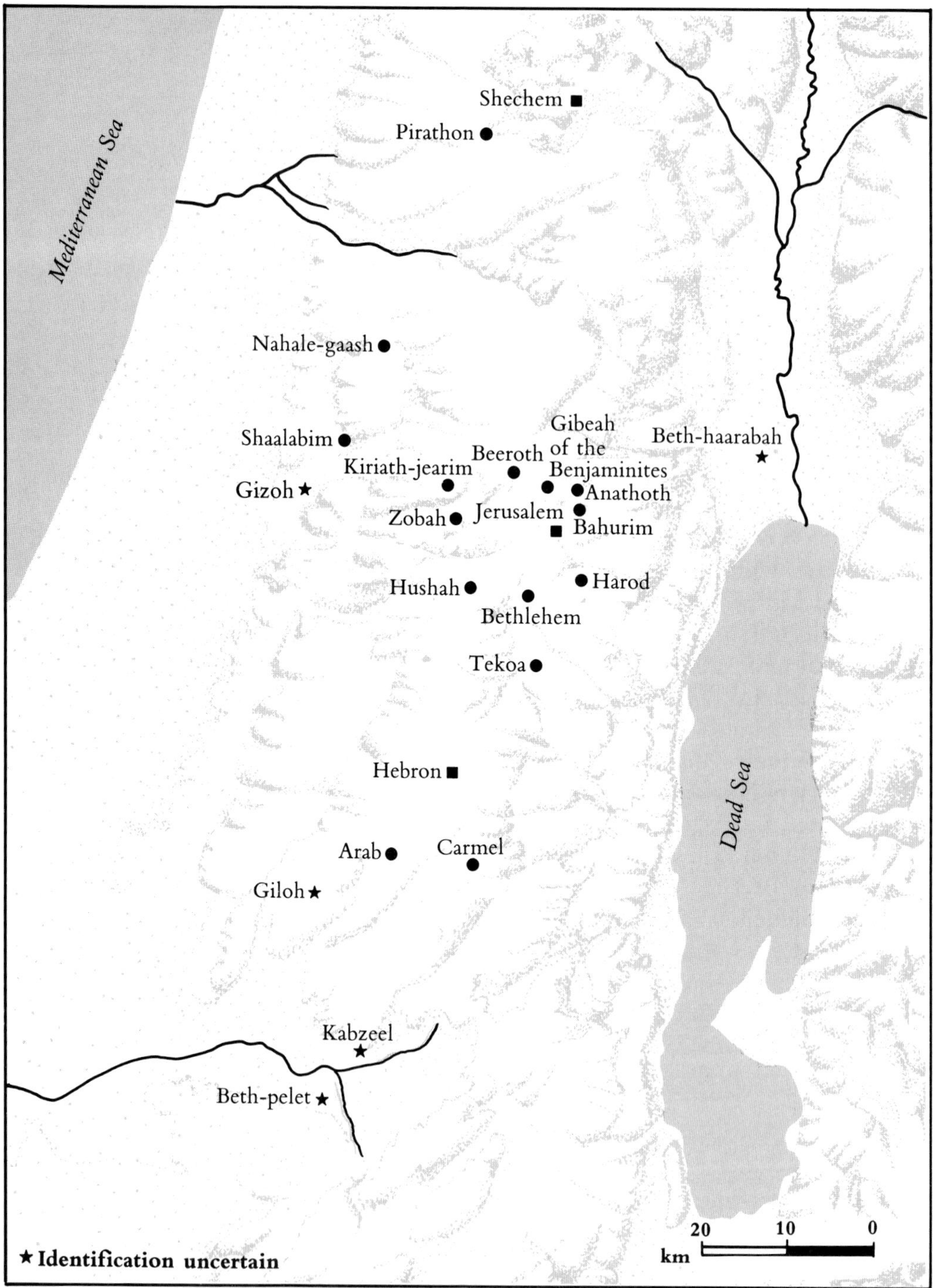

The birthplaces of King David's "heroes"

unique character of the heroic fraternity, but from numerous textual allusions we may deduce a good deal, especially about the stages in the development of the élite and its general character.

It appears that the élite of heroes was established by David during the time of his wanderings in the Judean borderlands when he was captain of a band. A group of close associates and "mighty men" who did David's bidding, grew up around him in that early period and served as a supreme command. From the cycle of Davidic stories it emerges that, at the outset, David's band differed very little, if at all, from the other bands of "poor and shiftless men" who roamed the land. Such men were usually of a lower social status than that of the Israelite citizen (*ʾezraḥ*); generally many among them were landless and relatively unprotected *gerim* who assembled around a chief (*śar*) particularly in times of social or political unrest. Together, they would engage in unrestrained pillage, and sell their services and protection against enemies and marauders to local lords and powerful owners of flocks and land. Occasionally, the *śar* at the head of such a band had authority, influence and political aspirations which exceeded those of a mere bandit chief. Such a commander may have had designs on the powers that be. He might attract warriors of reputation, entire companies of mercenaries, and persons who bore a grudge against the incumbent regime. He might turn his band into a large and well-organized army, aimed at ultimately usurping the throne.[4] Such bands are mentioned in the El-Amarna Letters, and in the biblical stories of Abimelech (Judg 9) and Jephthah (Judg 11). An illuminating example is the 15th century B.C.E. autobiographical account of Idrimi, son of Ilmilam, King of Alalakh, ruler of Mukish, Niʾ and ʿAmu in northern Syria, whose capital was at Alalakh.[5] The inscription tells how Idrimi and his brothers fled a revolution in their native country to find refuge with his mother's family in Emar, on the Euphrates.[6] A quarrel with his brethren forced Idrimi to leave Emar and to return to Canaan (*Kinani*) by way of the desert. In the town of Ammia he was joined by a few countrymen, and

each. Here the round number is, therefore, *ten* not thirty. See K. Sethe, *Von Zahlen und Zahlworten bei den alten Aegyptern* (1916), 40; and in this volume, "King David's Scribe and the High Officialdom of the United Monarchy of Israel" (henceforth "King David's Scribe"), p. 127, n. 4.

4 See A. Malamat, *Enc. Miq.* 2, 432–434. On the subject in general, see R. de Vaux, *Ancient Israel* 2 (1961), 218ff.

5 See S. Smith, *The Statue of Idrimi* (1949), and illuminating comments by W.F. Albright, *BASOR* 118 (1950), 14ff. On Niʾ and ʿAmu, see Albright, *ibid.*, 15. He makes a very interesting suggestion that ʿAmu (Amea) is the same as the land of the ʿAmo, wherein lay Pethor, native city of Balaam (Num 22:5; see also B. Mazar, *Enc. Miq.* 2, 178, s.v. בני עמו). This identification is now in doubt. For discussion, see A. Rofe, *The Book of Balaam* (1980), 34f. (Hebrew).

6 On the location of Emar north of the bend of the Euphrates, see A. Goetze, *BASOR* 147 (1957), 22ff.; also W.W. Hallo, *JCS* 18 (1964), 57ff.

finally reached a group of Habiru. He served as their leader for seven years.[7] When he had grown sufficiently strong, Idrimi had a ship built, and with his men sailed as far as Baal-zaphon (Mount Hazi, Jebel el Akraᶜ), from whence he recaptured his native throne.

Concerning David, it should be noted that besides his kin, who were probably in fear of revenge by Saul, he was joined by "everyone who was in straits and everyone who was in debt and everyone who was desperate, ... and he became their leader; there were about four hundred men with him" (2 Sam 22:1–2). In another story (2 Sam 25:10) David and his band are called by Nabal the Carmelite "slaves ... who run away from their masters", i.e. men beyond the bounds of organized society. They sought refuge from Saul in the borderlands of the Judean Desert, dwelling in stone-enclosed camps and inaccessible caves. But from the very beginning, David was also joined by men of standing who were enemies of Saul, such as Abiathar, son of the most respected priestly family in Israel and sole survivor of the massacre of the priests at Nob. He became David's priest and bearer of the *ephod*, which he had brought from the temple at Nob (1 Sam 22:20, etc.) Another noteworthy addition to David's band was Gad, the prophet (1 Sam 22:5) or seer (1 Chr 29:29), of whose origins no details have been preserved.

While still in the service of Saul, David had already gained much personal respect and a reputation as a successful military commander and contender for the throne. This is attested by his ties with the Moabite king, who may have been his kinsman, by his marriage policy, which forged a strong bond with the noble families of Judah and the borderlands,[8] and by the fact that

7 Prof. B. Landsberger has kindly pointed out to me that in line 27 in the inscription one should read *sa-ra-ak* (instead of *u-ra-ak*), i.e. "I was a *śar* (captain)" among the Hapiru men. The author has borrowed a West Semitic word in order to express the role of the captain of a band. On the Ḫapiru, see especially G. Bottero, *Le problème des Ḫabiru* (1954); M. Greenberg, *The Ḫab/piru* (1955); *idem*, in B. Mazar (ed.), *The World History of the Jewish People*, 2: *Patriarchs* (1970), 188ff.

8 Abigail, whom David took as a wife when the band wandered in the wilderness of Maon, had previously been the wife of Nabal the Calebite, a "very great" man, who owned large flocks at Maon, and "whose possessions were in Carmel" (1 Sam 25:2ff.). The house of Nabal at Maon was probably descended from the Calebite line of Rekem (1 Chr 2:43–45); see also S. Klein, *Studies in the Genealogical Lists in the Book of Chronicles* (1930), 18 (Hebrew); Mazar, *Cities and Districts*, 61ff. David's second wife was Ahinoam of Jezreel (1 Sam 25:43), the name of a town in the Judean hill country, in the same province as Carmel and Maon (Josh 15:55; cf. 1 Chr 4:3). Of particular interest is the passage in 1 Chr 2:17, according to which Amasa, Absalom's military commander (2 Sam 17:25) and commander of Judah after Absalom's revolt (2 Sam 20:5; 1 Kgs 2:32), was the son of Jether the Ishmaelite and David's sister Abigail (compare also 2 Sam 19:14).
The various versions of 2 Sam 17:25 are obscure: Jithra the Israelite who had married Abigal (אשר בא אל אביגל) daughter of Nahash (Septuagint: Ιεσσαι); also see S.R. Driver, *The Books of Samuel* (1913), 372. According to one view, the name Nahash (instead of Jesse) had been erroneously copied here from v. 27 ("Shobi son of Nahash"). David's connection with the Ishmaelites, the large confederation of nomadic tribes of the southern and eastern borderlands and the desert, is attested by the fact that Obil the Ishmaelite was in charge of David's camels (1 Chr 27:30). It should be

he became the trusted vassal of King Achish of Gath, who gave him the town of Ziklag to dwell in. Also among David's principal heroes during his days in the wilderness of Ziph, was Ahimelech the Hittite, who may have been a liaison officer or even the commander of a group of foreign warriors that had joined David *en masse* (1 Sam 26:6). We hear nothing more of him in later sources.[9] Another important allusion to the presence of foreign mercenaries in David's service is in Ps 57. The psalm bears the title "For the leader *al tashheth*, of David, a *michtam*, when he fled from Saul into a cave" (v. 1). There is no reason to date the psalm to a later period as some have proposed. Verse 5 speaks of mercenaries called *lᵉbaʾim*, "lions", apparently referring to members of a military unit whose emblem was a lion-goddess. This verse describes them vividly as fiery men "whose teeth are spears and arrows, whose tongue is a sharp sword". These warriors may be identified as professional archers. They resemble the type referred to in the inscriptions as *ḥṣ ʿbdlbʾt* (i.e. "the arrow of the servant of the lion-goddess"). Their names appear on arrows from the 11th century B.C.E. that have been found at the village of el-Khadr near Bethlehem,[10] and in an administrative list of archers from Ugarit.[11]

The sources telling about David's élite of thirty heroes before his accession at Hebron, and about the origin and lives of individual members thereof are diverse and fragmented, and are usually incorporated in other historical accounts. It appears that, although the élite of thirty heroes had been in existence from the earliest days of the band, the constitution of its membership varied, and the chiefs of the Thirty were replaced more than once. Of particular interest in this respect is the list of men who came to David at Ziklag (1 Chr 12).[12] A passage appended to the list (vv. 17–19) reads:

stressed, however, that the disintegration of this organization of tribes, which at one time "dwelt from Havilah, by Shur, which is close to Egypt, all the way to Asshur" (Gen. 25:18), had already begun by the period in question, as had their assimilation (and that of the Hagrites) into the tribal organizations collectively known as Arabs. Some of them assimilated into the nomadic or semi-nomadic tribes of the Judean borderlands, such as Mibsam and Mishma, the "children" of Ishmael (Gen 25:13–14) who later appear as the names of families (or lineages) in the tribe of Simeon (1 Chr 4:25; see J. Liver, *Enc. Miq.* 3, 902ff.).

9 According to Josephus Flavius (*Ant.* VII, 12, 2), David's hero Sibbecai (2 Sam 21:18; 1 Chr 11:29) was a Hittite. Nonetheless, it is very clear that he mistook חשתי, "Hushathite" (i.e. coming from Hushah) for חתי, "Hittite".

10 See J.T. Milik and F.M. Cross, *BASOR* 134 (1954), 5ff.; *ADAJ* 3 (1956), 15ff. The inscriptions probably date from the second half of the 11th century B.C.E., and are therefore among the earliest examples of the standard alphabetical script from which the Phoenician-Hebrew writing of the 10th century B.C.E. developed.

11 C.H. Gordon, *Ugaritic Textbook* (1965), no. 321:III, 38.

12 The majority view does not doubt the reliability of this document, which draws on a very old tradition. See A.C. Welch, *The Work of the Chronicler* (1939), 14; W. Rudolph, *Chronikbücher* (1955), 103ff.

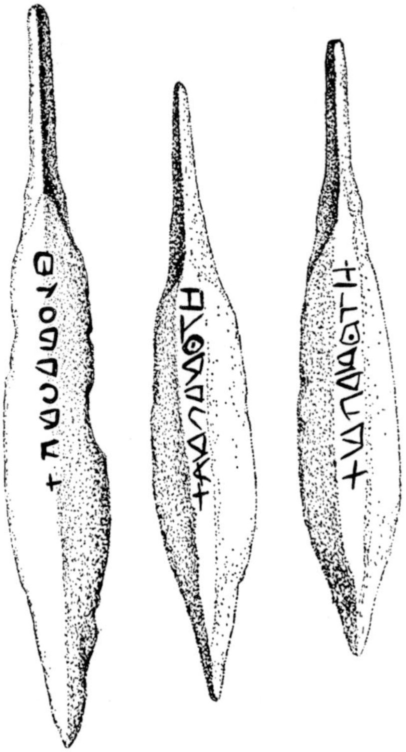

The javelin-heads from el-Khadr bearing the inscription: "the arrow of the servant of the lion-goddess" [F.M. Cross and J.T. Milik, *BASOR* 134 (1954), 7]

> Some of the Benjaminites and Judahites came to the stronghold to David, and David went out to meet them, saying to them, "If you come on a peaceful errand, to support me, then I will make common cause with you, but if to betray me to my foes, for injustice on my part, then let the God of our fathers take notice and give judgement". Then the spirit seized Amasai, chief of the Thirty:[13]
>
> We are yours, David,
> On your side, son of Jesse;
> At peace, at peace with you,
> And at peace with him who supports you.
> For your God supports you.
>
> So David accepted them and placed them at the head of his band.

This source indicates that the men who came to David at his stronghold (probably at Adullam) and whom he placed at the head of his band were of

13 The *qere*: שלישים (also in 1 Chr 11:11, versus the *kethib*: שלושים) derives from the term שליש, *shalish*, a position which still existed in Israel at the time of David and certainly before then. The Septuagint, the Peshitta and the Vulgate read שלושים. On the term *shalish*, see de Vaux, *Ancient Israel* (note 4), 23.

the tribes of Judah and Benjamin. It accords with other sources, all of which indicate that the vast majority of heroes in the élite came from Judah and from Benjamin (see below). 1 Chr 12 also mentions Amasai as chief of the Thirty, the senior hero in the unit, but nothing more is heard of him, unless it is assumed that he was the same person as Amasa, son of Jether the Ishmaelite and David's sister Abigail, but this is rather unlikely.[14] Earlier in the same chapter (v. 4) another hero, Ishmaiah the Gibeonite, is mentioned as "a warrior among the thirty, leading the thirty". He is named immediately after the professional warriors in the service of David, those who were "armed with the bow and could use both right hand and left hand to sling stones or shoot arrows with the bow".[15] Interestingly, the latter were "kinsmen of Saul from Benjamin" (v. 2), "formerly, protecting the interests of the house of Saul" (v. 30). For reasons unknown they had defected to David's camp. The fact that Ishmaiah was from Gibeon, and probably a man of standing, also brings to mind an important yet obscure episode connected with this town, namely the massacre of its inhabitants by Saul. These people were descended from the autochthonous population and were slaughtered by Saul "in his zeal for the people of Israel and Judah" (2 Sam 21:2). It is not impossible that there was a causal relationship between the massacre and the rise of a Gibeonite[16] to the position of chief of the Thirty under David at Ziklag. Like Amasai, Ishmaiah the Gibeonite is not heard of again. Later, during the time of David's reign at Hebron, we find Abishai, the brother of Joab, son of Zeruiah, at the head of the Thirty (2 Sam 23:18 and below). Another source also lists Benaiah son of Jehoiada (1 Chr 27:6).

14 On Amasa, see note 8. If one presupposes that Amasai and Amasa son of Jether are one and the same, one must also assume that Jether the Ishmaelite took Abigail for a wife long before David first arrived at the court of Saul; at that time Amasa lost his position as commander in the service of David. He again served as commander of the army of Israel only during the time of Absalom's insurrection (2 Sam 17:25).

15 According to the list in 1 Chr, the archers in the armies of both Saul and David came from Gibeah, Azmaveth, and Anathoth, all in the territory of Benjamin. Further on in the list one finds men of Calebite extraction, namely Korahites [1 Chr 2:43; see Klein, *Genealogical Lists* (note 8), 17ff.; Mazar, *Cities and Districts*, 60ff.], Harephites (i.e. sons of Hareph son of Caleb, father of Beth-gader, 1 Chr 2:51), and men of Gedor (which, perhaps, may be identified with Beth-gader). On Gedor (1 Chr 12:8), as well as on Gederah (1 Chr 12:5), see relevant entries in *Enc. Miq.* 2, 69–70, 447. The document also includes a list of professional warriors "of the Gadites", who had crossed the Jordan "when it was at its crest" and "withdrew to follow David to the wilderness stronghold" (vv. 9–15).

16 The importance of Gibeon, particularly of its famous high place, at the time in question is attested by 1 Kgs 3 [a passage about Solomon; cf. S. Yeivin, *RHJE* 1 (1974), 143ff.]. There is also reference to "the Tent of Meeting", *Ohel Moed*? and of the "shrine at Gibeon" (2 Chr 1:3); and to "Zadok the priest and his fellow priests before the Tabernacle of the Lord at the shrine that was in Gibeon" (1 Chr 16:39).

Dating the establishment of the élite of thirty heroes to the time of David's wanderings in Judah's borderlands is supported by information concerning the organization of the band at large. The Davidic cycle indicates that even before David came to Ziklag the size of the band had grown from 400 to 600 men at arms (1 Sam 25:13; 27:2), which comprised a regular regiment in Israel and Philistia.[17] The band was composed of three columns, two of which formed the fighting force while the third "remained with the baggage" (1 Sam 25:13; 30:9–10). It is very likely that the tripartite division of the force, which undoubtedly reflects an early pattern,[18] is the origin of what became the structure of the supreme command. It consisted of three senior commanders, "the three" (*hashelosha*) who are mentioned at the top of the list, one of whom was "head of the three". Their heroic exploits in the company of the *śar* became an inspiration, the subject of many folk legends, some of which are preserved in the Davidic cycle.

The main sources of information on the heroes are the above-mentioned lists of their names preserved in 2 Sam 23:8–39 and 1 Chr 11:10–47. These lists have been studied extensively for the valuable information they provide on the history of the Israelite Monarchy, particularly in the time of David. The structure and evolution of the personal names of the heroes, which are usually accompanied by a patronymic or family name, or place of origin, add further information. It has usually been assumed that the two lists are versions of a single early source, but no agreement has been reached concerning the particulars of the changes, additions, and omissions affecting the lists, or the divergence between the Masoretic and Septuagint versions.[19] The following analysis demonstrates that despite the corruptions and juxtapositions that affect the two biblical versions, it is generally possible to reconstruct a common, early source, leaving only few disparities unresolved.

Below are the lists in juxtaposition:

17 See especially Judg 18:11; 1 Sam 13:15; Judg 2:31; 2 Sam 15:18.

18 The division into three parts probably reflects the method of raiding and offensive warfare practiced by these columns. It was common in Israel and Philistia (e.g. 1 Sam 11:11; 13:17), and was customary as well among the desert tribes (Job 1:17). David's innovation was that one of the columns remained with the baggage, and the distribution of booty was determined accordingly (1 Sam 30:21–25). This corresponds with C.H. Gordon, *HUCA* 26 (1955), 83, on the Homeric Triad of officers, one of whom was more senior than the others. Gordon goes as far as to conclude that "each East Mediterranean military contingent had three officers".

19 See especially K. Elliger, *PJb* 31 (1935), 29–75; S. Klein, *Yediot* 7 (1940), 95–106 (Hebrew); B. Mazar, *Enc. Miq.* 2, 398–400, and the commentaries on 2 Sam and 1 Chr.

2 Sam 23:8–39	1 Chr 11:10–41
אלה שמות הגברים אשר לדוד:	ואלה ראשי הגיבורים אשר לדויד
ישב בשבת תחכמני[20] ראש השלשי[21]	המתחזקים עמו במלכותו עם כל ישראל
הוא עדינו העצנו[22]	להמליכו, כדבר ה' על ישראל.
על שמנה מאות חלל בפעם אחד.	ואלה מספר הגברים אשר לדויד:
ואחרו אלעזר בן דדי[23] בן אחחי,	ישבעם בן חכמוני[20] ראש השלושים[21],
בשלשה גברים	הוא עורר את חניתו
עם דוד בחרפם[24]	על שלש מאות חלל בפעם אחת.
בפלשתים נאספו שם למלחמה,	ואחריו אלעזר בן דודו האחוחי,
ויעלו איש ישראל.	הוא בשלושה הגברים.
הוא קם ויך בפלשתים	הוא היה עם דויד בפס דמים[24]
עד כי יגעה ידו	והפלשתים נאספו שם למלחמה
ותדבק ידו אל החרב,	
ויעש ה' תשועה גדולה ביום ההוא,	
והעם ישֻבו אחריו אך לפַשט.	
ואחרו שמה בן אגא הררי[25],	
ויאספו פלשתים לחיה,	

20 The Lucian recension of the Septuagint has in 2 Sam: Ἰσβααλ for ישב בשבת<ישבשת<ישבעל, and Ἰσσεβααλ for ישבעם in 1 Chr. This enables us to reconstruct the original name, which was Yeshbaal (see J. Liver, *Enc. Miq.* 3, 892). His name, therefore, is the same as that of Saul's son, Eshbaal, אשבעל (אישבשת, Ishbosheth). I have shown (see in this volume, "King David's Scribe", p. 135, n. 41) that the name is composed of two elements: אש — יש (Ugaritic: *ʾiṯ*) and *baʿal*, and that ישי (Jesse) — אישי (1 Chr 2:13) is merely the abbreviation of the same theophorous name. As in 1 Sam 14:49, we find ישוי instead of Eshbaal (Septuagint Lag.: Ἰεσσιου, ישיו). It appears that the king's original name was Yeshbaal, whereas his official name was ישיו, or ישיהו, which is the Israelite adaptation of the same name. This also holds true for Yeshbaal son of Hachmoni, mentioned in the list. It appears to me that he is the same person as ישיהו, one of the Korahites who joined David at Ziklag (1 Chr 12:7; cf. also note 15). He may even have been the brother of Jehiel son of Hachmoni, who was "with the king's sons" (1 Chr 27:32), i.e. their military instructor. On Jashobeam in 1 Chr 12:7; 27:2, see J. Liver, *Enc. Miq.* 3, 892. On the Korahites, see note 15.

21 The *qere* in 1 Chr is השלושים. According to the Septuagint Lag., השלושה is the correct rendition.

22 1 Chr is preferable, since the text in 2 Sam is corrupt. Perhaps the corruption stems from the words ועץ חניתו כמנור ארגים, "the shaft of his spear was like a weaver's bar", which is found in the stories about Elhanan son of Jaare, and about David and Goliath (1 Sam 17:7; 2 Sam 21:19). Under the influence of the above two passages, the words חנית כמנור ארגים slipped into 1 Chr 11:23. P. Dohrme, *Les livres de Samuel* (1910), *ad loc.*, has suggested the reading ערר חצינו from the Arabic חצין (Syrian: חצינא), meaning battle-axe.

23 *Qere*: Dodo; in 1 Chr 27:4: Dodai the Ahohite.

24 The source of this corruption probably also lies in the stories in 1 Sam 17 and at the end of 2 Sam 21. Pas-dammim in 1 Chr is the same as Ephes-dammim, mentioned in 1 Sam 17:1.

25 In the Lucianic recension of the Septuagint, Ἠλα, Ela, is the same as the name of Solomon's prefect in the land of Benjamin (1 Kgs 4:18). It is not impossible that he is identical to Shammah the Harodite mentioned later in the list (2 Sam 23:25; the parallel in 1 Chr is Shammoth the Harorite), but the evidence is inconclusive. Yet further in the list we find Jonathan (son of) Shammah the Ararite, who may have been his son (see below note 50). There is no doubt, however, that הררי, הארורי, ההררי, אררי, and החרודי all refer to the same place, namely Harod, in the vicinity of Bethlehem, or Beth-harodo in the Judean Desert, "about three [Roman] miles from Jerusalem" (*Mishnah Yomma* 2:8). Ch. Clermont-Ganneau has identified the site with Khirbet el-Ḥaridan, 6 km south-east of Jerusalem [see S. Klein, *Erez Yehudah* (1939), 86 (Hebrew); B. Mazar, *Enc. Miq.* 3, 280–281].

2 Sam 23:8–39	1 Chr 11:10–41
ותהי שם חלקת השדה	ותהי חלקת השדה
מלאה עדשים[26],	מלאה שעורים[26]
והעם נס מפני פלשתים.	והעם נסו מפני פלשתים.
ויתיצב בתוך החלקה ויצילה,	ויתיצבו בתוך החלקה ויצילוה,
ויך את פלשתים,	ויכו את פלשתים,
ויעש ה' תשועה גדולה.	ויושע ה' תשועה גדולה
וירדו שלשים[27] מהשלשים ראש[28],	וירדו שלושה מן השלושים ראש[28]
ויבאו אל קציר אל דוד	על הצָר אל דויד,
אל מערת[29] עדלם,	אל מערת[29] עדלם,
וחית פלשתים	ומחנה פלשתים
חֹנה בעמק רפאים.	חנה בעמק רפאים.
ודוד אז במצודה,	ודויד אז במצודה,
ומצב[30] פלשתים אז בית לחם.	ונציב פלשתים אז בבית לחם.
ויתאוה דוד ויאמר,	ויתאו דויד ויאמר,
מי ישקני מים	מי ישקני מים
מבֹּאר בית לחם אשר בשער.	מבור בית לחם אשר בשער.
ויבקעו שלשת הגברים	ויבקעו השלשה
במחנה פלשתים,	במחנה פלשתים,
וישאבו מים מבאר בית לחם	וישאבו מים מבור בית לחם
אשר בשער,	אשר בשער,
וישאו ויבִאו אל דוד,	וישאו ויבִאו אל דויד,
ולא אבה לשתותם	ולא אבה דויד לשתותם,
ויסך אותם לה'.	וינסך אתם לה'.
ויאמר חלילה לי ה'	ויאמר חלילה לי מאלהי
מעשׂתי זאת,	מעשות זאת,
הדם האנשים ההלכים בנפשתם[31],	הדם האנשים האלה אשתה בנפשתם
	כי בנפשותם הביאום,
ולא אבה לשתותם,	ולא אבה לשתותם,
אלה עשו שלשת הגברים.	אלה עשו שלשת הגבורים.
ואבישי אחי יואב בן צרויה	ואבשי אחי יואב
הוא ראש השלשי[32],	הוא היה ראש השלושה[32],
והוא עורר את חניתו	והוא עורר את חניתו

26 Compare "and he has barley there" in the story of Joab's field (near Bethlehem?) which the servants of Absalom set on fire (2 Sam 14:30).

27 According to the *qere*, 1 Chr and both Masoretic and Septuagint Mss., one should read here שלושה.

28 The text is corrupt and may be reconstructed with the aid of 1 Chr. If one assumes that a letter *mem*, prefixed to the word ראש, had been dropped due to the *mem* at the end of the word preceding it, and that the word אל or על has been mistakenly introduced before הצר, the original should have read: מראש הצר אל דוד.

29 It is commonly accepted that the word מערת is a scribal error and should be corrected to read מצדת (cf. 1 Sam 22:1). It refers to David's fortified camp near Bethlehem, possibly at el-Khadr, situated in a good strategic position 5 km south-west of Bethlehem (see above, p. 87 and note 10). In 1 Sam 22:4, "and David was then in the stronghold" probably refers to the fortress of Zion.

30 מצב is the more feasible version (compare 1 Sam 10:5 to 1 Sam 13:23; 14:1, etc.).

31 1 Chr is preferable to 2 Sam, which has been much abbreviated and corrupted.

32 Here one should read השלשים, in accordance with the Masoretic Mss. of 2 Sam, and the Peshitta version of both 2 Sam and 1 Chr.

2 Sam 23:8–39	1 Chr 11:10–41
על שלש מאות חלל[33],	על שלש מאות חלל[33],
ולו שם בשלשה[32].	ולו שם בשלושה[32].
מן השלשה הכי נכבד[34],	מן השלשה בשנים נכבד[34],
ויהי להם לשר,	ויהי להם לשר,
ועד השלשה לא בא[35].	ועד השלשה לא בא[35].
ובניהו בן יהוידע	בניה בן יהוידע
בן איש חי	בן איש חיל
רב פעלים מקבצאל,	רב פעלים מן קבצאל,
הוא הכה את שני	הוא הכה את שני
אראל[36] מואב,	אריאל[36] מואב,
והוא ירד והכה	והוא ירד והכה
את האריה בתוך הבֹּאר[37]	את הארי בתוך הבור
ביום השלג.	ביום השלג.
והוא הכה את איש מצרי	והוא הכה את האיש המצרי,
אשר מראה[38],	איש מִדה חמש באמה,
וביד המצרי חנית,	וביד המצרי חנית כמנור ארגים[39],
וירד אליו בשבט,	וירד אליו בשבט,
ויגזל את החנית מיד המצרי,	ויגזל את החנית מיד המצרי,
ויהרגהו בחניתו.	ויהרגוהו בחניתו.
אלה עשה בניהו בן יהוידע,	אלה עשה בניהו בן יהוידע,
ולו שם בשלשה[40] הגברים.	ולו שם בשלושה[40] הגברים,
מן השלשים נכבד,	מן השלושים הנו נכבד הוא,
ואל השלשה לא בא[35]	ואל השלושה לא בא[35],
וישׂמהו דוד אל משמעתו.	וישימהו דויד על משמעותו.
	וגבורי החילים,
עשהאל אחי יואב בשלשים,	עשהאל אחי יואב,
אלחנן בן דודו בית לחם[41],	אלחנן בן דודו מבית לחם[41].

33 This is undoubtedly a gloss, taken from the description of Shammah the Harodite (2 Sam 23:25; 1 Chr 11:27), which interrupts the continuous sequence of the original.

34 In mistakenly writing השלשה instead of השלשים the scribe was probably influenced by the preceding passage; see 1 Chr 11:25: מן השלושים הנו נכבד (הוא), and compare the Septuagint version. The word בשנים is more obscure.

35 M. Tsevat, *HUCA* 29 (1958), 127, has found an interesting analogy in the Alalakh documents (at the conclusion of lists of veteran soldiers) in the expression *ana naphari la irubu*, "were not counted among the above mentioned" (in our case, among the three).

36 Perhaps we should read אראלי. The meaning of the word אריאל/אראל is probably hero (cf. Isa 33:7). According to Albright [*BASOR* 83 (1943), 16], in the ancient Phoenician inscription from Cyprus [published by A.M. Honeyman, *Iraq* 6 (1939), 106ff.] one should similarly read אראלם; however, see the interpretation by N.H. Tur-Sinai, *Enc. Miq.* 1, 558ff. In the Mesha inscription, line 12: ואשב.משם.את.אראל.דודה.

37 As in vv. 15–16, 2 Sam reads באר for בור in 1 Chr; also compare Jer 2:13.

38 1 Chr is preferable as the text here has been corrupted and abbreviated. One should also note another source in 1 Chr (27:6) that is relevant to the list: הוא בניהו גיבור השלשים ועל השלשים.

39 See note 22.

40 Should read בשלשים as implied by the context, and by 1 Chr 27:6.

41 According to one view, Elhanan son of Dodo from Bethlehem is the same as Elhanan son of Jaare (-orgim) the Bethlehemite, and probably also identical to Elhanan son of Jair, mentioned in 1 Chr 20:5. On the other hand, the great resemblance between the stories of Elhanan and of David and

2 Sam 23:8–39	1 Chr 11:10–41
שמה החרדי[25],	שמות ההרורי[25],
אליקא החרדי[25],	
חלץ הפלטי[42],	חלץ הפלוני[42].
עירא בן עקש התקעי,	עירא בן עקש התקועי,
אביעזר הענתתי,	אביעזר הענתותי,
מבני[43] החשתי,	סבכי[43] החשתי,
צלמון[44] האחחי,	עילי[44] האחוחי,
מהרי הנטפתי,	מהרי הנטופתי,
חלב[45] בן בענא הנטפתי,	חלד[45] בן בענה הנטופתי
אתי בן ריבי מגבעת בני בנימן,	איתי בן ריבי מגבעת בני בנימן,
בניהו פרעתני,	בניה הפרעתני,
הדי[46] מנחלי געש,	חורי[46] מנחלי געש,
אבי עלבון[47] הערבתי,	אביאל[47] הערבתי,
עזמות הברחמי[48]	עזמות הבחרומי,
אליחבא השעלבני,	אליחבא השעלבני,

Goliath suggests that the patronym had been corrupted in the copying, and that, palaeographically, the reading ישי, Jesse, is more likely. Therefore, Elhanan son of Jaare is the original name of David son of Jesse [see S. Goldschmidtt, *Yediot* 14 (1941), 122 (Hebrew)].

42 It is likely that the text here refers to a native of Beth-pelet in the Negeb, so named after the family of Pelet, descended from Caleb (1 Chr 2:47). Like many others in David's circle, Helez was, therefore, of Calebite extraction (see B. Mazar, *Enc. Miq.* 2, 98). It is surprising that Helez the Pelonite of the 1 Chr version is also named in 1 Chr 27:10 as one of David's chiefs, and is said to be of the Ephraimites. It is possible, however, that the editor of the list in 1 Chr confused Helez the Peletite with Helez the Pelonite as a result of the passage in 1 Chr 27.

43 Namely, Sibechai, also in the Septuagint; in 2 Sam 21:18 and 1 Chr 27:11: Sibechai the Hushathite, i.e. from the town of Hushah (today Ḥūssān, ca. 6 km west of Bethlehem). According to the genealogy in 1 Chr 4:4, the residents of Hushah and Bethlehem were kinsmen.

44 According to the Septuagint (B) of 1 Chr, ʿΗλει; the original version has been preserved in 2 Sam. The family of Ahoah traced its lineage to Bela, the first born of Benjamin (1 Chr 8:4).

45 Heled is the obvious preference, referring to "Heldai the Netophathite, of Othniel", mentioned in 1 Chr 27:15. Netophah, a town in the area of Bethlehem, has not been identified to date.

46 1 Chr more likely preserves the original form of the name. Nahale-gaash probably refers to the area of Mount Gaash (cf. the הנחלים ארנון, Num 21:14; also Deut 10:7), in the hill country of Ephraim (Josh 24:30; Judg 2:9; Jub 34:4); see also Z. Kallai, *Enc. Miq.* 2, 540; B. Klein, *ZDPV* 57 (1935), 12ff. According to Abel, *GP* 1, 399, it refers to Wadi ʿEin ez-Zerqā, near Timnah. An assumption of kinship between Hurai of Nahale-gaash and Ben-hur, Solomon's prefect for the district of Ephraim (1 Kgs 4:8), is very hypothetical.

47 The name Abi-albon in 2 Sam appears to be a corruption of אביבעל בן; therefore, the original must have read: אביבעל בן הערבתי, Abibaal son of the Arbathite. Compare substitutions in other theophorous names, e.g. Beeliada, a brother of David (1 Chr 14:7) and Eliada (2 Sam 5:16); see in this volume, "King David's Scribe", pp. 126–138. Beth-Haarabah, the native town of this hero, was located near the oasis of Jericho in the northern part of Judean Desert (Josh 15:6 and 61), close to modern el-Ghrbeh south-west of Jericho [see A. Alt, *PJb* 21 (1925), 26f.]. The list of Benjamite towns in which it is included (Josh 18:22) probably dates from the period of Abiah; see Z. Kallai, *The Northern Boundaries of Judah* (1960), 11, 33–34 (Hebrew).

48 The name in 2 Sam is a corruption. It has been suggested (Abel, *GP* 2, 260) that Bahurim, mentioned in the Bible several times as a settlement on the eastern slopes of the Mount of Olives, to the east of Jerusalem, be identified with Ras et-Tammim. Cf. I. Press, *A Topographical-Historical Encyclopedia of Palestine* 1 (2nd ed, 1951), 65–66.

2 Sam 23:8–39	1 Chr 11:10–41
בני ישן[49]	בני השם הגִזוני[49],
יהונתן. שמה[50] ההררי,	יונתן בן שגה[50] ההררי,
אחיאם בן שרר[51] האררי[25],	אחיאם בן שכר ההררי[25],
אליפלט בן אחסבי[52] בן המעכתי,	אליפל בן אור. חפר[52] המכרתי[53],
אליעם בן אחיתפל[54] הגִלני,	אחיה[54] הפלֹני[55],
חצרו[56] הכרמלי,	חצרו[56] הכרמלי,
פערי[57] הארבי,	נערי[57] בן אזבי[58],

49 It is unclear whether בני is merely a repetition of the end of the preceding word השעלבני, or indicates the personal בני(ה) (Septuagint B of 1 Chr: Βενναιας), in which case the emendation is בני [בן]. השם or ישן (Septuagint: ᾿Ασαν, ᾿Ασαμ) seem to me to be corruptions of חשם, a name which appears in the genealogies of both Dan and Benjamin (see Mazar, *Cities and Districts*, 89–90;S.E. Loewenstamm, *Enc. Miq.* 3, 66). Concerning the appellation הגזוני, the Gizonite, preserved in 1 Chr, one view holds that it should be read הגוני, on the basis of the Septuagint (A), whereas Elliger [*PJb* 31 (1945), 31, 53] has suggested emending it to הגמזוני. According to Y. Ben-Zvi [*Haolam* 35 (1948), 606 (Hebrew)], a vestige of the name is manifest in Beth-Jiz, near Aijalon (in the territory of Dan); see S.E. Loewenstamm, *Enc. Miq.* 2, 463.

50 The Septuagint Luc. of 1 Chr is Σαμαια. The passage probably refers to Jonathan son of Shammah the Harodite; see note 25.

51 1 Chr: "Sachar" is preferable, on the basis of Septuagint Luc. for 2 Sam: ᾿Ισσαχαρ, and the mention of the name Sacar in 1 Chr 26:4. It is likely that the name שכר (Sachar) is a short form of Issachar.

52 Eliphelet has been shortened to Eliphal, אליפל, in 1 Chr. With regard to the patronym, it is generally accepted that both versions are corruptions [see K. Elliger, *PJb* (1945), 56–57]. The name אחסבי is unlikely as nowhere else do we encounter סבי as a component of names. On the other hand, no emendation of 1 Chr אור חפר can be related or connected to Ahasbai. Neither do the various Septuagint versions shed more light on the subject (see B. Mazar, *Enc. Miq.* 1, 229). As to the appellation בן המעכתי, son of the Maachathite, it may be reasonably taken to refer to the large family which traced its lineage to Maachah, the concubine of Caleb (1 Chr 2:48; 4:19; 2 Kgs 25:23), and which probably dwelled in the south of the Judean Hills and in the northern Negeb. Mentioned in 1 Chr 27:16 is a Shephatiah son of Maachah, officer over the tribe of Simeon.

53 A scribal error for המעכתי.

54 Eliam was the son of the king's counselor Ahithophel the Gilonite (i.e. from the town of Giloh in the province of Debir in the hill country of Judah — Josh 15:51). According to one view, Eliam was the father of Bathsheba [2 Sam 11:3 — Eliam; 1 Chr 3:5 — Amiel; see also S. Yeivin, *Studies in the History of Israel and Its Country* (1960), 200ff. (Hebrew)]. There is no doubt that the element *tophel* in Ahithophel is a derogatory version of "baal" similar to "bosheth". The original name, therefore, must have been Ahibaal (see B. Mazar, *Enc. Miq.* 1, 226–227). It seems to me that the text in 1 Chr is a truncated form of [אליעם בן]אחיה הגלני, ["Eliam son of] Ahiah the Gilonite", which must have been the original. In other words, Ahibaal (= Ahithophel) in 2 Sam is the same person as Ahiah in 1 Chr. It should be noted that the custom of replacing the pagan element in theophorous names with יהו is especially typical of the early period of the Israelite Monarchy, when national-religious sentiment ran high among the ruling class in Israel; see in this volume, "King David's Scribe", pp. 126–138. Ahithophel's original name, therefore, was Ahibaal or Ahiah(u) in its Israelite adaptation. See also note 20.

55 The discrepancy (הפלני instead of הגלני) is resolved palaeographically.

56 *Qere*: חצרי, also in the Septuagint. He came from Carmel in the Calebite area of the southern Judean Hills (Josh 15:55; 1 Sam 25:2).

57 The original name appears to be נערי (נעריה).

58 1 Chr: בן אזבי is a corruption of בן ארבי, i.e. from Arab in the vicinity of Hebron (Josh 15:52). It has been suggested that Arab be identified with the modern er-Rabieh, east of Dumah.

2 Sam 23:8–39	1 Chr 11:10–41
יגאל בן נתן מצֹבה[59],	יואל אחי נתן[59],
בני הגדי[60],	מבחר בן הגרי[60],
צלק העמוני,	צלק העמוני,
נחרי הבארתי,	נחרי הברתי,
נשאי כלי יואב בן צרויה[61],	נשׂא כלי יואב בן צרויה[61],
עירא היתרי[62],	עירא היתרי[62],
גרב היתרי,	גרב היתרי,
אוריה החתי,	אוריה החתי,
	זבד בן אחלי[63].
כל שלשים ושבעה.	

59 The original version (יואל instead of יגאל) emerges from Septuagint B of 1 Chr: Ἰωηλ υἱὸς Ναθάν, and the Septuagint of 2 Sam. His native town was Zobah, which is mentioned in the Septuagint addition to Josh 15:59 as a town in the district of Bethlehem [Σωβηε, Σωβης); see M.L. Margolis, *The Book of Joshua in Greek* (1931), 317]. It has been identified with absolute certainty as Suba, and the suggestion that it refers to the Aramean Zobah [K. Elliger, *PJB* 31 (1945), 33] is entirely unfounded. See also Press, *Topographical-Historical Encyclopedia* 4 (1955), 781.

60 The first name must have been elided in 2 Sam. The name Mibhar in 1 Chr is also doubtful (Septuagint: Μεβααλ). 2 Sam could be read with equal likelihood בן הגדי, "son of the Gadite", or בן הגרי, "son of Hagri", as in 1 Chr. Here it is impossible to arrive at a conclusive reconstruction of the original as, on the one hand, Gadites were among those who came to David at his desert stronghold (1 Chr 12:9f.), but on the other hand, the Hagrites, genealogically related to the Ishmaelites, were an important confederation of nomadic tribes in the borderlands (1 Chr 5:10, 18–22), and a Hagrite, Jaziz, was in charge of King David's flocks (1 Chr 27:31). Septuagint B: υἱὸς Γαλααδδεί, "son of the Gileadite", is surprising, as it has no source in any of the Masoretic versions.

61 *Qere*: נשא, in both 2 Sam and 1 Chr, meaning that only Naharai the Beerothite was arms-bearer to Joab. Beeroth was one of four Hivite towns whose inhabitants, although of non-Israelite stock (compare 2 Sam 21:2), were included within the tribal organizations of Benjamin ["... sons of Rimmon the Beerothite — Benjaminites, since Beeroth too was considered part of Benjamin" (2 Sam 4:2); on the name Naharai, see in this volume, "King David's Scribe", p. 129, note 11]. The fact that the two sons of Rimmon the Beerothite were company commanders in the service of Saul, and that Joab's arms-bearer came from the same town confirms that the Beerothites were famous as professional warriors.
After the murder of Eshbaal, the two sons of Rimmon the Beerothite fled across the border of Israel to Gittaim, which was under Philistine rule (2 Sam 4:3). This is the source of the place name Gath-rimmon in the territory of Dan (Josh 19:45). With the expansion of the United Monarchy during Solomon's reign, Gath-rimmon was annexed to the territory of Dan and became a Levitical town (Josh 21:24). See Mazar, *Canaan and Israel*, 222ff.; and in this volume, "The Cities of the Territory of Dan", pp. 104–112.

62 היתרי, "the Ithrite", was the principal family of Kiriath-jearim, of Hivite extraction, later assimilated into Judah (1 Chr 2:53). See also H.L. Ginsberg and B. Mazar (Maisler), *JPOS* 14 (1934), 260.

63 According to the genealogies in 1 Chr 2, Ahlai was the son of Sheshan, a respected Jerahmeelite line about which we have contradicting information (1 Chr 2:31f.). Jerahmeel was a nomadic and semi-nomadic tribe in the Negeb, that later assimilated into Judah [compare "the Negeb of the Jerahmeelites" (1 Sam 27:10); "the towns of the Jerahmeelites" (1 Sam 30:29); see also J. Liver, *Enc. Miq.* 3, 851ff.]. It is not impossible that Aabad son of Ahlai joined David as early as Ziklag, when the latter came into close contact with the elders of Judah and the heads of the borderland tribes (1 Sam 30:26–30).

The discrepancies between the sources are usually only matters of spelling and metathesis, and may be resolved with the aid of the Septuagint and other sources. Both versions also suffer from omissions and scribal errors that stand out clearly under comparison. I therefore suggest below a reconstruction of the ancient origin of both versions, conceding that several instances are yet unresolved pending new findings:

These are the names of David's heroes:	אלה שמות הגבּרים אשר לדוד:
Ishbaal son of Hachmoni, the chief of the three.	ישבעל בן חכמני ראש השלושה.
He wielded [the shaft of] his spear against three hundred and slew them all on one occasion.	הוא עורר את [עץ] חניתו על שלש מאות חלל בפעם אחת.
Next to him was Eleazar son of Dodo, the Ahohite; he was one of the three heroes.	ואחריו אלעזר בן דדו האחֹחי בשלשה הגבּרים.
He was with David at Ephes dammim	הוא היה עם דוד ב[א]פס דמים.
when the Philistines gathered there for battle.	והפלשתים נאספו שם למלחמה.
The Israelite soldiers retreated	ויעלו איש ישראל.
but he held his ground. He struck down Philistines until his arm grew tired and his hand stuck to his sword;	הוא קם ויך בפלשתים עד כי יגעה ידו ותדבק ידו אל החרב.
and the Lord wrought a great victory that day.	ויעש ה' תשועה גדולה ביום ההוא.
Then the troops came back to him — but only to strip [the slain].	והעם ישֻׁבו אחריו אך לפשט.
Next to him was Shammah son of Ela the Harodite.	ואחריו שמה בן אלא החרדי.
The Philistines had gathered in force.	ויאספו פלשתים לחיה.
There was a plot of ground full of barley there;	ותהי שם חלקת השדה מלאת שׂערים.
and the troops fled from the Philistines.	והעם נס מפני פלשתים.
But he took his stand in the middle of the plot and	ויתיצב בתוך החלקה ויצילה.
defended it, and he routed the Philistines.	ויך את פלשתים.
Thus the Lord wrought a great victory.	ויעש ה' תשועה גדולה.
Three of the Thirty went down from the rock(?) to	וירדו שלשה מהשלשים מראש הצֻר(?)
David, at the stronghold(?) of Adullam,	ויבאו אל דוד אל מצדת(?) עדלם.
while a force of Philistines was encamped in the Valley of Rephaim.	וחית פלשתים חֹנה בעמק רפאים.
David was then in the stronghold, and a Philistine garrison was then at Bethlehem.	ודוד אז במצֻדה ומצב פלשתים אז בבית לחם.
David felt a craving and said:	ויתאוה דוד ויאמר:
"If only I could get a drink of water from the cistern which is by the gate of Bethlehem!"	מי ישקני מים מבאר בית לחם אשר בשער.
So the three heroes got through the Philistine camp,	ויבקעו שלשת הגבּרים במחנה פלשתים.
and drew water from the cistern which is by the gate of Bethlehem, and they carried it back to David.	וישאבו מים מבאר בית לחם אשר בשער וישאו ויבִאו אל דוד.

But David would not drink it, and he poured it out as a libation to the Lord.	ולא אבה דוד לשתותם ויסך אתם ליהוה.
For he said,	ויאמר:
"God forbid that I should do this!	חלילה לי מיהוה מעשׂתי זאת.
Can I drink the blood of these men who risked their lives?" — for they had brought it at the risk of their lives,	הדם האנשים האלה אשתה בנפשתם כי בנפשתם הביאום.
and he would not drink it.	ולא אבה לשתותם.
Such were the exploits of the three heroes.	אלה עשו שלשת הגבֹּרים.
Abishai, the brother of Joab son of Zeruiah, was head of the Thirty. He won a name among the Thirty.	ואבשי אחי יואב בן צרויה הוא ראש השלשים ולו שם בשלשים.
Among the Thirty he was more highly regarded and so he became their commander. However, he did not attain to the three.	מן השלשים הנו נכבד ויהי להם לשר ועד השלשה לא בא.
Benaiah son of Jehoiada, from Kabzeel, the son of a brave soldier who performed great deeds(?).	ובניהו בן יהוידע בן איש חיל רב פעלים(?) מקבצאל.
He killed the two Ariels of Moab.	הוא הכה את שני אראלי מואב.
Once, on a snowy day, he went down into a pit and killed a lion.	והוא ירד והכה את האריה בתוך הבֹּאר ביום השלג.
He also killed an Egyptian, a giant of a man five cubits tall.	והוא הכה את איש מצרי איש מדה חמש באמה.
The Egyptian had a spear in his hand,	וביד המצרי חנית.
yet he went down against him with a club,	וירד אליו בשבט.
wrenched the spear out of the Egyptian's hand, and killed him with his own spear.	ויגזל את החנית מיד המצרי ויהרגהו בחניתו.
Such were the exploits of Benaiah son of Jehoiada; and he won a name among the Thirty heroes.	אלה עשה בניהו בן יהוידע. ולו שם בשלשים הגבֹּרים.
He was highly regarded among the Thirty, but he did not attain to the three.	מן השלשים הנו נכבד ואל השלשה לא בא.
David appointed him to his bodyguard.	וישימהו דוד אל משמעתו.
Among the Thirty were Asahel, the brother of Joab,	עשהאל אחי יואב בשלשים.
Elhanan son of Dodo [from] Bethlehem.	אלחנן בן דֹּדו [מ]בית לחם.
Shammah the Harodite.	שמה החרֹדי.
Elika the Harodite.	אליקא החרֹדי.
Helez the Paltite.	חלץ הפלטי.
Ira son of Ikkesh from Tekoa.	עירא בן עקש התקועי.
Abiezer of Anathoth.	אביעזר הענתֹתי.
Sibbechai the Hushathite.	סִבכי החֻשתי.
Ilai the Ahohite.	עילי האחֹחי.
Maharai the Netophathite.	מהרי הנטֹפתי.
Heled son of Baanah the Netophathite.	חלד בן בענא הנטֹפתי.
Ittai son of Ribai from Gibeah of the Benjaminites.	איתי בן ריבי מגבעת בני בנימין.
Benaiahu of Pirathon.	בניהו הפרעתני.

English	Hebrew
Hurai of Nahale-gaash.	חורי מנחלי געש.
Abibaal (Abiel) [son of...] the Arbathite	אביבעל (אביאל) [בן ...] הערבתי.
Azmaveth the Bahrumite.	עזמות הבחֻרמי.
Eliahba of Shaalbon.	אליחבא השעלבֹני.
[Benaiah son of] Hashem the Gizonite.	[בניה בן] חשם הגזוני.
Jonathan son of Shammah the Harodite.	יהונתן בן שמה החרֹדי.
Ahiam son of Sachar the Harodite.	אחיאם בן שכר החרדי.
Eliphelet son of [...] the Maachathite.	אליפלט בן[...] המעכתי.
Eliam son of Ahibaal (Ahia) the Gilonite.	אליעם בן אחיבעל (אחיה) הגלוני.
Hezrai the Carmelite.	חצרי הכרמלי.
Naarai [son of ...] the Arbite.	נערי [בן ...] הארבי.
Joel son of Nathan from Zobah.	יואל בן נתן מצֹבה.
Mibhar [the] Hagrite (Gadite?).	מבחר [ה]הגרי (הגדי?).
Zelek the Ammonite.	צלק העמוני.
Naharai the Berothite, the arms-bearer of Joab son of Zeruiah.	נחרי הבארֹתי נושא כלי יואב בן צרויה.
Ira the Ithrite.	עירא היתרי.
Gareb the Ithrite.	גרב היתרי.
Uriah the Hittite.	אוריה החתי.
Zabad son of Ahlai:	זבד בן אחלי.
thirty-seven in all.	כל שלשים ושבעה.

The list of heroes consists of two parts. The first part names "the three" (Hebrew: השלושה): Ishbaal son of Hachmoni, chief of the three, Eleazar son of Dodo, and Shammah son of Ela, and two others who had gained renown among the Thirty yet were not officially numbered among the first three. These were Abishai, the brother of Joab, son of Zeruiah, chief of the Thirty, and Benaiah son of Jehoiada, who was in charge of David's bodyguard (Hebrew: משמעת). The list also provides several details pertaining to their origins, and records memorable events in their careers. The second part enumerates the remaining heroes, who are termed in Chronicles "the valiant warriors" (gibborei haḥayalim) (1 Chr 11:26). They are mentioned by name, patronymic, and place of origin.

It may seem surprising that in both biblical versions, the list includes thirty-seven names,[64] and concludes with the postscript "thirty-seven in all". Yet the number thirty is repeated both here and in other sources as the fixed number of heroes within the élite. A close examination of the texts reveals that one should distinguish between the first thirty heroes, the three included, and the remaining seven. Of the first thirty heroes, thirteen[65] are from Bethlehem in

---

64 1 Sam lists only thirty-six heroes, but the name of Zabad son of Ahlai, which had been mistakenly elided, has been preserved in 1 Chr.

65 At least twelve, if Shammah son of Ela the Harodite is the same person as Shammah (שמהות/שמות), chief of the three, which is doubtful; see note 25 above.

Judah and its environs (either from Bethlehem itself or from the towns of Netophah, Harod, Tekoa, Hushah, or Zobah). Five more are from other Judean towns (Arab, Giloh, Carmel), or bear names indicating that they came from the Calebite families of the Judean hill country (Korahites and Maachathites). One is from Beth-haarabah in the Judean Desert, and two more are from the northern Negeb (Kabzeel, Beth-pelet),[66] and probably belonged to the tribe of Simeon. The distribution of the remaining heroes included in the first thirty is as follows: five are of the tribe of Benjamin (Gibeah of the Benjaminites, Anathoth, Bahurim, and from the family of Ahoah), two are from Mount Ephraim (Pirathon, Nahale-gaash), and two are from Dan (Shaalbim, Gizoh).

The places and family names show very clearly that the first thirty heroes came from the pale of Israelite settlement west of the Jordan, in this case within an area between Ephraim and the Negeb, with a majority from the Judean hill country. This information provides no support whatsoever for the theory that the list reflects the state of affairs during David's reign over the United Monarchy, and even less for the suggestion that the list dates from the time after David had moved his capital from Hebron to Jerusalem. Furthermore, the mention of Asahel, Joab's brother, gives us a *terminus ad quem* for the list. We know that Asahel was slain by Abner in the war of Yeshbaal against David, during the early days of his reign at Hebron (2 Sam 2:19ff.).[67]

In the light of all this, it seems likely that the first thirty heroes were of Israelite stock, including families assimilated into the tribes of Israel during the settlement period. They were warriors of fame who supported David during his reign at Hebron, i.e. after he was annointed king of Judah (2 Sam 2:1–4), but some time before his coronation as monarch of all Israel (2 Sam 5:1–3). At that time, Joab was already commander-in-chief of the Judean army.[68] His

66 Y. Aharoni, in *Judah and Jerusalem* (1957), 58 (Hebrew), has suggested identifying Kabzeel (Jekabzeel) with Tell Ghāra, a conspicuous tell 20 km east of Beer-sheba. The identification of Beth Pelet is more difficult: I have hypothetically suggested Khirbet el-Medhbeh, a large area of ruins about 15 km south-east of Beer-sheba (*Enc. Miq.* 2, 98).

67 Prof. I. Eph'al has brought to my attention that Asahel, the brother of Joab, is mentioned also in 1 Chr 27:7 among the chiefs in charge of the divisions, most of whom were heroes, members of the élite. However, his name is accompanied there by "and his son Zebadiah after him", which may be taken to indicate that he was succeeded as hero and chief of a division by his son. This resembles the mention of Ammizabad, after his father Benaiah son of Jehoiada in the preceding verse (27:6), which should very likely be emended similarly to עמיזבד בנו [ואחריו], "[after him] his son Ammizabad", to the effect that he, too, inherited his father's position.

68 Joab presents us with a difficult problem: he appears as commander-in-chief of David's army and rival to Abner, commander of the army of Israel, as early as the battle near Gibeon (2 Sam 2:12f.), but in 1 Chr 11:6, in the account of the conquest of Jerusalem: "David said, 'Whoever attacks the Jebusites first will be chief officer'; Joab son of Zeruiah attacked first, and became the chief". Joab is mentioned as David's chief officer already in the stories relating to the reign at Hebron, but not before. The view

brother Abishai was chief of the Thirty, and their younger brother, Asahel, was a member of the élite.[69]

Unlike the thirty, all the valiant warriors from number thirty-one onwards came either from distant provinces or were of autochthonous, non-Israelite stock.[70] They were professional warriors who, together with their men, entered the service of David as early as the period of Hebron. They were not associated with the Cherethites and Pelethites who formed David's bodyguard after his accession and who were under the command of Benaiah son of Jehoiada (compare 2 Sam 8:18; 20:23; to 2 Sam 23:23; 1 Chr 11:25). Among them was one Ammonite (Zelek), and three were of Hivite extraction (Naharai the Beerothite, and Ira and Gareb of the family of Ithri of Kiriath-jearim).[71] One was a Hittite (Uriah).[72] In addition, there was one hero of the Ishmaelite family of Ahlai, a Hagrite (descended from Hagar) or, according to 2 Sam 23: 36, בן הגדי, "the Gadite".

Another unresolved question concerns the sequel to the list in 1 Chr. It mentions "Adina son of Shiza the Reubenite, a chief of the Reubenites, and thirty with him" (1 Chr 11:42), after which are listed fourteen men with patronymics or places of origin. Rothstein and Klein have suggested that whereas the author of 2 Sam 23 had before him only the early list of David's élite of intimates, the author of 1 Chr 11 was acquainted with the complete list, some of whose names he copied. That list also included warriors from the Transjordanian provinces.[73] Furthermore, Klein has found a resemblance be-

that is generally accepted [see, M. Noth, *Geschichte Israels* 2 (1953), 166ff.; J. Bright, *A History of Israel* (1960), 174ff.] is that David conquered Jerusalem towards the end of his reign at Hebron, and established himself there as king over the whole of Israel shortly afterwards. However, the proximity of the accounts of the two events (the conquest of the city and its establishment as capital) should in no way be taken as evidence of a chronological proximity between them. The notion that David waited until the eighth year of his reign before attacking Jerusalem, and with his men only (2 Sam 5:6) — without recruiting "all Israel" — for the sake of securing the main road from Hebron to the north, seems to me utterly groundless. It is not impossible that the conquest took place at the beginning of his reign, which explains, among other things, certain accounts of his wars against the Philistines and his attitude to the Jebusites who remained in the city. Only after becoming more established in power did he build the "City of David" and make it his metropolis. See B. Mazar, in *In the Time of Harvest, Essays in the Honour of A.H. Silver* (1963), 235ff.

69 In this matter David followed the example of Saul, who placed his kinsmen at the head of his army (his son Jonathan and his cousin Abner). Other relatives of David held important administrative positions.

70 On the "Canaanite" residents of the land in the service of David, see in this volume, "King David's Scribe", pp. 126–138; Yeivin, *Israel and Its Country* (see note 54), 178ff.

71 See preceding notes on the names of the heroes; note 62, and in this volume, "King David's Scribe", pp. 126–138.

72 Yeivin, *Israel and Its Country* (see note 54), 198–199, assumes that he was one of Jerusalem's Jebusite inhabitants who were probably of Hittite extraction (cf. Ezek 16:3, 45); see *Enc. Miq.* 1, 178–179.

73 See W. Rothstein and J. Hanel, *Kommentar zum erster Buch der Chronik* (1927), 241; Klein, *Yediot* 7 (1940), 97f. (Hebrew).

tween the addition in 1 Chr 11 and the genealogies of the Israelite families in Transjordan. This supports the view that the addition is not an invention of the author.[74]

We must bear in mind that as their source, the authors of both 2 Sam 23 and 1 Chr 11 had a single list of the heroes of David, one which included thirty-seven names. There are no grounds for the assumption that there were several such enumerations, or that the common source of both biblical versions was a fragment of a larger list. Adina son of Shiza, a chief of the Reubenites, is mentioned in the verse immediately following the list of heroes in 1 Chr 11 (v. 42). This indicates only that at a certain time, perhaps during David's wars in Transjordan,[75] the armies of the King of Israel were reinforced by a band of Reubenites, headed by Adina. This band had its own élite of thirty, who had experience in warfare against local and neighbouring marauders (compare 1 Chr 5:10, 18–19; 12:38). On the other hand, the appended list of fourteen "Reubenite" men (1 Chr 11:43–47) does not provide any insight into its date. While Klein has successfully proved that all fourteen heroes are Transjordanian, from the tribes of Reuben and Gad, from the Bashan, and even one from Moab, and that there is some resemblance between this list and the genealogies of the Transjordanian tribes of Israel (1 Chr 5:3ff.), it is not certain that it dates from the time of David. It may just as well be attributed to the census of Jeroboam II and Jotham (v. 17). For our purposes it clearly has no bearing on the heroes of David, and was probably appended because it mentioned the chief of the Reubenites after the names of the heroes.

Not much is known about the élite after the kingdom of David came into being, when Jerusalem became the metropolis of Israel, the capital of a centralized government and the main seat of a complex military and civil establishment. It appears that this period saw a certain decline in the authority and influence of the élite of heroes in comparison with the previous one, coterminous with a rise in the power of the military commander-in-chief. The commander-in-chief had at his disposal an entire regiment, "Joab's men", including the commander of the Cherethites and Pelethites (David's bodyguard), and the military commander of Judah, in charge of the Judean reserve forces (see 2 Sam 20:4ff.; cf. 1 Kgs 2:32). There is no doubt, however, that even then, the élite of heroes enjoyed great importance within the regular army, that was loyal to the king. It played a cardinal role in the wars against Israel's neighbours (2 Sam 10:7), in the suppression of Absalom's mutiny

74 Unlike the view held by K. Elliger, *PJb* 31 (1935), 36, and M. Noth, *Überlieferungsgeschichtliche Studien* 1 (1934), 136, who do not accept the antiquity of the addition. See also Rudolph, *Chronikbücher* (note 12), 101.

75 According to the chronological table suggested by S. Yeivin (*Enc. Miq.* 2, 641–642), David's wars east of the Jordan began in the twelfth year of his reign and ended in the seventeenth.

(2 Sam 16:6), and in putting down the uprising of Sheba son of Bichri.[76] Finally, it figured in the struggle for succession after the death of David. We find Benaiah son of Jehoiada supporting Solomon instead of the rightful heir, Adonijah, who was backed by Joab (1 Kgs 1:8,10).[77]

No information has been preserved concerning the fate of the élite during the reign of Solomon.[78] That period saw far-reaching changes in the structure of the Israelite army, most notably the establishment of a chariotry. There was extensive fortification of the metropolis and of other cities along the major routes (see in particular 1 Kgs 9:15–19; 2 Chr 8:46). These projects continued throughout the reigns of all the kings of Israel and Judah. The fate of the élite of the heroes who served the House of David after David's death is beyond the scope of the present discussion. Let me just note that the location of the hall of heroes in the City of David was known as late as the time of Nehemiah (Neh 3:16).[79]

76 We learn about the composition of David's army from 2 Sam 20:7: "Joab's men, the Cherethites and the Pelethites, and all the warriors, marched out behind him. They left Jerusalem in pursuit of Sheba son of Bichri". At about the same time Amasa was sent to call up the men of Judah (2 Sam 20:4–5).

77 It is likely that towards the end of David's reign Benaiah son of Jehoiada, who was in charge of the king's bodyguard (the Cherethites and the Pelethites), rose to the position of chief of the Thirty. We find evidence of this in 1 Chr 27:6: "That was Benaiah, one of the thirty and over the thirty". This source confuses Jehoiada, the father of Benaiah, with Jehoiada, the chief priest. See S.E. Loewenstamm, *Enc. Miq.* 2, 262f.

78 Only hypothetically may one interpret the passage in the Song of Songs (3:7) "There is Solomon's couch, sixty heroes are around it, from the heroes of Israel" as indicating the existence, during the reign of Solomon, of an elite inner circle of sixty heroes.

79 On the location of the hall of heroes in the City of David, see B. Mazar, *Enc. Miq*. 3, 821.

The Cities of the Territory of Dan

The results of the archaeological survey carried out by Naveh[1] at Khirbet el-Muqanna' (Tel Miqne) mark an important advance towards the solution of one of the most difficult problems encountered in the study of the historical topography of the Land of Israel, namely the identification of the Philistine city of Ekron and also of the Danite cities in the region of the Valley of Sorek (Wādi Ṣarār). From this systematic study, which was accompanied by accurate drawings of the surface remains of buildings and the collection of potsherds from all over the site, a fairly clear picture emerges of the character of the city and its fortifications. It seems probable — in so far as any definite conclusions can be reached solely on the basis of an archaeological survey, without any actual excavation — that the city was founded at the beginning of the Iron Age in the 12th century B.C.E., that it reached the height of its prosperity and power in the 10th to 6th centuries B.C.E., and that it declined and finally fell into ruins in the Persian period, possibly in its early part.

Not only do these data conform admirably with what we are told of Ekron in the Old Testament, but it is particularly noteworthy that the site in question is of larger dimensions than all the other Iron Age settlements discovered to date in Israel. The area of Khirbet el-Muqanna' is approximately forty acres, and in addition, outside the walls visible on the surface there are various structures which appear to be the ruins of towers and outlying quarters. Other specially notable remains are those of the large edifice on the northern spur which rises above the rest of the tell (perhaps the site of the acropolis), and those of the city gate and its towers in the centre of the southern wall. It should further be mentioned that Khirbet el-Muqanna' stands at the junction of several important roads and that it is surrounded by copious underground springs and fertile soil.

* This study is a revised version of the article published in *IEJ* 10 (1960), 65–77.

1 J. Naveh, *IEJ* 8 (1958), 87–100, 165–170.

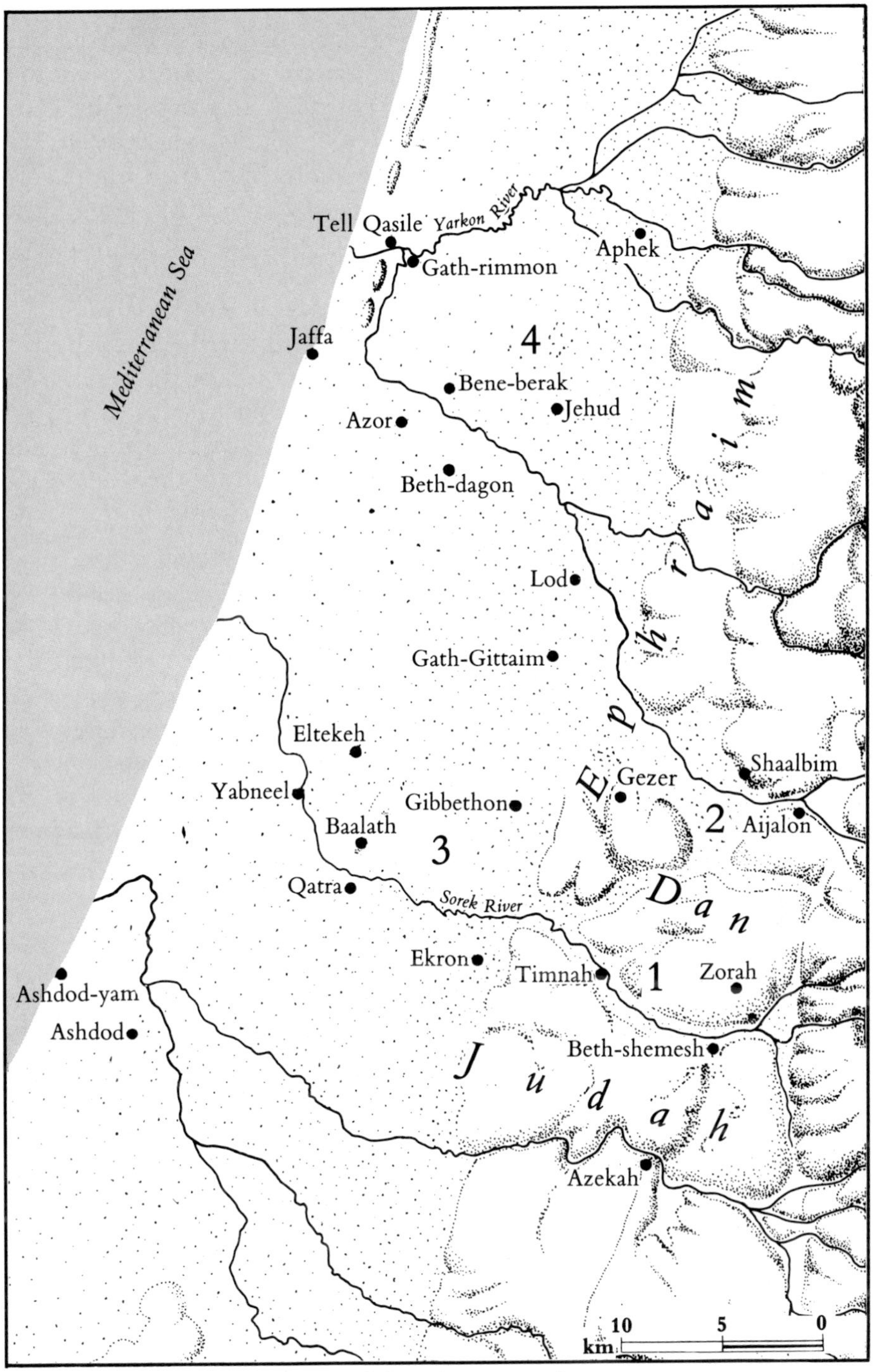

The cities of the inheritance of Dan

Thus the archaeological data and the evidence from the Bible and non-biblical sources contemporary with the Old Testament period all point to the identification of Ekron with Khirbet el-Muqannaʿ, as proposed by Naveh, despite the difficulties involved in the location of the Maccabean estate Ekron and of the Jewish village of Ekron in the time of Eusebius.[2] This automatically disposes of previously suggested identifications of Ekron and Eltekeh, including Albright's proposal that Ekron is Qatra[3] and Eltekeh is Khirbet el-Muqannaʿ,[4] and likewise the proposal made by this writer to place Ekron at Tel Batashi.[5] It is inconceivable that Ekron, which was one of the five principal Philistine cities and a large population centre, should have been much smaller and much less important than Eltekeh or any other city in the region of the Sorek Valley. Moreover, the identification of Ekron with Khirbet el-Muqannaʿ foregoes a conclusion that Timnah is Tel Batashi,[6] thus providing a clear and consistent picture of the historical topography of the whole region. In particular, it clarifies the description of the northern border of the territory of Judah which ran along the Sorek Valley:

> ... and went down to Beth-shemesh, and passed on to Timnah. And the border went out into the side of Ekron northward; and the border was drawn to Shicron,[7] and passed along to Mount Baalah,[8] and went out unto Jabneel; and the goings out of the border were at the sea (Josh 15:10–11).

Any attempt to establish the location of the other cities of the Sorek Valley region must start from a study of the list of Danite cities given in Josh 19:

2 Cf. *ibid*., 166–170. It is to be hoped that the remains of the later city of Ekron will one day be discovered in the neighbourhood of Khirbet el-Muqannaʿ. The village of Gallaa, mentioned by Eusebius [*Onomasticon* (ed. Klostermann), 72. 6ff.] as being near Ekron, is the abandoned Arab village of Jilya, one and a half kilometers south-east of Khirbet el-Muqannaʿ. The excavations at Tel Miqne were begun in 1981; cf. Trude Dothan and S. Gitin, *IEJ* 32 (1982), 150–153; 33 (1983), 127–129; 35 (1985), 67.

3 W.F. Albright, *AASOR* 2–3 (1923), 1–7.

4 W.F. Albright, *BASOR* 15 (1924) 8; *idem*, *BASOR* 17 (1925), 5–6; *idem*, *JBL* 59 (1940) 540ff.

5 B. Mazar, *EI* 2 (1953), 171 (Hebrew); cf. *idem*, *Yediot*, 16 (1951), 51 (Hebrew). Tel Batashi is located in the Sorek Valley, about 7.5 km north-west of Beth-shemesh and about 5 km from Khirbet Tibneh. The area covered by the tell is about four acres, and the remains found in it testify to the existence of a large settlement there in the Iron Age and a smaller one in the Hellenistic and Roman periods. The tell was examined by the writer of this article together with Dr. J. Kaplan, and the proposed identification with Ekron was put forward on the basis of this examination. The excavations at Tel Batashi, conducted since 1977, substantiate the site's identification with Timnah; cf. G.L. Kelm and A. Mazar, *IEJ* 27 (1977), 167f.; 28 (1978), 195f.; 29 (1979), 241ff.; 32 (1982), 153; 33 (1983), 126, 269; 35 (1985), 200; *Qadmoniot* 13 (1981), 89–97 (Hebrew).

6 See J. Naveh, *IEJ* 8 (1958), 167; Y. Aharoni, *PEQ* 90 (1958), 28–30. Z. Kallai, *VT* 8 (1958), 145.

7 The location of this ancient settlement is beset with difficulties. Aharoni [*PEQ* 90 (1958), 30] proposed identifying it with the small Tell el-Fūl; cf. the comments of J. Kaplan, *Yediot* 17 (1953), 138; 21 (1957), 206 (Hebrew).

8 Generally agreed by most scholars to be on the ridge of the hills above el-Mughar; cf. below, p. 108 on Baalath.

40–46. This list contains four groups of towns, or to be more precise, four districts, which together comprise "the territory of Dan" (see Map on p. 105):
1. Zorah, Eshtaol, and Ir-shemesh (Beth-shemesh) — in the north-eastern part of the Shephelah in the area of the point at which the Sorek Valley debouches from the Judean Hills;
2. Shaalbim, Aijalon, Ithlah, Elon (Elon-beth-hanan, 1 Kgs 4:9) — in the region of the Valley of Aijalon;
3. Timnah, Ekron, Eltekeh, Gibbethon, and Baalath — in the region of the Sorek Valley and to the north of it.
4. Jehud (Septuagint: ᾿Αζωρ), Bene-berak, Gath-rimmon, and Me-jarkon and Rakkon — in the region of Wadi Muṣrara and up to the Yarkon and the confines of Jaffa.

The first district consists of territory occupied by the tribe of Dan during the period of the Israelite conquest of Canaan (Zorah, Eshtaol), in close proximity to Timnah which was a Philistine city in Samson's days (Judg 13:1, 25; 14:1ff.). Also included in this district was the Israelite city of Beth-shemesh (1 Sam 6:12). The second district had a mixed population during the period of the conquest, and the struggle for control between the Israelite and non-Israelite elements continued down to the time of David:

> And the Amorites forced the children of Dan into the mountain: for they would not suffer them to come down to the valley. But the Amorites would dwell in Mount Heres,[9] in Aijalon, and in Shaalbim, yet the hand of the house of Joseph prevailed, so that they became tributaries (Judg 1:34–35).[10]

These two districts, together with the non-Israelite cities that subsequently became Israelite, formed a single administrative unit in David's reign, namely the second in the list of the nomes into which Solomon is said to have divided the country at the beginning of his reign (1 Kgs 4:9).[11]

The other two districts in the territory of Dan would seem to have been added to the Israelite kingdom as a result of the extension of its borders

9 It has been proposed to identify "Har Heres" with Beth-shemesh, but there is no warrant for such a conjecture. On Mount Heres, see Z. Kallai, *Enc. Miq*. 2, 853.

10 An enigmatic piece of information is preserved in 1 Sam 7:14 about the cities that had at some time been captured by the Philistines and were later regained for Israel by Samuel: "and the coasts thereof did Israel deliver out of the hands of the Philistines. And there was peace between Israel and the Amorites". The mention of Ekron and Gath (Gittaim) in this passage suggests that it is a reference to the obscure events connected with the struggle between the tribe of Ephraim and the inhabitants of Gath, in the period before the Israelite Monarchy; cf. B. Mazar, *IEJ* 4 (1954), 227–235.

11 The order in which the nomes of the United Monarchy are listed in 1 Kgs 4 actually reflects the sequence of Israelite conquests, the gradual expansion of the kingdom on both sides of the Jordan, and finally the severance of the territory of Benjamin from Ephraim in the reign of David. This view of mine has been accepted by S. Yeivin (see *Enc. Miq*. 2, 632–633, s.v. "David"), and also Z. Kallai, *VT* 8 (1958), 160, n. 3; cf. F.M. Cross and G.E. Wright, *JBL* 75 (1956), 216.

westwards, at the expense of the areas under Philistine control. This expansion apparently took place after the conquest of Gath (Gittaim), and after the annexation of Gezer and its dependencies to the Israelite kingdom at the beginning of Solomon's reign.[12] Moreover, the inclusion of Ekron in the list of Danite cities is no doubt to be interpreted as indicating that the kingdom of Ekron, which was apparently co-terminous with the third district, had accepted the suzerainty of Israel and was, to all intents and purposes, annexed to Solomon's domain.[13]

The assumption that the list is from the time of Solomon is borne out by both the biblical sources and the archaeological data. First of all we must note that, after the division of the monarchy, the first district — the cities of Zorah, Eshtaol and Beth-shemesh — formed an integral part of the kingdom of Judah. This means that at a certain period — apparently in the latter part of Solomon's reign — this district was detached from the territory of Dan and joined to Judah, a process that was accompanied by the settling of Judahites in its cities.[14] It is also worth noting that Gibbethon, which is mentioned as being located in the third district and was one of the Levitical cities in the territory of Dan, had already in the time of Jeroboam's dynasty become a Philistine stronghold ("Gibbethon, which belonged to the Philistines", 1 Kgs 16:15).

Perhaps a similar conclusion about the date of the list may be drawn from the mention of Baalath in the third district (Josh 19:44 — after Eltekeh and Gibbethon), if it is true, as has been conjectured, that the reference is to the fortified city of that name built by Solomon at the same time as Gezer and

12 The biblical sources leave no room for doubting the presence of Ephraimites in the territory of Gezer at the time of the occupation of Canaan, and its consequent annexation by Solomon; cf. Josh 16:3,10; Judg 1:29; 1 Chr 7:28. In Josh 16:10 it is stated that "they drove not out the Canaanites that dwelt in Gezer: but the Canaanites dwell among the Ephraimites unto this day, and serve under tribute". In the list of the Levitical cities, Gezer is mentioned amongst the cities of Ephraim (Josh 21:21). On Gath (Gittaim), see my article, *IEJ* 4 (1954); *idem*, *Enc. Miq*. 2, 574.

13 Cf. A. Malamat, *JNES* 22 (1963), 16.

14 Zorah and Eshtaol are included in the cities of the second district of Judah in Josh 15:33. Moreover, the families of the Zorahites and Eshtaolites, mentioned in 1 Chr 2:53; 4:2 as coming from Kiriath-jearim, were no doubt Judahite clans which had settled in Zorah and Eshtaol. Rehoboam fortified Zorah as one of the Judean siege cities (2 Chr 11:10). As for Beth-shemesh, its connection with Judah is evident from the list of the Levitical cities (Josh 21:16), and it is also explicitly described as belonging to Judah in 2 Kgs 14:11–13 (in the reign of Amaziah) and in 2 Chr 28:18 (in the reign of Ahaz). This raises the question of the date at which the Judean city at Beth-shemesh (stratum IIa) was built. As against the view expressed by Wright in E. Grant and G.E. Wright, *Ain Shems Excavations* 5 (1939), 15; F.M. Cross and G.E. Wright, *JBL* 75 (1956), 215–217, that it was started at the beginning of David's reign [cf. Z. Kallai, *VT* 8 (1958), 149ff.; Y. Aharoni, *VT* 9 (1959), 244–246], I am inclined to bring its date down to the latter part of Solomon's reign. In my opinion, this was the Levitical city of Beth-shemesh in Judah. See also Y. Aharoni, *BASOR* 154 (1959), 35–39, where he adds more evidence for ascribing stratum IIa of Beth-shemesh to Solomon's reign.

Beth-horon to defend the approach routes to Jerusalem from the west (1 Kgs 9: 17–18).[15] Finally, it is worth remarking that Gath-rimmon, which also appears in the list of the Levitical cities in the territory of Dan and which I have proposed to identify with Tell Jerishe, was razed to the ground during Shishak's campaign and never rebuilt.[16]

Before we can finally determine the date of the Josh 19 reference to the Danite cities, the historical background of the list of the Levitical cities in Josh 21 and 1 Chr 6 requires clarification. If it is correct to assume that the Levitical cities were in fact administrative and fiscal centres built by Solomon,[17] in which he settled Levites "for all the work of the Lord and for the service of the king" (1 Chr 26:30–32), this would also be an indication of the date of the Danite city list. For all the four Levitical cities in the territory of Dan — Aijalon, Gibbethon, Eltekeh and Gath-rimmon — are mentioned there (Josh 21:23–24), while, on the other hand, there is evidence that after the division of the monarchy the Levites left their cities in Israel and took up residence in Judah (2 Chr 11:14).

It follows from the foregoing discussion that the administrative division of the country described in 1 Kgs 4 actually took place in the time of David but was assigned to the beginning of Solomon's reign; whereas the list of Danite cities in Josh 19, and likewise that of Levitical cities in Josh 21, both date from the time of Solomon, the period of the United Monarchy's greatest glory. At the end of Solomon's reign the territory of Dan was reduced by the annexation of the first district to Judah, while after the division of the monarchy (in the reigns of Jeroboam and Rehoboam), the third and fourth districts ceased to be under Israelite rule, no doubt in the aftermath of Pharaoh Shishak's campaign[18] and the consequent weakening of the kingdom of Israel. Dan thus lost its status as a tribal and administrative unit in the heart of the country. The Danites were assimilated into other Israelite tribes — Judah, Benjamin and Ephraim — and the name Dan was henceforth used exclusively to designate the city Laish-Dan and the district around it, in the north of the country which was part of the territory of Naphtali. This change, incidentally, is reflected in

15 It seems that the site of Baalath must be sought in the neighbourhood of Mount Baalah. Z. Kallai has therefore proposed [*Yediot* 17 (1952), 63 (Hebrew)] identifying it with al-Mughar, while Y. Aharoni, *PEQ* 90 (1958), 30, has tentatively suggested locating it at Qatra which had a settlement of considerable size in the Iron Age. There is, however, still a possibility of equating Baalath with Kiriath-jearim, precisely with Gibeath-kiriath-jearim.

16 Cf. B. Maisler (Mazar), *IEJ* 1 (1950–1951), 63, n. 6.

17 For this conjecture of the writer's, following Klein and Albright, who assign the list to the period of the United Monarchy, see *VT Suppl.* 7 (1960), 193ff.

18 On his march, Shishak took and sacked — in addition to other cities — Gezer and Aijalon. The former remained in ruins, while Aijalon was rebuilt by Rehoboam as one of his siege cities (2 Chr 11:10).

the Blessing of Moses (Deut 33:22), as well as in other biblical passages. The second conclusion to be drawn from the discussion of the Danite cities and those of the Levites in the territory of Dan is that in any identification must be substantiated by remains, especially sherds, dating to the early Iron Age III (10th century B.C.E.) at the sites proposed.

One of the most important places in the third district was Gibbethon, which is also mentioned in the list of Levitical cities. Von Rad long ago persuasively suggested that Gibbethon should be identified with Tell el-Malāt, about 5 km west of Gezer, on the basis of an analysis of the biblical passages referring to these two fortified towns.[19] The remains from this tell, which dominates the surrounding flat countryside, include potsherds from all historical periods, especially from the early and middle Iron Ages.[20]

Confirmation of von Rad's proposal would also seem to be provided by the records of Sargon. In the annals of this Assyrian monarch, we are informed that in the course of his military operation against the kingdom of Ashdod in 712 B.C.E., he captured Gath (Rās Abu Ḥamid near Ramleh), Ashdod, and Ashdod-yam. Moreover, as Tadmor has shown,[21] it is this same campaign that is recorded on the reliefs from the royal palace at Khorsabad, which portray the capture of the cities *Gab-bu-tu-nu* (Gibbethon) and *ʾA-am-qa-[ar]-ru-[na]* (Ekron).[22] These data enable us to reconstruct the course of the campaign with a high degree of certainty. Most probably the Assyrian army marched along the Via Maris through the Sharon Plain from Aphek to Lod, and then continued its advance through Gath and Gibbethon to Ekron. At this point some of Sargon's forces turned westward to attack Ashdod, which was captured together with Ashdod-yam, while another column split off south-eastwards into the Judean foothills and reduced Azekah.[23] Assuming that it is correct to infer from this evidence that the site of Gibbethon lies between Gath and Ekron, we have here further proof of the identification of Gibbethon with Tell el-Malāt. This conjecture also enables us better to understand the constantly repeated attempts made by the Israelite kings (1 Kgs 15:27; 16:15) to gain control of this city, which dominated a vital line of communication and was one of the strongholds of the kingdom of Ekron.

The problems involved in the identification of Eltekeh (Septuagint: ʾΕλθεκω), which was also in the third district of the territory of Dan and one of the Levitical cities (Josh 19:44; in Josh 21:23: אלתקא), are more difficult to

19 See G. von Rad, *PJb* 29 (1933), 30ff.
20 See B. Maisler (Mazar), *Yediot* 16, 3–4 (1952), 49–50 (Hebrew).
21 H. Tadmor, *JCS* 12 (1958), 83.
22 See M. El-Amin, *Sumer* 9 (1953), 36–40, and also H. Tadmor, *JCS* 12 (1958), 83, n. 243.
23 See *ibid.*, 81ff.

solve. The main source of our information is the Annals of Sennacherib[24] in which the Assyrian monarch gives a detailed description of his military campaign to the Land of Israel in the year 701 B.C.E. In contrast to the forces of his predecessor, Sargon, Sennacherib's troops entered the Land of Israel from the Phoenician coast, apparently advancing along the coastal road through the province of Dor as far as the district of Jaffa, which was at that time subject to the king of Ashkelon. After taking the cities of Jaffa, Bene-berak, Azor, and Beth-dagon, Sennacherib appears to have continued his march southwards by the shortest and easiest route to Ashdod, in order to confront the Egyptian reinforcements which the leaders of the anti-Assyrian confederacy — Hezekiah, King of Judah, and Ṣidqa, King of Ashkelon — had summoned. In the decisive engagement which took place on the battlefield of Altaqu (Eltekeh), Sennacherib inflicted a severe defeat upon the Egyptians. He then reduced Eltekeh and Timnah and stormed Ekron, where the leading nobles of the city had seized power in the political confusion prior to his campaign, joined the anti-Assyrian alliance and handed over their King Padi, who had remained loyal to Assyria, to Hezekiah, King of Judah. After these victories, the Assyrian army advanced from the region of the Sorek Valley into the Judean foothills, thus launching the Assyrian invasion of the kingdom of Judah.

From Sennacherib's description, the site of Eltekeh must be on the line of the main highway running from the environs of Jaffa and Beth-dagon southwards to Philistia, and close to the point at which the road turned eastwards to the cities of the Sorek Valley (including Timnah) and Ekron. There is no warrant for the supposition that both the Assyrian and the Egyptian armies followed a route to the east of this main highway.

When we set about locating the exact position of Eltekeh in accordance with the Annals of Sennacherib and biblical references, the first place to claim our attention must be an important site on the road from Jabneel northwards to Beth-dagon, north of the Sorek Valley and north-west of Mount Baalah, namely Tell esh-Shalaf. This tell, which covers an area of about six acres, is located near the abandoned Arab village of Qubeibeh, approximately 4 km north-east of Yavneh (biblical Yabneel), at the junction of two ancient roads leading out of Yavneh, one of which runs north to Beth-dagon, while the other turns off to Ramleh and Lod. Tell esh-Shalaf has been examined by J. Kaplan[25] who found there many potsherds from the early and middle Iron

24 See the translations of D.D. Luckenbill, *The Annals of Sennacherib* (1924); A.L. Oppenheim, in *ANET*, 287–288; and cf. my survey in *EI* 2 (1953), 172ff. (Hebrew); I. Ephaʿl, *Enc. Miq*. 5, 1063–1069, s.v. "Sennacherib".

25 J. Kaplan, *Yediot* 21 (1957), 202–203 (Hebrew). I visited Tell esh-Shalaf, together with J. Naveh and Z. Kallai, on August 16, 1959. What we saw fully confirmed Kaplan's survey. The whole area of the tell is covered with middle Iron Age sherds which testify to the existence of a large settlement

Ages and a few from the Late Bronze Age and from the Persian and Hellenistic periods. This identification of Eltekeh, which has been shown to be also archaeologically satisfactory, completes the mapping of the great majority of the cities in the territory of Dan known to us from the Old Testament and from contemporary non-biblical sources.

on the site, especially in the eighth century B.C.E. We also picked up sherds characteristic of the early Iron Age, including Philistine specimens. It is also worth remarking that the proposed identification of Eltekeh with the small ruined site at el-Mughar [first put forward by Abel, *GP*, 313, and revived by M. Naor, *EI* 5 (1958), 127–128 (Hebrew)], is totally unacceptable. Abel could produce no evidence for his conjecture besides one of the names given to the *wali* at el-Mughar, viz. Abu Ṭaqah ("the father of the window"); see Ch. Clermont-Ganneau, *Archaeological Researches* 2 (1896), 192–193.

Geshur and Maachah

The Geshurites and Maachathites, according to biblical tradition, were inhabitants of Transjordan who were not dispossessed by the Israelites, either at the time of the actual conquest of Canaan or during the subsequent occupation of the country. This tradition is reflected in three separate, but interrelated and complementary, passages. In the summary provided in the Book of Joshua of the territories allocated to the tribes in Transjordan (Josh 13:8–13), it is stated that "the people of Israel did not drive out the Geshurites and the Maachathites; but Geshur and Maachath dwell in the midst of Israel to this day" (v. 13). This verse gives expression to the view generally accepted in Israel for hundreds of years after the conquest, that as a result of the victories won by Moses over Sihon, the Amorite king, with his capital at Heshbon, and Og, the King of Bashan, whose capital was Ashtaroth, the whole of Transjordan — from the river Arnon up to and including Mount Hermon — had fallen to the Israelites and been allocated to the tribes of Reuben, Gad, and half Manasseh. The only exceptions were the kingdom of the Ammonites in the region of the upper Jabbok River, and the territory of the Geshurites and Maachathites — between Gilead and Mount Hermon (*ibid*., v. 11) — which had remained a foreign enclave in Israel "to this day". Again, in the parallel description of the various lands conquered by the Israelites (Josh 12:1–6), we are told that the territory ruled over by Og, comprising the whole of Bashan, the district of Salcah and Mount Hermon, extended "to the boundary of the Geshurites and Maachathites". This is also implied by Deut 3:14: "Jair the Manassite took all the region of Argob, as far as the boundary of the Geshurites and Maachathites".[1]

* This study is a revised version of the article which appeared in *JBL* 80 (1961), 16–28.

1 On the widespread ramifications of the family of Jair, see my article in *Tarbiz* 15 (1944), 63–64 (Hebrew), and *Enc. Miq*. 3, s.v. "Jair" and "Havvoth-jair".

The Israelites thus regarded the domain of the Geshurites and Maachathites as "land that remained to be possessed" within the area conquered and occupied by them; that is to say, land that was not included in any of the tribal portions and which, before the conquest, had been a geographical and ethnic unit, independent of the rulers of the kingdoms adjacent to it. This territory can be located with a high degree of certainty — on the basis of such data as Josh 12:5; 13:11 — between Gilead on the south, Bashan on the east, and Mount Hermon to the north — that is, in the Golan.[2] We must assume that the Geshurites occupied the southern part, and the Maachathites the northern part,[3] of this mountainous region which was heavily wooded and enjoyed a relatively high annual rainfall. Here a violent volcanic eruption in the Pleistocene epoch gave rise to widespread flows of basalt lava, and to the formation of the many volcanic cones which are characteristic of the whole area. From the earliest times the Golan has reserved a special character of its own, geographically distinct from the rest of Eretz-Israel, within the boundaries set for it by nature: to the north, Mount Hermon; on the west, the upper Jordan Valley over which the Golan ridges tower; to the south, the Yarmuk depression which separates the Golan from Gilead; and on the east, the fertile plateau of Bashan stretching away beyond Wadi er-Ruqqād.

That Geshur and Maachah were part of Canaan in the period preceding the Israelite conquest can be deduced, first and foremost, from the description of the borders of Canaan given in Num 34. I have elsewhere tried to show that the term "Canaan", as used in this particular biblical source, is simply the designation then customary for the Egyptian province in Syria and Eretz-Israel, the limits of which, after frequent fluctuations from the reign of Tuthmosis III to the period of the El-Amarna Letters, were eventually more or less stabilized by the treaty signed between Ramesses II and the Hittite king in ca. 1270 B.C.E.[4] The Israelites at the

2 M. Noth's conjecture, in *Beiträge zur biblischen Landes und Altertumskunde* (1951), 1ff. [= *ZDPV* 68 (1949–1951)], that the mountains of Bashan are to be identified with the mountains of Jolan, and the territory of Maachah and Geshur with the northern and north-eastern part of the Golan up to the Hermon, finds no warrant in the sources. On the contrary, these clearly imply that Geshur bordered on Gilead; see especially Josh 13:11, where "Gilead" and "the region of the Geshurites and Maachathites" are listed side by side, and "Mount Hermon" and "all Bashan" only afterwards.

3 On Abel Beth-maachah, at the northern extremity of Galilee, which had apparently belonged to Maachah before the time of David, see below, p. 124.

4 According to the "low" chronology of M.B. Rowton (accession of Ramesses II in 1290 B.C.E.); but see his later view in *JCS* 13 (1959), 8ff.; *idem*, *JNES* 19 (1960), 15ff., where he shows on the basis of new evidence that 1304 B.C.E. is a more plausible date for the accession of Ramesses II. For a resumé of the problem, cf. H. Tadmor, in B. Mazar (ed.), *The World History of the Jewish People* 2: *The Patriarchs* (1970), 88, 265, n. 84. An extremely "low" chronology is preferred by K.A. Kitchen, *Pharaoh Triumphant: The Life and Times of Ramesses II* (1982), 239.

time of the conquest thus merely adopted the term.[5] This ancient source, despite the later alterations and additions made to it, can be taken as evidence that the boundary between Canaan and the land of the Hittites (cf. Josh 1:4) followed the line of Mount Hor (one of the Lebanon ridges)–Lebo-hamath[6]–Zedad, then took in the region of Damascus and the whole of Bashan, and finally extended "to the shoulder of the sea of Chinnereth on the east; and the boundary shall go down to the Jordan, and its end shall be at the Salt Sea" (Num 34:11–12). In other words, the Golan was included in the territory of Canaan, whereas Gilead and the regions bordering on the desert (Ammon, Moab, and Edom) were regarded as being outside the sphere of Egyptian domination.

In any attempt to trace the history of the territory occupied by the Geshurites and Maachathites in the period before the Israelite conquest, we must turn first of all to the El-Amarna Letters dating to the first half of the 14th century B.C.E. From these documents it emerges that the Golan was both a bridge and a barrier between three vassal "kingdoms" in the area ruled by Egypt: Hazor in Upper Galilee, Ashtaroth in Bashan, and Piḫilu in the Jordan Valley.[7] From a letter of Ayyab (Job), the prince of Ashtaroth, we learn that the prince of Hazor had seized a favourable opportunity to capture three cities from him.[8] It would thus seem that Hazor had become powerful enough to extend the limits of its rule to the east of the upper Jordan, apparently in the region occupied by the Maachathites which was regarded as disputed territory between the two Canaanite "kingdoms" on either side of the river. It is noteworthy that both Ashtaroth and Hazor managed to increase their power to such an extent that Hazor became known as "the head of all those kingdoms" (Josh 11: 10), i.e., of the political units that survived in Canaan down to the beginning of the Israelite occupation of Galilee,[9] while Ashtaroth was the capital of Bashan at the time of the Israelite conquest of Transjordan.

Of greater interest is another of the Amarna letters,[10] which was sent by Mut-baʿlu, the prince of Piḫilu, to Yanḫamu, the Canaanite agent of Pharaoh Amenḥotep IV (1370–1353 B.C.E.). In this letter Mut-baʿlu stresses his own loyalty and that of his ally, Ayyab, to the king of Egypt. He states

5. Cf. in this volume, "Lebo-hamath and the Northern Border of Canaan", pp. 189–202.

6 Cf. *ibid.*; O. Eissfeldt, *Forschungen und Fortschritte* 12 (1936), 51ff.

7 Pella in the Decapolis, today Khirbet Faḥil; cf. N. Glueck, *AASOR* 25–28(1951), 254ff.; R.W. Funk and H. N. Richardson, *BA* 21 (1958), 82ff.

8 EA 364; cf. A. Alt, *PJb* 20 (1924), 30ff.

9 For a different view, see A. Malamat, *JBL* 79 (1960), 12ff. On the excavation of Hazor, cf. Y. Yadin, *Hazor* (1972).

10 EA 256; cf. W.F. Albright's translation and interpretation of the document in *BASOR* 89 (1943), 7ff.

that Ashtaroth came to his assistance when the cities of the Land of Garu were hostile to him and took from him the two cities of Ḫayyānu and Yabilīma, which apparently had previously been subject to his rule. Albright has, plausibly, suggested that Ḫayyānu be identified with Ijon, which is known to us from the Roman period as a small Jewish town in the district of Susitha (Hippos), modern ʿAyyūn north-west of el-Ḥamma; and Yabilīma with Abel-Abila, one of the cities of the Decapolis, today Tell Abil.[11] Hence, from this Amarna letter it may be inferred that the Land of Garu stretched northwards from the Yarmuk River, which formed the northern boundary of the region under the control of Piḫilu, and westwards from Bashan, of which Ashtaroth was the political centre.

Such an inference is made particularly acceptable by two of the names that appear in the list of the cities of Garu contained in the document — Ḫeni-anabi and Adūru. The first of these is apparently none other than ʿEin-Nāb (en-Nāb) in the central Golan, which in Roman times was a small Jewish town called Nāb, in the district of Susitha, while the second may perhaps be identified with Dūra, a ruined site beside natural springs, about 3 km south-east of Jisr Bināt Yaʿqūb.[12] Aharoni has already pointed out that both these towns are also mentioned in Papyrus Anastasi I from the reign of Ramesses II (1290–1224 B.C.E.), the first under the name of *Qrt ʿnb*, and the second as *ʾdrn*,[13] and that, according to this document, they were both located on the highway from Damascus to the Jordan Valley. *Qrt ʿnb* also occurs in the topographical lists of Seti I (1308–1290 B.C.E.).[14] Of the other cities named in the above Amarna letter, mention should be made of Magdalu, which may be identified either with the Migdal Ṣabāyyā found in talmudic sources, as proposed by Albright, or with Migdal-geder,

11 *Ibid.*, 14–15, 43 and 44. It is noteworthy that no remains from before the Hellenistic period have yet been found at Tell Abil. Another possibility is to identify Yabilīma with one of the ancient sites near the Arab village of Yubla, e.g. Rujm el-Adʿam [on this site, see N. Glueck, *AASOR* 25–28 (1951), 128ff.].

12 See W.F. Albright, *BASOR* 89 (1943), 14, no. 41.

13 It is now obvious that the name mentioned in Papyrus Anastasi I is not *ʾdrn* but Edreʿi, as attested by the Turim fragment; cf. S. Aḥituv, *Canaanite Toponyms in Ancient Egyptian Documents* (1984), 90–91.

14 See Y. Aharoni, *The Settlement of the Israelite Tribes in Upper Galilee* (1957), 59, 124 (Hebrew). There is little probability in Aharoni's conjecture that the site of *Qrt ʿnb* is to be sought at Tell es-Shihāb in Bashan where a stele of Seti I was found. ʿEin-Nāb, which was located on the main road from the Jordan Valley to Damascus, between Fīq and Khasfīeh, must have been a place of great importance in antiquity. See C. Epstein and S. Gutman, in M. Kochavi (ed.), *Judea, Samaria and the Golan: An Archaeological Survey 1967/8* (1972), 285, no. 162 (Hebrew). The site of the ancient settlement is probably Ain eṭ-Ṭarūq, south-east of en-Nāb, which was occupied in the Middle and Late Bronze Ages and also during later periods; and cf. *ibid.*, 286, no. 177.

which I have suggested locating at Tell ed-Duweir, at the confluence of the Yarmuk and the Jordan.[15]

An interesting question arises in connection with another city in the Land of Garu, namely, Araru. Though a settlement by this name is not known from any other source, there may be reference to it in the Story of Sinuhe, from the beginning of the second millennium B.C.E.[16] There *ʾ33* is mentioned as a district at the furthest limits of the territory controlled by the great ruler of the Land of Upper Retenu (i.e., Canaan), where Sinuhe rose to be a tribal chief. The territory designated *ʾ33* which, according to the laws of Egyptian transliteration in the time of the Middle Kingdom, corresponds exactly to *ʾrr*,[17] is described as a region blessed with plentiful crops, olive oil, cattle, and extensive hunting grounds, whose population enjoys a high living standard thanks to its well-developed agricultural economy. Occasionally, however, the peace of the country was disturbed by armed conflicts between its inhabitants and the nomad and semi-nomad tribes who tried to force their way into the settled areas. The location of the district of *ʾrr* in the region of the Yarmuk, with its fertile soil and abundant supplies of water, is also probable on archaeological grounds, in view of the many remains there of MB I settlements, as proved by the surveys of N. Glueck.[18]

In the light of all these data, it may be taken as certain that the Land of Garu mentioned in the Amarna letter under discussion was a large tract of territory in the Golan, as suggested by Albright, stretching southwards as far as the Yarmuk and identical with biblical Geshur. It is true that the name Garu does not occur in any other source and that scholars have, not without reason, been puzzled by its connotation. However, it would seem that the problem can be solved by assuming a scribal error which has resulted in the omission from the word of one cuneiform sign, so that it was written as *Ga-ri* (genitive) instead of *Ga-šu-ri*. Omissions of this kind are fairly common in the El-Amarna Letters, as is shown by the following examples: *Gu-la* for *Gu-ub-la* (Byblos), *Na-aḫ-ma* for *Na-aḫ-ri-ma* (Naharaim), *Su-ri* for *Su-ba-ri*, *Ṣi-na* for *Ṣi-du-na* (Sidon).[19]

15 See B. Mazar and S. Yeivin, *Yediot* 10 (1944), 99ff.; 11 (1945), 20ff. (Hebrew); N. Glueck, *AASOR* 25–28 (1951), 140f. While it is true that in our survey at Tell ed-Duweir no sherds antedating the Iron Age were found, there may still be Bronze Age remains buried beneath the later strata.

16 See J.A. Wilson's translation in *ANET*, 18ff.

17 See B. Mazar (Maisler), *RHJE* 1 (1947), 40; *EI* 3 (1954), 21.

18 See N. Glueck, *AASOR* 25–28 (1951), 125ff., and the summary on p. 423. Glueck's comment on the remains from MB II and LB in the Jordan Valley should be noted (*ibid*., 250): "MB and LB were definitely represented, but settlements were apparently not as numerous as in earlier and later periods".

19 See the index of place names in J.A. Knudtzon, *Die El-Amarna Taflen* (1915). Attention may be

The Land of Garu is peculiar in having a form of political organization quite different in a general sense from that of other regions of Canaan in the Amarna period, but very similar to that of biblical Geshur. The letter in question makes no reference to the existence of a royal capital or a single ruler in this territory; on the contrary, it is implied that the supreme authority in the Land of Garu was vested in a kind of federation of seven cities which, as a system of government, calls to mind the union of the four Hivite cities described in Josh 9–10. We thus see that the political organization of *Ga[šu]ru* = Geshur remained constant from the Amarna period, in the first half of the 14th century B.C.E., right down to the time of the Israelite conquest and the occupation of Canaan in the 13th and 12th centuries B.C.E. For the biblical sources do not speak of Geshur and Maachah as kingdoms in the latter period either, but refer to them as ethnic and territorial units, viz., areas occupied by the Geshurites and Maachathites which remained, after the conquest, as foreign enclaves inside Israel.[20]

As regards Maachah, attention should first of all be paid to a biblical source in which we catch a glimpse of an ancient historical tradition current among the Western Semitic peoples. In the genealogical table of the twelve children of Nahor (Gen 22:20–24), Maachah is mentioned, together with Tebah, Gaham, and Tahash, as one of the sons of Nahor's concubine Reumah. It seems probable that this list of the four "sons" of Nahor and Reumah represents a territorial and ethnic unit in southern Syria which was affiliated to the "family" of Nahor, the latter being a confederacy or league of eight tribes in the region of the middle Euphrates and in north-western Mesopotamia, with its central sanctuary at Harran.[21]

This list accords well with the evidence provided by the Mari documents from the second half of the 18th century B.C.E. and may reflect the political and ethnic situation that existed probably in the first half of the 17th century B.C.E., when the Western Semitic tribes of nomads and semi-nomads reached the height of their power in the lands of the Fertile Crescent and dominated the roads leading from Mesopotamia to Syria and Eretz-Israel.[22] Tebah is known to us, from both the El-Amarna Letters and

drawn to the fact that Weber, in Knudtzon, *ibid*. 2, 1319, had already considered the possibility of a scribal error, namely *Ga[-az]ri*, but was apparently misled by the contents of the letter into assuming that the city referred to was Gezer.

20 The Geshurite enclave in the south of the country (1 Sam 27:8) may have been ethnically connected with the Geshurites in Transjordan. A separate problem is raised by the mention, in the description of "the land still to be possessed", of "all the Geshurites" immediately after "all the regions of the Philistines" (Josh 13:2). It is difficult to decide whether this is simply a gloss referring to Geshur in Transjordan, or whether the Geshurites in the south are meant.

21 For details, see *Zion* 11 (1946), 8 (Hebrew).

22 See J.-R. Kupper, *Les nomades en Mesopotamie* (1957); A. Malamat, *JBL* 79 (1960), 15ff.

from other Egyptian documents, as an important city in southern Syria, and was one of the political centres of power in the kingdom of Aram Zobah at the beginning of the 10th century B.C.E.[23] Tahash, which also occurs in Egyptian inscriptions and in cuneiform documents, is to be located in the region between Kadesh-on-the-Orontes and the Oasis of Damascus.[24]

Maachah, which was no doubt the most southerly of the lands of the "sons" of Nahor and Reumah, appears to be mentioned already in Egyptian sources from the end of the 19th or beginning of the 18th century B.C.E., i.e., in the Execration Texts which were published by Posener in 1940 and which contain a list of rulers and princes in Syria and Eretz-Israel.[25] One of the geographical names in this list is *Mʿkʾw*, which must denote the territory occupied by the tribes of *Mʿkyw* who are mentioned there.[26] It is noteworthy that, in this source, the name of the land of *Mʿkʾw* occurs together with city-states and territories in southern Syria and northern Transjordan, such as Ashtaroth, the two lands of Āpum (Damascus), Sirion, and others. Only one possible conclusion can be drawn from these various pieces of evidence from different sources: from at least as early as the beginning of the second millennium B.C.E., the group of Maachah tribes occupied a tract of territory in northern Transjordan which was called by its name. Some time in the 17th century B.C.E., the large tribal confederacy of the sons of Nahor, whose centre lay in the neighbourhood of Harran and the regions of the upper Euphrates, succeeded by expansionist pressure in extending its sphere of influence as far as southern Syria and in absorbing various ethnic units, including the Maachah tribes. These latter were now regarded, within the framework of the enlarged patriarchal federation, as the "sons of the concubine". It may even be conjectured that the ancient etiological story in Gen 31 about the covenant made by Laban and Jacob on the mountain of Gilead (in its northern part), in witness of which they built a cairn of stones, set up a memorial pillar (מצבה) and called on the god of Abraham and the god of Nahor (vv. 44–54), is probably an echo of the historical relations between the two groups of tribes that traced their descent to Abraham and Nahor respectively.

From the biblical and non-biblical sources we can obtain only the merest

23 See A. Gardiner, *Ancient Egyptian Onomastica* 1 (1947), 139*. Its location was apparently in the region of Baalbek in the Lebanon Valley.

24 See *ibid*., 150ff.; A. Alt, *Kleine Schriften* (1953), 236ff. Cf. M. Noth, *Die israelitischen Personennamen* (1928), 23.

25 See G. Posener, *Princes et pays d'Asie et de Nubie* (1940); and my remarks in *RHJE* 1 (1947), 33ff.; Mazar, *Canaan and Israel*, 20.

26 *Ibid.*, 32, 39 (Hebrew). The alternative form מעוך is also found in the Bible; cf. 1 Sam 27:2; 1 Kgs 2:39. The ending in the name *Mʿky*, *Mʿkyw* is simply the genitival suffix which is common in the Execration Texts.

glimpse of the history of the Geshurites and Maachathites in the regions occupied by them in the Golan in the period prior to the settlement of the Israelite tribes in Canaan and the beginnings of the expansion of the Arameans in Syria. Fresh epigraphic material, as well as systematically conducted excavations and archaeological surveys, is required to throw new light on the history of the early settlements in the Golan, which played an important part in the political and economic life of Eretz-Israel at various times in the Canaanite period. The natural conditions and geographical position of the land of Geshur and Maachah enabled its inhabitants to develop a flourishing agriculture, to take full advantage of the extensive pastures, and to establish cities in the most populated areas and on the vital lines of communication.

As regards the history of this territory at the time of the Israelite occupation of Canaan and later, in the period of the United Monarchy, no complete picture can be pieced together from the fragments of information preserved in the Bible. However, from the little contained in the historiographical sources of the books of Samuel and Chronicles, we do learn of certain changes that occurred in Geshur and Maachah in this period, in consequence of the expansion of the Arameans in Syria in the 11th century B.C.E., and the founding of the kingdom of Aram Zobah by the dynasty of Beth-rehob. In the narratives about David's wars against the confederacy of kings led by the king of Aram Zobah, Hadad-ezer the son of Rehob, the king of Maachah appears in the confederate ranks (2 Sam 10:6; 1 Chr 19:7), whereas Geshur is not mentioned at all. Conversely, in 2 Sam 3:3 and 1 Chr 3:2 we are informed that, while David was still at Hebron, a friendship developed between him and Talmai, King of Geshur, and that David married Talmai's daughter, Maachah.

If my earlier conjecture about the political organization in force in Geshur and Maachah during the period of the Israelite conquest and occupation is correct, then there should be a causal connection, on the one hand, between the rise of the Arameans, the setting up of the Aramean kingdoms including Aram Zobah in Syria, and the establishment of the Israelite monarchy, and the change which took place in the regimes of Geshur and Maachah, on the other. The most likely explanation, to my mind, is that, as a result of the general political situation in the 11th century B.C.E., the Geshurite and Maachathite tribes were able to set up independent kingdoms of their own. We do not know whether it was Talmai who founded the reigning dynasty at Geshur, or possibly his father Ammihud[27] before him (2 Sam 13:37). What is certain is that, as early as

27 Or Amihur (*kethib*); cf. Noth, *israelitischen Personennamen* (see note 24), 77, 146. On the name

the beginning of David's reign, the policy followed by Talmai was independent of the Arameans and probably remained so throughout his lifetime, as may be inferred from his non-participation in the anti-Israelite confederacy led by the king of Aram Zobah. There is no reason for supposing that the relations between the two kingdoms were adversely affected by the flight of Absalom, David's son by Talmai's daughter Maachah, to Geshur, and the asylum given him there by his grandfather. The Old Testament gives no explicit indication of the position taken by the king of Geshur in the conflict between David and Absalom, least of all during the decisive battle in the woodland of Ephraim in Transjordan. It can only be inferred, from what is related about David's stay at Mahanaim, that Talmai was not among those who offered him assistance (2 Sam 17:24–29), and it may well be that the king of Geshur remained strictly neutral throughout the revolt. At all events, there is not the faintest suggestion of armed conflict between Geshur and Israel at any time during the reigns of David and Solomon.

The piece of historical information inserted into the genealogical tables of Judah, to the effect that Geshur and Aram took Havvoth-jair and also Kenath and its villages, "sixty towns" (1 Chr 2:23),[28] is no doubt of later date than the division of the Israelite kingdom. It may refer to the end of Baasha's reign, when Ben-hadad I marched on Israel (ca. 886 B.C.E.). It is true that, in 1 Kgs 15:16–22 and 2 Chr 16:1–6, we are told that Ben-hadad sent his forces to Galilee, where they attacked the store cities of Naphtali in response to an appeal for help from Asa. But even so, this by no means rules out the conjecture that Geshur and Aram[29] took advantage of the opportunity thus offered them to make themselves masters of Bashan.[30] Certainly it may be inferred from the verse in question in 1 Chr that, at the time when the fortunes of the newly created kingdom of Israel were at a very low ebb after the division of the monarchy, Geshur and Aram Damascus detached the districts of Bashan from it, and that the kingdom of Geshur was then still separate from Damascus

Talmai, which is apparently Hurrite, see Mazar, *Cities and Districts*, 60. Attention may also be drawn to the remarks of R.J. O'Callaghan, *Aram Naharaim* (1948), 125. On the basis of the Septuagint rendering of 2 Sam 13:37 (where Geshur seems to be described as being "in the land of Maachah"), O'Callaghan tentatively conjectures that Geshur was, from the first, a part of Maachah. However, it is probable that the Septuagint version is corrupt.

28 The author of this passage is presumably referring to Havvoth-jair in the territory of Argob in Bashan, although in the previous verse he speaks of twenty-three cities of Jair, the son of Segub, in Gilead; cf. 1 Kgs 4:13; Deut 3:14; Josh 13:30. See also B. Mazar, *Enc. Miq*. 3, s.v. "Havvoth-jair"; and J. Simons, *The Geographical and Topographical Texts of the Old Testament* (1959), 123ff.

29 In both the biblical and non-biblical sources, viz., the Assyrian documents and the Aramean inscriptions, the kingdom of Aram Damascus is frequently designated by the name Aram alone.

30 See W.F. Albright, *BASOR* 87 (1942), 23ff.

and apparently the latter's ally. The Israelite territory conquered by Geshur presumably comprised the western part of the district of Argob in Bashan, i.e., the region on either side of Wadi el-ʿAllan which flows into the Yarmuk, east of Wadi er-Ruqqād. The latter wadi apparently marked the border between Geshur and the territory of Havvoth-jair in Bashan (cf. Deut 3:14). At the same time, Aram Damascus conquered and annexed the remaining areas of Bashan and, it would seem, shortly afterwards — probably during the reign of Ben-hadad II - created out of them the two administrative districts of Karnaim and Hauran, well known from later sources.

In connection with the area conquered by Geshur, the question arises whether this was not the same as the Israelite administrative district whose capital in the time of the United Monarchy was the city of refuge and Levitical city of Golan in Bashan,[31] which is usually identified with Shaḥm el-Jolân.[32] In that case there might be grounds for the further conjecture that, with the annexation of this territory, Golan became the capital of Geshur; hence the name Golan[33] was probably applied to the whole area of the western part of northern Transjordan.

The Bible provides no direct information about the decline and disappearance of the kingdom of Geshur. However, from the accounts of the wars between Israel and Aram in the last years of Ahab's reign (ca. 856–852B.C.E.), we can infer certain fundamental changes in the structure of the kingdom of Aram Damascus, which resulted in its absorption of various Aramaic kingdoms formerly allied to it, including Geshur, and its rise to the position of the leading Aramean state. Especially noteworthy in this connection is the narrative describing the first attack of Ben-hadad II and "the thirty-two kings that were with him" against Israel, the Arameans' penetration into the heart of the kingdom and their laying siege to Samaria — a large-scale military campaign that ended in the defeat of the Arameans before the gates of Samaria (1 Kgs 20). According to the prophetical source on this point contained in the Bible, Ben-hadad, acting on the advice of his ministers, carried out a very important political and military reform immediately after this defeat: "And do this: remove the kings, each from his post, and put governors (פחות) in their places; and muster an army like the army that you have lost, horse for horse and chariot for chariot" (1 Kgs 20:24–25). There is no good reason for regarding

31 Deut 4:43; Josh 21:27 (where the *kethib* reads "Galon" for "Golan"); 1 Chr 6:56. In Eusebius (*Onomast* 64, 6.7) — Γουλων.

32 On Shaḥm el-Jôlan, see G. Schumacher, *ZDPV* 9 (1886), 169ff. There is little probability in Albright's conjecture [in *L. Ginzberg Jubilee Volume* (1947), 57] that the site of this city, Golan, is to be found in the district of Golan.

33 I.e., Γαυλανῖτις. Cf Abel, *GP* 2, 158; and M. Avi-Yonah, *Historical Geography of Palestine* (1951), 29 (Hebrew).

this story as devoid of all historical basis. On the contrary, it is very likely that such a reform, like that carried out by David at a different time and in different circumstances, should have been pushed through by Ben-hadad at an opportune moment after the defeat of the Aramean coalition at Samaria and when the danger from Assyria was so very close. It was only about two years later — in 853 B.C.E. — that an enlarged confederacy of the kings of Syria and Eretz-Israel, led by the king of Aram, had to fight the armies of Shalmaneser III near Qarqar, in the country of Hamath. It is therefore probable that Ben-hadad succeeded in turning the satellite kingdoms into administrative districts, each ruled by a governor after the Assyrian manner, and that, by thus concentrating absolute power in his own hands, he established the administrative and military regime of Aram Damascus for generations to come.

Imperial Aramaic also probably originated at this time in the Aramaic dialect of Damascus, the capital of the kingdom of Aram. From then onwards, Aram Damascus appears in both biblical and non-biblical sources as a united kingdom, the kingdom of Aram, and an inscription of Tiglath-Pileser III has preserved for us information about the division of the state into administrative regions.[34] It was in these fateful days, no doubt, that Geshur, the former satellite of Ben-hadad, also became an integral part of Aram, being attached, it would seem, to the province of Karnaim probably as a secondary district bearing the name of Golan. This is also implied even more forcefully in the narrative about the second war with Ahab (1 Kgs 20:26 ff.), where it is related that Ben-hadad and his forces took refuge in the city of Aphek. From the biblical data it would appear that this Aphek remained a fortified city in the possession of Aram even after Ahab's time and down to the reign of Joash, the son of Jehoahaz, at the beginning of the 8th century B.C.E. (2 Kgs 13:17). Moreover, from the account of Ahab's last battle and his death (852 B.C.E.) we learn that the Arameans also managed to gain control of the district of Ramoth-gilead, and that Ahab and his son Joram (842 B.C.E.) twice failed in their attempts to regain this vital area, together with the stronghold of Ramoth-gilead itself, for Israel.

In the light of the foregoing analysis, we can now explain the addition of the words "in Aram" in Absalom's statement: "For your servant vowed a vow while I dwelt in Geshur in Aram..." (2 Sam 15:8). Evidently "in Aram" (בארם) was added to the original text of the verse by a copyist or recensionist at a later period, when it was already necessary to explain to the reader that Geshur was located in Aram, i.e., in Aram Damascus.[35] In fact, Geshur did not actually

34 Luckenbill, *AR* 1, 279. Cf. in this volume, "The Aramean Empire and Its Relations with Israel", pp. 151–172.

35 It is probable that Aram, as the name of the kingdom of Aram Damascus, came into general use only in the reign of Ben-hadad II, after the completion of the reform discussed above.

become a district of Aram until the days of Ben-hadad II, and the Geshurites were subsequently merged into the Arameo-Israelite population of the province of Karnaim.

As for Maachah, we do not possess sufficient information to enable us to follow its history after the period when the Arameans overran southern Syria and began to establish their kingdoms there. From the sparse data contained in the Bible it seems probable that Maachah's fate was similar to that of Geshur, despite the open conflicts which divided them in the eventful period that decided their future. Maachah apparently became a kingdom at about the same time as Geshur. However, in contrast to Geshur which, as already stated, entered into an alliance with David when the latter was still reigning at Hebron, Maachah joined the confederacy of kings led by Hadad-ezer, King of Aram Zobah. There appear to have been two reasons for this: first, the fact that Maachah was nearer to the kingdom of Aram Zobah and its satellites, especially to Aram Beth-rehob which bordered on the territory of Dan;[36] and secondly, the hostile relations then prevailing between the kingdoms of Maachah and Geshur.

It is even possible that, supported by the confederacy, Maachah gained control of the areas adjacent to it and also expanded into northern Galilee, whence the name Abel Beth-maachah (today Tell Abil, between Metulla and Kfar Gilʿadi). The addition of the appellative Beth-maachah is a sure sign that, before its conquest by the Israelites, Abel had belonged to Beth-maachah, i.e., the kingdom of Maachah.[37] As in the case of Geshur, it is not to be inferred from the Bible that Maachah was an Aramean kingdom already in David's day; nor is there any warrant for the assumption that another of Hadad-ezer's allies in his war against David, the men of Tob, were Arameans and that their country, Tob, had an Aramean population in the time of David.[38] As we know from the prologue to the story about David's war against the allied forces of Aram and Ammon, the Ammonites hired "the Arameans of Beth-rehob, and the Arameans of Zobah, twenty thousand foot soldiers, and the king of Maachah with a thousand men, and the men of Tob, twelve thousand men" (2 Sam 10:6). It is quite clear from this that the epithet Aramean does not apply to Maachah and Tob, even though, in the sequel, all the allies are collec-

36 This was apparently the territory controlled by the Beth-rehob mentioned in Judg 18:28. On the relations between Aram Zobah and Aram Beth-rehob mentioned in Judg 18:28, see K. Elliger, *PJb* 32 (1936), 36; A. Dupont-Sommer, *Les Araméens* (1949), 25; A. Malamat, *Enc. Miq.* 2, 577.

37 B. Maisler (Mazar), *Enc. Miq.* 1, s.v. "Abel Beth-maachah".

38 It was to the land of Tob in Transjordan that Jephthah the Gileadite fled to escape from his brothers (Judg 11:3). On the various attempts made to locate it, see B. Mazar, *JPOS* 9 (1929), 83ff., and Abel, *GP* 2, 10; and for another view, M. Noth, *BBLA* 1 (1949), 27ff. [= *ZDPV* 68 (1949–1951)]. Cf. A. Jirku, *ZAW* 62 (1950), 319. This may explain the escape of Sheba son of Bichri of Benjamin from Mount Ephraim to Abel Beth-maachah.

tively referred to as Arameans, since the army of Hadad-ezer, King of Aram Zobah, constituted the majority of the forces employed. As for the statement in 1 Chr 19:6: "Hanun and the Ammonites sent a thousand talents of silver to hire chariots and horsemen from Mesopotamia, from Aram Maachah and from Zobah", it is self-evident — especially by comparison with 2 Sam 10:6 and 1 Chr 19:7 — that the present text is corrupt, and that the true reading is not "from Aram Maachah and from Zobah", but "from Aram Zobah and from Maachah".

What happened after the battle of Madeba, in which the allied states were routed by Israel, and after the other defeats inflicted by David upon Hadad-ezer and his satellites, is fairly well known. The Aramean kingdoms of Aram Zobah and Aram Beth-rehob, together with Aram Damascus, became vassals of Israel, as did the kingdom of Maachah. It was presumably in consequence of this that David lopped off Abel, i.e., Abel Beth-maachah, from the territory of Maachah and that the city then became an Israelite stronghold guarding the northern extremity of the land of Naphtali, with an Israelite population (perhaps from Ephraim and Benjamin),[39] so that it was known, at the end of David's reign, as "a city which is a mother in Israel" (2 Sam 20, especially v. 19). In later times too it was still one of the important store cities of Naphtali (1 Kgs 15:20), and remained so until conquered by the armies of Tiglath-Pileser III. At the same time, the actual territory of Maachah presumably became a vassal state of Israel. It may have been annexed to Aram Damascus when the Aramean kingdom of Damascus was founded at the end of Solomon's reign, or at the latest during Ben-hadad I's campaign at the end of Baasha's reign, and have subsequently become one of the Aramean territories bordering on the administrative district of Naphtali, which included the tribal portion of Dan, at the northern extremity of the kingdom of Israel. Maachah thus disappeared from the historical scene in much the same way as its neighbour, Geshur. Both of them were absorbed into Aram, and were so completely forgotten as separate national and political entities that there is no further reference to them in the chronicles of the time.[40]

39 In the inscription of Tiglath-Pileser III it is mentioned as "Abil[ma]aka, which is located in the border area of the land of Bīt Ḫumria" [see P. Rost, *Die Keilschrifttexte Tiglathpilessers III* 1 (1983), 78]. Cf. also H. Tadmor, in *All the Land of Naphtali* (1967), 65–66 (Hebrew).

40 Some of the historical-geographical assumptions of this study should be re-examined in the light of the archaeological surveys conducted in the Golan by C. Epstein and S. Gutman, especially as there are only few sites which show traces of settlement in the Late Bronze Age. Cf. Epstein and Gutman, *Judea, Samaria and the Golan* (see note 14), 244ff.

King David's Scribe and the High Officialdom of the United Monarchy of Israel

Scholars of Israelite history in the biblical period have often discussed the subject of the high officials in the military and civil service of the early kingdom. One of the problems encountered concerns the origins of the complex administrative system instituted by David and Solomon, Israel's two great kings. De Vaux and Begrich tried to prove that David patterned his senior administration mainly after an Egyptian model. They pointed to a meaningful relationship or a resemblance between a number of key offices and the distribution of duties in the 10th century B.C.E. Israelite civil service, and important offices in the ancient and highly developed administrative system of the Egyptian kingdom.[1] With regard to the three main offices of *mazkīr* (recorder), *sōfēr* (scribe), and *rēʿa hammelek* (associate of the king), they have not, however, succeeded — despite their extensive efforts — in proving any direct influence by analogue to positions in the Pharoanic court. Albright accepted their view in principle, and suggested that the Egyptian models reached David through Phoenician and other mediators.[2] The present author proposes an altogether different approach.

One must first take note of the fact that even before the conquest of Jerusalem, David had set up a military service according to a pattern already long established in the land. This emerges from the fact that the most important office in the realm was commander of the army, exactly as it was in the Canaanite, Philistine, and Aramean states and as it had been during the reigns

1 See R. de Vaux, *RB* 48 (1939), 394–405; J. Begrich, *ZDMG* 86 (1933), 10*; *idem*, *ZAW* 58 (1940–1941), 1–29.

2 W.F. Albright, *Archaeology and the Religion of Israel* (1942), 120.

A scribe depicted standing before the king in the stele of Bar-Rakib, King of Samʾal, found at Zenjirli and dating from the second half of the 8th century B.C.E. (*Enc. Miq.*)

of Saul and Eshbaal.[3] Furthermore, from the very beginning, the principal military force under David was the Thirty Heroes, an institution deeply rooted in the society of the Land of Israel and the Israelite people.[4]

3 See in particular Gen 21:22; Judg 4:2; 1 Sam 14:50; 2 Sam 10:16. In Assyria, the *turtanu*, the commander of the army, was also considered the first among the princes, second only to the king.

4 See Judg 10:4; 12:19; 14:11; 1 Sam 9:22; 1 Chr 11:42. The abundant evidence in the Bible indicates a very long-standing tradition in Israel. The opinion of K. Elliger, *PJb* 31 (1935), 62f., that the number thirty indicates Egyptian influence, is based on a tomb inscription from Thebes, in which

As for the civil administrative system, one should look to David's own conquests, which included most notably Jerusalem, the capital of the Jebusites, the Canaanite city-states on the coast and in the valleys, the Transjordanian kingdoms of Edom, Moab, and Ammon, the Aramean states in southern Syria, and the Philistine principalities. In proclaiming Jerusalem his capital, he was influenced by its long history as an independent or semi-independent city-state. He also retained some of the concepts of political order held by Jerusalem's previous rulers. This conclusion is supported by the fact that the king of Israel was recognized to some extent as successor to Melchizedek, King of Salem and priest of *ʾEl ʾElyōn* (El Most High), who was a revered, almost mythical figure. He was a *heros eponymos* to the rulers of the city, and he later assumed the title of the king of Jerusalem (Ps 110). In addition, the conquered territories in Philistia, the Canaanite towns, and the Transjordanian kingdoms presented David with good models of central government. There were experienced Canaanite and other[5] ministers and officials upon whom he may have drawn in the organization of his administrative system.

It is a fact that of the twelve districts of Solomon, at least four were composed of smaller political units which had been conquered by David.[6] The others also included former city-states (e.g. Shechem, Tirzah, Aphek, etc.). An additional factor which could have influenced the civil administrative system is the marital policy pursued by David and Solomon. Both married into the ruling families of the conquered and vassal states and into the royal houses of the neighbouring lands.[7]

It appears that together with the various institutions of government — the Jurisdiction of the King (1 Sam 8:11–17),the corvée, the Royal Sanctuary and

a company of thirty in the entourage of Ramesses II is mentioned [K. Sethe, *ZAS* 44 (1907), 32]. However, in K. Sethe, *Von Zahlen und Zahlworten bei den alten Ägyptern* (1916), 40, already it is noted that this is a reference to the thirty judges, later mentioned by Diodoros as representing the three capitals of Heliopolis, Memphis, and Thebes, ten from each city. Therefore, the round number here is "ten", not "thirty". This does not provide a good analogy to the Thirty Heroes of David. The same holds true for the 600 men in David's company during his stay in Ziklag. This number has no particular significance in Egypt, but recurs several times in the stories of the Settlement period (Judg 18:11, 16–17; 20:47; cf. Judg 3:31, and even Ex 14:7: "six hundred of his picked chariots, and the rest of the chariots of Egypt"!). Also note that the band of Ittai the Gittite in the service of David included 600 men of Gath (2 Sam 15:18).

5 I use the term "Canaanite" with a dual significance: (1) the autochthonous and permanent West Semitic population of the Land of Israel and Phoenicia, as distinguished from the Hebrews, Horites, Hittites, and Philistines; (2) the non-Israelite population (including Horite, Hittite, and other such elements) who had been the residents of Canaan before the Israelite settlement. They mainly used the "Canaanite", West Semitic language, which had always been the language of the inhabitants of the land. The Bible refers to the latter population by the term "Amorite". On the origin of the name "Canaan", see B. Mazar, *BASOR* 120 (1946), 7ff.; M. Astour, *JNES* 24 (1965), 346ff.

6 The second to fifth districts, 1 Kgs 4:7–20.

7 See S. Yeivin, *Studies in the History of Israel and His Country* (1960), 195ff. (Hebrew).

the Domain of the Realm in Jerusalem, there emerged a complex administrative system which combined Canaanite principles of government with the Israelite patriarchal-tribal mode in its mature stages. It also seems that in that system non-Israelite courtiers and officials, in particular from the Canaanite population, served side by side with their Israelite counterparts.

The number of officials in both the civil and military service recruited by David and Solomon from the non-Israelite population, in particular from the Canaanites, is remarkably large. An officer of Edomite origin is already to be found in the court of Saul (1 Sam 21:8; 22:9) along with two captains of bands from Beeroth (2 Sam 4:2), who were probably Hivites, or, as emerged later, Horites.[8] In the same period we find a Hittite (1 Sam 26:6) in David's service. As for the Heroes (*haggibborīm*) of David,[9] they included Uriah the Hittite, most likely from the Jebusite aristocracy of Jerusalem;[10] Naharai[11] the Beerothite; two Ithrite men, apparently from a Hivite (Horite) family from Baalath(?) which is Kiriath-jearim;[12] another man from Shaalbim (Judg 1:35; 1 Kgs 4:9); an Ammonite; and others (2 Sam 22:23ff.; 1 Chr 11:35ff). Ittai[13] the Gittite, who led the six hundred men of Gath in the service of King David, was certainly non-Israelite. If there were non-Israelites in King David's military service, it is all the more likely that they were also employed in his civil service. Thus we find, among the Property of Stewards, Obil the Ishmaelite

8 Beeroth was one of the towns of the Hivites (Jos 9:17), who, like the Gibeonites, were not of Israelite stock, but a remnant of the Amorites (2 Sam 21:2). The statement "for Beeroth too was considered part of Benjamin" (2 Sam 4:2) should perhaps be interpreted as a remark by the scribe to the effect that the residents of Beeroth were included in the tribal-territorial organization of Benjamin (as were Shechem, Tirzah, and Hefer in Manasseh). For more on this, see B. Maisler (Mazar), *A History of Eretz-Israel* 1 (1938), 224–225, 267 (Hebrew). The Septuagint version Χορραῖος, "Horite", should be preferred to the Masoretic "Hivvite", as has been suggested by Ed. Meyer, *Die Israeliten und ihre Nachbarstämme* (1906), 331; and particularly in E.A. Speiser, *AASOR* 14 (1931–1932), 27ff. Also see H.L. Ginsberg and B. Maisler (Mazar), *JPOS* 14 (1934), 255ff.

9 Concerning the Heroes of David, see in this volume, "The Military Elite of King David", pp. 83–103.

10 According to Yeivin [*History of Israel* (see note 7), 199–200], Uriah may have been the crown prince or, at least, one of the military commanders of the last Jebusite king, who later came to serve David. In addition, Yeivin mentions a number of sources which, in his opinion, gave rise to the assumption that Bathsheba (Bath-shua) and Ahithophel the Gilonite, who may have been her father's father (according to 2 Sam 11:3; 23:34), were also of non-Israelite stock (Yeivin, *ibid*., 200ff.)

11 The name appears to me to be Hurrian, *Ne/iḫria*, which is common in the Nuzi documents and in other sources. The divine attribute *Ne/iḫr* often appears as a component in Hurrian first names such as *Ne/iḫri-Tešup*, *Ne/iḫri-tilla*, etc. See I.J. Gelb, P.M. Purves and A.A. McRae, *Nuzi Personal Names* (henceforth *NPN*) (1943), 105, 239a. The interpretation of M. Noth, *Die Israelitischen Personennamen* (1928), 228, as "fleissig, intelligent" (*naḫāru* in Arabic) is unfounded.

12 See 1 Chr 2:53; Jos 9:17, and also A. Reuveni, *Shem, Ham and Jephet* (1932), 142, 147 (Hebrew); H.L. Ginsberg and B. Maisler, *JPOS* 14 (1934), 260.

13 See 2 Sam 15:18–19; in the Septuagint his name is ʾΕθθει, which is the Hurrian name Eteia, Etiia [see *NPN* (note 11), 49, 211b]. This was also the name of the governor of Ashkelon in the El-Amarna period (see EA 320:5; 321:5; 322:4; 323:3; 324:4; 325:3; 326:3; 370:1).

in charge of the camels and Jaziz the Hagrite responsible for the flocks,[14] both probably from the border provinces of the Israelite state. In addition, it is possible that Ethan the Ezrahite and Heman the Ezrahite, the two great singers in David's service, the progenitors of families of temple singers, were from noble Canaanite families. They assimilated into Israel and were later included, together with their progeny, in the Levite genealogical lists.[15]

One of the important officers in the service of David and Solomon was Adoram who was in charge of the levy, and who is identified with Adoniram son of Abda, in one source also named Hadoram.[16] In biblical sources there is no indication that this official was of non-Israelite origin. The system of the corvée was, however, the product of a socio-economic order typical of Canaanite city-states and adopted by the kings of Israel.[17] David may well have selected the officer to be in charge of the levy from among the Canaanite nobility who were better acquainted with its regulations. In addition, Adoram is a Canaanite name[18] which may be indicative of the officer's origin, while it appears that Adoniram is merely a Hebraized form, considered more euphonious to the Israelite ear. This is further supported by the fact that *ʾadōn* (lord) is not only etymologically derived from *ʾadd-*, but was originally also synonymous with it.[19] It likewise appears that Baanah son of Ahilud, one of the prefects of the districts of Solomon, was of Canaanite origin. He was in charge of the fifth district, which encompassed Taanach, Megiddo, and all Beth-shean, and consisted mainly of the Canaanite valley kingdoms. His theophorous name is Canaanite.[20] Ahilud, on the other hand, is not mentioned at all

14 See 1 Chr 27:30–31. On the origin of Amasa, see 1 Chr 2:17.

15 See 1 Kgs 5:11; Ps 88:1; 89:1; on the genealogies of Ethan (Jeduthun) and Heman, see K. Mohlenbrink, *ZAW* 52 (1934), 202f., 229f., and especially Albright, *Archaeology and Religion* (note 2), 126ff., according to whom the original designation of "Ezrahite" is "a member of a pre-Israelite family" (see also *ibid*., 210, n. 95). It is my opinion that "Ezrahite" (*ʾezraḥi*) refers to a native of the land (*ʾezraḥ ha-ʾareṣ*) such as a free man of non-Israelite (Canaanite) stock who joined Israel, similar to the proselytes of the Second Temple period — in this case, the class of Levitical poets. Later, the term *ʾezraḥ* came to specify the landowning class, as distinguished from resident aliens and foreigners. On the term *ʾezraḥ ha-ʾareṣ*, in the Septuagint αὐτόχθων τῆς γῆς, see Ex 12:48; Num 9:14.

16 See 2 Sam 20:24; 1 Kgs 12:18 (Adoram); 1 Kgs 4:6; 5:28 (Adoniram); 2 Chr 10:18 (Hadoram). According to 1 Chr 18:10, the son of Toi, King of Hamath, was also named Hadoram (instead of Joram, 2 Sam 8:10). The name Hadoram comprises the name of the god, Haddu Hadad.

17 See I. Mendelsohn, *BASOR* (1942), 14ff.

18 See *N.H. Torczyner Volume* = *Lešonenu* 15 (1947), 38–39 (Hebrew) and note 16 above.

19 See H.L. Ginsberg, *OLZ* 37 (1934), 473–474. Abda, as well, is an abbreviated, theophorous Canaanite name, and appears with the same spelling in Phoenician inscriptions [see, e.g. *Lešonenu* 14 (1946), 168 (Hebrew)]. It was used in Israel and is mentioned in one of the Samaria ostraca (no. 57).

20 See 1 Kgs 4:12; the name should probably be construed as B(in-)Ana; it appears in the El-Amarna Letters (Bin-Ana) and in documents in Ugarit (*bn.ʿan*); see B. Maisler (Mazar), *JPOS* 16 (1936), 152ff.; and *Lešonenu* 14 (1946), 172–173 (Hebrew). Also see J. Lewy, *ZA* N.F. 4 (1929), 272; *idem*, *RHR* 110 (1934), 42ff. on the West Semitic god Ana (*ʿan*). Baanah was also the name of one of

in the other sources except in 1 Kgs 4:3[21] where he is listed as the father of Jehoshaphat, King Solomon's recorder. The uniqueness of the name Ahilud makes it difficult to separate Jehoshaphat son of Ahilud from Baanah son of Ahilud, prefect of the valley district. The two may be reasonably presumed to have been brothers, of Canaanite origin, who served under both David and Solomon. The one who served at court merely assumed an Israelite name.

In the light of all the above, one may approach the matter of King David's scribe, who is mentioned in the list of the monarch's officials and who is known as the father of two scribes in the court of Solomon. According to Begrich, de Vaux, and others, the important functions of recorder and scribe were modelled by David directly on the Egyptian examples of *whm.w*[22] and *sẖ-nśw.t* ("the king's scribe"; compare 2 Kgs 12:11). De Vaux also draws conclusions from the name of the scribe, which, in his opinion, is Egyptian.[23] However, such a view encounters many difficulties. It should first be noted that "king's scribe" was the ordinary title of any Egyptian official of rank, needless to say of any prince in Pharaoh's court, and does not specifically designate a particular office.[24] In Israel, things were different. Already in David's administration as in the service of all the subsequent kings of the House of David, we often find mentioned next to the "Recorder", "Officer over the House", or "Head Priest", an important official whose title is "Scribe" (*sōfēr*) or "the king's scribe". Only from the reign of Solomon is there mention of two scribal brothers. This office was distinguished from those of all other officials, among whom were included scribes, i.e. experts in the art of writing and men of books.[25] One should note that an actual class of scribes already existed in Canaan long before the Israelite conquest, and not only in the royal or governor's court. Every town may have had a trained scribe, a master of a fair hand, or a "guild" of scribes (a company of scribes, analogous to "a company of prophets"), or even families of scribes, the likes of which are found

the sons of Rimmon the Beerothite (2 Sam 4:2) and of the father of one of David's Heroes (2 Sam 23:29).

21 The different versions of the Septuagint ᾿Αχειλιαδ, ᾿Αχειλουϑ, ᾿Αχιμα(χ), ᾿Ελουδ do not recommend any emendation of the Masoretic version. In theory the name could be theophorous, but we have no knowledge to date of a deity named "Lud", and only new documents may throw more light on this name.

22 The original sense of the term is "herald", and it seems to me that in Babylonia its parallel is the *nāgiru* (in Sumerian *nimgir*) who publicizes the king's orders. The connection between these offices and that of the recorder is, nevertheless, still unclear.

23 See R. de Vaux, *RB* 48 (1939), 497ff., and also W.F. Albright, *From the Stone Age to Christianity* (2d ed, 1946), 367.

24 See e.g. H. Kees, *Aegypten* (1933), 211f. See also W.F. Albright, *JNES* 5 (1946), 29–21, on *sẖ-šʿ.t*, the scribe in charge of the royal correspondence.

25 Such a person was Jonathan, David's uncle, a counselor, a master, and a scribe (1 Chr 27:32).

1) An Aramean scribe writing with a brush on a papyrus or parchment scroll (Pritchard, *ANEP*) and 2) An Assyrian scribe incising cuneiform characters on a clay tablet with a stylus

elsewhere in the ancient Near East.[26] We have interesting evidence of scribal families of Kenite origin in the south of Judah, probably descended from an ancestor named Jabez, "who was more honourable than his brothers".[27] It may also be that the Canaanite-Hebrew term *sōfēr* occurs in the Ugaritic writings.[28]

26 The Nuzi documents give some interesting details on the scribes and scribal institutions in the Hurrian towns of Mesopotamia during the 14th–15th centuries B.C.E. See P.M. Purves, *AJSL* 57 (1940), 162ff.; more details are in the Ugaritic documents.

27 See 1 Chr 2:55; 4:9–10. There is no basis for the assumption that the expression משפחות סופרים, "scribal families", refers to "Schriftgelehrte" [see e.g. J.W. Rothstein and J. Hänel, *Kommentar zum ersten Buch der Chronik* (1927), 35] or to "Gesetzeskundige" [R. Kittel, *Die Bücher der Chronik* (*HKAT* 1902), 20]. See also S. Klein, *Research on the Genealogical Chapters in the Book of Chronicles* (1930), 9 (Hebrew) and *MGWJ* 70 (1926), 410ff. The source in Chronicles appears to refer to the Settlement period, or to the early period of the Israelite monarchy. If the name Kiriath-sepher or, as is more likely, Kiriath-sopher, was given to the Canaanite city-state of Debir after its conquest by the Kenizites, it was possibly in connection with scribal families, who were of Kenite stock, and who were related to the Kenizites. [For Septuagint πόλις γραμμάτων, see W.F. Albright, *AASOR* 17 (1936/37), 5, n.7; H.M. Orlinsky, *JBL* 8 (1939), 255ff.] Regarding the common opinion that the early (Canaanite) name of Debir was Kiriath-sepher, based on Judg 1:11 (cf. Judg 1:10, concerning Hebron), see Mazar, *Cities and Districts*, 45ff.

28 See especially C.H. Gordon, *Ugaritic Text-Book* (1965), 177. He reads the beginning of the colophon of the tale of Baal: *spr. ʾilmlk šbny* as "the scribe *ʾIl-mlk* the *Šbn*-ite" [H.L. Ginsberg, *The Ugarit Texts* (1936), 43, 68 (Hebrew) differs: *sapar* = wrote].

It is undoubtedly mentioned in Egypt as a Canaanite word *ṯ(u)-p(i)-(i)r*, *sōfēr*, already in the 19th Dynasty.[29]

In the cuneiform literature written in the Akkadian *lingua franca*, there is evidence of the function of a king's scribe, held by an official or prince, existing in the court of every ruler in western Asia during the Middle and Late Bronze Ages, titled *ṭupšar šarri*, "king's scribe". Even after the introduction of alphabetical writing in Canaan, cuneiform remained the ordinary medium of negotiation. By the 11th century B.C.E. the Canaanite language and alphabetical script were gaining predominance in the Land of Israel, Phoenicia, and Syria, and accordingly, the kings' scribes started to use them. It is not impossible that a scribe would know still another language considered necessary for international relations. Illuminating testimony of the status of the king's scribe in Phoenicia is to be found in the tale of Wen-Amon dating from the second quarter of the 11th century B.C.E., according to which the scribe held an important position in the court of Zakarbaʿal, King of Byblos. The king seems to have entrusted him not only with his correspondence, but also with foreign negotiations. The scribe apparently also kept the commercial accounts and performed other economic and political functions.[30]

From a later date, we have more detailed information about royal scribes in Mesopotamia and Syria. Such is preserved in extra-biblical documents and in various depictions, such as the famous one of a scribe standing before Bar-Rakib, King of Samʾal.[31] It is likely that in the royal court of Jerusalem, David bestowed the office of scribe on a person who had previous experience in that office in one of the conquered city-states, such as Jebusite Jerusalem. As such offices were often inherited, it is not surprising that the sons of this scribe would have carried on his duties in the service of Solomon. The name of David's own scribe appears in various biblical sources, with widely divergent spellings. In the Masoretic text we find שריה, "Seraiah" (2 Sam 8:17); שוא, "Sheva" (2 Sam 20:25, spelled שיא); שישא, "Shisha" (1 Kgs 4:3), and שושא, "Shavsha" (1 Chr 18:16). Noteworthy versions in the Septuagint are: Σαραιας (A — 2 Sam 8:17); ʾΑσα (B — 2 Sam 8:17, a corruption); Ιησους, ʾΙσους (A and B — 2 Sam 20:25, a corruption of "Shavsha"?); Σουσα, "Shavsha" (Lag. — 2 Sam 20:25); Σεισα, "Shisha" (A — 1 Kgs 4:3); Σαβα, "Sheva" (B — 1 Kgs 4:3); Σουσα, "Shavsha" (A — 1 Chr 18:17); ʾΙησους (B — 1 Chr 18:17, see above); Σους, "Shavsha" (S). In the Vulgate, we find *Susa*, "Shavsha". A review of all the source material reveals that there is no possibility of reducing all three

29 See W.F. Albright, *The Vocalization of the Egyptian Syllabic Orthography* (1934), 42. Note also the designation *rb. spr*, "master scribe"? of the Ugaritic documents.

30 See S. Yeivin, *The Journey of Wen-Amon* (1930), 17, 25 (Hebrew). His title was *sḫ-šʿ.t*; see also notes 23 and 24.

31 See e.g. H. Schäfer and W. Andrae, *Die Kunst des alten Orients* (1935), Pl. 35.

forms: "Sheva", "Shavsha" and "Seraiah". In view of the numerous versions, the reading "Shisha" seems less likely. The widely held opinion that one should choose only the one form, "Shavsha" (or "Shisha"), and that all the other versions are but corruptions or scribal errors, is unacceptable. It is quite clear that the forms שושא, "Shavsha" (שישא, "Shisha") and שיא, "Sheva" (שיא, "Sia") cannot be traced to any West Semitic name,[32] whereas שריהו(ו), "Seraiah(u)", is typically Israelite and common in the Bible.[33]

How, then, is one to explain these puzzling phenomena? It appears to me that King David's scribe bore a Hurrian name, one from which all three forms preserved in the biblical sources derive. I suggest a name such as *Šewe-šarri*, already encountered in the Nuzi documents.[34] This name is composed of the element *šew(e)*, which is identifiable with *šaw(a)*, a component of many Hurrian personal names, both masculine and feminine.[35] Several scholars have suggested that the name of the Hurrian goddess *Šawuška*, mentioned also in the Ugaritic writings, and which they have identified with Ishtar of Nineveh, is composed of this element.[36] As for the *šarri* element, it is none but the Hurrian word *šar(ri)*, or in Ugaritic *žr*, signifying king (especially as an attribute of a god), and one of the most common components of personal names.[37]

The name *Še/awe/a-šarri* could easily have been shortened in ordinary usage to *Še/awr/a-ša* and written in the Hebrew alphabet as שושא, "Shavsha". It is likely after all that *-ša* as a second component in a number of Hurrian names is merely an abbreviation of *-šarri*, in the same way that *-še* is of *-šenni* (brother)

32 See Noth [*Israelitschen Personennamen* (note 11), 40f.], who discusses names such as "Shavsha". He states: "Hier haben wir mit aus der Kinderstube erwachsenen Kosennamer zu tun, die so stark entstellt sind, dass die zugrundeliegenden Vollnamen nicht mehr ermittelt werden Können". In other words, Noth did not find a solution to the meaning of this and several similar names. Similarly, other scholars only find the form "Shavsha" acceptable [see, e.g. Rothstein and Hänel, *Ersten Buch der Chronik* (note 27), 347], which gave J. Marquardt, *Fundamente israelitischer und judischer Geschicht* (1896), 22, the thought that *Šawšu* is *Šamšu*, "sun"!; R. de Vaux, *RB* 48 (1939), 399, suggests that it is an Egyptian name like *ša*, *šši'*, *ššw*.

33 See, Noth, *Israelitischen Personennamen* (note 11), 191, 208.

34 See *NPN* (note 11), 133a, 257a.

35 *Ibid.*, 252–253, 257a.

36 On this goddess and regarding the origin of her name see, in particular, B. Hrozny, *Archiv Orientální* 4 (1932), 127; *NPN* (note 11), 253a; E.A. Speiser, *AASOR* 20 (1940/41), 15f., 19, 36f.

37 The most common form is *Eweri-šarri*; in Nuzi *Erwi-šarri*; in Ugaritic *'wr-žr*, "Adonimelek". On *šar(ri)*, in Ugaritic *žr*, as a theophorous element in Hurrian names, see, in particular, H.L. Ginsberg and B. Maisler, *JPOS* 14 (1934), 250f.; Z. Harris, *JAOS* 55 (1935), 95ff.; E.A. Speiser, *JAOS* 58 (1938), 176ff.; *idem*, *AASOR* 20, 127, 204; *NPN* (note 11), 251f. The special Hurrian sign *ž*, a separate form of the letter *š* in the Ugaritic script, was discovered by Ginsberg and the present author in 1934, and accepted by the above-mentioned authors. One should note the view of F. Thureau-Dangin, *Syria* 12 (1931), 254, that the Hurrians borrowed *šar(ri)* (*žarri*) from the Akkadian *šarru* even though it may also have been borrowed from West Semitic שר. Still other scholars are of the opinion that originally it was a Hurrian word.

or *-te* (also *-teššelа*) of (the god) *Tešup*.[38] The name could have been abbreviated even further, to become *Še/awe/a*, omitting the *-šarri* component completely. This shortened form appears in the Nuzi documents, and is reflected in the biblical spelling שוא, "Sheva".[39] The two forms "Shavsha" and "Sheva", then, are abbreviations of the same Hurrian name, which in the Hebrew alphabet should have been written שושר*, *"Shavshar". If this is correct, the third form, "Seraiah", could be easily explained. Here is a typical example of the deliberate conversion of a non-Israelite name into an Israelite one: the Hurrian element *šar(ri) (žr)* is presented in its Hebrew form *śar*, and the component *Še/awe/a* was replaced by *-iah(u)*, thus giving the name an explicitly Israelite ring.[40] The forms "Shavsha" and "Sheva", then, represent the scribe's Hurrian name in two different abbreviations as they were used in speech, whereas "Seraiah" is his official Israelite name, which, in fact, is an Israelite adaptation of the Hurrian original.

There is, therefore, no need to suppose that the name of David's scribe was corrupted in the various biblical sources. The tendency to convert foreign into Israelite names, or to replace the pagan element therein by *-iah(u)*, or by a theophorous element which could not be suspected of "foreignness", seems to be characteristic of the early phase of the Israelite kingdom.[41] It should be remembered that during that period religious and national sentiments were strong among the tribes of Israel. The belief in the God of the Fathers, not

38 On the component *-ša* in Hurrian names, see A.L. Oppenheim, *WZKM* 44 (1937), 204 ff.; Purves in *NPN* (note 11), 249b. I have found the abbreviation *ša* instead of *-šarri* also in names such as *Ḫuti-ša*, composed of the common verb *ḫut*. [Compare the name *Ḫutip-šarri* (on the verb form *ḫutip*, see Purves, *ibid*, 188) and *Šatu-ša* which is composed of the common element *šat(u)* (compare names such as *Šatu-senni*, *Šatu-tae*, etc.].

39 In the genealogies of the Calebites, who mingled with the autochthonous inhabitants, there is mention of a certain Sheva, father of Machbenah and Gibea (1 Chr 2:49) [on the mixed population of West Semites and Horites in the south of the country, see H.L. Ginsberg and B. Maisler, *JPOS* 14 (1934), 256ff.]. As Hurrian names are particularly numerous in these lists, it appears to be the same abbreviated Hurrian name [see also Reuveni, *Shem, Ham and Jephet* (note 12), 137ff.].

40 The appearance of the theophorous element in the second position, rather than in the first, should not raise any problem. Similar metatheses are found in other theophorous names, such as Jehoahaz-Ahaziahu, Jehojachin-Jechaniah, Eliam-Amiel (the father of Bathsheba). Furthermore, one case involves an adaptation to the explicitly Israelite name Seraiah(u).

41 The same phenomenon may be noted in the name of Saul's son and heir-apparent Eshbaal (1 Chr 8: 33; 9:39), known as Ish-bosheth in 2 Sam. The name is probably composed of אש = יש (compare 2 Sam 14:19; Micha 6:10), and the element "baal" [see Albright, *Archaeology and Religion* (note 2), 207, n. 26 on Ugaritic *ʾiṯ*]. The forms אישי = ישי (1 Chr 2:12–13) are probably also abbreviated theophorous names composed of the same element. Here, instead of Eshbaal or Ishbosheth, we find in the official record in 1 Sam 14:49: Ishvi. According to the Septuagint (Lag. Ἰεσσιου), it should be emended to ישיו, i.e. ישיהו = אשיהו. The names ישיה and ישיהו should perhaps be vocalized accordingly. It may be that whereas the original name was Ishbaal/Eshbaal, the official name was Ieshiah/Eshiahu. Note other metatheses in the names of David's son Beeliada (1 Chr 14:7) = Eliada (2 Sam 5:16ff). [On this name, see *J. Klausner Volume* (1937), 51 (Hebrew).] There are many more examples of this phenomenon.

solely as Israel's only God, protecting His people and His Messiah, but as the only God of all peoples, ruler of all beings, watching over the fate of men and nations, served as a tremendous motivating force in the creation of the Israelite state and in the evolvement of its political and social order. This process explains the adoption of the spiritual life of Israel by non-Israelites and quasi-Israelites in the service of David and Solomon, one of the expressions of which was the Hebraization of personal names. At the same time, external influences and those of the local Canaanite culture continued to have their effect on the developing character of the United Monarchy.

I have already cited the typically Canaanite name of Adoram, David's minister in charge of the levy, which was converted into Adoniram, a form which cannot be foreign.[42] Similarly, it appears that the name of Uriah the Hittite, one of David's Heroes,[43] was of foreign stock. Gustavs suggested that his original name was Hurrian: *Ariia*. Vieyra, on the other hand, proposed another Hurrian name such as *Ewiria*. The present author has in mind the form, *Ewriia*, and Purves preferred the form *Ewariia*. The three latter forms are all abbreviations of a Hurrian name derived from *ewri* or *ewar*, meaning "lord".[44] Notwithstanding this explanation, one should not neglect the fact that the name as it appears in the biblical source, Uriah(u), seems to be purely Israelite. Is it not reasonable to suppose that the original name was Hurrian, composed of an *ewri-* (or *ewar-*) element and a pagan name or title [such as *Ew(a)ri-šarri* or *Ew(a)ri-Tešub*, etc.] which was later replaced by the Israelite theophorous element *-iah(u)*? This conclusion finds support in the account of the building by David of the altar on Mount Zion.[45] There, the last Jebusite governor of Jerusalem is called in one source "Arawnah" (ארונה)[46] and in another "the Awarnah" (האורנה), indicating that Arawnah-Awarnah is not a personal name but the title of the ruler of Jebusites: ארונה המלך, i.e. "Arawnah the king" (2 Sam 24:23).[47] This seems to be another derivation of the Hurrian element

42 On *ʾadōn* as an attribute of the God of Israel, similar to king, see W.W.S. von Baudissin and O. Eissfeldt, *Kyrios als Gottesname* 3 (1927), 179; Noth, *Israelitischen Personennamen* (see note 11), 177f.

43 On Uriah, see above, p. 129.

44 See A. Gustavs, *ZAW* 33 (1913), 201f.; M. Vieyra, *RHA* 5 (1938–1940), 113ff.; Purves in *NPN* (note 11), 210ff. Purves distinguishes between two elements which often appear as components of personal names: *ewri* (in Nuzi *erwi*), signifying "king", and *ewar*, signifying "lord", owner. He interprets the Hurrian word *ewaru* as "inherited feudal property". Therefore the meaning of *ewar* is "feudal lord". Instead of the accepted reading *Ewri-šarri* (Ugaritic: *ʾwržr*; in the Qaṭna documents the name is expressed by the ideogram EN.LUGAL), Purves suggests the reading *Ewari-šarri*. The two readings appear to be closely related.

45 My assumption was briefly presented, in Yeivin, *History of Israel* (see note 7), 198–199; see also *Torczyner* (note 18), 42, n. 2.

46 2 Sam 24:20, 23–24; in v. 18 the *kethib* is ארניה, the *qere* is ארונה, "Arawnah".

47 The spelling אורנה is reflected in all Septuagint versions (Ὀρνα); and in Josephus, *Antiq.* VII, 13.4 (Ὀροννα). The form Arnan, appearing only in the Masoretic version of Chronicles, is exceptional.

ewri- (or *ewar-* in Nuzi also with the metathesis *erwi*), meaning "lord". Here in the sense of owner of the town, a feudal lord, it appears in conjunction with the genitive suffix *-ne*, which in some cases also serves as a definite article.[48] Together they become the common Hurrian word *Ewri-ne* (or *Ewar-ne*), or as in Ugaritic documents *ʾewrn*. If the Hurrian title of the ruler of Jerusalem, *Awarnah* (*Arawnah*), was in use until the time of David, it is not surprising to find a Hittite nobleman of Jerusalem with a name composed of the element *ewr*, "lord", which he nevertheless adapted so as to make it sound more Israelite upon entering the service of David.[49]

The view suggested here, that King David's scribe was of one of the "Canaanite" inhabitants (אזרח), and that his original name was typically Hurrian, raises another problem. It involves "Elihoreph and Ahija, the sons of Shisha — scribes" (1 Kgs 4:3), during the reign of Solomon. The etymology of Elihoreph has not been suitably explained to date.[50] On the basis of Septuagint B — ʾΕλιαφ, it has been suggested that it is a Hebrew theophorous name grafted onto the name of the Egyptian deity *Ḥʿpy* (Apis).[51] However, a single version of the Septuagint is not sufficient basis for emending the Masoretic text on the assumption that the letter "r" (ר) was mistakenly introduced into the name.[52] I propose that the second component of the name is the god

It should be noted that the Septuagint has ʾΟρνα instead of Arnan, not only in 1 Chr 21:15, 18, and 2 Chr 3:1, but also in 1 Chr 3:21. The hypothesis proposed by Wellhausen and others, that v. 23 should be emended as ארונה עבד המלך, "Arawna servant of the king", is groundless, since Arawnah was not an official of the Israelite king. Others have suggested the emendation עבד אדוני המלך, "servant of my master, the King", instead of ארונה המלך, "Arawnah the king", which is likewise groundless. A solution suggested by N.H. Tur-Sinai (Torczyner), *Lešonenu* 13 (1945), 105 (Hebrew), is that , "the threshing floor of Arawnah the Jebusite" is also the threshing floor of the god Jebus(?), and that this may have to do with the ark (*ʾārōn*) of the god. I find these hypotheses unreasonable.

48 On the suffix *-ne*, see E.A. Speiser, *AASOR* 20, 98ff.; also see F. Thureau-Dangin, *Syria* 12 (1913), 254ff., according to whom *-ne* is the definite article in Hurrian. On *ewerne*, see Speiser, *ibid*., 218b (index).

49 The fact that the king of Jerusalem during the El-Amarna period bears a Hurrian name, *Abdi Ḫeba*, indicates that there was a Hurrian element within the nobility of Jerusalem. This is very compatible with the general picture of the "Canaanite" population of the land, particularly around Jerusalem. See bibliography in note 39 above; also W.F. Albright, *From the Pyramids to Paul* (1935), 9ff.; W. Feiler, *ZA* 45 (1939), 216ff. The fact that Uriah, a native of Jerusalem, was a Hittite, agrees with several statements in the Bible which suggest that the Jebusites, masters of the city in the time of the Israelite Settlement, were considered Hittites (see, in particular, Ezek 16:3, 45). On this matter in general, see B. Maisler (Mazar), *JPOS* 10 (1930), 189ff.; *AJSL* 49 (1932/3), 252ff.; for a different view, see E. Forrer, *PEF QSt* 1936, 190ff.; 1937, 100ff. However, Hurrian influence was very marked among the Hittite population particularly in Syria and in the Land of Israel; see I.J. Gelb, *Hurrians and Subarians* (1944), 68f.

50 According to Noth, *Israelitischen Personennamen* (see note 11), 237, no. 151, no interpretation of the second element of the name has been found to date.

51 See R. de Vaux, *RB* 48 (1939), 399. A similar hypothesis had already been suggested by Marquardt, *Israelitscher und judischer Geschicht* (see note 32), 22.

52 In A: ʾΑναρεϑ, apparently a corruption of ʾΕλιαρεφ, אליחרף.

Ḫarpa/e. This deity was worshipped by the Kassites in Babylonia, and identified by them with Enlil, the lord of the gods. He was also worshipped by the Hurrians, and his name appears as a component in personal names from Nuzi.[53] Some identify him with the god *Ḫaurpa/i*, already known in Elam in the early period. *Ḫaurpa/i* also serves as a component in Hurrian names in Nuzi.[54] In any case, it is not impossible that the name Elihoreph is "Canaanite" and comprises the name of the Hurrian deity, *Ḫarpa*. As for his brother, Ahija, his name is typically Israelite.[55]

In the light of the above, there are grounds for the assumption that, like other officials in the service of the first monarchs of Israel, King David's scribe was of "Canaanite" origin. He was one of the non-Israelite, native inhabitants, among whom the Hurrian element was very pronounced. This conclusion is supported by his original name, and perhaps also by that of one of his sons. When he came to serve David at the royal court in Jerusalem, he assimilated the spirit of the people whom he served, and converted his name into an Israelite one. He probably also gave his second son a typically Israelite name.[56]

53 See *NPN* (note 11), 214.

54 Thus A.L. Oppenheim, *AfO* 12 (1937–1939), 31; see also Purves in *NPN* (note 11), 218, who distinguishes between the two, and Gelb in *ibid*., 51, n. 12.

55 Some suggest reading אחיה = אחיו, since the passage refers to Elihoreph and "his brother" who is not named. See R. de Vaux, *RB* 48 (1939), 399–400.

56 A. Cody, *RB* 72 (1965), 381–393, suggested that the name of King David's scribe was Seraiah, whereas the names Shisha, etc. are none other than the Egyptian title *sḫ-šʿ.t*, "a scribe of epistles". On the rejection of his hypothesis, see S. Aḥituv, *IEJ* 23 (1973), 126. On the scribe in the biblical period, see A.F. Rainey, in *Enc. Miq.* 5, 1010f. including detailed bibliography. T.N.D. Mettinger, in his *Solomonic State Officials* (1971), tries to present additional supporting evidence for the opinion that the administrative system of the United Monarchy was influenced decisively by Egypt.

Pharaoh Shishak's Campaign to the Land of Israel

The Sources

The campaign of Pharaoh Shishak I was an event of decisive importance in Israelite history during the period following the reign of Solomon. According to 1 Kgs 14:25, it took place in the fifth year of Rehoboam, King of Judah (926 B.C.E.). This was soon after the division of the United Monarchy, which resulted in political complications and brought about a weakening of authority both in Israel and in Judah. The time was propitious for Shishak, founder of the 22nd Lybian Dynasty in Egypt, to enhance the prestige of his monarchy. It was his chance to appear as an important political force in the regions of western Asia bordering Egypt, and at the same time to enrich his kingdom with spoils taken from the cities of the Land of Israel. Before undertaking the military venture, Pharaoh Shishak made recurrent attempts to interfere in the internal affairs of the Israelite kingdom: he supported Jeroboam's attempt to rebel against Solomon (1 Kgs 11:40), stirred up political unrest in Edom, and extended his power over Philistia.[1] In his last years, Solomon built fortresses and storage-cities like Gezer, Beth-horon and Baalith (1 Kgs 9:17–18). Apparently this was a reaction to the aggressive policy pursued by Shishak against the United Monarchy, which was in marked contrast to the line followed by the pharaohs of the preceding 21st Dynasty.[2]

What were the results of Shishak's campaign? Our knowledge of the operation stems not only from the few surviving written accounts, but also from

1 Cf. I. Goldwasser, *Yediot* 16 (1949), 82–84 (Hebrew); A. Malamat, in E.F. Campbell and D.N. Freedman (eds.), *The Biblical Archaeologist Reader* 3 (1964), 94ff.

2 On the 21st Dynasty in Egypt, see A. Gardiner, *Egypt of the Pharaohs* (1961), 316ff.; J. Cerny, in *CAH* 2, Part 2, 643ff.

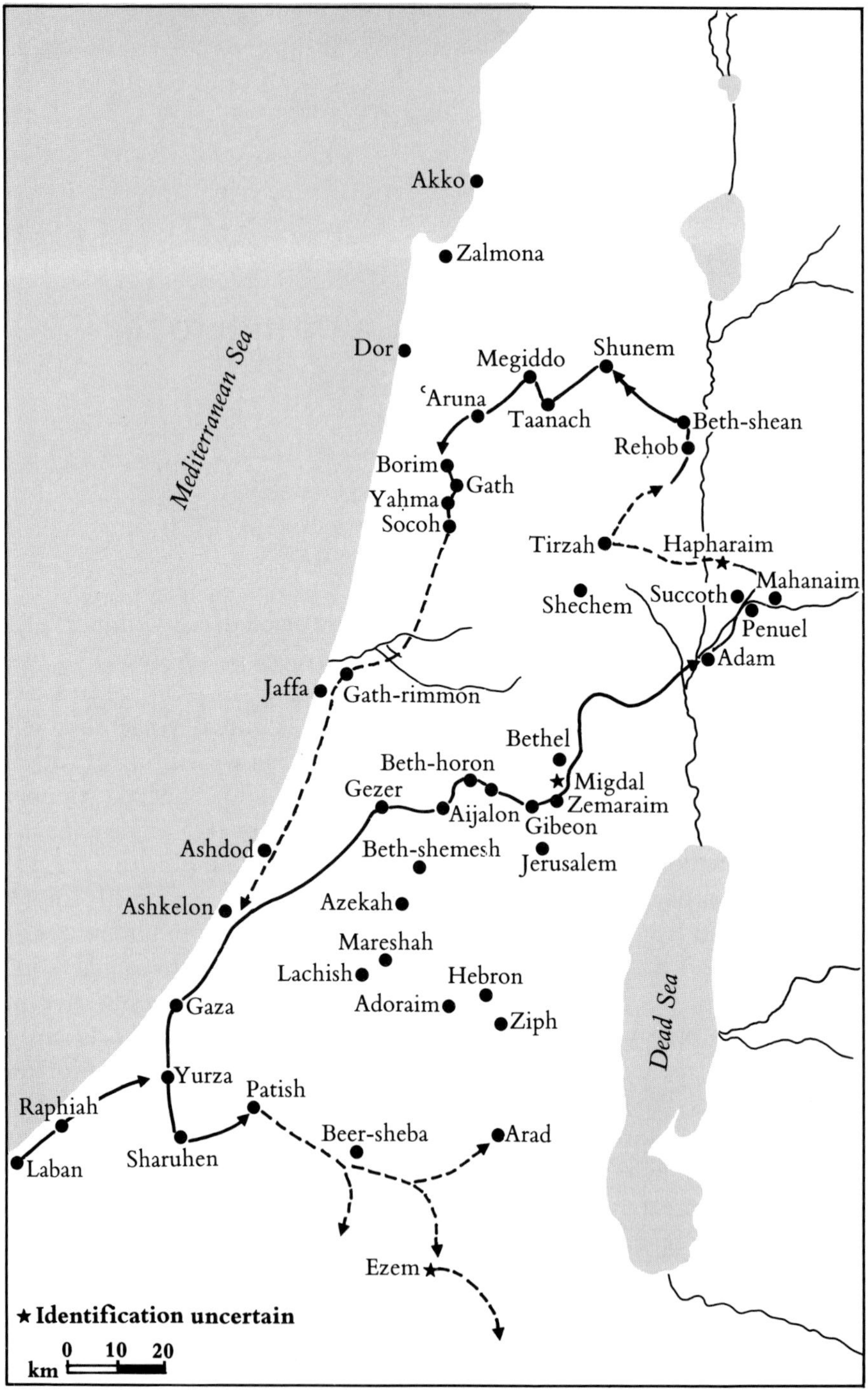

The route of Pharaoh Shishak's campaign to the Land of Israel

archaeological finds in various parts of Israel. These archaeological discoveries reveal the complete or partial destruction of many fortresses and settlements in border areas and along the main lines of communication occurring towards the end of the early Iron Age,[3] and evidently the result of devastation and pillage by the Egyptian troops.

Shishak's campaign is mentioned in two biblical sources, both of which refer to it only in passing. One source, preserved in 1 Kgs 14:25–28and 2 Chr 12: 9–12,is apparently derived from a Chronicle of the Temple of Jerusalem.[4] It tells how Shishak king of Egypt attacked Jerusalem in the fifth year of King Rehoboam and exacted heavy tribute from the king of Judah: "... and he carried away the treasures of the House of the Lord, and the treasures of the royal palace. He carried off everything; he even carried off the golden shields that Solomon had made" (1 Kgs 14:26). The second source, in 2 Chr 12:2–8, is distinctly prophetic in tone and apparently derived from the "Acts of the Prophet Shemaiah".[5] It includes interesting information as to how Jerusalem escaped destruction when "Shishak king of Egypt marched against Jerusalem ... with 1200 chariots, 60,000 horsemen" and a horde of Libyans and Nubians.[6] The lords of Judah, unable to defend their cities against the invading hosts, fled to Jerusalem. Jerusalem itself was saved, but in fact only because Rehoboam hastened to pay the heavy tribute. It is worth noting that the biblical sources mention only Jerusalem and Judah; they do not provide information regarding Shishak's campaign as a whole, or his army's line of march.

What can archaeological evidence tell us about Pharaoh Shishak's military operations and their aftermath? Megiddo has yielded a fragment of the commemorative stele erected by Pharaoh Shishak in that important, fortified city. Evidence from levels VA–IVB at Megiddo, and from Gezer, built by Solomon on the ruins of the Canaanite city (1 Kgs 9:16–19), shows that both were totally destroyed shortly after the Solomonic period — very likely at the time of Shishak's attack. Similar suppositions have been advanced about other settlements (for example, Beth-shean V) but without sound evidence.

We can learn a great deal, however, from the hieroglyphic inscriptions of Shishak preserved on the southern entrance of the temple of Amon at Karnak,[7]

3 See below and G.E. Wright, *BASOR* 155 (1959), 28.

4 On the historical sources used by the authors of the Books of Kings and Chronicles, see B. Mazar, *IEJ* 2 (1952), 82ff.; J. Liver, *Studies in Bible and Judean Desert Scrolls* (1971), 221ff. (Hebrew); B. Dinur, in A. Malamat (ed.), *The Kingdoms of Israel and Judah* (1961), 9ff. (Hebrew).

5 A source called "the chronicles of the prophet Shemaiah" is mentioned in 2 Chr 12:15; the story relates that it was Shemaiah the prophet who came to Rehoboam and the lords of Judah and rebuked them for their sins while they were gathered in Jerusalem under threat of attack by Shishak (*ibid.*, v. 5).

6 In the words of 2 Chr 12:3: לובים, סוכיים וכושים "Lybians, Sukkites and Kushites".

7 The document, accompanied by learned commentaries, has been published many times since the 19th

The reliefs of Pharaoh Shishak on the southern wall of the Amon temple at Karnak listing the cities he conquered in the Land of Israel (Lines 1–10) (B. Grdseloff)

in which the sites conquered by the Egyptians are registered. This list is divided into two parts: the upper part, which has five lines, begins with the conventional recording of the "nine peoples of the bow". The word for "list" (or "copy") is followed by the names of the conquered cities (nos. 11–65). The lower part has five, much longer lines containing a great number of place names. Scholars referring to the Bible and other sources have been able to identify many geographical names appearing in the upper part with known sites in the central and northern parts of the Land of Israel. They have not, however, managed to find the key to the order followed by the scribe, and consequently the character and meaning of the register have remained obscure. According to some scholars, the second part bears the names of places and regions in the Negeb, but generally, this part has also remained a riddle.

I made an attempt to clarify the contents of the list in 1947, in cooperation with the late Bernhard Grdseloff, on the basis of new photographs and copies made by him.[8] As a point of departure I assumed that the first group of places — the first four lines — should be read *boustrophedon* (i.e. the first line from left to right, the second line from right to left, etc.). In fact, the last two names in the first line are *Gezer* (no. 12) and *Rubute* (no. 13), while the second line ends with *Aijalon* (no. 26). Now, in the El-Amarna Letters, the town of Rubute is mentioned as lying near Gezer on the way to Jerusalem, so that if the first two lines are read *boustrophedon*, they give a consecutive list of sites. The sequence becomes still clearer when we read the first name in the second line, *Taanach* (no. 14), and the first entry in the third line, *Megiddo* (no. 27). Reading the inscription in this way, and assuming that the localities in line 5 were omitted from line 2 and added at the end of the first part, we obtain a consecutive and logical list of towns and camping places lying in the path of the Egyptian army on its march through the Kingdom of Israel. Of course, a considerable number of names are completely or partially erased or blurred, and there are various difficulties in deciphering some others. The following is a list of sites in correct order, inasmuch as they can be read with certainty or (in a few cases) with probability:

No. 11 Gaza	22 Mahanaim	28 ʾAdar
No. 12 Gezer	21 Šut	29 Yad Hammelek
No. 13 Rubute	[20 erased]	30 —

century. See J. Simons, *Handbook of the Study of Egyptian Topographical Lists Relating to Western Asia* (1937), 89–101, 178–186; M. Noth, *ZDPV* 61 (1938), 227ff.; *ANET*, 242ff. The serial numbers of the names in the list follow Simons, *ibid*. [See also Y. Aharoni, *The Land of the Bible* (2d ed, 1979), 323ff.; K.A. Kitchen, *The Third Intermediate Period in Egypt* (1973), 293ff., 432ff.]

8 In the interim, excellent photographs and copies of the inscriptions have been produced and published under the auspices of the Oriental Institute of the University of Chicago; see G.R. Hughes and C.P. Nims, *Reliefs and Inscriptions at Karnak* (1954), in particular Pls. X and XI.

No. 26 Aijalon	19 Adoraim	31 Honim
No. 25 Kiriathaim	18 Hapharaim	32 ʿAruna
No. 24 Beth-horon	59 Tirzah	33 Borim
No. 23 Gibeon	[60–64 erased]	34 Gath-patalla
No. 58 Migdal	65 p3-ʿemeq ("The Valley" with the Egyptian article)[9]	35 Yaḥma
No. 57 Zemaraim	17 Reḥob	36 Beth-ʿolam
No. 56 Adam	16 Beth-shean	37 Qqrw?
No. 55 Succoth	15 Shunem	38 Socoh
No. 54 Qedesh or Qodesh	14 Taanach	39 Beth-tappuaḥ
No. 53 Penuel	27 Megiddo	

Nos. 41–52 are erased and cannot be deciphered.

The Campaign to the Kingdom of Israel

In analyzing the above list I shall discuss only the principal points. At the outset, we note that immediately after Gaza, which was the starting point of the campaign, there follows Gezer, the frontier outpost city of Israel, facing Philistia. The biblical story about Gezer, according to which Solomon received it from Pharaoh as his daughter's dowry (1 Kgs 9:16), may be taken as evidence that Philistia was already under Egyptian domination at the time of the 21st Dynasty. Very possibly it had been dominated by Egypt since the days of Pharaoh Siamon, whose campaign against the "Sea Peoples" is alluded to in a relief from Tanis.[10] The strategic importance of Gezer is attested by the fact that it is listed among the principal fortresses built by Solomon as a barrier against Egypt (1 Kgs 9:17). The route leading from Gezer to Aijalon–Beth-horon–Gibeon, and from there to Zemaraim, in the southern region of the Ephraimite Mountains, is quite clear. This is the well-known road, often mentioned in the Bible, that led from the Shephelah via Beth-horon into the mountain region of Benjamin and Ephraim, north of Jerusalem. This route demonstrates the fact that Shishak advanced on Jerusalem from the north, and that probably he received the tribute paid by Rehoboam in one of the cities to the west or north of the capital, such as Aijalon or Gibeon. From Gibeon, Shishak proceeded to Migdal[11] and from there to Zemaraim. From Zemaraim

9 The name appears with the Egyptian article *p3*, equivalent to the article *ha* in Hebrew.

10 See I. Goldwasser, *Yediot* 14 (1948), 82–84 (Hebrew); P. Montet, *Le drame d'Avaris* (1940), 185ff.

11 S. Aḥituv is of the opinion, which I accept, that the name does not refer to Majdal Beni Fāḍil (Fadel) on the eastern borders of the Ephraim Mountains, 12 km east of Lebonah (al-Luban), as thought by Abel and Noth [F.M. Abel, *Mélanges Maspero* 1 (1935), 33; M. Noth, *ZDPV* 61 (1938), 288 =

the Egyptian army descended to the Jordan Valley, more precisely to the Valley of Succoth — a fertile and densely populated area. The first point reached was Adam (Tell ed-Damiyeh). The following places in the list are all known to have been important towns in the Jabbok region during the period of the early Monarchy. They are Succoth (Tell Deir ʿAlla), Penuel (perhaps Tell el-Ḥarma) and Mahanaim (identified with Tulul edh-Dhaḥab). Some of the names that follow are unknown from any other source. Adoraim and Hapharaim, which subsequently appear, may yield a clue if we link the latter with Ephron on the Jordan (mentioned in 1 Macc 5:46–52 and 2 Macc 2:12, and identifiable as Tell es-Saʿidiyeh, located at one of the fords of the Jordan).[12] After Adoraim and Hapharaim, I propose, reading "[T]irzah", identified as Tell el-Farʿah.[13] If this suggestion is correct, the Egyptian army crossed the Jordan near Tell es-Saʿidiyeh and arrived at Tell el-Farʿah, continuing from there to the Beth-shean Valley (*p3-ʿemeq*; no. 65). Henceforth, the route of Shishak's march is clear: Reḥob (Tell eṣ-Ṣarem in the Beth-shean Valley)–Beth-shean–Shunem–Taanach–Megiddo.

There is much interest in the sites that follow immediately after Megiddo, which were certainly connected with this important fortress city: ʾAdar (no. 28), to judge by its name, was probably the threshingfloor of the city; Yad

A fragment of Pharoah Shishak's commemorative stele found at Megiddo [C.S. Fisher, *The Excavations of Armageddon* (1929), Fig. 7b]

Aufsätze zur biblischen Landes und Altertumskunde 2 (1971), 81] and S. Herrmann [*ZDPV* 80 (1964), 62ff.]. Aḥituv believes that the place referred to is Migdal-eder, south of Bethel and south of Rachel's grave (1 Sam 10:2). On Rachel's tombstone at Zelzah, see Mazar, *Cities and Districts*, 80ff. The location of Migdal-eder near Bethlehem is based on the later tradition that places Rachel's tomb near Bethlehem.

12 On Tell es-Saʿidiyeh, see N. Glueck, *AASOR* 25–28(1951), 290ff., where he makes the unacceptable suggestion that it should be identified with Zaraten; see Mazar, *Canaan and Israel*, 33; S. Yeivin, *Yediot* 14 (1949), 87 (Hebrew). A more likely possibility is that Tell es-Saʿidiyeh should be identified with Zaphon, as proposed by W.F. Albright, *AASOR* 6 (1926), 45–47. On the excavations of Tell es-Saʿidiyeh, cf. J.P. Pritchard, *EAEHL* 4, 1028–1032, and now, *idem*, *Tell es-Saʿidiyeh, Excavations in the Tell, 1964–1966* (1985).

13 The reading "Tirzah" is doubtful, but not impossible. On its identification with Tell el-Farʿah, see R. de Vaux, *RB* 56 (1949), 102ff. According to 1 Kgs 14:17, Tirzah was already the capital of Israel in the days of Jeroboam.

Hammelek (no. 29) was perhaps a royal monument which stood at the entrance to Wadi ʿArah, serving as a landmark and possibly also as a holy place;[14] *Hnm* (no. 31) by its meaning seems to have been a resting or camping area for caravans in Wadi ʿArah on the approaches to the city of ʿAruna (no. 32) (Tell ʿArah). Next to be recorded is Borim (no. 33), identical with Burin near Baqʿa el-Gharbiye; it is followed by Gath-patalla (no. 34), which is known from the El-Amarna Letters and from the Egyptian lists, and can be identified with Jatt in northern Sharon. In the Late Bronze Age, Gath-patalla and Yaḥma (no. 35) had already become important stations along the Via Maris. Of the names that follow, Socoh (no. 38) is known to have been an important centre on the Via Maris. It is also mentioned in 1 Kgs 4:10, and is today identified as er-Rās, near Shuweika. The location of the next entry, Beth-tappuaḥ (no. 39) is unknown, unless it is Tappuaḥ, the royal Canaanite city (Josh 12:17).

This entire section of Shishak's inscription shows that the Egyptian army made a circular march through the main northern regions of the Kingdom of Israel, destroying the cities and fortresses on the main roads and returning by the Via Maris to Philistia. We can hardly deduce from this list that the Egyptians invaded the northern and central parts of Judah. On the contrary, the rich areas of the Kingdom of Israel seem to have been the main objective of the expedition. Shishak may also have intended to teach the Kingdom of Israel a lesson. Perhaps he was motivated by the fact that Rehoboam, now established as king, refused to acknowledge Egyptian suzerainty, revoking an agreement made during his stay in Egypt and/or at the time of his revolt. In any event, it is a fact that the first part of Shishak's list does not contain a single place name that can definitely be located within the Kingdom of Judah (Aijalon was probably annexed to Judah after Shishak's campaign).

Shishak's register provides numerous data concerning the main roads of Israel during that period, and about the settlements located on them. It shows that Benjamin and south Ephraim, the Jordan Valley, the northern valleys, and the Plain of Sharon were densely inhabited during the days of Solomon and at the beginning of Jeroboam's reign. The destruction brought about by Shishak's armies is attested by the archaeological finds at the sites identified with the cities mentioned. Thus it appears from the excavations that Gezer was razed at the end of the early Iron Age and was only rebuilt centuries later. At Megiddo, the Solomonic city (levels VA–IVB) was destroyed, and the structures found in the next level (IVA) are markedly inferior. At Beth-shean a sharp decline is also evident during the transition from the early to the middle Iron Age (level IV). Taanach, too, was reduced to ruins at that time.[15]

14 See in this volume, "The Aramean Empire and Its Relations with Israel", p. 162, note 26.

15 On the archaeological finds at Gezer, Beth-shean, Taanach and Megiddo, see the appropriate entries in *EAEHL*.

Archaeological exploration and research in the Yarkon area, through which the returning Egyptians certainly passed, show that at Tell Jerishe — which I suggest is the biblical Gath-rimmon (Josh 19:45) — the settlement was destroyed at the end of the early Iron Age,[16] while at Tell Qasile on the Yarkon River the transition from the early Iron Age (level IV) to the middle Iron Age (level VIII) is marked by a burnt layer.[17]

We note as significant the decline in the importance of the Succoth Valley and Mahanaim after the time of Solomon. The absence of the names Mahanaim, Penuel and Succoth from the sources after the Monarchy was divided cannot be accidental. We may also attribute to Shishak's expedition the final decline of such cities as ʿAruna, Yaḥma, and Gath-patalla in the Sharon, Reḥob in the Beth-shean Valley, Rubute in the northern Shephelah, etc. Only a thorough archaeological survey will confirm whether there was a complete change in settlement during the transition from the early to the middle Iron Age at these sites.

The Expedition to the Negeb

The second and much longer part of Shishak's list deals with the Negeb and adjacent areas. Some of the places mentioned are known, for example Ezem (no. 66), which is mentioned as one of the cities of Simeon (Josh 19:3),[18] and Arad (no. 113). Certain place names in the inscription are prefixed with the Egyptian article *p3* and *Negeb* (*p3-Negeb*). There is a parallel biblical usage, with the Hebrew article *ha*,[19] such as in *Negeb ha-Keni* (1 Sam 27:10) and *Negeb ha-Krethi* (1 Sam 30:14). We may assume that the second element in such geographical terms is the name of a family, or clan of nomads (or semi-nomads) living in the wilderness or grazing lands of the south. Thus, for example, we may explain nos. 92–93, *p3-Negeb ʾAsḥt*, as the Hebrew *Negeb ha-Shuḥati*. In fact the genealogical list in 1 Chr 4:11 contains the family name Shuhah.

Another element appearing as a component of geographical terms in this second part of Shishak's list is *p3-ḥaqar* or *p3-ḥagar*, i.e. *ḥagar* with the Egyptian article *p3*. *Ḥagar*, meaning "fort", is used with this connotation in Aramaic (*ḥagra*), in post-biblical Hebrew, and in Arabic.[20] No less than seven place

16 See B. Mazar, *IEJ* 1 (1950–1951), 63, n. 6.

17 *Ibid*., 139ff.

18 See E. Oren, *IEJ* 24 (1974), 26.

19 See note 9 above.

20 On the meaning of the term *ḥagar*, see Mazar, *Cities and Districts*, 132ff. Evidently in post-biblical Hebrew (*Mishnah Gittin*, Ch. 1, 1–2; *Bereshith Rabba*, 79:7) it has the same meaning as *limes* in the Roman province of Palaestina.

names in the second part of the list comprise this element, once in the plural form *p3-ḥagarim*, החגרים. In nos. 107–112 we read: *p3-ḥagarim ʿArad rabath, ʿArad n Beth Yeroḥam*, "The *Ḥagarim* (forts) Great Arad, and Arad of the House of Yeroham". The first-mentioned *ḥagar*, "Great Arad", is identical with biblical Arad (Tel Arad), important in the defence of southern Judah against the desert nomads.[21] The second, "Arad of the House of Yeroham", may be interpreted as referring either to the Jerahmeel family (1 Chr 2:25ff.) or to the Calebite clan of Raham (1 Chr 2:44). Among the other *ḥagarim*, we find *p3-ḥagar Ḥnn*, "the fort of Hanan" (nos. 94–95), and *p3-ḥagar twlwn*, "the fort of Tholon" (nos. 101–102) — the forts of the two families Ben-hanan and Tolon (*qere:* Tilon) mentioned together in the genealogical list of Judah in 1 Chr 4:20. It appears, therefore, that Shishak's list of *ḥagarim* fits the biblical network of *ḥaṣerim*, or fortified settlements in the Negeb. It is not improbable that the inhabitants of the Negeb called their fortified settlements *ḥagarim*, and that the Nabateans adopted the term *ḥagar* or *ḥagra* and continued its use into later times.

From the many places referred to as part of the Negeb, I shall mention only those that help us understand Shishak's campaign. Besides Tilon, Hanan and Shuhah, we find several family names from the Negeb that are known to us from the genealogical lists in the Chronicles: for example, *fltm* (no. 121), the Jerahmeelite clan Peleth (1 Chr 2:33) and *wnm* (no. 140) which is Onam, another Jerahmeelite family (1 Chr 2:26). Terms like ʾAbel, Beʾer, ʾAdar, Goren, Shibboleth appear as place names or as elements in geographical terms in this region. Shishak's list also mentions Adummim and Shilḥim. Shilḥim appears in Josh 15:32 (in place of Sharuhen, in Jos 19:6). Among the other toponyms recorded in this section, we can identify Yurza (no. 133) with the town of that name mentioned in the El-Amarna Letters and in the geographical lists of the kings of Egypt from the 19th and 20th Dynasties. I propose that Yurza be identified as Tell Jemmeh.[22] On the other hand it is difficult to pinpoint Elimoth and Beth-ʿanat.

A few entries which have been preserved at the end of the list show that Shishak returned home by way of Yordan (no. 150) which seems to correspond to Yorda, located on the southern border of Judah, mentioned by Josephus Flavius (Bell. III, 3:5). From there, he proceeded on his homeward march through Raphiah to Laban, a town near the Brook of Egypt known from an inscription of Sargon.[23]

21 The earliest of the series of fortresses uncovered by the Arad expedition appears to have been built by Solomon and destroyed by the armies of Shishak; see Y. Aharoni, *Enc. Miq*. 6, 375.

22 See B. Maisler (Mazar), *PEQ* 1952, 48f.

23 See A. Alt, *Kleine Schriften* 2 (1953), 226ff. Perhaps Laban is Tell Abu Sleima.

The second part of Shishak's inscription lists a great number of sites, regions, settlements, forts and families in the Negeb, and along the southern coastal plain of the Land of Israel. The bulk of the Egyptian army must therefore have advanced along the Via Maris. At the same time, and in order to protect his rear from the semi-nomadic tribes in the southern desert and to enable the main force to advance along the narrow coastal strip without hindrance, Pharaoh Shishak dispatched some troops into the Negeb, who penetrated deeply into the area as far as the region of Arad. They most certainly invaded these regions, and also struck at the southern defensive installations of the Kingdom of Judah.

The penetration of Shishak's forces into the Negeb and the destruction of so many settlements, forts and fortified camps along the caravan routes is well supported by other evidence. It is a fact that from the days of Tuthmosis III in the 15th century B.C.E., the rulers of Egypt always made sure that in their campaigns into Canaan they commanded the main highway ("the way of the land of the Philistines", Ex 13:17) and the roads branching off from it. They did this by digging wells, building forts and sending troops along the desert trails to the centres of the "marauders" (the *š3św* nomads) in the Negeb, to subdue them and bring them under Pharaoh's suzerainty. From the reign of Seti I, and throughout the 14th century B.C.E., the Egyptian sources refer profusely to such punitive expeditions against the nomads of the desert who were gaining in strength with the movement of nomadic tribes into the borders and the interior of Canaan. A particularly interesting document from the days of Ramesses II describes one such expedition, and provides a list of places in the land of Seir conquered by the Egyptians.[24] Shishak's dispatch of strong military forces to the Negeb, bringing ruin and destruction to its settlements and to the whole southern defensive network of Judah, is understandable. It came against the background of the policy followed by David and Solomon of intensively populating this area, and establishing forts and settlements along the main routes leading from Judah to Egypt, to Eloth (Elath) and Edom. The Egyptian forces did their work thoroughly, so thoroughly that, after Shishak's campaign, Rehoboam was forced to set up a new line of fortifications, encircling the Shephelah and mountains of Judah from the south and the south-west (2 Chr 11:5–10).[25]

24 See B. Grdseloff, *RHJE* 1 (1947), 63ff. It should be mentioned that Aharoni, *Land of the Bible* (see note 7), 328, suggests that *gbr* (in the combination: *šblt n-gbr*, "Shibboleth of Geber") should be identified with Ezion-Geber; this would mean that the Egyptian invaders reached the coast of Elath.

25 On Rehoboam's fortifications, see Abel, *GP* 2, 113–134; G. Beyer, *ZDPV* 54 (1931), 84ff.; M. Gichon, in J. Liver (ed.), *The Military History of the Land of Israel in Biblical Times* (1964), 410–425 (Hebrew). Alt's theory [*Kleine Schriften* (see note 23), 313f.] that the list refers to the time of Josiah must be rejected as groundless. See Z. Kallai, *EI* 10 (1971), 245ff. (Hebrew).

The Aramean Empire and Its Relations with Israel

The Rise of Aram

Mutual relations between Aram and Israel in the course of many generations are vividly described in the Bible. These ties were not merely the result of political contact through prolonged periods of time, in war and peace, but in a great measure were also the product of related origins and language, and of common traditions from time immemorial. This fact is amply documented in biblical sources, primarily in ancient patriarchal traditions about Israelite and Aramean ancestors who roamed the extensive region between Naharaim and Canaan sustaining themselves mainly from livestock breeding, and in the genealogical lists which emphasize consanguinity and common fate from patriarchal days down to division and settlement in separate and distant regions. An investigation of genealogies pertaining to Aram preserved in Genesis shows, first of all, that they are not of one piece and period; they reflect to some degree a historical development from which the wandering Aramean tribes emerged as an important factor in the political and economic life of the ancient Near East. This process effected important changes in the relations between Aram and Israel and related ethnic groups.

The oldest genealogy is that of Nahor (Gen 22:20–24), Abraham's brother. It affords us a glimpse of an ancient historical tradition about a cluster of nomadic and semi-nomadic tribes who had apparently reached the zenith of their strength in the 18th century B.C.E. The area of their

* This study is a revised version of the article published in *BA* 25 (1962), 97–120 and in *Biblical Archaeologist Reader* 2 (1964), 127–151.

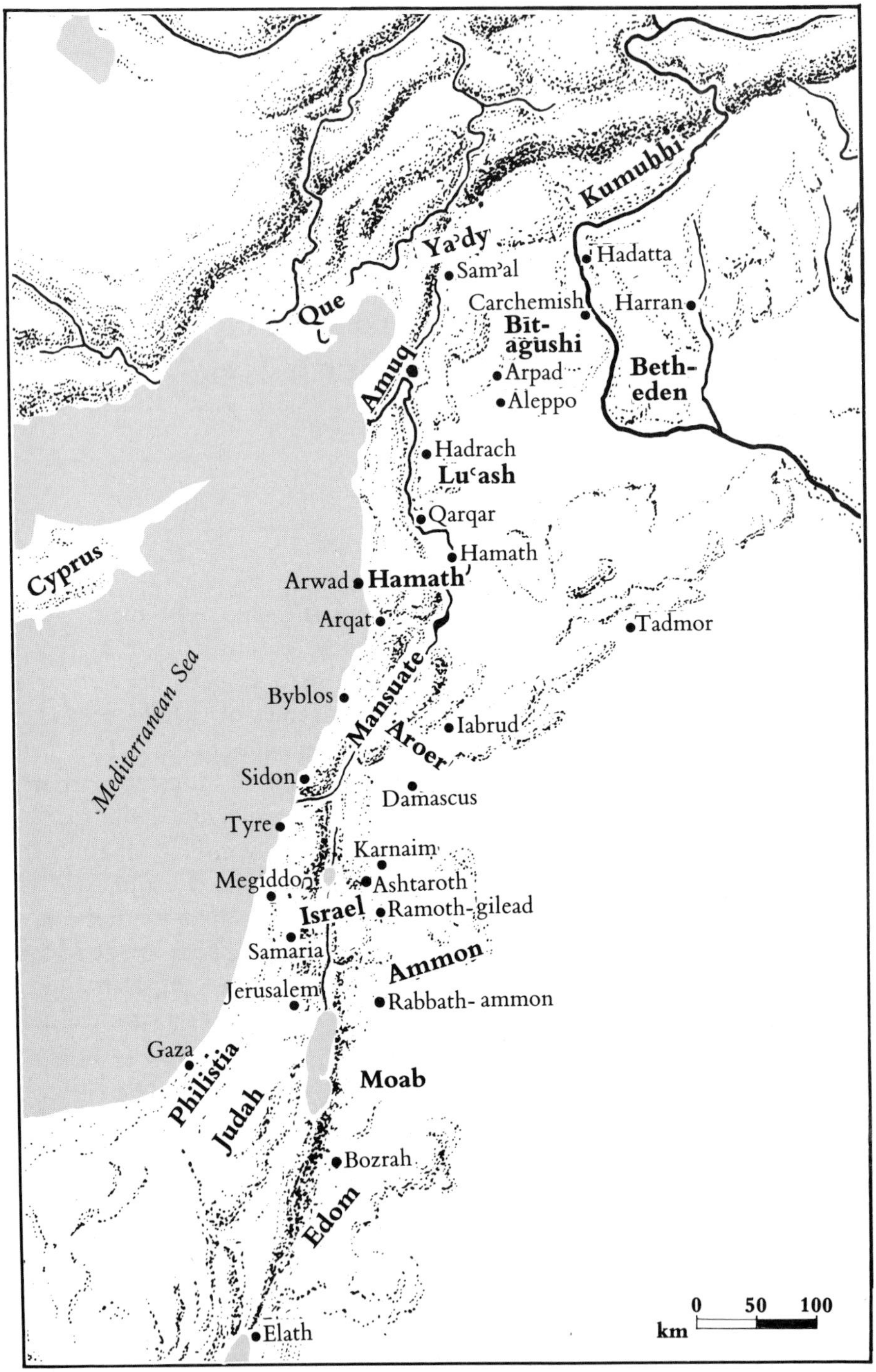

Syria and Eretz-Israel in the 9th–8th centuries B.C.E.

expansion stretched from the political-religious centre of Harran, where Nahor lived, to the Valley of Lebanon (Tebah and Tahash) and to northern Transjordan (Maachah).[1] In this list Aram is the son of Kemuel,[2] one of Nahor's sons; that is, Aram, the eponym of the Arameans, a younger branch in the organization of the Nahor tribes, was the grandson of Nahor, just as Jacob, the eponym of the Israelites, was the grandson of Abraham, "the father of many nations".

Another tradition, prevalent in Israel, bestows a position of great importance on Laban,[3] the son of Bethuel and the father of Leah and Rachel. In the genealogy of Gen 22, Bethuel[4] appears as Nahor's son and brother of Kemuel the father of Aram (v. 22), whereas in the cycle of stories about Jacob and Laban, the latter is described as an Aramean who lives in Aram Naharaim or Padan Aram,[5] that is, in Harran (Gen 27:43ff.) and in the neighbouring town, Nahor (Gen 24:10).[6] The Israelite folk tradition apparently ascribed to Jacob's father-in-law Laban the position of eponym of the Aramean tribes, who spread from their centre into the land of the "People of the East" (*Bene Qedem*) as far as eastern Transjordan, and there conspired against Israel (Gen 29:1).[7] Surely the story in Gen 31 deserves attention here. This narrative tells about the covenant between Laban the Aramean and Jacob at Mount Gilead, where they fixed the boundaries of their territorial possessions; as a witness thereof, they built

1 On several of the geographical conclusions here, see *Zion* 11 (1946), 1ff.; Mazar, *Canaan and Israel*, 11ff.; and in this volume, "The Historical Background of the Samaria Ostraca", pp. 173–188.

2 Kemuel is not found in extra-biblical sources. It is a West Semitic name mentioned in the Bible as that of the leader of the tribe of Ephraim (Num 34:24). Cf. the Transjordanian toponym "Kamon" (Judg 10:5).

3 On Laban as an epithet for the moon-god and his relation to Harran, the cultic centre of the mood-god Sin, see J. Lewy, *HUCA* 18 (1944), 434, n. 39, and 455f. It is noteworthy that Laban appears as a component in West Semitic names and in the geographical name, Mount Lebanon.

4 Bethuel, like Kemuel, is an ancient West Semitic theophoric name; see S. Loewenstamm, *Enc. Miq.* 2, s.v. "Bethuel".

5 On Padan Aram, "Field of Aram", see R. T. O'Callaghan, *Aram Naharaim* (1948), *passim*.

6 The town Nahor, which is in the vicinity of Harran, is known as an important city already from the Cappadocian Tablets (19th century B.C.E.) and in particular from the Mari Documents (18th century B.C.E.). It is also mentioned in inscriptions from the middle Assyrian empire (14th–12th century B.C.E.). See W.F. Albright, *BASOR* 78 (1940), 29f.; *idem*, *From the Stone Age to Christianity* (1957), 236f.; J.-R. Kupper, *Les nomades en Mesopotamie* (1957), 8ff.

7 In Genesis, "Qedem" is the name of the vast area from the eastern borders of Eretz-Israel to the vicinity of Harran, including the Syrian Desert (Gen 25:6). Balak, King of Moab, called "Balaam from Aram, from the mountains of Qedem" (Num 23:7), that is "from Pethor, which is near the River [Euphrates] in the land of Amu" [Num 22:5; see W.F. Albright, *BASOR* 118 (1950), 15], that is, Pethor of Aram Naharaim (Deut 23:5). As early as the Middle Kingdom, the Egyptians used this name; this we know mainly from the Sinuhe story (*ANET*, 19). On Qedem of the Egyptian documents, see S. Aḥituv, *Canaanite Toponyms in Ancient Egyptian Documents* (1984), 158.

a stone cairn, set up a pillar, and swore by their ancestral gods, "the God of Abraham and the god of Nahor" (vv. 44ff.).

The latest genealogical list is given in the "Table of Nations" (Gen 10: 22–23), where Aram, Asshur, Arpachshad, and others are counted with Shem; Aram's firstborn is Uz, the eponym of the large tribe. Uz appears in the older genealogy of Gen 22:21 as the firstborn of Nahor. The Table of Nations evidently reflects the period of large-scale expansion by the Arameans and their settlement throughout the countries of the Fertile Crescent, which began about the end of the 2nd millennium B.C.E. Therefore, in this author's time, Aram, the father of the Arameans, was considered to be the son of Shem and the grandson of Noah, and not, as in the older genealogy, the grandson of Nahor.

The cuneiform sources testify that the Arameans were but a relatively late ethnic group among the West Semitic nomadic tribes; they are designated *Aḫlamu* in Assyrian documents from the 14th century B.C.E. Only towards the end of the 12th century are they mentioned explicitly in the combination *aḫlamē-ʾaramaya* as nomadic and semi-nomadic tribes. At that time they spread through the Syrian Desert[8] and the border areas of Mesopotamia and Syria. The Assyrian king Tiglath-Pileser I (1114–1076 B.C.E.) fought them fiercely, mainly to weaken their pressure upon regions conquered by the Assyrians and to wrest from them the control over lines of communication to Syria and the Mediterranean shore.[9]

In the course of time, however, the Arameans not only gained enough strength to swallow up many West Semitic tribes, to gain control over vast regions in the Euphrates area and in north-west Mesopotamia (Aram Naharaim), and to break into southern and northern Syria, but also to impose their authority on Babylonia. This process initiated far-reaching changes in the ethnic and political scene of the ancient Near East. Already in the second half of the 11th century B.C.E. the Arameans had attained great power in large areas on both sides of the Syrian Desert and had even succeeded in settling and taking possession of them, in adjusting to living

8 Palmyra (Tadmor) certainly was an important centre of wandering Arameans, mentioned in the inscriptions of Tiglath-Pileser I as "Tadmar". On Palmyra, see E. Dhorme, *RB* 33 (1924), 106. Here we find an explanation for the mention of Palmyra as one of the cities built by Solomon, "Tadmor in the desert" (1 Kgs 9:18, following the qere; 2 Chr 8:4), because it served as the main station for caravans between the Euphrates and Damascus. Palmyra was in existence already in the time of the Cappadocian and Mari Tablets; cf. J. Lewy, *Symbolae Hrozny* 4 (1950), 369, n. 19.

9 It appears that it is from this period that the term "Aramean" in the sense of "nomad" was retained in the Israelite and Assyrian tradition: "A vagrant(?) Aramean was my father" of Deut 26:5, and "the fugitive, wandering Aramean" in Sennacherib's Taylor Prism, Col. 5, II, 22f. For the origin of the names "Aram" and the "Arameans", see R.A. Bowman, *JNES* 7 (1948), 65ff.; Kupper, *Les nomades* (note 6), 112ff.; A. Dupont-Sommer, *VT Suppl.* 1 (1953), 40ff.; S. Moscati, *JSS* 1 (1959), 303ff.

conditions in their adopted lands and in establishing ruling dynasties in the conquered countries. Having seized control of caravan routes, the lifelines of the ancient Near East, leading from Mesopotamia to Anatolia and Syria (including the desert roads) and having gained a foothold in the large centres and important stations for merchant caravans and nomadic tribes with their enormous flocks, they secured for themselves ever greater importance in international trade.

In their expansion to the south-west, the Arameans clashed with the Israelites who, already in preceding generations, had extended the borders of their settlement to the distant regions in northern Transjordan. This confrontation produced bloody and protracted wars for domination and over boundary disputes; it also gave rise to mutual influence and intermarriage in times of peace. Concerning this eventful period detailed information is preserved in the Bible.

Israel and Aram from the Bible

In the 11th century B.C.E., the Arameans penetrated en masse the countries of the Fertile Crescent which had a rich material and spiritual culture, and an ancient royal tradition; gradually they widened their area of settlement and control. It ought to be noted that during this time the great empires suffered notable decline. Already at the beginning of the 12th century B.C.E., the Hittite empire was shattered into fragments. Its large districts in Syria were inherited mainly by comparatively small Hittite kingdoms, such as Carchemish on the Euphrates and Hamath in middle Syria. The Egyptian empire fell from its mighty position during the second third of the 12th century B.C.E. and ceased to be a significant political factor in Canaan in the 11th century B.C.E. Babylon fell prey to its neighbours and to the Aramean tribes, while Assyria declined after Tiglath-Pileser I and was reduced to narrow borders. At the same time, three West Semitic nations, the Arameans, the Israelites, and the Phoenicians, were rising. These nations attained a great measure of power at the beginning of the first millennium B.C.E.

As far back as the end of the 11th and the beginning of the 10th century B.C.E., we encounter an important Aramean kingdom in southern Syria, Aram Zobah, ruled by the dynasty of Beth-rehob. Aram Zobah established a federation of Aramean and non-Aramean states in Syria and northern Transjordan, thus controlling the roads leading to Mesopotamia (see 2 Sam 8:3, 10:16, 1 Chr 19:10). The focal point of the Zobah kingdom, which included in its boundaries also Mount Senir (Anti-Lebanon), was probably located in the northern part of the Lebanon Valley. There we should look for the three main cities of Hadad-ezer ben-Rehob, the King of Aram Zobah, namely Tebah, Cun, and Berothai, which were conquered by David in his decisive battle with Hadad-ezer.[10]

The region of Damascus was one of the Aramean districts in the confederation under the leadership of Aram Zobah, whereas the kingdom of Maachah and the land of Tob in the northern part of the eastern Transjordan were presumably not Aramean as yet, but along with the kingdom of Ammon, an ally of Hadad-ezer's, were among the satellites. It is my opinion that in his wars with David, and especially in his great military expedition to Transjordan which brought him as far as the Valley of Madeba (1 Chr 19:7), Hadad-ezer sought to gain control over the "King's Highway" (see Num 20:17; 21:22), one of the essential caravan routes in international commerce, which led from Damascus along eastern Transjordan to Elath and Arabia. It is worthy of note that the kings of Aram Damascus[11] subsequently followed the same policies. However, these ambitions of Aram Zobah were frustrated by the young kingdom of Israel.

David, who firmly established the Israelite Monarchy founded by Saul, and around it consolidated the Israelite tribes in a permanent and lasting political-military and social regime, succeeded not only in conquering the countries bordering Israel but also in subjugating the confederacy of Aramean kings and their satellites up to the border of the Hittite kingdom of Hamath, the adversary of Aram Zobah. Hamath established intimate relations with David and apparently acknowledged his suzerainty (2 Sam 8: 9–11; 1 Chr 18:9–11) in southern Syria[12] and as far as the Euphrates in the north-east. Control over the extensive territories from the River of Egypt up to Lebo in the Lebanon Valley (Lebo-hamath), and over the main caravan routes to Mesopotamia and Arabia, raised the young Israelite kingdom to the level of one of the important states in the ancient Near East. David's

10 See A. Malamat, *BA* (1958), 82ff.; M.F. Unger, *Israel and the Arameans of Damascus* (1957), 42ff. For the disputed explanation of Hamath-zobah, see J. Lewy, *HUCA* 18 (1944), 443ff.

11 One ought to mention Hazael's military expedition to Gilead and his conquest up to its southern border at the Arnon River (2 Kgs 10:33). It is not unlikely that he proceeded southwards across Israel's border to Moab and Edom. This is borne out, indirectly, by a list of Adadnirari III's tribute payers after his expedition to Damascus, in which Edom is mentioned (Luckenbill, *AR*, 739f.). That Rezin reached Elath is explicity stated: "And he drove the man of Judah from Elath" (2 Kgs 16:6). After having conquered Damascus and incorporated it into their empire, the Assyrians continued the same policy. This accounts for the extreme importance of Damascus in Syria and its strong ties with Arabia under the Assyrians and in later periods. On trade with Arabia, see G. W. Van Beek, *BA* 23 (1960), 70ff.; W.F. Albright, *EI* 5 (1958), 7*, 9*.

12 See in this volume, "Lebo-hamath and the Northern Border of Canaan", pp. 189–202; and A. Malamat, *BA* 21 (1958), 101.

treaty with Toi, King of Hamath, and with Hiram, King of Tyre (the Sidonian kingdom), as well as the friendly relations with the rulers of Arabia in the days of Solomon and the development of trade relations with them (1 Kgs 10:1–13, 15), added much to Israel's political stature and economic power. According to a source preserved in 2 Chr 8:3–6, Solomon even succeeded in strengthening and broadening his control over Syria.

The districts under Israelite rule in the days of David and Solomon can be divided into countries in which David set up governors and states subject to Israel. About Aram Damascus we are told: "Then David put governors in Aram of Damascus; and the Arameans became servants to David and brought tribute" (2 Sam 8:6), whereas the story about the defeat of the armies of Aram Zobah and its satellites under the leadership of Shobach, Hadad-ezer's general, concludes with the words: "And when all the kings who were servants of Hadad-ezer saw that they had been defeated by Israel they made peace with Israel and became subject to them" (2 Sam 10:19). Especially noteworthy is the fact that in dealing with the kingdom of Solomon, Israelite historiographers emphasize that "Solomon ruled over all the kingdoms from the river [Euphrates] to the land of the Philistines and to the border of Egypt" (1 Kgs 5:1; 2 Chr 9:26).

It seems that late in Solomon's reign, when his rule weakened and the state was disintegrating internally and externally, the position of several conquered nations and particularly that of the Arameans changed. In this period of weakness, when Egypt's power waxed under the leadership of Shishak, the founder of the 22nd Dynasty, and a rebel movement was afoot in Israel, Aram Damascus took advantage of the opportunity, throwing off the yoke of the House of David in the period of Israel's decline. The reigning dynasty in Damascus, founded by Hezion,[13] made Aram Damascus the most important Aramean state in Syria. Hezion's grandson Ben-hadad I initiated aggressive policies against Israel. It is possible that he founded the coalition of Aramean states in Syria under the leadership of Aram Damascus which attained great power in the time of Ben-hadad II. This king of Damascus is mentioned in several interesting historiographical sources in the Bible. According to 1 Kgs 15:18–20, and 2 Chr 16:2–4, Ben-hadad I availed himself of the opportunity to interfere in a Judean-Israelite dispute and broke through the line of fortified cities in Naphtali, from Ijon and Dan to Chinneroth. This war most certainly took place in the twenty-sixth

13 Some time ago, in *Lešonenu* 15 (1944), 42f. (Hebrew), I expressed the opinion that Hezion ought to be taken as the proper name of the founder of the dynasty, and Rezon (cf. Prov 14:28) as his royal title. Some scholars assume that, after Rezon, Hezion was the founder of a new dynasty in Damascus.

year of Asa's reign (886 B.C.E.; 2 Chr 16:1 "the 36th year of the reign of Asa" is an error) which was Baasha's[14] last ruling year.

It seems that one ought to attribute to the period of Israel's decline after Baasha's death the historical information interpolated in the genealogical list of Judah to the effect that Geshur and Aram took Havvoth-jair as well as Kenath and its settlements — "sixty towns" (1 Chr 2:23). Evidently Aram Damascus and its satellite Geshur wrested Bashan from Israel — to be exact, from the district of Ramoth-gilead founded by Solomon (1 Kgs 4: 13) — and joined it to their states.[15] Undoubtedly the pressure of Aram Damascus on Israel did not slacken in the days of Omri. According to the testimony of 1 Kgs 20:34, Ben-hadad II's father Ben-hadad I captured cities from Ahab's father Omri and established bazaars in Samaria.[16] However, the assumption that Bir-hadad, the king of Aram, who dedicated to Melqart the stele found in the vicinity of Aleppo, is Ben-hadad I is problematic. This premise was based on Albright's proposed restoration of a break in the text, which is not satisfactory. The inscription seems to refer to Ben-hadad II instead.[17]

Much information about Ben-hadad, Ahab's contemporary, apparently Ben-hadad II, has been preserved in the Bible. It stands to reason that this Ben-hadad is none other than Adad-idri (Hadad-ezer), King of Aram, known from the inscription of Shalmaneser III, King of Assyria. It is even likely that Ben-hadad (Bir-hadad) is not a personal name but a title common to kings of Aram Damascus; it means "son of the god Hadad" (Hadad-rimmon, the god of Damascus).[18] Under Ben-hadad II, wrangling between

14 See H. Tadmor in *Enc. Miq*. 1, 469f., contra W.F. Albright, *BASOR* 100 (1945), 20. Albright accepts the Chronicler's date and proposes a new chronological scheme differing from the one accepted by most scholars, even identifying Ben-hadad of Baasha's time with Ben-hadad of Ahab's time.

15 See in this volume, "Geshur and Maachah", pp. 113–125. An excavation at Tell ʿEin Gev on the eastern shore of the Sea of Galilee uncovered evidence of the destruction of an Israelite city fortified by a casemate wall and its subsequent occupation by Arameans. Cf. *EAEHL* 2 (1976), 382ff.

16 1 Kgs 20:34; see G. Bostrom, *Proverbiastudien* (1935), 91ff., referring to the right given to the stronger ally to build business quarters for merchants in the large cities and especially in the capital of the state.

17 The inscription was published by Dunand in *BMB* 3 (1939), 65ff. Cf. W.F. Albright, *BASOR* 87 (1942), 23ff. See R. de Vaux in *BMB* 5 (1943), 9, n. 1; J. Starcky, in A. Dupont-Sommer, *Les inscriptions araméennes de Sfiré* (1958), 135, n. 1; and cf. F.M. Cross, *BASOR* 205 (1972), 36ff.

18 W.F. Albright, *BASOR* 87 (1942), 28, n. 16, is of the opinion that the kings of Damascus, like the kings of Israel, took on an additional name upon coronation. In my opinion, the parallel expressions "the house of Hazael" and "the palaces of Ben-hadad" in Am 1:4 allude to Hazael as the founder of a new Aramean dynasty. In a later Assyrian document Aram Damascus was referred to as *Bīt-Hazaeli*, "the House of Hazael", reflecting the name of the dynasty, in the same way as Israel became known as *Bīt-Ḫumri*, "the House of Omri" [see D.J. Wiseman, *Iraq* 13 (1951), 120–121], from which we infer that Ben-hadad was the title of Aramean kings in general. Also

Israel and Aram Damascus evolved into a protracted war which put Israel to a severe test. During the last years of Ahab's rule, when the kingdoms of Judah and Israel were enjoying some measure of political and economic prosperity, Ben-hadad II exerted extreme pressure on Israel in hopes of gaining control over the whole state. At that time Shalmaneser III (859–829 B.C.E.) was already terrorizing Syria with his military expeditions to the region of Samʾal (858) and his war with Beth-eden (857–855) which resulted in the conquest of this important Aramean kingdom in the Euphrates and Baliḫ regions and its annexation to Assyria. It is not unlikely that Ben-hadad's aggressive policy towards Israel and his attempt to gain control over it were intended primarily to secure his rear by turning the strong and flourishing kingdom of Israel into one of Aram Damascus' satellites[19] before the Assyrian king began his decisive battle for the conquest of Syria.

From a highly interesting historiographical source in the Book of Kings, we draw enlightening information about the Aramean incursion into the centre of Israel and about Ben-hadad's siege of Samaria, where Ahab had entrenched himself. This military expedition ended with defeat for Ben-hadad and his allies. The biblical story describes Ben-hadad as the head of the Aramean kingdoms: "Ben-hadad the king of Aram gathered all his army together; thirty-two kings were with him, and horses and chariots; and he went up and besieged Samaria and fought against it" (1 Kgs 20:1). There is no reason to assume that the number thirty-two was invented by the author. Among Ben-hadad's vassals were apparently not only the rulers of small states in southern Syria and Transjordan (as for instance Geshur and perhaps even Ammon), but also tribal princes from all over the Syrian Desert as well as the Aramean kings of northern Syria. This view gains force if one accepts the proposition that Ben-hadad II set up the Melqart stele found near Aleppo.

The dramatic description of the Aramean defeat by "the servitors of the governors of the districts" who were besieged with Ahab in Samaria, contains several interesting details. According to this story, which is part of a cycle of prophetic tales of the period of the Omrite dynasty, the attack surprised the Aramean kings while they were drinking in their booths: "And each killed his man and the Arameans fled" (1 Kgs 20:20). It is not unlikely that a bloody dispute broke out among Ben-hadad's followers, completely undermining the basis of the political alliance and precipitating its dissolution.

worthy of note is the parallel in Jer 49:27: "And I will kindle a fire in the wall of Damascus, and it shall devour the palaces of Ben-hadad".

19 It stands to reason that the Egyptians supported these policies of Ben-hadad.

Another narrative in the above-mentioned cycle (1 Kgs 20:22ff.) provides us with explicit information about basic changes in the structure of the kingdom of Aram Damascus. These changes resulted in the absorption of satellite kingdoms into Aram, following the defeat at the gates of Samaria. According to this source, Ben-hadad, on the advice of his ministers, instituted political and military reforms in order to renew with greater vigour the war against Israel: "And do this: remove the kings each from his post, and put governors (*pāḥōt*) in their places: and muster an army like the army that you have lost, horse for horse and chariot for chariot" (1 Kgs 20:24–25). One is not to assume that these words are bereft of historical basis,[20] for not only does the Israelite historiographer report them in all innocence, but they also fit the events which occurred between the fall of Beth-eden in 855 B.C.E. (echoes of which were still reverberating strongly in a much later period: Am 1:5) and the battle of Qarqar in the land of Hamath, where the coalition of Syrians, Phoenicians and Israelites headed by the King of Damascus lined up against Shalmaneser III (853 B.C.E.). The biblical story leads to the conclusion that the reform primarily accomplished the conversion of the loose coalition of Aramean kings under the leadership of Ben-hadad into the great united and sovereign Aramean empire, with Damascus as its capital. The satellite states were liquidated and turned into administrative districts headed by governors appointed by the king of Aram. Administrative reforms were followed by military reforms. Ben-hadad unified under his command the various armies of the satellite kings, and welded them into a mighty force. According to Shalmaneser III's testimony in his description of the battle of Qarqar, the army of Aram was composed of 1200 chariots, 1200 cavalry, and 20,000 infantry.

Results and Implications of Unification

The results of these military and political reforms, which for generations shaped the image of the Aramean regime, are clearly discernible in the subsequent period. It is important to note that biblical and Assyrian sources make no further mention of satellite kingdoms of Aram Damascus. In the battle of Qarqar, Hadad-ezer, who certainly is none other than Ben-hadad II, with a mighty army under his command, heads the coalition of twelve allies among which only one Aramean state — Damascus — is mentioned.

20 See among others, A. Alt, *Kleine Schriften* 3 (1959), 223f. Alt is not unaware of the fact that the author was acquainted with the life of the period, but he disqualifies the trustworthiness of the testimony concerning the establishment of a unified empire ("Einheitsstaat").

Beginning with the 9th century B.C.E., Aramean kingdoms in southern Syria, as well as non-Aramean satellites of Damascus, simply disappear from the historical arena. What is more, names of Aramean administrative districts, previously unknown in sources, begin to be mentioned. For example, the administrative unit Karnaim does not appear in the sources before the 9th century B.C.E.; it was named after the new capital of the district which was located in Sheikh Saʿad, not far from Ashtaroth, previously the capital of Bashan. Geshur, formerly an Aram Damascus satellite, was apparently absorbed into this district. It is not unlikely that Ben-hadad II not only founded the district Karnaim (Assyrian: *Qarnīni*) in Bashan but also its capital Karnaim, while Ashtaroth declined and became merely one of Karnaim's towns.[21] This, by the way, explains the name Ashteroth-karnaim in Gen 14:5; Karnaim here is used to locate the ancient city in the administrative division of later times.

Presumably the foundation of the administrative districts of Hauran in east Bashan and Manṣuate in the southern part of the Lebanon Valley[22] dates back to this time. Hauran is first mentioned in an inscription of Shalmaneser III describing his campaign against Hazael, and Manṣuate is known from Adad-nirari III's military expeditions. Both districts subsequently became Assyrian prefectures under Tiglath-Pileser III. It is enlightening that when the Assyrian scribe depicts the conquest of Damascus by Tiglath-Pileser III, he counts sixteen districts of the Aramean empire, despite the great changes in the political scene of Syria after the truncation of the empire. The Assyrians obviously did not change the administrative division introduced by the Aramean kings, which originated with Ben-hadad II as he centralized power in his own hands.

Ben-hadad's reform undoubtedly affected other spheres of life. Damascus became the metropolis of a mighty empire, the seat of civil and military government, and it dominated major lines of communication, the life arteries of east Asia. It became *the* city of Aram,[23] first in national, religious, and economic significance for the Arameans. It became "the famous city, the joyful city" (Jer 49:25; cf. Ezek 27:18), like Jerusalem, *the* city of Israel under David and Solomon. Not much is known about Damascus as a religious centre. By inference from several sources, one can conclude that Hadad, worshipped in Damascus under the name Raman (biblical Rimmon),[24] be-

21 Cf., Abel, *GP* 2, 413f.

22 Cf. M. Noth, *PJb* (1937), 42f.

23 It is likely that one of Damascus' names was *ʿīr ʾarām*, "the city of Aram" (to be compared with the designation of Jerusalem as "the city of Judah"). This is apparently the reading in Zech 9:1 for *ʿyn ʾdm* [A. Malamat, *IEJ* 1 (1951), 82, n. 13]. The variant reading *ʿyn/ʿyr* is frequent in the Bible (e.g., Josh 19:29, 41).

24 The epithet or divine title *Rāmān* known from Assyrian sources and personal names is undoubtedly of Aramaic origin. In the Bible, the vocalization has been adjusted to the Hebrew word *rimmon*

came prominent in the 9th century B.C.E. His temple, the remains of which are now covered by the Omayyad Mosque, was famous for hundreds of years down to Roman times as that of "Jupiter Damascinus".[25]

It is not at all unlikely that the use of the name Ben-hadad as the common title for Damascus kings originated in the cultic-religious relationship between the rulers of the locality and their god. We encounter the composite name of the god Hadad-rimmon in Zech 12:11, where reference is made to mourning for him in the Valley of Megiddo. This certainly was a religious ceremony performed regularly in the sanctuary on the crossroads near Megiddo and derived from the cult practiced in the royal temple of Hadad-rimmon in Damascus,[26] which is referred to as Beth-rimmon (2 Kgs 5:18). It stands to reason that the priest Uriah patterned the altar in the temple of Jerusalem which he built by order of Ahaz, King of Judah (2 Kgs 16:10–13), after the altar in Beth-rimmon. Furthermore, the story about Ahaz emphasizes the high esteem in which the Damascene cult was held in Jerusalem: "He sacrificed to the gods of Damascus which had defeated him and said: 'Because the gods of the kings of Aram helped them, I'll sacrifice to them that they may help me'" (2 Chr 28:23). The divine title Rimmon which we encounter as a compound of the theophoric name of King Tabrimmon, son of Hezion, and which was common among the Arameans at least from the beginning of the 9th century B.C.E., gained particular importance after Damascus became the metropolis of Aram.[27]

("pomegranate"), which is appears in the names of several places in Eretz-Israel. In my opinion, *rāmān* is an extended form of *rām* with the suffix *-an*; at first it was a divine title like *Rām* or *ʿElyōn* (in the Sefire treaty *ʿlyn*). It stands to reason that from time immemorial the deity of Damascus was Hadad, one of whose major cultic centres was in Aleppo; the Aramaic epithet *rāmān* was attached to him after the Arameans took Damascus. But cf. J. Greenfield's opinion (*Enc. Miq*. 7, 377, s.v. "Rimmon") that the correct form is *Rammānu* from *ramāmu*, "to roar", an epithet of the thunder god.

25 For the place of Hadad's temple in Damascus, see R. Dussaud, *Syria* 3 (1922), 219ff.; worthy of note is the orthostat from Damascus' heyday as the capital of Aram, depicting a "cherub" in Syrian (Aramean) style. It was found, not *in situ*, in one of the ancient walls on the grounds of the Omayyad Mosque [Djafar Abel-Kadr, *Syria* 25 (1949), 191ff.].

26 According to Jerome in his commentary on Zechariah, Hadad-rimmon is the ancient name of Maximianopolis (Legio) that took the place of Megiddo; Jerome may have been influenced by a folk tradition which linked Hadad-rimmon with Gath-rimmon (Josh 21:25). There was presumably a sanctuary of Hadad-rimmon on the crossroads of the Megiddo plain, not far from the Assyrian district capital of Megiddo. There may have been some connection between this sacred ground and the threshing floor (Adar, no. 28 and Yad Hammelek, no. 29) mentioned alongside Megiddo (no. 27) in the Shishak inscriptions (see in this volume, "Pharaoh Shishak's Campaign to the Land of Israel", pp. 139–150).

27 On Rāmān, see H. Schlobies, *MDOG*, I:3 (1925), 9. In one list of gods [see O. Schröder, *Keilschrifttexte aus Assur verschiedenen Inhalts*, 64, V, 5], "Rāmān of the Mountain" is identified with Amurru, which raises him to the status of the god of the west (Syria), apparently because of the

The formation of the Aramean empire raises the problem of the official language used in royal offices in Damascus, in the districts throughout the empire, in trade, and in contact with neighbouring states. This problem is linked with the origin and dissemination of imperial Aramaic which, as is known, was current as the *lingua franca* in the Persian empire from India to Ethiopia, and to a lesser degree was the official language of diplomacy, administration, and business under the Assyrians and Babylonians in the 8th to 6th centuries B.C.E. We shall merely point to the fact that already in the 8th century B.C.E. Aramaic had spread well beyond the boundaries of Aramaic-speaking countries. Assyrian documents from the 8th–7th centuries B.C.E. mention Aramean scribes in the service of the Assyrian government. Also the officers of Hezekiah, King of Judah, turn to Rabshakeh saying: "Pray speak to your servants in the Aramaic language, for we understand it; do not speak to us in the language of Judah within the hearing of the people who are on the wall" (2 Kgs 18:26).[28] Evidently Aramaic emerged as the official language of the Aramean empire by the second half of the 8th century B.C.E. and spread all the way to Ya'dy (Sam'al) in the north and to the Euphrates regions of the Khabur and Baliḫ (for example in Gozan and Ḥadatta) in the north-east.

Of particular importance is the stele of Bir-hadad, King of Aram, dedicated to Melqart, which was found at Apis in the vicinity of Aleppo. It testifies that Bir-hadad's domain included the northern districts of the Arameans. Also worth mentioning is the ivory plaque from a bed board found at Ḥadatta (Arslan-tash) on the Euphrates, with an Aramaic inscription dedicated "to our

The ivory plaque from a bed board found at Ḥadatta (Arslan-tash) on the Euphrates, with an Aramaic inscription dedicated "to our lord Hazael"

unique position attained by the Aramean empire and its metropolis, Damascus. *Rāmān*, the epithet of Hadad, is clearly of Aramean origin, and Schlobies' view that he was originally the ancient pre-Semitic god of Damascus cannot be accepted.

28 For official or imperial Aramaic, see the summaries of F. Rosenthal, *Die aramaistische Forschung* (1939), 24ff.; A. Dupont-Sommer, *Les araméens* (1949), 82ff. For the Aramean scribes in the Assyrian

The stele of Bir-hadad, King of Aram (Musée National Syrien d'Alep)

lord Hazael" (*lmrʾn ḥzʾl*), [29] in all probability none other than Hazael, King of Aram, who ruled in Damascus after the death of Bir-hadad II, founding a new dynasty and appreciably extending Aramean dominion. Also, the stele of Zakur, King of Hamath and Luʿash, inscribed in official Aramaic, is to be attributed to the end of the 9th century B.C.E., or at the latest to the first quarter of the 8th century[30].

administration, see J. Lewy, *HUCA* 25 (1954), 188ff. H. Tadmor brought to my attention the fact that an Aramean epistle (*egirtu armītu*) is mentioned in a document from the second half of the 9th century B.C.E., in a letter of an Assyrian clerk to *Ashur-dan-apli*, son of Shalmaneser, most likely Shalmaneser III. See A.T. Olmstead, *JAOS* 41 (1921), 382.

29 See F. Thureau-Dangin et al., *Arslan-Tash* (1931), Pl. XLVII, 112a; R.D. Barnett, *A Catalogue of the Nimrud Ivories* (1957), 126f.

30 J. Lewy, *Orientalia* 21 (1952), 418; M. Noth, *ZDPV* 52 (1929), 124ff. In the Aramean inscription, Zakur describes his victory over Bir-hadad, King of Aram, that is Ben-hadad III, son of Hazael, who

The theory that official Aramaic was first instituted in the offices of the small Aramean kingdoms in the Euphrates region, or in those of the Assyrian government, is not convincing. It is more reasonable to assume that it originated in the Aramean idiom of Damascus where it developed and crystallized into a written language. When Ben-hadad II founded the Aramean empire, Aramaic began to be used as the administrative language in all of its provinces. Then it became the official language of diplomacy and business, and thus spread beyond the borders of that empire. With the expansion and consolidation of Assyrian rule over Trans-Euphrates, and in particular over the provinces of Aram, the Assyrian administration inherited official Aramaic as one of the languages of the empire. This view is supported by the fact that official Aramaic has none of the characteristics of east Aramaic dialects.

The preceding discussion does not exhaust all the implications of the establishment of a united Aramean empire in the middle of the 9th century B.C.E. Particularly deserving of mention is the cultural impact of the Aramean empire upon the neighbouring countries, including Israel and Judah. As is known, Eretz-Israel was for a long time under the political and cultural influence of the Phoenicians, from the time of David to the end of the Omrite dynasty. Traces of this, viewed against the alliance between the courts of Israel and Tyre, are clearly discernible in Israel's economic, religious, and cultic life, as well as in architecture, court practice, and upper class manners, and are strongly reflected in biblical literature and in material remains discovered throughout the country. When the Israel-Tyre alliance ended with the bloody purge of Jehu, Phoenician impact on Israel and Judah waned. Political, economic, and military pressure from Damascus brought Israel under the influence of Aram, and mutual relations affecting all areas of life developed between them. This explains the great changes in the culture of the country during the second half of the 9th century B.C.E., particularly towards the end of that century, as evidenced by archaeological excavations on the one hand and biblical literature on the other. The Aramean culture was eclectic, blending ancient Syrian with Phoenician and neo-Hittite ele-

had, with his allies, laid siege to Hadrach (Zech 9:1), Zakur's fortress in the land of Luʿash. Luʿash, which was populated by Arameans, was part of the Aramean empire, but after Adad-nirari's defeat of Damascus it was attached to Hamath, which was at that time an Assyrian ally. As can be gathered from the inscription, Ben-hadad III did not succeed in retrieving Luʿash for Aram, and it remained under the authority of Hamath, a fact attested by Zakur's title: King of Hamath and Luʿash. It seems that due to the annexation of this important Aramean country, Aramaic became the official language of Hamath alongside hieroglyphic Hittite; in the course of time Hittite was discontinued. This is an illuminating example of the spread of Aramaic as the official language of Syria. Some Aramaic inscriptions discovered at Hamath are from the 8th and 7th centuries B.C.E.

ments, as well as a constant stream of material and spiritual influence from Assyria.[31]

The biblical source discussed above (1 Kgs 20) implies that after the defeat of the Arameans at the gates of Samaria and the implementation of Ben-hadad's reforms, Aramean pressure on Israel did not cease, but was renewed with greater vigour. "In the spring Ben-hadad mustered the Arameans and went up to Aphek to fight against Israel" (1 Kgs 20:26). The battle took place in the plain south-west of Aphek, the border fortress of the former kingdom of Geshur, which was subsequently annexed to the Aramean empire. The Aramean army was again defeated and negotiations between Ben-hadad, who was entrenched in Aphek, and Ahab ended with an agreement and a peace treaty (1 Kgs 20:26–34). It appears that this treaty was concluded in anticipation of the great showdown at Qarqar (853 B.C.E.). There, Hadad-ezer was joined by his two sworn adversaries, Ahab, King of Israel, and Arḫilenu, King of Hamath, as well as Gindibu the Arab and Baasha the Ammonite and auxiliary forces from the coastal cities (north of Byblos) and from Egypt. Such an alliance testifies to large-scale and thorough planning, the result of Ben-hadad's initiative.[32]

This coalition, however, was created only to meet a crisis. Aram's pressure on Israel was renewed and even intensified, and Ben-hadad succeeded in gaining control over Ramoth-gilead and its district, undoubtedly for the purpose of imposing his authority on Transjordan and perhaps also on the whole kingdom of Israel. When Shalmaneser III's expeditions against Damascus in the years 841 and 838 B.C.E. weakened the Aramean empire, the old alliance fell apart. Hazael was left to stand alone against the mighty Assyrian army, while Jehu, the founder of the new Israelite dynasty, chose a policy of submission to Assyria. But when Assyrian pressure on Syria subsequently ceased, the empire under Hazael revived its strength. It succeeded not only in regaining control over Aramean districts in northern Syria and the Euphrates region, but also in conquering Israelite territories in Trans-

31 The clarification of this highly important problem in the cultural history of Syria and Eretz-Israel calls for a large-scale and exhaustive study of Syrian architecture, sculpture, pottery, ivories [see Barnett, *Nimrud Ivories* (note 29), 44ff.], and seals in the 9th and 8th centuries B.C.E. and their influence on Israel in that period. On the basis of indications from ceramic chronology, Y. Aharoni and R. Amiran [*IEJ* 8 (1958), 171ff.] proposed a tripartite division of the Iron Age in Israel: 1) Iron I — 1200–1000 B.C.E.; 2) Iron II — 1000–840 B.C.E.; and Iron III — 840–587. However, G.E. Wright [*BASOR* 154 (1959), 13ff.] argued convincingly that a date round about 800 B.C.E. (or 815 more correctly) rather than 840 is the critical transition point from Iron II to Iron III. From the cultural-historical point of view, the transition from Iron II to III is expressive of the decline of Phoenician influence and the rise of the Aramean empire before Syria and Eretz-Israel became an integral part of the Assyrian empire.

32 See W.W. Hallo, *BA* 23 (1960), 39f.

jordan (2 Kgs 10:32–33; Am 1:3) and perhaps in dominating the "King's Highway" along its entire length to the Gulf of Elath. In 815–814 B.C.E., Hazael launched his great campaign into western Eretz-Israel, proceeding along the coast to Gath on the border of Judah. Joash, King of Judah, was forced to capitulate to Aram and to pay Hazael a heavy tribute (2 Kgs 12: 18–19); the Philistine principalities possibly also became Aramean dependencies at this time. That is the indirect implication of the inscriptions of Adadnirari III, who obviously aimed at gaining control not only of Aram but also of its dependencies. Adadnirari mentions the fact that Israel (*Bīt Ḫumri,* "the House of Omri"), Philistia, and Edom were among the states which paid him tribute after his expedition to Damascus.

Consolidated by an efficient imperial regime and dominating the major trade routes, the Aramean kingdom thus reached its zenith as the strongest and most influential power in the western Fertile Crescent. The biblical historiographer is justified: "Hazael, king of Aram, oppressed Israel all the days of Jehoahaz" (2 Kgs 13:22; cf. 2 Kgs 8:2), "and the anger of the Lord was kindled against Israel, and he gave them continually into the hands of Hazael. Then Jehoahaz besought the Lord ... and the Lord gave Israel a savior, so that they escaped from the hand of the Arameans" (2 Kgs 13:3–5). This saviour was none other than Adadnirari III, King of Assyria, who by his military expeditions to Syria and Eretz-Israel succeeded in raising Assyria again to the level of a mighty military-political force and in weakening the power of the Aramean empire.[33]

In summary, we can say that, beginning with the mid-9th century B.C.E., the kingdom of Israel was severely tried by the mighty Aramean empire which had attained the level of a decisive ethnic, political, and cultural force in Syria. This took place at a time when the Assyrian giant had already begun to overawe the Trans-Euphrates region, being ultimately destined to swallow up Aram and Israel. Aram-Israel relations from the end of Ahab's rule down to Joash's time become clear if we bear in mind that Ben-hadad II consolidated the Aramean kingdoms in Syria into one state, officially named Aram, with its capital at Damascus. This was a vast empire occupying a central position in the political and economic life of the ancient Near East. Aram achieved this position by its successful consolidation of all the Aramean tribes, its excellent organization of civil and military administration, and the spread of Aramaic as the official language of business and diplomacy. Hazael, the founder of a new dynasty in Damascus, not only managed to preserve the stability of the empire, but also to broaden and strengthen it internally and externally.

33 See in this volume, "The Historical Background of the Samaria Ostraca", pp. 173–188.

The turning point in the fate of the Aramean empire came during the reign of Ben-hadad III, Hazael's successor. The campaigns of Adadnirari III, King of Assyria, brought about the dissolution of the empire; Damascus declined and was even conquered by Jeroboam II of Israel, only regaining some of its strength under Rezin several years before it was finally conquered by Tiglath-Pileser III when it became a district capital, a stronghold of Assyria in Trans-Euphrates.

The Sefire Treaty and Aram in the 8th Century B.C.E.

An impressive phenomenon in the history of the Arameans in Syria is their tradition of unity and distinctiveness, which remained unimpaired even when they were split up into small kingdoms and northern Syria replaced Damascus as their major centre. This is strongly attested in a treaty between Mattiel, King of Arpad, and Birgaʾyah, King of *Ktk*, dating approximately to 745 B.C.E. This treaty was written in Aramaic and preserved on three stelae which were discovered at Sefire about 24 km south-east of Aleppo.[34] We are informed that Mattiel, of the aggressive Bir-gush Aramean dynasty, succeeded in raising Arpad to a position of leadership in the Aramean empire in Syria; the ruler of *Ktk* was probably a vassal of the mighty state of Ararat (Urartu) which from 749 B.C.E. ruled over southern Anatolia and began to compete with its enemy Assyria for dominion over northern Syria.[35] According to this document, Mattiel represented not only Arpad (stele AI, line 4), but all of the Aramean states (*ʾrm klh*, "All Aram") separated into two regions, "Upper Aram" in northern Syria including Arpad, and "Lower Aram" in southern Syria (*kl ʿly ʾrm wtḥth*). The decisive passage, however, appears in stele BI, lines 9–10. It explicitly informs us that "All Aram" — with its upper and lower division — includes all of the provinces previously in the Aramean empire.

Regrettably, this important passage is defective, and its restoration is highly problematic. It undoubtedly contains a detailed description of Aram's boundaries, patterned after parallel biblical descriptions delineating the boundaries

34 A. Dupont-Sommer, *Les inscriptions araméennes* (see note 17), for stelae I and II; *idem*, *BMB* 13 (1956), 23ff. (stele III). Stele I was first published by P. Ronzevalle, *Mélanges de l'Université Saint-Joseph* 15 (1930–1931)as a stele from Sujin in the vicinity of Sefire, and has hence been known as the "Contract from Sujin". See also Alt, *Kleine Schriften* (note 20), 214ff., and J.A. Fitzmyer, *JAOS* 81 (1961), 178ff.

35 Dupont-Sommer at first proposed identifying *Ktk* with Kaška mentioned in Assyrian documents together with Tubal and Halah, but later postulated that Birgaʾyah is the title of Sardur II, King of Ararat.

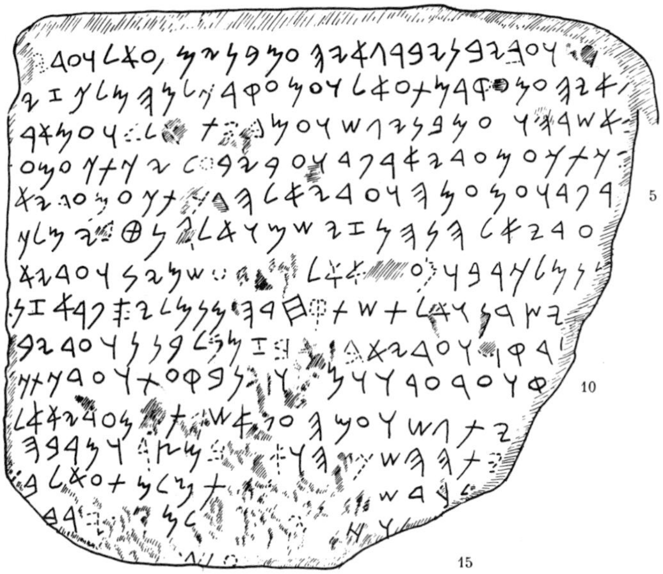

Stele BI from Sefire (lines 1–15) [A. Dupont-Sommer, *Les inscriptions araméennes de Sfiré* (1958), Pl. VIII]

of Canaan and the Land of Israel. Dupont-Sommer published the following transcription of the text with some restorations:

9. *mn]rqw wʿḋ yʾd[y w]ḃz mn lbnn wʿd yb-*
10. *[..........]q wʿrʿrw wm..w.[wm]n bqʿt wʿd ktk*

The uncertain letters are indicated by a dot above them. On the basis of a careful analysis of the photograph published in Dupont-Sommer's book, and in the light of biblical, Akkadian, and Greek sources for the historical geography of Syria, I propose emendations in the reading and an attempt to restore the two lines as follows:

9. *mn ʿ]rqw wʿd yʾḋ[y] w.z mn lbnn wʿd yb*
10. *[rdw wdms]q wʿrʿrw wm[nṣ]wṫ [m]n bqʿt wʿd ktk*

Here again the uncertain letters are indicated by a dot above them. The translation that emerges, then, is "from Arqu to Yad[iya and .]z, from Lebanon to Iab[rud, and Damas]cus and Aroer and Ma[nṣ]uate, from the Valley [of Lebanon] to Ktk".

Should this restoration of the text prove correct, it would contain a delineation of the boundaries of Upper and Lower Aram, in sum, of "All Aram". "Upper Aram" is the region stretching from Arqu (which is Arqa in the vicinity of Zumur on the coast, known from Tiglath-Pileser III's inscriptions and from the Arkite of Gen 10:17, and now Tell ʿArqa not far from the basin of the Nahr el-Kabir[36]) up to Aramean Yaʾdi-land, the capital of which was Samʾal (now Zenjirli), and thence to a place or province the name of which is not explicable in any satisfactory way.[37] As for "Lower Aram", its boundaries are well defined in spite of the defects in the document. Its north(western) border is marked by Mount Lebanon,[38] whereas the southern border is demarcated by four place names only one of which, Aroer, has been preserved intact.

Aroer brings to mind the passage in Isa 17:1–2: "An oracle concerning Damascus. Behold, Damascus will cease to be a city and will become a heap of ruins. The cities of Aroer are deserted; they will be for flocks, which will lie down, and none will make them afraid". Thus it is clear that Aroer is the fertile stretch of land in the vicinity of Damascus; hence, the word ending in *q* may be restored to read *Dmśq*, "Damascus". This would suggest that the other two words refer to cities or districts east and west of Damascus. Accordingly, the first, the first two letters of which are *yb*, can be read as *ybrd*, the city Iabrud, known from an Assyrian source and from the Hellenistic-Roman period.[39] Even now Iabrud is the name of a village located in an area rich in springs on the eastern slopes of Mount Senir in the vicinity of Nebk on the main road from Damascus to Aleppo, which branches off east to Palmyra. As to the fourth name, of which only the letters *m...wt* are preserved, I propose to restore it to read *m[nṣ]wt*, referring to Manṣuate of the Assyrian documents, located in the south of the Valley of Lebanon, west of the Oasis of Damascus.[40] To outline the boundaries, the author uses names of countries and of political and administrative units.[41] It is noteworthy that

36 This is the city ʿArqata mentioned in the Amarna Letters and Egyptian documents. In the inscriptions of Tiglath-Pileser III, the spelling is "Arqa", and in the Greek sources "Arke". The nominative suffix (cf. "ʿArʿarw" in line 10) deserves special attention.

37 While Dupont-Sommer's proposed restoration *yʾd[y]* is acceptable, his supposition, offered with some hesitation, that the second name is *bz* (that is, Buz, known from Jer 25:23ff.), is doubtful. More likely it is *ḥzz*, mentioned in the Sefire inscription (face A, 1. 35) as a "daughter-city" of Arpad and known as *Hazāzu* from Assyrian texts (Arabic: ʿAzāz, to the north of Arpad).

38 It is noteworthy that Mount Lebanon serves, in many instances in the Bible, to demarcate the northern border of Canaan (Deut 11:24, Josh 1:4), analogous to the fixed border point Lebo-hamath which is north of the Valley of Lebanon.

39 Iabrudu is mentioned in Ashurbanipal's campaign to Arabia (together with Zobah, Ammon, Edom, etc.; see *ANET* 298). Cf. also A. Rust, *Die Höhlenfunde von Jabrud* (1950), 3ff.

40 Manṣuate is mentioned in Assyrian sources beginning with Adad-nirari III who led military expeditions to Manṣuate in order to gain control over this important district of the Aramean empire which was blessed with rich iron deposits. Manṣuate was a district in the Assyrian empire [see M. Noth, *PJb* 33 (1937), 42f.].

41 This approach brings our document quite close to Ezek 47–48. Ezekiel outlines the future borders of Israel on the basis of the ancient "land of Canaan in its full extent" (Num 34), but intersperses

Iabrud, Damascus, Aroer, and Manṣuate are, in all likelihood, counted among the sixteen districts of the Aramean state mentioned by Tiglath-Pileser III in connection with the conquest of its metropolis. At the end of the passage, the author sums up the whole area of Aram by emphasizing its extreme borders; from the "Biqaᶜt" to "Ktk", that is from the Valley of Lebanon[42] in the south to the border of Anatolia. We have thus exhausted the content of the passage in stele I which spells out, in detail, the boundaries of Aram, and which indicates that as late as the third quarter of the 8th century B.C.E. "All Aram" was an accepted ethnic-territorial concept in Syria, though two or three generations had already passed since the united Aramean empire had disintegrated.[43]

"All Aram" and "Upper and Lower Aram"

These territorial expressions, "All Aram" and "Upper and Lower Aram", coined in the days of the Aramean empire, were preserved, surprisingly enough, down to the Hellenistic period. It appears that already in the Persian period the Greeks were accustomed to use the term "Syria" in a double sense: a) for Trans-Euphrates including Syria, Phoenicia, and Eretz-Israel (with Philistia), a name established apparently in the time of Sargon and current in the Persian period as the designation of the fifth satrapy; b) for Aram, that

his description with names of districts to bring the reader closer to the realities of his time. Cf. H. Tadmor, *IEJ* 12 (1962), 114ff.

42 In Josh 11:17, 12:7, 13:5, in place of Mount Hermon, Baal-gad in the Valley of Lebanon marks the northern border of Canaan. In contrast, our document refers not to a particular border point, but to the whole valley. The Valley of Lebanon is now called *el-Biqaᶜ*, "the Valley".

43 In the light of the Sefire inscriptions and a renewed investigation of the cuneiform sources [cf. H. Tadmor, *Scripta Hierosolymitana* 8 (1961), 232ff.], the events during the years 748–738 B.C.E. unfold as follows:

748/7 B.C.E.: The death of Jeroboam II, disorder in Israel; the end of Israel's rule over Damascus (the beginning of Rezin's reign?); the ascendancy of Arpad in Upper Aram to the chief Aramean state in Syria.

746/5 B.C.E. Sardur II's expedition to Kumuhhu and its transformation into satellite state; Carchemish a protectorate of Ararat; Tiglath-Pileser III ascends the throne of Assyria; establishment of the Aramean states' league ("All Aram" headed by the king of Arpad).

745/4 B.C.E.: Tiglath-Pileser fights the Chaldeans in Babylon and Namri on the Medean border; the treaty between Mattiel, King of Arpad, and Birgaʾyah, King of *Ktk*.

743 B.C.E.: Tiglath-Pileser's war against Sardur II: defeat of the Ararat army and its Syrian allies in the vicinity of Arpad.

742/1 B.C.E.: Tiglath-Pileser's march on northern Syria; the siege of Arpad.

740 B.C.E.: The fall of Arpad.

739 B.C.E.: Tiglath-Pileser's march on Syria; disintegration of the alliance and the defeat of Judah; conquest of Calneh; organization of Assyrian prefectures in northern Syria and on the sea-coast; tribute paid to Tiglath-Pileser by Menahem, King of Samaria, and Rezin, King of Damascus; Damascus' recovery and rise to the level of political centre of Lower Aram.

is, the territories of the Arameans in Syria, without Phoenicia and Eretz-Israel. This is the reason why Aram is generally translated in the Septuagint as Syria. The composite term *Koile Syria* appears already in the first half of the 4th century B.C.E. as the name of Syria proper in its restricted meaning, whereas the coastal area is called *Phoinike*, "Phoenicia". This is the case in the *Periplus* of Pseudo-Scylax, which gives a description of "Syria and Phoenicia". This division reflects the ethnic-territorial difference between the population of interior and northern Syria and the Phoenicians on the seashore.[44]

The etymology of the word *Koile* is interesting. E. Schwarz had already postulated that it is a Greek form of the Hebrew word *kol*.[45] A. Shalit[46] added further evidence and proved convincingly that *Koile Syria* is identical in meaning with the normal expression in Greek for "All Syria". However, the Greeks probably formed the name *Koile Syria* on the basis of the ancient term *arām kolā*, "All Aram", current among Aramaic-speaking people, the antiquity of which is attested by the Sefire inscription discussed above. Furthermore, the division of Syria into "Upper Syria" stretching from the Cilician border to the Orontes River and "Lower Syria" south of the Orontes, was still prevalent in the Hellenistic period. It is amply clear that this geographical partition reflects a tradition prevalent in Aramaic Syria and based on the old division found in the Sefire inscription.

After the conquest of southern Syria by Ptolemy I (Lagos), the term *Koile Syria* began to be used to designate the area of the Ptolemaic conquest; such usage of this name was consistent with Lagos' claim to the right of ruling all of Syria. The name was thereby given a new meaning from the point of view of the Ptolemaic rulers, and it was emphasized in this new sense by Diodorus, who actually uses *Koile Syria* for "Lower Syria" in distinction from "Upper Syria" which was under Seleucid rule.

The entire discussion of these names demonstrates that the concepts "All Aram" and "Upper and Lower Aram" were used in Syria from the time of the Aramean empire through the Assyrian, Babylonian, and Persian periods, down to the time of the Diadochi, except that in Greek "Syria" was substituted for "Aram".

44 Cf. K. Galling, *ZDPV* 61 (1938), 69ff.; E. Bickerman, *RB* 54 (1947), 257.
45 E. Schwarz, *Philologus* 86 (1931), 309.
46 A. Shalit, *Scripta Hierosolymitana* 1 (1954), 64ff.

The Historical Background of the Samaria Ostraca

The group of ostraca found in the area of one of the buildings at Samaria (the "Ostraca House") by the Harvard Expedition of 1908/1910[1] has justly attracted considerable attention among scholars. This epigraphical source consists of sixty-three Hebrew documents, some complete and some fragmentary, as well as a quantity of insignificant sherds. They represent invoices sent with jars of oil and wine, a tax in kind, to the court of the kings of Israel. The many problems connected with this discovery have naturally produced a rich controversial literature.[2] They relate to the administrative division of the kingdom of Israel, the system of taxing the rural population, and the topography of the Samaria region, besides linguistic and palaeographic questions.

The actual historical background of this source, however, and especially the problem of the date of the sherds, do not appear to have been dealt with hitherto in an entirely satisfactory manner. The excavators considered the ostraca to

* This study is a revised version of the article which appeared in *JPOS* 21 (1948), 117–133.

1 G.A. Reisner, C.S. Fisher and D.G. Lyon, *Harvard Excavations at Samaria (1908–1910)* 1–2 (1924) (henceforth *HES*).

2 W.F. Albright, *JPOS* 5 (1925), 38ff.; 11 (1931), 241ff.; M. Noth, *ZDPV* 50 (1927), 219ff.; B. Maisler (Mazar), *JPOS* 14 (1934), 96ff.; D. Diringer, *Le iscrizioni antica-ebraiche palestinesi* (1934), 21–74 (with bibliography on pp. 66–68, 339); Abel, *GP* 2, 95–98; S. Yeivin, *History of the Hebrew Script* (1939), 127ff. (Hebrew); S.A. Birnbaum, *PEQ* 1942, 107f; S. Moscati, *Epigrafia ebraica antica 1935–1950* (1951), 27–37; Y. Yadin, *IEJ* 9 (1959), 184–187; 12 (1962), 64–66; *idem*, *Scripta Hierosolymitana* 8 (1960), 9–17; F.M. Cross, *BASOR* 163 (1961), 12–14; A.F. Rainey, *IEJ* 12 (1962), 62–63; *idem*, *PEQ* 1967, 32–41; Y. Aharoni, *IEJ* 12 (1982), 67–69; *idem*, *BASOR* 184 (1966), 13–19; *idem*, *The Land of the Bible* (rev ed, 1979), 356–368; C.L. Gibson, *Hebrew and Moabite Inscriptions* (1971), 5–13; R. Gophna and Y. Porath, in M. Kochavi (ed.), *Judaea, Samaria and the Golan, an Archaeological Survey 1967/8* (1972), 200 (nos. 66, 80, 105, 132, 142, 148, 157) (Hebrew); W.H. Shea, *IEJ* 27 (1927), 16–27; A. Lemaire, *Inscriptions hebraiques* 1: *Les Ostraca* (1977), 23–81, 245–250 (with extensive bibliography).

date from the days of Ahab (first half of the 9th century B.C.E.). Most of the other scholars who dealt with the subject followed their opinion. However, Albright has — on palaeographical and historical grounds — proposed to assign them to the time of Jeroboam II (8th century B.C.E.).[3] J.W. Crowfoot, the director of the Samaria expedition from 1931 to 1935, was of the same opinion for palaeographic reasons and also in consideration of the ceramics.[4]

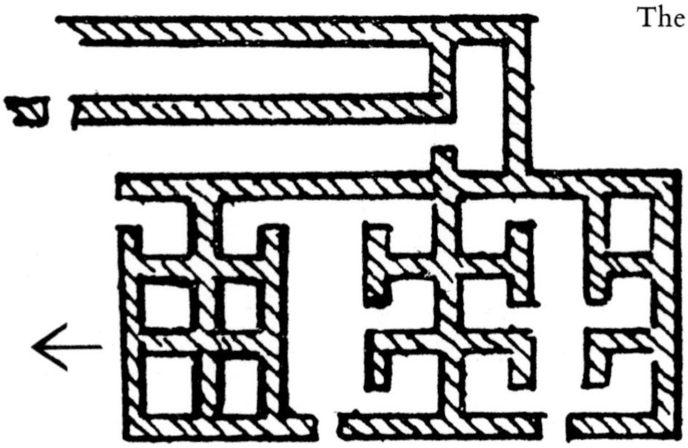

The "Ostraca House" (*EAEHL*)

In considering the chronological aspect, we should first pay attention to the "Ostraca House" itself.[5] The remains of this structure were found inside the acropolis of Samaria adjacent to the south-western corner of the casemate wall. The building and its courtyard, which lay to the north, were separated from the royal palace by a wall running from north to south. The western side of the "Ostraca House" was entered through two openings leading to two corridors. From these corridors, entrance was gained to three groups of square chambers, two of which each consisted of six rooms, while the third had only three chambers. The eastern side of the "Ostraca House" included two long rectangular halls (each approximately 21 m in length and barely 3 m wide) and one broad oblong chamber which adjoined them across their breadth. Although it is clear that the eastern and western sides of the "Ostraca House" were erected at the same time and are part of one building plan, no traces of a door connecting them have been found.

While there is still some doubt regarding the purpose of the three groups of square rooms, there can be none with respect to the two long and narrow

3 W.F. Albright, *From the Stone Age to Christianity* (1940), 314, n. 17; *idem*, *Archaeology and the Religion of Israel* (1942), 41, 122, 141, 160, 214, n. 41, 220, n. 110; *idem*, *AASOR* 21–22 (1943), 59.

4 J.W. Crowfoot, K.M. Kenyon and E.L. Sukenik, *The Buildings at Samaria* (1943) (henceforth *BS*), 8.

5 Fisher in *HES* 1, 114ff. and Figs. 42–43.

ones. It becomes more and more evident that they served for the storing of the oil and wine received at the royal palace in Samaria, in short that they were government storehouses of the type found in various Israelite cities.[6] The ostraca themselves were found in these two long chambers and in the part of the courtyard nearest to them. According to Reisner, they were found in "the lowest part of the debris of occupation"[7] of the "Ostraca House". It appears therefore that 1) the ostraca were collected in storehouses, perhaps together with the wine and oil jars; and 2) that they belong to the earliest phase of the building prior to changes and repairs, e.g., dividing walls in the long rectangular rooms.

As regards the architectural character of the "Ostraca House", it is worthwhile recalling the words of Fisher:[8] "The masonry was of totally different character from that of any of the preceding or following periods, and, so far as the excavations have been carried, was peculiar to this building". It seems, therefore, that, as far as the construction is concerned, there is no possibility of assigning the "Ostraca House" to the Omrite period; but at the same time we may not date it in the late period of the Israelite Monarchy. It seems that — following Crowfoot[9] — we should place it in the fourth (Period IV) of the six periods (I–VI) distinguished by the joint Samaria expedition. These periods comprise the time during which Samaria was the capital of Israel, from its foundation by Omri to its capture by Sargon II (viz. 880–721 B.C.E.).[10] The excavators assign Periods I–II to the dynasty of Omri, III — as it seems — to the time of Jehu, and VI to the end of the Israelite Monarchy. In fact the uncertainty exists only as regards Periods IV and V.

The excavators assign Periods IV and V — together with VI — to the 8th century B.C.E., down to the capture of the city by the Assyrians. Various considerations enable us, however, to establish with a fair degree of certainty a more exact synchronism between the history of Samaria, as known from literary and epigraphical sources, and the archaeological finds made by the joint expedition. First of all, a quite clear distinction may be made between the "fine masonry" of periods I–II and the masonry of III–IV; in the words of the excavators: "The new constructions which date from periods III–VI are built in a very different style". This difference may be explained by the cessation of Phoenician influence at the end of the Omrite dynasty, and the beginning of a new period — Period III — with the accession of Jehu.[11]

6 These buildings, mostly of the 10th century B.C.E., are discussed by W.F. Albright, *AASOR* 21–22 (1943), 22ff.

7 Reisner in *HES* 1, 227.

8 *HES* 1, 116.

9 Crowfoot in *BS*, 8.

10 *BS* 8, 93ff.

11 *Ibid.,* 8–9.

As regards Period IV, we should remember that, according to Dame Kenyon, "From the pottery the most important break would appear to be between Periods III and IV, but it is difficult to say whether this coincides with an important political event or not".[12] It appears, therefore, that the transition from III to IV is connected with some great crisis in the life of Samaria. This would agree well with the time of Jehoahaz, beginning with the great campaign to the Land of Israel undertaken by Hazael in 814/3 B.C.E., when the country suffered greatly from the Aramean invaders and the armies of Assyria appeared for the first time on its soil (806 B.C.E.). It was a period of decline in the history of the Israelite kingdom, to be followed by a revival in the days of Jehoash (early 8th century B.C.E.). This view is in good agreement with Dame Kenyon's opinion as regards the pottery of Period IV: "A date of about 800 B.C. would suit...."[13] This was also the period in which various repairs were made in the casemate wall[14] in order to strengthen the defences of the city, which during the period under consideration was certainly besieged more than once. On the occasion of one of these repairs to the wall, the "Ostraca House" was constructed. From these considerations it follows that we may assign Period IV (and IVa) to the reigns of Jehoahaz and Jehoash. Period V is marked *inter alia* by "a fairly complete reconstruction of the buildings on the north of the courtyard".[15] Apparently this was a time of renewed prosperity, such as fits well the reign of Jeroboam II.

Yet, although the archaeological data discussed serve to fix with a fair degree of certainty the date of the "Ostraca House" — and in consequence that of the ostraca themselves — at the end of the 9th century B.C.E., an exact determination can be reached only by an examination of their script, and in particular, of their content. As mentioned above, both Albright and Crowfoot based their datings of the ostraca in the reign of Jeroboam II on the script. However, the palaeographic examination has met with many difficulties. The ostraca were written in ink, while the only comparative material in our possession consists of incised script on stelae.

The comparison of the ostraca with the Mesha stele (ca. 845 B.C.E.) is of special interest (see Table opposite). The Mesha script is clearly more archaic, even if we discount the monumental character of the inscription. It is much more similar to the classical Phoenician of the documents from Byblos, Cyprus and Sardinia from the 10th–9th centuries B.C.E. It suffices to compare the letters *waw, samekh, ṣade* and *qof*, in order to note the great difference between the Mesha stele and the ostraca. On the other hand, the ostraca script appears

12 *Ibid.,* 105.
13 *Ibid.*
14 *Ibid.,* 99f., 103.
15 *Ibid.,* 106ff.

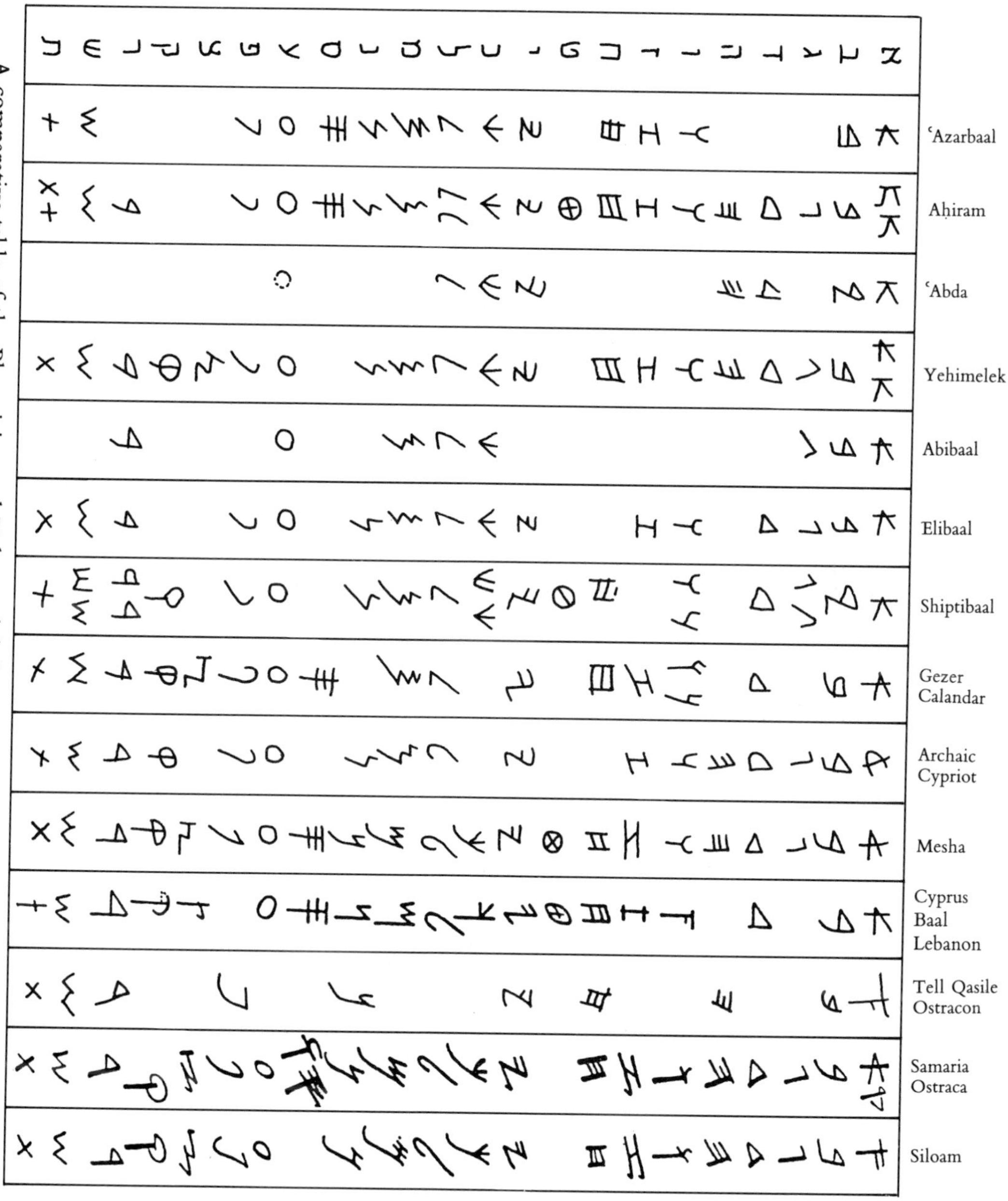
ʿAzarbaal
Aḥiram
ʿAbda
Yehimelek
Abibaal
Elibaal
Shiptibaal
Gezer Calandar
Archaic Cypriot
Mesha
Cyprus Baal Lebanon
Tell Qasile Ostracon
Samaria Ostraca
Siloam

A comparative table of the Phoenician and Hebrew alphabetic writing in the 11th–8th centuries B.C.E.

in the following period in Israel and Judah, as is shown, *inter alia*, by that of the Siloam inscription, which is very much later (ca. 700 B.C.E.). The above may be explained as follows:

a) There is a difference in time between the Mesha stele and the ostraca, although we are not able to determine it.

b) From the time of David and Solomon till the end of the Omrite dynasty, the classical Phoenician script was used in Israel, and we should attribute this fact to the continuation of the Sidonian-Phoenician influences throughout this period. And whereas Moab formed a part of the Israelite monarchy till the death of Ahab, there is nothing astonishing in the fact that this script was employed in the Mesha stele, which was inscribed a short time after the liberation of Moab from Omrite rule.

c) It is by no means impossible that the flowing script which we find in Israel and Judah in the 8th and 7th centuries B.C.E. was first developed by the Israelite scribes after the cessation of the Phoenician influence. The classical Phoenician script was not forgotten, but was employed mainly for monumental inscriptions.

It follows from the above that the script cannot serve as a firm basis for the dating of the Samaria ostraca; the palaeographic study can only show that the ostraca should not be assigned to the period of the Omrite dynasty, and especially not to the period of Ahab, which preceded the Mesha stele.

When the attribution of the ostraca to the time of Ahab is thus definitely discarded, there remain only three possible reigns to which they can be assigned, viz. those of Jehu, Jehoahaz the son of Jehu, and Jeroboam II. The regnal years mentioned in the ostraca themselves eliminate other possibilities. Usually the receipts begin with a dating formula: "In the ninth year from *Šptn* to *Baᶜalzemer* a skin of old wine" (*Bšt.htšᶜt/mšptn lbᶜl/zmr. nbl yn/yšn*). At least eight ostraca date from the ninth year, fourteen from the tenth year, twenty-six from the fifteenth year, and one from the seventeenth year.[16] As undoubtedly all of them belong to the reign of one and the same Israelite king (despite slight changes in the formulae), the king can only be either Jehu, who reigned twenty-eight years (2 Kgs 10:36), or Jehoahaz, who reigned seventeen years (*ibid.*, 13:1), or Jeroboam II, who reigned forty-one years (*ibid.*, 14:23). No other Israelite king following Ahab reigned seventeen years or more.

16 On the year seventeen in ostracon 63, see Reisner in *HES* 1, 243; Diringer, *Le iscrizioni* (note 2), 57f.; Albright, *Archaeology and the Religion* (note 3), 220, n. 110; N.H. Torczyner, *Lachish Letters* (1940), 203ff. (Hebrew). Although the sign for five in this ostracon is different from the usual one, the above scholars were obviously right in their identification, as there is no other number between one and ten for which a special sign is used. The ostraca from Arad as well as from Kadesh-barnea provide conclusive evidence for the use of Egyptian hieratic numerals in the Hebrew script.

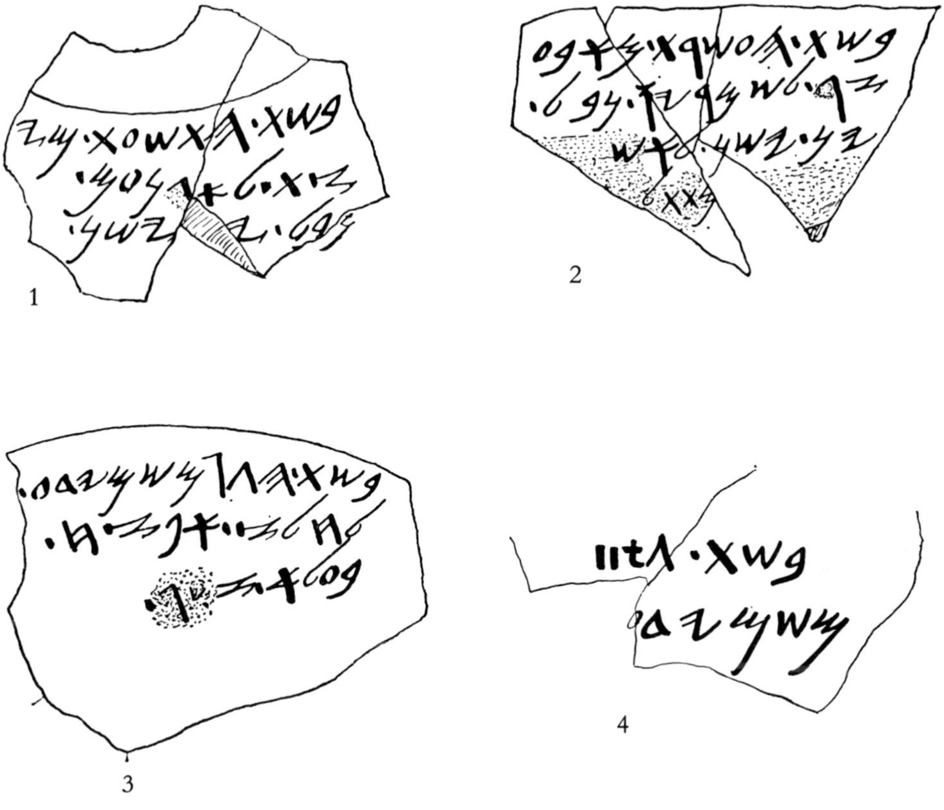

Ostraca from Samaria: 1) no. 9 from the ninth year; 2) no. 13 from the tenth year; 3) no. 31 from the fifteenth year; and 4) no. 63 from the seventeenth year

If we come to consider which of the three kings mentioned above is the most likely candidate, we arrive at the conclusion that it is Jehoahaz the son of Jehu. For, in addition to the archaeological data stated above, which point to the reign of this king, we must also consider that none of the ostraca date from before the ninth or after the seventeenth year. As for the terminal date, this is especially decisive as regards Jeroboam II, but hardly less so in the case of Jehu. It does not affect the case of Jehoahaz, who was king for seventeen years. The considerable number of ostraca (sixty-three, of which forty-eight are dated certainly) shows that these date limitations are not accidental. If the ostraca had been written in the days of Jeroboam, we should expect at least a few dated from the eighteenth to the forty-first regnal year.

It seems that on the basis of the historical information available from the Assyrian inscriptions and the Bible, we are able to explain not only the fact that the last date mentioned in the ostraca is the year seventeen, but even why the earliest is the year nine. In other words, the "Ostraca House" — or, more exactly, the three long rooms — was first used as a royal storehouse in the ninth year of Jehoahaz and it ceased to serve as such in the last year of this king. Jehoahaz began to reign after the death of his father Jehu in the twenty-third year of Joash, King of Judah (2 Kgs 13:1). This was a year of crisis in the history of the Israelite kingdom. Hazael, King of Damascus, who had succeeded in conquering the whole of Gilead (2 Kgs 10:33), crossed into western Eretz-Israel, defeated the Israelite army and invaded the land of the Philistines. He captured, among other cities, Gath (= Gittaim — Rās Abu Ḥamid)[17] and prepared to attack Jerusalem. The latter was saved through the payment of a heavy tribute by Joash (2 Kgs 12:18–19). The story told in Ch. 12 of 2 Kgs makes it quite clear that it refers to the twenty-third year of Joash, the year in which Jehu died, and it is possible that the death of Jehu is connected with these historical events. According to the most probable dating, that of E.R. Thiele,[18] these events must be fixed between Tishri 814 and Nissan 813; according to other calculations, they took place in 815–814 B.C.E.[19]

The first years of the rule of Jehoahaz were a time of decline and abasement in Israel: "But Hazael king of Aram oppressed Israel all the days of Jehoahaz" (2 Kgs 13:22). The general situation is well reflected in the prophecy uttered by the prophet Elisha to Hazael in 2 Kgs 8:12. As long as Hazael was alive, and for some time in the reign of his son Ben-hadad, the hand of Aram was heavy upon Israel: "Neither did he, the king of Aram, leave of the people to Jehoahaz but fifty horsemen and ten chariots and ten thousand(?) footmen; for the king of Aram had destroyed them and had made them like the dust by threshing" (2 Kgs 13:7). We should undoubtedly assign to this period many of the stories of the Elisha cycle, such as that about Naaman, which points clearly to the subjection of the king of Israel to the king of Aram (2 Kgs 5:1–7), the story of Dothan, which goes to show that at this time Aramean rule extended as far as this city in the northern part of the mountains of Samaria (2 Kgs 6:7–20), and the narrative describing the siege of Samaria (2 Kgs 6:24–7:20).[20]

17 Cf. B. Mazar, *IEJ* 4 (1954), 227–235.

18 E.R. Thiele, *JNES* 3 (1944), 152, 184; *idem*, *The Mysterious Numbers of the Hebrew Kings* (2d ed, 1965), 72.

19 According to J. Morgenstern [*Amos Studies* 1 (1941), 382], Jehoahaz reigned from 814–798 B.C.E., while W.F. Albright [*BASOR* 100 (1945), 21] suggested that he ruled from 815–801 B.C.E.

20 These stories cannot by any means be attributed to the time of the Omrite dynasty, for instance to the days of Jehoram, because till the death of this king (i.e., till the end of the dynasty) the area of Ramot-Gilead was still the boundary between Israel and Aram, and there is no mention of any

Unquestionably, the Israelite kingdom was reduced during this period to very narrow boundaries, practically to the district of Samaria alone, the neighbourhood of the capital. However, as early as the reign of Jehoahaz Israel's position improved: "And Jehoahaz besought the Lord ... and the Lord gave Israel a saviour so that they went out from under the hand of Aram..." (2 Kgs 13:4–5);this favourable turn in events lasted till the end of the rule of Jehoahaz, when again there was a change for the worse in the history of Israel and Judah. For, according to 2 Chr 24:23ff., a great historical event took place during the reign of Joash, King of Judah: the army of Aram invaded Judah and approached Jerusalem "and destroyed all the princes of the people from among the people and sent all the spoil of them unto the king of Damascus ... and when they were departed from him [Joash] (for they left him in great diseases) his own servants conspired against him ... and slew him on his bed and he died". There is no reason for denying the authenticity of this story or for regarding it as another version of the events in the twenty-third year of Joash. It refers expressly to the end of his reign, and it gives the background of the revolt, as a consequence of which Joash perished and his son Amaziah began to reign in his stead.

It seems that Joash died in 797/6 B.C.E., while the death of Jehoahaz occurred in 798.[21] In any case the interval between their deaths was not a long one, as is indicated in 2 Kgs 14:1. There it is stated that Amaziah the son of Joash, King of Judah, began to reign in the second year of Joash son of Jehoahaz, King of Israel. In my opinion there exists a close connection between the invasion of Ben-hadad, as told in 2 Chr 24, and the death of Jehoahaz. We may attempt to reconstruct the events as follows: at an opportune moment, when the Assyrian campaigns in the west had ceased for a long time, Ben-hadad attacked the kingdom of Israel and Jehoahaz perished in this war or as a consequence of it. The army of Aram continued southwards, invaded Judah, and perpetrated a great massacre in Jerusalem and Judah. This caused a revolt in Jerusalem and Joash perished during this revolt about a year after the Aramean invasion. The account in 2 Kgs 13:24–25 is in accordance with what has been stated above: "So Hazael king of Aram died and Ben-hadad his son reigned in his stead. And Jehoash the son of Jehoahaz took again out

expansion of Aram in western Eretz-Israel. It is clear that the catastrophe came only at the end of Jehu's reign. It should also be noted that the friendly relations between Elisha and the king of Israel in these stories belong rather to the time of Jehu and his dynasty. The only reign which fits this context is, therefore, that of Jehoahaz. Cf. Morgenstern, *Amos Studies* (see note 19), 368, n. 269. It appears also that the ruin of Megiddo IV should be assigned to the great campaign of Hazael in the years 814/3 B.C.E.; cf. W.F. Albright, *AASOR* 21–22 (1943), 2, n. 1.

21 For the chronological problems of this period, cf. E.R. Thiele, *JNES* 3 (1944), 152ff; H. Tadmor, *Enc. Miq*. 4, 279–280.

of the hand of Ben-hadad the cities which he had taken out of the hand of Jehoahaz his father by war". It appears that Jehoash restored to Israel the cities which had been captured by Ben-hadad from Jehoahaz apparently in the course of the Aramean campaign of 798 B.C.E., which led to a change of kings at Samaria.

Information derived from the Assyrian sources from the time of Adadnirari III conforms with the biblical narrative outlined above. Adadnirari began to reign in 810 B.C.E. According to the Sabaʿa stele,[22] Adadnirari commanded his armies to attack the land of *Ḫatti* — the common name for Syria in Assyrian documents[23] — in his fifth regnal year, viz. 806/5 B.C.E.[24] According to the Eponymic Chronicle,[25] he warred against Arpad in northern Syria in 805 B.C.E., advanced to the sea shore in 802, and in 796 again marched to the west, this time against Manṣuate, a district of the kingdom of Damascus in the south of the Lebanon Valley.[26] The aim of these campaigns[27] was to weaken the Aramean kingdoms of Arpad and Damascus, which were prominent in the last quarter of the 9th century B.C.E. The war against Manṣuate was certainly undertaken to restrain the king of Damascus, who had defeated Jehoahaz in 798 B.C.E. (as suggested above), and Adadnirari's campaign against the king of Aram in 796 B.C.E. was the opportunity for Israel to make headway against the enemy in the north and to entirely throw off the yoke of Damascus.[28] It seems that the inscription of Zakur, the King of Hamat and Luʿash,

22 Luckenbill, *AR*, 1, 261, §§734–735. The stele was published by E. Unger, *Reliefstele Adadniraris III aus Sabaʿa und Semiramis* (1916); H. Tadmor, *Iraq* 35 (1973), 144–145.

23 On the reading *Ḫatti* and not *Palaštu* (Unger's reading), cf. H. Tadmor, *IEJ* 19 (1969), 47.

24 See A. Poebel, *JNES* 2 (1943), 78, for the chronological problems involved.

25 Luckenbill, *AR* 2, 433, §1198; A. Ungnad, *RLA* 2, 429.

26 On Manṣuate, cf. in this volume, "The Aramean Empire and Its Relations with Israel", pp. 151–172, n. 26.

27 More details pertaining to Adadnirari's campaign in northern Syria against Arpad and Damascus may be gleaned from the stelae of Tell er-Rīmaḥ [S. Page, *Iraq* 20 (1968), 139–153] and Tell Sheikh Ḥamad [A.R. Millard and H. Tadmor, *Iraq* 35 (1973), 57–64]. As for the relation between the information in Adadnirari's stelae and the Eponymic Chronicle, cf. Millard and Tadmor, *ibid.* (with bibliography); B. Oded, in B. Oded, U. Rappaport et al., *Studies in the History of the Jewish People and the Land of Israel* 2 (1972), 25–34 (Hebrew); A. Malamat, in *ibid.*, 35–37.

28 According to the stele from Tell er-Rīmaḥ [S. Page, *Iraq* 20 (1968), 139–153], Adadnirari received the tribute of *Ia-ʾa-su* ^{māt}*Sa-me-ri-na-a-a*, "Joash the Samaritan", viz. Jehoash, King of Israel. Malamat [in *History of the Jewish People* (see note 28), 36–37] proposed reading the name *Iu-ʾa-su*, suggesting that the appellative "the Samaritan" refers to the restricted territory of the kingdom of Jehoash at the beginning of his reign. When Jehoash paid this tribute to the Assyrian king is a matter for debate. H. Cazelles (*CRAIBL* 1969, 106–118) proposed that it was in 802 B.C.E. According to E. Lipiński [*Proceedings of the 5th World Congress of Jewish Studies* 1 (1969), 164–165], he did so in 803 B.C.E. But according to H. Tadmor [*Qadmoniot* 2 (1970), 136 (Hebrew); *idem*, *Iraq* 35 (1973), 35], Jehoash paid the tribute in 796 B.C.E. while Adadnirari campaigned in Manṣuate. This view is in accord with our suggestion that Jehoahaz died in 798 B.C.E., and Jehoash then ascended the throne.

belongs to the same time; it describes how Zakur succeeded in severing his allegiance with Ben-hadad, King of Aram.[29]

These facts enable us to understand the historical background of the Samaria ostraca. We have already noted that archaeological data cause us to fix their date near the end of the 9th century B.C.E. There is a surprising concurrence between the ninth year of the ostraca — in our opinion the ninth year of Jehoahaz, viz. 806/5 B.C.E. — and the year in which Adadnirari undertook his great campaign to the land of *Ḫatti* (806/5). This is the year in which a "saviour" of Israel appeared (2 Kgs 13:5), quite clearly Adadnirari, who delivered Israel from the heavy yoke of the kings of Damascus. It seems that as soon as matters improved in this year, Jehoahaz hurried to reorganize the method of collecting taxes in his kingdom; tax-collection had obviously been neglected in the years in which the troops of the king of Damascus were despoiling the countryside. For this purpose he erected in the citadel of Samaria a storage house for the oil and wine received from the villages. It is by no means impossible that in the last year of Jehoahaz, i.e., the seventeenth year of his reign, the storehouses ceased to be used because of the renewed invasion by Damascus. Such is our explanation of the fact that no ostraca were found dating from the reigns of other kings, and that the storehouses underwent considerable reconstruction.

We pass now to a discussion of the extent of the area from which the taxes in kind were collected, and its political and territorial significance. Most scholars consider that the "Ostraca House" served a particular province of the Israelite kingdom, that is the territorial and administrative unit of the Manassites. We should, however, consider the possibility that the ostraca refer to the whole of the kingdom of Israel in its reduced state in the days of Jehoahaz, and not to only one of its districts. Moreover, it is possible that between the ninth and the fifteenth–sixteenth years of Jehoahaz there was an increase of territory. The ostraca from the years nine and ten mention the following places from which taxes were collected in kind:[30]

ʾAzāh — apparently Khirbet Zawāta, 5 km south-east of Samaria.
ʾAz[n]ōth-paran — not yet identified.[31]

29 M. Noth, *ZDPV* 52 (1929), 124ff.; E. Lipiński, *RB* 78 (1971), 88; A.R. Millard, *PEQ* (1973), 161–164.

30 On the topographical material in the Samaria ostraca, see W.F. Albright, *JPOS* 11 (1931), 241ff; M. Noth, *PJb* 28 (1932), 54ff.; B. Mazar (Maisler), *JPOS* 14 (1934), 96ff; Gibson, *Hebrew and Moabite Inscriptions* (note 2), 5–13; Aharoni, *The Land of the Bible* (note 2), 368.

31 Reisner had already proposed to read in ostracon 14:1–2, *ʾz/t prʾn*, while other scholars (Noth, Albright) proposed *ʾ/t prʾn* or *ʾ[l]/t prʾn*. Some identified the place with Farʿūn south of Tūl Karm (Dussaud) or Khirbet Beit Farʿah (Albright). I consider Reisner's version the correct one, but the name must be completed as *ʾaz[n]t*. ʾAznôth-paran may be explained as a place name, such as ʾAznôth-tabor; then Paran would be the extended form of *prʾ*, "wild ass".

*Geba*ᶜ — now Jabaᶜ, 9 km north of Samaria.
Ḥaṣerōt — apparently to be identified with ᶜAṣīret el-Ḥaṭab, 7.5 km south-east of Samaria.
Yaṣīt — now Yaṣīd, 8 km north-north-east of Samaria (Abel).[32]
Sefer[33] — now Safōrim, 8 km west of Samaria (Cross).
Poraim — perhaps Khirbet Kafr ᶜEin Fārāt, 2.5 km south-east of Samaria (Mazar).[34]
Qōṣō — Qūṣin, 3 km south of Samaria (Abel, Albright).[35]
Sftn — perhaps Šūfa, 9 km west of Samaria (Abel).
Ttl — identification unknown.[36]

Equally unidentified are the Kerem Hattel and the Kerem Yeḥawᶜeli, two "vineyards", apparently private estates in the Samaria district. In the tenth year the two territorial units Šemyedaᶜ (*Šemîda*ᶜ) and Abiᶜezer also appear. They were the territories of two great clans which belonged to the tribe of Manasseh.

This survey of the area indicates that it was limited to that surrounding the city of Samaria (see map below), or, more exactly, the district of the Israelite capital proper. On the other hand, we note a considerable increase of territory in the year fifteen. In the ostraca of this year, we find, in addition to the above, the following localities:
ʾElmatān — Immātīn, 10 km west-south-west of Shechem (Albright).
Hattel — perhaps Khirbet et-Tell, south of Immātīn (Avi-Yonah).
Yâšib — Khirbet Kafr Sīb near Šuweika (Albright), or *Yāsif* — 19 km south of Samaria (Aharoni).[37]
ᶜšr[38] — probably Bīr ᶜAšayir near the above (Alt).
Šekem — Shechem, the great centre of Mount Ephraim, now Tell Balāṭa
We also encounter the name of one person designated *Baᶜal Maᶜoni* (ostracon 27), "he who came from Baᶜal Maᶜon",[39] and another called *Hyhd[y]*, "the Judean" (ostracon 51).[40]

32 The large mosaic inscription from the synagogue of Rehob (Tell eṣ-Ṣarim), south of Beth-shean, mentions *Yaṣīt* in the district of Sebaste [Y. Sussman, *Tarbiz* 43 (1974), 138 (Hebrew)].
33 Proposed by F.M. Cross [*BASOR* 163 (1961), 12–14] — not *sq*!
34 The common reading *Beʾrim* is mistaken, and in consequence the identification with Burin near Farᶜâta (Abel) should be discarded. *Pʾrym* (Poraim) can be perhaps explained as derived from *pôʾrah*, "branch", although this word has accidentally been preserved only in its female gender. The suggested identification is purely hypothetical.
35 W.F. Albright, *JBL* 58 (1939), 185.
36 Perhaps we should assume *Ttl*<*tltl* (Songs 5:11, *Taltalim*; Septuagint: ἐλάται "waving palm branches"; *BDB*, 1068).
37 Aharoni, *The Land of the Bible* (see note 2), 368, 384, n. 122.
38 The name is obscure; perhaps it is connected with Ugaritic *ᶜšrt*; cf. H.L. Ginsberg, *The Legend of King Keret* (1946), 45.
39 S. Klein [*Studies in the Genealogical Chapters of the Chronicles* (1930), 10–11 (Hebrew)] thinks that this is a reference to a man from Baᶜal Meᶜôn beyond the Jordan, but this need not be so.
40 Y. Yadin [*Yediot* 16/3–4 (1952), 61–62 (Hebrew)] suggested that this person came from a locality

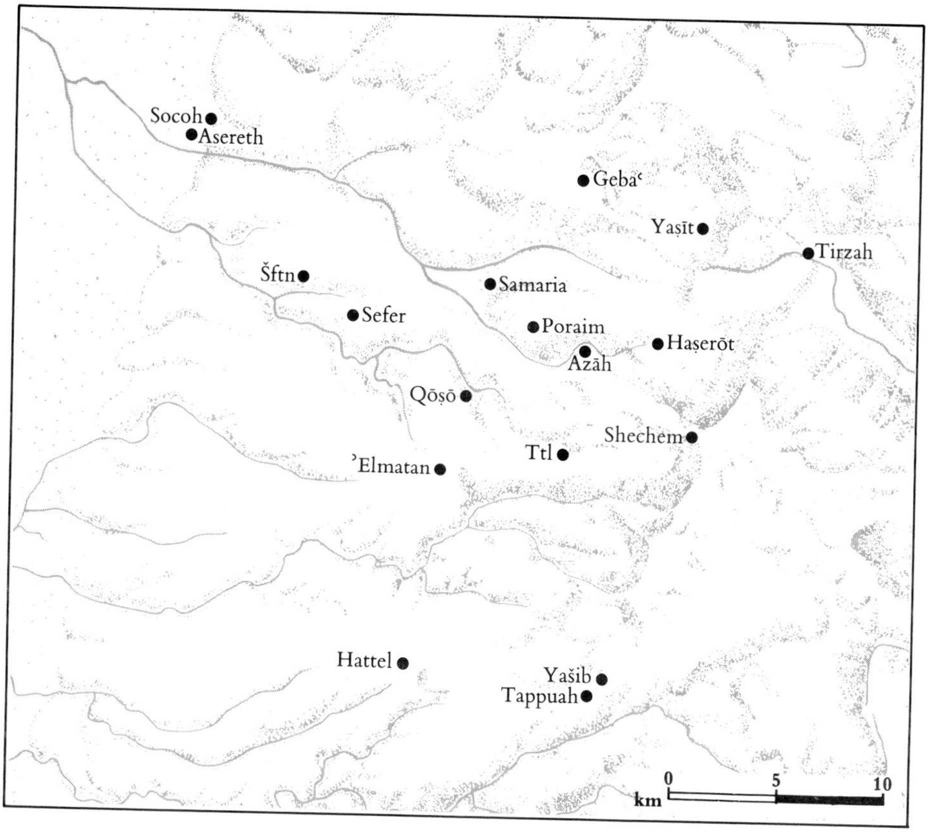

Mount Ephraim according to the Samaria Ostraca

As regards the clan territories mentioned in this group of ostraca, we find, in addition to Abiʿezer and Šemyedaʿ, also Ḥoglah, Ḥeleq, Noʿah, all of which are clans of Manasseh, and perhaps also Shechem and ʾAsrʾel,[41] which may be understood either as territorial or as place names. Thus the area which was taxed in the year fifteen extended from Sānūr (or at least from Gebaʿ) in the north to the neighbourhood of Tappuaḥ — if this locality can be identified with Tell Abu Zarad (Abel) in the south — and to the vicinity of Šuweika and Tūl-Karm along the line of the Via Maris in the west. The eastern boundary

named *Yehud* in Samaria, which he proposed to locate at Khirbet Yahūda, north of Taluza. His suggestion is confirmed by the large mosaic inscription from the synagogue of Rehob which mentions Kefar Yehudith in the district of Sebaste [Y. Sussman, *Tarbiz* 43 (1974), 138].

41 *(ʾ)šrʾ[l]* suggested already by W.F. Albright [*JPOS* 11 (1931), 249f.] and not *šrq*, "Soreq", as I proposed in the first version of this study. There I identified it with Tūl Karm. F.M. Cross [*BASOR* 163 (1961), 14; 165 (1962), 36, n. 10] confirmed Albright's suggestion to read *šrʾ[l]*. He compared the *aleph* to that of the inscription in the tomb of the royal steward from Siloam village. Cf. N. Avigad, *IEJ* 3 (1953), 149, Fig. 149 and Pl. 9.

cannot be defined. In comparison with the administrative division of Solomon, we note that this area comprises not only the northern part of District I (Mount Ephraim, 1 Kgs 4:8), but also part of District III (v. 10).

As stated above, there arises the question whether the ostraca do not happen to reflect a political situation in which the area of the kingdom of Israel was reduced to that surrounding the city of Samaria. The ostraca from the years nine–ten would then indicate roughly its boundaries during one stage, and those of the year fifteen during another. We should take into account what has been said above about the political decline of the kingdom in the time of Jehoahaz, especially just before the invasion of Eretz-Israel by Adadnirari, and about the small size of the army left to the king (2 Kgs 13:7). If the explanation of 2 Kgs 6:13 given above is the correct one, then even the city of Dothan, which was situated only 6 km north of Sānūr, was in Aramean hands. As regards the southern part of Mount Ephraim, we may assume that the king of Judah profited from the weakness of Israel and annexed most of it, as happened on other such occasions (cf. 2 Chr 13:19; 15:8–9).

This would also explain the attitude of Amaziah as regards Jehoash and the attempt of the former to extend his rule over the whole of Israel (2 Kgs 14:9). Moreover, it seems to me that there is a clear indication of the expansion of the kingdom of Judah northwards in 2 Chr 25, in the story of the Ephraimite troops hired by Amaziah in his war against Edom, but which he sent back before the war had begun. There it is written (v. 13): "But the soldiers of the army which Amaziah sent back fell upon the cities of Judah [Septuagint: ἐπὶ τὰς πόλεις ᾿Ιούδα], from Samaria even unto Beth-Horon". This can refer only to the cities of the kingdom of Judah in the area from Beth-Horon in the south to the boundaries of the territory of Samaria in the north, viz. the former territory of the tribe of Ephraim (cf. Josh 15:5–8). Only after the war between Jehoash and Amaziah was all this area returned to the kingdom of Israel. We may also conclude from this that "Samaria", in the political-territorial sense, referred to the limited area round the capital of the Israelite kingdom; this is alluded to as early as the time of the dynasty of Jehu (cf. e.g. Am 3:9: "the mountains of Samaria"; Hos 14:1: "Samaria"). The identification of this Samaria with the kingdom of Israel dates from the days of decline in the time of Jehoahaz (cf. also "the cities of Samaria", 1 Kgs 13:32). The creation of the district of Samaria as a territorial-administrative unit dates to the Assyrian period in the time of the provincial reorganization of Sargon II.

It appears therefore that the ostraca reveal to us a political situation which corresponds closely to the reign of Jehoahaz at the end of the 9th century B.C.E., when the extent of the kingdom of Israel did not exceed the boundaries of the district of the capital proper, i.e. the mountain (or land) of Samaria. Accordingly, the storehouses in which the ostraca were found served for the collection of the wine and oil taxes from the whole kingdom, which flourished from the year nine, when Jehoahaz threw off the yoke of Damascus, till the year seventeen. Indeed, as regards the extent of the territory, there is some justification for the common view that the taxes referred to were collected from the territory of Manasseh alone, as the region of Samaria did not then extend beyond the area occupied by the families of this tribe.[42]

The onomasticon of the personal names mentioned in the ostraca is also of considerable importance for the establishment of their date. It is well known that in the Samaria ostraca, many names are compounded with the theophoric *-baʿal*, side by side with others compounded with *-yau*.[43] Albright has already discussed this problem.[44] He pointed out that the ratio of the names formed with *-baʿal* to those formed with *-yau* is roughly 11:7. As he, however, dated the ostraca in the time of Jeroboam II, he had to explain how in the second half of the 8th century B.C.E., a long time after the revolution of Jehu (841) when the cult of Baal had been rooted out of Samaria, there were still so many people whose names were combined with that of the fallen deity. According to him, "...yahwism had, indeed, triumphed politically in the Northern Kingdom with Jehu's victory, but it was apparently unable to command the adhesion, even nominally, of over two-thirds of the population". There are, however, several discrepancies in this supposition. First of all, there is no hint in our sources that the cult of Baal continued in Israel after the revolution of Jehu; even Amos does not mention the existence of this cult in the time of Jeroboam II. Secondly, in the seals and inscriptions preserved from Judah and Israel and dating from the 8th century B.C.E., there are no personal names compounded with Baal. Thirdly, the fact is noteworthy that among the six officials engaged in collecting the taxes in the years nine to ten, there are two whose names are compounded with *-baʿal* (Baʿala and Baʿalzemer), while among the eleven (or at least ten) officials of the year fifteen there is not even one.[45]

It seems, therefore, that the number of persons who bore names compounded with *-baʿal*, especially among government officials, declined from

42 As regards the idea of Noth [*ZDPV* 50 (1927) 219–244; *PJb* 28 (1932), 54–68] that the ostraca are memoranda of shipments of oil and wine from crown properties to the court of the Israelite king, see W.F. Albright, *JPOS* 11 (1931), 249. There is no foundation for Noth's theory in the documents under consideration.

43 The shortened form *-yau* for *-yahu* in the theophoric names also occurs in some seals of the 8th and 7th centuries B.C.E., especially from Judah, such as *l'byw ʿbd ʿzyw* and *lšbnyw ʿbd ʿzyw* [Diringer, *Le iscrizioni* (note 2), 221, 223], both officials of Uzziah, King of Judah. Cf. also A. Reifenberg, *PEQ* 1938, 114–115.

44 Albright, *Archaeology and the Religion* (note 3), 160–161.

45 On the other hand, the father of one of the officials, Hanan (ben) Baʿra (ostraca 45–47), has a shortened name which apparently contains the element *baʿal* [M. Noth, *Die Israelitischen Personennamen* (1928) 40].

the tenth to the fifteenth year. All these details substantiate the assumption that these people lived in the time of Jehoahaz, as between the revolution of Jehu and the year nine of Jehoahaz only thirty-five years elapsed, and obviously there were many still alive who had been born and had received their names before that revolution. As time passed, however, their number diminished, especially among government officials. From this point of view also there are good grounds for dating the ostraca to the reign of Jehoahaz, King of Israel.[46]

46 Cf. N. Avigad, in *EAEHL* 4, 1032ff. (with bibliography).

Lebo-hamath and the Northern Border of Canaan

The geographical term or place name Lebo-hamath is often mentioned in the Bible as the northernmost limit of the Land of Canaan. Its identification remains one of the most difficult problems facing geographers and historical-topographers of the Land of Israel. Not only is there no unanimity as to the exact location of Lebo-hamath, but opinions vary regarding its meaning. The name usually appears in one of two formulas: "from Lebo-hamath until ...", and "from ... until Lebo-hamath".

The most commonly accepted interpretation of the name Lebo-hamath is represented in the following: τῆς εἰσόδου ʿΗμάθ, ἕως τῆς εἰσόδου ʿΕμάθ, εἰσπορευομένων εἰς ʿΕμάθ (Septuagint); *introitus Emath* (Vulgate); למטי חמת (Targum Onkelos); and ממעלנא חמת (Targum Jonathan). All of these renderings interpret לבוא as deriving from the Hebrew root בוא. On this basis, the name is understood as בואך חמת, "approaching Hamath", "towards Hamath", "the entrance to Hamath", "the road to Hamath", etc. This "entrance" or "approach" has been sought in the Valley of Lebanon, in the Marj ʿAyūn, and even along the road from the Mediterranean coast to the city of Hamath on the Orontes River.[1] Another view is that Lebo-hamath denotes a specific place, Lebo being the name of a settlement, and Hamath, that of a region or of a regional metropolis, added in order to distinguish this Lebo from other settlements with the same name. Lebo-hamath has been sought in the extreme north of the Golan, near the sources of the Jordan.[2] It has also been identified with the village of Labweh which is

1 See in particular, Abel, *GP* 1, 300ff.; K. Elliger, *PJb* 32 (1936), 40ff. Also see B. Mazar (Maisler), *Israel in Biblical Times*, Maps 3 and 15. The name Lebo-hamath does not appear in G.E. Wright and F.V. Filson, *The Westminister Historical Atlas to the Bible* (1945).

2 M. Noth, *ZDPV* 58 (1935), 242ff.; *idem*, *PJb* 33 (1937), 36ff.

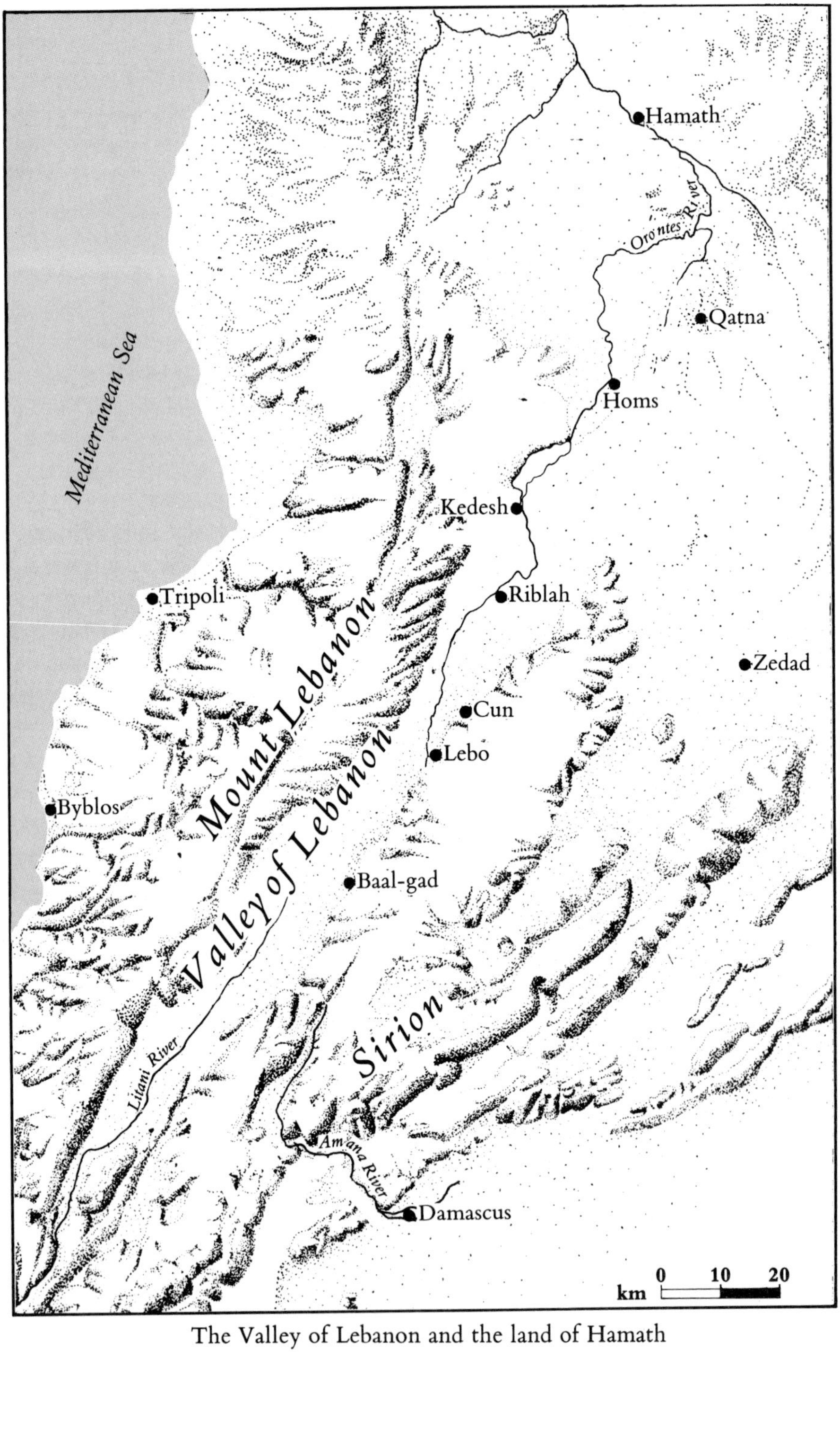

The Valley of Lebanon and the land of Hamath

situated north of Rās Baalbek, near one of the sources of the Orontes.[3] According to yet another hypothesis, Lebo is a metathesis of the Hebrew name of a stream or river, more specifically the Litani,[4] and there is even a suggestion that it was a town or river in the vicinity of Antioch, not far from the Euphrates.[5] The last interpretation is based on Targum Jonathan and the Talmud of Jerusalem, which identify biblical Hamath with Hellenistic Antioch.

The view that Lebo is the name of a specific settlement is based on the following:

1. The *lamed* in לבוא, "Lebo", clearly is a radical letter. Nowhere in the Hebrew Bible do we find the combination בואך חמת or בואך חמתה, parallel to מצידון באכה גררה, "from Sidon as far as Gerar" (Gen 10:19) or מערוער ועד באכה מנית, "from Aroer as far as Minnith" (Judg 11:33). Instead of מבוא חמת מלבוא חמת (מן לבוא), always appears.[6]
2. The name "Lebo" occurs unaccompanied by "Hamath" (Ezek 47:15).[7]
3. It is unlikely that the term refers to a road or a pass in the south of the Valley of Lebanon or in the Marj ʿAyūn leading towards Hamath on the Orontes, as the Marj ʿAyūn is 200 km from Hamath, and in no way could be considered as leading to it.
4. A definition as vague as that stated in no. 3 is inconsistent with the specific character of the other names of towns and mountains listed as boundaries.[8]

The Septuagint of Judg 3:3 provides further support for this view. There, עד לבוא חמת is translated as ἕως Λαβὼ ʿΕμάθ (Λοβω Ημαθ, Λοωβ Ημαθ). In deviating from the traditional interpretation, the translator obviously had in mind a specific place called לבוא, "Lebo".

Scriptural sources alone do not provide sufficient data to allow for a clear identification of Lebo-hamath. We must turn to external documents, and rely on our knowledge of the general historical-geographical context that produced this complex name. But first, let us examine the data in the Hebrew Bible.

One of the main scriptural sources on this subject is Num 34, which provides a detailed description of "the land of Canaan, this is the land that

3 O. Eissfeldt, *Forschungen und Fortschritte* 12 (1936), 51ff.

4 J. Jaffe, *Studies in the Bible and the Geography of Eretz-Israel* (1934), 3ff. (Hebrew). On the ancient name of the Litani River, see F.M. Abel, *JPOS* 13 (1933), 156ff.

5 H. Bar-Droma, *Yavneh* 1 (1939), 59ff. (Hebrew).

6 The expression עד לבוא occurs only twice in the Bible without reference to Hamath: in 1 Chr 5:9 (see the Septuagint *ad loc.*) and in 2 Chr 26:8, which is probably an abbreviation or corruption of לבוא חמת עד נחל מצרים.

7 But see below, p. 200.

8 E.g. in Num 34 and Ezek 46–48.

shall fall to you as your portion, the land of Canaan with its various boundaries" (v.2). This introduction to the list of boundaries clearly indicates that the narrator intended to chart the borders of Canaan, not those of the kingdom of David[9] or of the Israelite Settlement.[10] It is my understanding that "the land of Canaan with its various boundaries" is a fixed administrative-territorial formula originating at a time long before the Israelite conquest, when Canaan, Phoenicia, and southern Syria constituted an Egyptian province. This useful formula was later adopted by the Israelites when they conquered the land.

From the list in Num 34 it appears that in the north, the frontiers of Canaan extended to Mount Hor and the sites called Lebo-hamath and Zedad. In the north-east, they reached settlements on the fringes of the Syrian Desert beyond Damascus. These boundaries encompass the northern part of Transjordan as far as the Sea of Galilee, and from there they follow the Jordan as far as the Dead Sea. The whole of Gilead and the kingdoms of Ammon, Moab, and Edom were therefore not included under the designation "the land of Canaan". Its southern limits incorporated the entire Negeb as far as the desert and the Wadi of Egypt.[11] Even taking into consideration the later expansion of the borders, it is clear from this source that "the land of Canaan" was at no time identical to the actual area of Israelite Settlement, or to the extent of the Israelite Monarchy. In fact the designation refers to the Egyptian province in Asia. The boundaries of this province fluctuated during the 18th Dynasty and the beginning of the 19th Dynasty. They were stabilized only as a result of the peace treaty signed between Ramesses II and the Hittites in the early 13th century B.C.E.

In the El-Amarna Letters, the Egyptian province in Asia is called *Kinaḫḫu/i* or *Kinaḫna/i* (Canaan).[12] In a letter to Pharaoh, the King of Alashya/Elishah (Cyprus?) mentions *piḫati ša Ki-na-ḫi*, "the provinces of Canaan", as territories belonging to Pharaoh,[13] and the King of Babylon writes to Amenḥotep IV: "*Kinaḫḫu* is thy land and her kings are thy

9 Thus K. Elliger, *PJb* 32 (1936), 34ff.

10 This is the opinion of M. Noth, *PJb* 33 (1937), 49.

11 It should be noted that according to Num 21:1ff. and 33:37ff., "the Canaanite, king of Arad, who dwelt in the Negeb" was prompted to take action against the Children of Israel when they set out from Kadesh-barnea and encamped at Mount Hor [identified by some as Jebel Maḍrah; see E. Robinson, *The Sarcophagus of an Ancient Civilization*, 263 ff.]. In other words, this occurred when they arrived at the southern tip of the Negeb in the wilderness of Zin on the border of Edom. According to the above biblical sources, the Negeb was considered part of Canaan. Similarly, all of the settled territories in the south of Eretz-Israel, as far as Gerar and the plain of the Jordan south of the Dead Sea, were considered part of Canaan. See Gen 10:19.

12 Also in the Boghazköy Documents (e.g. *KBo* I, 19, v. 8). See B. Mazar (Maisler), *Untersuchungen zur alten Geschichte Syriens und Palästinas* (1931), 54ff.

13 EA 36:15.

servants".[14] We also find recorded there the title of *amēlu tarbaṣi (PA.TUR) ša šarri ina* ^{mat}*Kinaḫḫi*, "the person in charge of the king's stables in Canaan".[15] In Egyptian sources from the time of Seti I (1316–1304 B.C.E.) onwards, there is also frequent mention of the territorial-administrative term *p3-knʿn*, "the Canaan", in conjunction with *Ḫuru*, the New Kingdom name for Egypt's Asian province.[16] The boundaries of the province are clearly defined in Papyrus Anastasi III: "the land of Ḫuru from Sile up to Upi", i.e. from the border post of Sileh near Qantara up to the region of Damascus.[17] The Syrian regions north of Canaan were Hittite: "from the wilderness and the Lebanon to the Great River, the River Euphrates — the whole Hittite country" (Josh 1:4).

At the time of the Israelite conquest, the Egyptian province of Canaan included the entire area of Cisjordan and the northern part of Transjordan,[18] most of Phoenicia, and southern Syria as far as the Valley of Lebanon and the area of Upi-Damascus.[19] On the basis of this information, one may assume that Lebo-hamath and Zedad were the northernmost points of the Land of Canaan along its border with the Hittite domain. Zedad, which appears both in Num 34:8[20] and in Ezek 47:15 is easily identified as the Christian Jacobite village of Zaddad (more specifically, a large tell at its southern end), located north of the Anti-Lebanon at the edge of the desert, some distance from the Damascus-Ḥoms-Hamath (Hamah) road.[21] The location of Zedad at the edge of the Syrian Desert may explain the following passage in the list of demarcations found in the Book of Numbers: "from Mount Hor draw a line to Lebo-hamath, and let the boundary reach Zedad" (Num 34:8).

Lebo-hamath must have been located midway between Mount Hor near the Mediterranean coast and Zedad on the edge of the desert. This would

14 EA 8:25.

15 EA 367:8.

16 See W.F. Albright, *From the Pyramids to Paul* (1935), 9ff.; Mazar, *Syriens und Palästinas* (see note 12), 58; and the summary by R. de Vaux, *Vivre et penser* 1 [= *RB* 50 (1941), 199].

17 On Upi, or Apu of the El-Amarna Letters, which is mentioned as early as the 19th and 18th centuries B.C.E., see W.F. Albright, *BASOR* 83 (1941), 34ff.

18 No town in the Gilead Mountains is, in fact, mentioned among the cities conquered by the Egyptians during the 18th and 19th Dynasties, although Moab is cited in the inscriptions of Ramesses II. See J. Simons, *Handbook for the Study of Egyptian Topographical Lists* (1937), 155–156 [K.A. Kitchen, *JEA* 50 (1964), 47–50; S. Aḥituv, *IEJ* 22 (1972), 141–142; Mazar, *Canaan and Israel*, 97–99].

19 It should be noted that the kingdom of Amurru in central Syria (cf. Josh 13:4 on the Amorite border) had always been considered part of the Hittite Empire from the El-Amarna period; see E. Forrer, *RLA* 1 (1928), 100ff.; A. Alt, *AO* 34/4 (1936), 23ff. According to the inscriptions of Seti I, the "land" of Kedesh (on the Orontes, today Tell Nebi Mind) belonged to Amurru [see M. Noth, *ZDPV* 60 (1937), 211, n. 6].

20 In Num 24:8 appearing with the ה (*h*) of direction as Zedada.

21 K. Elliger, *PJb* 32 (1936), 38.

explain the frequent mentions of Lebo-hamath as a frontier point, first of Canaan and later of the Israelite Monarchy in its floruit and at the time of its expansion in the direction of Damascus. In this sense we encounter it in the story of the spies sent by Moses from the wilderness of Paran to scout the Land of Canaan: "They went up and scouted the land, from the wilderness of Zin to Rehob, at Lebo-hamath" (Num 13:21). Here, as well as in Num 34, Zin and Lebo-hamath represent the respective southern and northern limits of Canaan. The term Rehob does not appear to designate the name of a city or "land" such as Beth-rehob near Dan (Judg 18:28) or Beth-rehob in the Aramean kingdom.[22] It is more likely that it was used here as a common noun meaning a square, the outskirts or vicinity of a town (compare *ribītu* in Akkadian), a passage, or a road. One should note that this is the interpretation of Targum Jonathan: פלטיות מעלך לאנטיוכיא (פלטיה = πλατεῖα), "The plazas at the entrance of Antioch".

The parallel passages in Josh 14:3-5 and Judg 3:3 are not clear and do not lead to unequivocal conclusions.[23] Both describe the regions and peoples of Canaan that were not conquered by the Israelites. In the north, they include "... the Sidonians ... and the land of the Gebalites [!] with the whole (Valley of the) Lebanon, from Baal-gad at the foot of Mount Hermon to Lebo-hamath on the east" (Josh 13:5).[24] From this it would seem that the border points, Baal-gad and Lebo-hamath, were distant from each other, but one may assume that the text is corrupted, or that the mention of Lebo-hamath appears here as parallel to Baal-gad at the foot of Mount Hermon. As an indication of Canaan's northern border, Baal-gad appears in contexts such as: "... from Baal-gad in the Valley of Lebanon to Mount Halak which ascends to Seir..." (Josh 12:7), or "from Mount Halak which ascends to Seir, all the way to Baal-gad in the Valley of the Lebanon, at the foot of Mount Hermon" (Josh 11:7).[25] Mount Halak is probably Jebel Halak, north-west of Wadi Marra in the wilderness of Zin,[26] whereas Baal-gad, probably an important cultic site in southern Syria, is located in the Beqaᶜ (the Valley of Lebanon) at the foot of Mount Hermon.[27] It is

22 With regard to Aramean Beth-rehob mentioned in 2 Sam 10:6, it has been shown by Ed. Meyer, *Die Israeliten und ihre Nachbarstämme* (1906), 539, that Beth-rehob is the name of the dynasty of (founded by) King Hadad-ezer son of Rehob of Zobah.

23 See Mazar, *Syriens und Palästinas* (note 12), 59ff., and K. Elliger, *PJb* 32 (1936), 40ff.

24 Judg 3:3 reads: "... and all the Canaanites, Sidonians, and Hivites who inhabited the hill country of the Lebanon from Mount Baal-hermon to Lebo-hamath". Concerning textual questions, see note 23 above.

25 B. Mazar, *Enc. Miq*. 2, s.v. "Baal-gad".

26 See A. Musil, *Arabia Petraea* 2/1 (1907), 170, 197. Nearby is Jebel Maḍrah, identified as Mount Hor.

27 Very often Mount Hermon is mistakenly identified with Jebel esh-Sheikh, the southern range of the Anti-Lebanon (see Abel, *GP* 1, 347ff.) More accurately, Mount Hermon refers to the entire

my opinion that Baal-gad and Mount Halak, representing the northernmost and southernmost limits of Canaan, are analogous to the frontier points of the land mentioned in the Book of Numbers (13:21; 34:4, 8, etc.): "the wilderness of Zin" and "Lebo-hamath".

The importance of Lebo-hamath as the northern limit of Canaan grew after the conquest of Damascus and of Zobah by David (1 Kgs 8:65; 1 Chr 13:5; 2 Chr 7:8) and during the ensuing floruit of the United Monarchy. From Assyrian sources we learn that the Land of *Ṣubatu* (also *Ṣubutu, Ṣubite*), which is the biblical Zobah, lay north of Damascus. It included vast areas to the north-west of the Anti-Lebanon[28] and north-east of it, as far as Tadmor (Palmyra) or even the Euphrates River. This is supported by the fact that Tebah, Cun and Berothai, the three cities of King Hadad-ezer of Zobah which were conquered by David, have been identified in the northern Valley of Lebanon, north-west of the Anti-Lebanon.[29]

Anti-Lebanon. Deut 3:9 reads to this effect: "Sidonians call Hermon Sirion, and the Amorites call it Senir". Senir, i.e. the Anti-Lebanon, already appears in 19th century B.C.E. Egyptian Execration Texts as *Šrynw* [see G. Posener, *Princes et pays de Syrie et de Nubie...* (1940), 62ff., E 30; Mazar, *Canaan and Israel*, 30]. *Šrynw* is mentioned in parallelism with Lebanon in Ugaritic [see C.H. Gordon, *Ugaritic Text-Book* (1965), 495, no. 2485], and in the contracts signed between the Hittite king and the kings of Syria [spelled *Šariyâna*; see E.F. Weidner, *Politische Dokumente aus Kleinasien* 1 (1923), 68, 74]; compare with Ps 29:6. It should be noted that *Sanîru* (Senir) in Assyrian documents (the *snyr* of Arab geographers) refers mainly to that part of the Anti-Lebanon which is north of Damascus, whereas Amana (in Assyrian *Am[m]ana*, *Ammūn*, *Ammanānu*) is that part of the range which is near the Zebdani, at the foot of which is located the source of the Amana River. The mention of Amana, Senir, and Hermon together, in a parallelism with Lebanon (Song 4:8), does not alter our conclusion. In light of the above, it is difficult to accept the identification of Baal-gad with modern-day Ḥaṣbaya (Abel, *GP* 2, 258), which is neither in the Valley of Lebanon nor does it mark a border of any kind. It may be that Baal-gad is Baalbek, which is probably mentioned as *Baʿli* in the inscriptions of Adadnirari III. It is in the Valley of Lebanon and north-west of Damascus [see E. Honigmann, *RLA* 1, 328; R. de Vaux, *RB* 43 (1934), 514]. On this matter, the suggestion by Eissfeldt [*Forschungen und Fortschritte* 12 (1936), 51ff.] that Baalbek is a later form of Baal Beqaʿ (the Valley of Lebanon) is groundless.

28 For details, see K. Elliger, *PJb* 33 (1937), 50ff.; M. Noth, *PJb* 33 (1937), 40ff.; W.F. Albright, *Archaeology and the Religion of Israel* (1942), 130ff., 211–212. On the term "Hamath Zobah" (Assyrian: *Ṣubut Hamâtu*), see below.

29 See 2 Sam 8:8 (corrupted: בטח); 1 Chr 18:8 (corrupted: טבחת). Tebah is *Tubiḫi* of the El-Amarna Letters, also mentioned in Egyptian sources from the New Kingdom. It is located in the north of the Valley of Lebanon. Albright (*ibid*., 212) identifies it with Baalbek. Cun is *Cunna*, on the road from Emessa (Ḥoms) to Heliopolis (Baalbek), and is to be identified with Rās Baalbek [see E. Honigmann, *ZDPV* 46 (1923), 179, n. 150]. Berothai (Ezek 47:16: Berothah) is widely believed to be Bereitan, south of Baalbek, and is certainly in the Valley of Lebanon (Abel, *GP* 2, 7). Comparison of 1 Kgs 9:18 (*qere*) to 2 Chr 8:3–4 and of 1 Kgs 5:1, 4 to 2 Sam 8:3; 10:16 gives rise to the assumption that Tadmor (Palmyra) too, and perhaps even Tiphsah (Tapsacos) on the Euphrates, were also originally part of Zobah. See E. Forrer, *RLA* 1, 134ff. The southern part of the Valley of Lebanon (the Litani area) is included in the Assyrian province of *Manṣuate*, listed by Hellenistic writers as Μασσύας αὐλών. See also M. Noth, *PJb* 33 (1937), 42ff.; E. Honigmann, *ZDPV* 47 (1924), 16; Mazar, *Canaan and Israel*, 255, n. 25, 266.

Sources, both biblical and Assyrian, attest that the Land of Hamath lay north of Zobah-Ṣubatu. Hamath was the dominant kingdom during the Israelite Monarchy. Its metropolis was Greater Hamath (Am 6:2) on the Orontes River, known in Assyrian as *Amātu, Ḫam(m)ātu*. In 2 Sam (8:9ff.) we read that King Toi of Hamath sent his son to David for the purpose of establishing relations and to congratulate him on his military victory over Hadad-ezer of Zobah, "for Hadad-ezer had been at war with Toi".[30] It is obvious that, after the conquest of Damascus and Zobah, the border of Israel reached the kingdom of Hamath, more specifically, Lebo-hamath (1 Kgs 8:65; 2 Chr 7:8). Hamath, according to Assyrian sources and as evidenced by the Hittite hieroglyphic inscriptions[31] found in its area, was unlike Damascus and Zobah. Zobah was a neo-Hittite state, one of several such kingdoms established in Syria after the destruction of the Hittite Empire by the Sea Peoples at the beginning of the 12th century B.C.E.[32]

In the 13th century B.C.E., Greater Hamath succeeded Kedesh on the Orontes as the regional metropolis. Politically speaking, the kingdom of Hamath inherited the Land of Amurru and became a vassal Hittite border-domain facing the Egyptian province of Canaan.[33] Once during the war of Qarqar (853 B.C.E.) we find Hamath joining forces with Damascus against the Assyrians, but in all subsequent generations the two kingdoms were bitter rivals striving for control over central Syria, and in particular the area of the Valley of Lebanon. This included Zobah (Hamath's rival in the days of David) which was incorporated within the realm of Damascus after its liberation from Israel's yoke during the reign of Solomon.[34] The Syrian campaigns of Adadnirari III of Assyria at the end of the 9th and in the early 8th century B.C.E. and the resulting political changes improved

30 See A. Malamat, in *The Hebrew Kingdoms* (1962), 24ff. (Hebrew).

31 The material has been collected by I.J. Gelb, *Hittite Hieroglyphs* 1 (1931); 2 (1932); 3 (1942), *passim*. The southernmost point in Syria where Hittite hieroglyphs have been found is er-Restān, 25 km south of Hamath.

32 Cf. 1 Kgs 10:29; see Mazar, *Canaan and Israel*, 77–78. For details on the Hittite and Aramean kingdoms in Syria, see A. Alt, *ZDMG* 88 (1934), 233ff.

33 See note 19 above. It is doubtful whether any of the places called Hamath in the lists of cities belonging to the pharoahs of the 18th and 19th Dynasties refers to Hamath on the Orontes River [certainly No. 16 in Tuthmosis III's list does not; contra M. Noth, *ZDPV* 6 (1938), 63, n. 3]. During the rule of Egypt in Canaan, Hamath was of no particular importance. The archaeological excavations carried out at Hamath in the years 1931–1938 prove this beyond doubt; see W.F. Albright, *AJA* 40 (1940), 163; E. Fugmann, *Hama* (1958).

34 1 Kgs 11:24–25. The inscription of King Zakur of Hamath and Luʿash [see M. Noth, *ZDPV* 52 (1929), 124ff.] bears witness to one of the wars between Damascus and Hamath. W.F. Albright, *AJA* 40 (1940), 13ff., dates it to 755 B.C.E. Since, however, according to the inscriptions, the king of Damascus was Bar-hadad son of Hazael (cf. 2 Kgs 13:3, 24–25), it may have to be dated earlier, to the campaigns of Adadnirari III (i.e. the end of the 9th and the beginning of the 8th century B.C.E.).

the fortunes of Hamath. Damascus suffered considerably from these campaigns, and it is not surprising that to the Israelites, Adadnirari appeared as a "saviour" who delivered them from the Arameans.[35] Jeroboam II[36] seized this historic opportunity and "restored the territory of Israel from Lebo-hamath to the sea of the Arabah [the Dead Sea]" (2 Kgs 14:25). In other words, he not only seized Damascus for Israel (1 Kgs 14:25), but also its northern territories including Zobah, up to the border of Hamath.[37] The Israelite kings did not have the power to maintain control over the vast Aramean territories.

During the reign of Tiglath-Pileser III (745–727 B.C.E.) we find Damascus reappearing on the political scene in Syria. The decline of Aram after the campaigns of Adadnirari had been exploited by Hamath in order to expand both its territory and its influence. Consequently, it had become a very large state extending as far north as Aleppo by the time the armies of Tiglath-Pileser III reached Syria in 743 B.C.E. The southern border of Hamath during the reign of Jeroboam II reached Lebo-hamath, and there is no reason to believe that this situation changed, even after Damascus had regained its political freedom. Of particular interest here is one of the inscriptions of Tiglath-Pileser III which lists the cities that he conquered in Syria.[38] The end of the inscription is missing, but the last city to be mentioned is *Labʾu*. Preceding it are all the cities of Hamath.[39] In other words, Tiglath-Pileser III mentions *Labʾu* as the first city in a kingdom — most likely Damascus — that lay south of Hamath. There is no question that the above-mentioned *Labʾu* was located very near the southern border of Hamath, and several scholars have suggested that, indeed, it should be identified with Lebo-hamath.[40]

Political conditions in Syria and Eretz-Israel changed radically after the campaigns of Tiglath-Pileser III in 738 and in 734–732 B.C.E. The kingdoms of Damascus and Israel became Assyrian provinces in 733/2, and in

35 2 Kgs 13:5 — in the reign of Jehoahaz.

36 See H. Tadmor, *Enc. Miq.* 5, s.v. "Chronology".

37 See also Am 6:14. M. Noth, *PJb* 33 (1937), 47ff., has examined the extra-biblical sources extensively, but incorrectly disregards the role played by the Kingdom of Israel in the reign of Jeroboam II. Thus he dismisses the possibility that Jeroboam II may have conquered Damascus (p. 50). See Mazar, *Israel in Biblical Times*, Maps 28–29; H. Tadmor, *Enc. Miq.* 3, s.v. "Jeroboam II".

38 See P. Rost, *Die Keilschrifttexte Tiglathpilesers III* 1 (1893), 83ff. (K1. Inschr. II); Luckenbill, *AR* 1, 294, 821.

39 The inscription lacks a beginning as well, and lists cities in the kingdoms to the north-west and west of Assyria (such as Enzi, Unqi, and according to H. Tadmor, also *Bīt A[gusi]*), which were conquered by Tiglath-Pileser III and which became his provinces.

40 See M. Noth, *PJb* 33 (1937), 50 ff. Noth's suggestion that the location of Labʾu (Lebo-hamath) should be sought near the sources of the Jordan is groundless; it is based on the assumption that at one time Hamath extended as far as the Galilee of the Gentiles, for which he provides no proof.

720 B.C.E. the last remnant of the kingdom of Hamath also met the same fate. The administrative system established by the Assyrians in Syria is known to us mainly from Assyrian eponymic lists[41] (the *lîmu*, in which each year was named after a prince or provincial governor), records of taxes levied on the provinces and other epigraphic sources, as well as from the Bible. It should be noted that the Assyrian administrative system remained very much the same under subsequent Chaldean and Persian regimes.[42]

Some of the provinces in southern Syria known to us are: *Ḫatrikka*,[43] Hamath, *Ṣubatu*,[44] *Manṣuate* (southern Valley of Lebanon), Damascus, *Qarnīni*, *Ḫaurīna* in northern Transjordan, and *Magiddu* in the north of Eretz-Israel.[45] Most of these provinces also appear in the Bible. Thus we learn that Riblah (modern Ribleh on the Orontes River, 35 km south of Ḥoms) was included in the province of Hamath.[46] We also learn that the Land of Hamath was included in the Assyrian province of Hamath, which extended as far south as the northern slope of the Anti-Lebanon and the Valley of Lebanon.

Ezekiel (chs. 46–48) provides clearer information on the southern and south-eastern borders of Hamath. The delineation of the borders of the Land of Israel was undoubtedly based on a "document" entitled "the land of Canaan with its various boundaries" (Num 34:2),[47] which we discussed above. But in order to make it more comprehensible to his audience, the author of Ezekiel used contemporary geographical names and terms. In Ezek 48:1 we find the following description: "along the Hethlon road, (from) Lebo-hamath to Hazar-enan — which is the border of Damascus,

41 The documents were first collected by E. Forrer, *Die Provinzeinteilung des assyrischen Reiches* (1921). Since then, research has advanced considerably, especially in the works of Alt, Noth, Elliger, Abel, Tadmor, Oded and others.

42 See especially the surveys by Abel, *GP* 2, 99ff.; A. Alt, *ZDPV* 52 (1929), 220ff.

43 Which is Hadrach; Zech 9:1.

44 Which is Zobah. It appears that for a certain time, prior to the conquest of Hamath by Sargon (720 B.C.E.), *Ṣubatu* was incorporated within Hamath. This may explain the usage "Hamath-zobah" (2 Chr 8:3), which is probably the same as *[alu]Ḫamātu*, *[alu]Ṣubut*, the name under which the province of *Ṣubatu* (*Ṣubut* in the construct form) appears in a list of provinces [see K. Elliger, *PJb* 32 (1936), 52]. A more daring hypothesis is suggested by Noth [*PJb* 33 (1937), 46ff.]. There is no further mention of the province of Ṣubatu-Zobah during the Babylonian-Persian periods. We may assume that it ceased to exist as an administrative unit and became part of the province of Damascus [see J. Lewy, *HUCA* 18 (1944), 450ff].

45 Qarnīni = Karnaim; Ḫaurina = Hauran; Magiddu = Megiddo, i.e. Galilee of the Gentiles; see Isa 8: 23. On the Assyrian provinces in Israel, see B. Oded, *JNES* 29 (1970), 2, 177ff.

46 2 Kgs 23:33; 25:6, etc. If it is correct to read Ezek 6:14 as מדבר רבלתה, "the wilderness as far as *Riblah*", instead of the Masoretic מדבר דבלתה, "the wilderness as far as Diblah", then we have yet another indication as to where Canaan's northern border lay with respect to Hamath. The wilderness of Riblah is the desert in the northern Valley of Lebanon, between Labweh and Riblah.

47 Above, pp. 193ff.; Mazar, *Canaan and Israel*, 267, n. 55.

with Hamath to the north". This clearly indicates that Damascus was included within the territory of the Land of Israel, and that Lebo-hamath and Hazar-enan were near the province of Hamath, or bordered on it. In Ezek 47:15–16 we read: "These are the boundaries of the land: As the northern limit: From the Great Sea by way of Hethlon, Lebo-hamath, Zedad, Berothah, Sibraim — which lies between the border of Damascus and the border of Hamath". The Masoretic version in fact reads לבוא צדדה חמת, which may reflect a scribal error. The Septuagint version implies that in the original text, Lebo-hamath had been listed immediately after Hethlon, whereas Zedad appeared either after Lebo-hamath, or after Sibraim.[48] The border points Zedadah/Zedad, Berothah/Berothai, and Sibraim appear in other sources as well, and are located in the northern Valley of Lebanon, north of the Anti-Lebanon.[49] Ezekiel (chs. 46–68) brings us closer to the exact location of Lebo-hamath in the northern Valley of Lebanon.

The Byzantine travel chronicle *Itinerarium Antonini*[50] mentions a place called "Libo", which is obviously similar in sound to "Lebo". According to this source, Libo lay on the road from Hemisa (Ḥoms) via Laudicea (Kedesh on the Orontes, today's Tell Nebi Mind) to Heliopolis (Baalbek). Its distance from both Laudicea and Heliopolis was "32 miles".[51] It may therefore be identified with absolute certainty as the village of Labweh, situated in a fertile area in the northern part of the Valley of Lebanon at the foot of the Anti-Lebanon, near the spring of Nabaᶜ Labweh, one of the main sources of the Orontes River. The present-day village is located on a tell which, according to potsherds found on the site, includes settlements from the Bronze and Iron Ages as well as from later periods.

48 Cf. Num 34:8; Ezek 47:20; 48:1; see K. Elliger, *PJb* 32 (1936), 35. According to M. Noth, *PJb* 33 (1937), 49, Lebo is mentioned here separately, without the addition of "Hamath", in a list of several towns.

49 On Zedad, see above, p.193; on Berothah-Berothai, see note 29 above. It had been widely thought that Sebraim is to be identified with *Šab/mara'in*. According to a Babylonian chronicle, the site was conquered by Shalmaneser V, the son of Tiglath-Pileser III [H. Winkler, in E. Schrader, *Die Keilinschriften und das Alte Testament* (3d ed, 1902), 63]. However, H. Tadmor [*JCS* 12 (1958), 39] has adduced evidence to show that the above source refers to *Šamrain*, i.e. *Shomron* (Samaria), represented by an Aramaic form of the name. Another suggestion is that *Sibraim* is Sepharvaim of 2 Kgs 17:31. See *Enc. Miq*. 5, s.v. "Sibraim; Sepharvaim".

50 See in particular K. Elliger, *PJb* 32 (1936), 44; Abel, *GP* 1, 300. Both accept the traditional interpretation of "Lebo-hamath". The identification of Lebo-hamath with Libo has been accepted by Eissfeldt [*Forschungen und Fortschritte* 12 (1936), 51ff]; M. Noth, [*PJb* 33 (1937), 50] distinguishes between Libo and Lebo-hamath, and assumes that there were other places called Lebo in southern Syria; see below.

51 See *Itineraria Romana* 1 (ed., Cuntz, 1929), 27, 198:3; E. Honigmann, in *Pauly-Wissowas Realenzyclopaedie* 25 (1926), 115. Some scholars suggest that *Heldo* in the *Tabula Peutingeriana* is a scribal error for Lebo; see *Itineraria Romana* (ed., Miller), 225.

In view of these facts, there is no doubt that Lebo-hamath is none other than Byzantine Libo, and that it was situated where Tell Labweh stands today.

The identification of Lebo-hamath with Labweh also sheds new light on the overall history of the area. Excavations at Memphis revealed a stele of Amenḥotep II,[52] the son of Tuthmosis III, which was later used to cover the tomb of Shishak, son of Osorkon III. The inscription on the stele includes an official report by the Pharaoh's scribes of the said Amenḥotep II's campaigns in Asia during the seventh and ninth years of his reign.[53] One detail of the campaign of the seventh year is noteworthy. On his return from northern Syria, Amenḥotep II reached Kedesh on the Orontes, and then continued south on a hunting expedition at "*Rbw*ʾ in the forest". In view of the Egyptian habit of transcribing the consonant *l* by Egyptian *r*, it is clear that this passage refers to לבוא, "Lebo", and that this "Lebo" should be identified with the biblical Lebo-hamath and with the Labʾu of Tiglath-Pileser III. The late B. Grdseloff called my attention to the fact that "Lebo in the forest" is also mentioned in the account of the war of Ramesses II against the Hittites at Kedesh, according to the Abu-Simbel version. In this source as well, "Lebo in the forest" was located some distance south of Kedesh.[54] It is very likely that the forests around Lebo, famous for hunting, were located on the slopes of the Anti-Lebanon or perhaps also on the slopes of Mount Lebanon, west of the Orontes, which are forested areas to this day.

It seems, then, that the area around Lebo, i.e. the upper reaches of the Orontes, was named after the town Lebo as early as the 18th Egyptian Dynasty. The town itself was known still earlier; it is already mentioned in the Egyptian Execration Texts dating from the 18th century B.C.E. These texts are inscribed on figurines, and include a list of the provincial governors in Asia.[55] One town (or district, or "land") mentioned is *Rbw*ʾ,[56] located between the Anti-Lebanon[57] and *Qn*ʾ*i*,[58] and the twin lands of *Āpum*.[59] According to the Execration Texts, Lebo was a major city during the Middle Kingdom. It may even have constituted a political unit. Its governor bore a Semitic name composed of two elements, but only the first of these, ʿ*pr*, has been preserved.

52 His reign was from 1450 to 1428 B.C.E.
53 See J.A. Wilson, in *ANET*, 245ff.; Mazar, *Canaan and Israel*, 84ff.
54 See *ibid.*, 87.
55 See G. Posener, *Princes et pays d'Asie et de Nubie* (1940), 62ff.
56 Which is Lebo (E 31); see Mazar, *Canaan and Israel*, 31.
57 E 30; see note 27 above; Mazar, *Canaan and Israel*, 30.
58 E 32; see Mazar, *Canaan and Israel*, 31.
59 The Oasis of Damascus (E 33–34); see note 17 above; Mazar, *Canaan and Israel*, 31.

It is also possible that the town of Lebo is alluded to in the El-Amarna Letters. I refer to the city of *La-b/pa-na* mentioned in the two letters[60] from the king of Qaṭna (today's Mishrefeh north-east of Ḥoms) to Amenḥotep III. According to these letters, the king of Labana joined forces with the treacherous king of Kedesh, who betrayed Pharaoh. He concluded a treaty with the Hittites, and endangered the peace of the whole of southern Syria, particularly of Upi. Scholars, searching for such a city south of Kedesh, have suggested identifying it with Labweh.[61] However, no one has considered the possibility that it might be the same as Lebo-hamath. This appears more likely if we assume that Labana is Labʾu/a with the addition of the Hurrian suffix *-na*. This suffix accounts for various toponyms, as in *Kinaḫ-na/i*, "Canaan",[62] *Api-na* (*Apu/i* in the Boghazköy Tablets),[63] *Kizzuwat-na*,[64] etc. If the Labana mentioned in the El-Amarna Letters is the same as Lebo(-hamath), this further supports the assumption that in the 18th Dynasty, Lebo was already the metropolis of a "land" lying in the southern part of Kedesh's sphere of influence.

It now becomes clear why in the Bible Lebo is called "Lebo-hamath". The name "Hamath" was not added in order to distinguish it from other towns with the same name,[65] but merely to indicate that it was included within the province of Hamath. The custom of appending the name of a province or region to that of cities is already encountered in the El-Amarna Letters,[66] and is very common in the Bible. An example can be found in Gen 14; among the places mentioned there is Ashteroth-karnaim, which is none other than Ashtaroth (*Ăstartu/i*), already known from Egyptian Execration Texts, from New Kingdom sources, from the El-Amarna Letters, and from the Bible, as the metropolis of the Bashan. "Karnaim" (Assyrian *Qarnīni*) was the name of the province under Aramean rule in the 8th century B.C.E., and in the Assyrian, Babylonian and Persian administration from the time of Tiglath-Pileser III.[67] Also mentioned in the same chapter are El-paran, meaning "El in the wilderness" or "land of

60 EA 53–54.

61 This was already suggested by G. Maspero, *RT* 19 (1897), 68; O. Weber, in J.A. Knudtzon, *Die El-Amarna Tafeln* 2 (1915), 1111; A. Jirku, *ZDMG* 87 (1933), 18; Abel, *GP* 2, 7. As an alternative identification, one could suggest *Rbn*, mentioned in the list of Tuthmosis III (no. 10).

62 See B. Maisler (Mazar), *BASOR* 102 (1948), 7–12.

63 See L.A. Mayer and J. Garstang, *Index of Hittite Names* 1 (1923), 3.

64 See A. Goetze, *Kizzuwatna* (1940), 5ff.

65 It should be noted that no knowledge of another Lebo has reached us.

66 I refer to examples such as Ziri-Bašani (*Zer-bashan*, EA 201), also mentioned in inscriptions from the period of Ramesses II, which is *Zrm* of the Middle Kingdom Execration Texts; see Mazar, *Canaan and Israel*, 28; also, below, p. 202

67 On the province of Karnaim, see A. Alt, *PJb* 29 (1933), 19ff.; Abel, *GP* 2, 102.

Paran", and Hazazon-tamar, probably to be understood as Hazazon in the region of Tamar. Other examples are Dibon-gad,[68] Jabesh-gilead, Moresheth-gath,[69] Ziri-bašani,[70] Jazer-gilead,[71] etc. Most of these were ancient towns, and some were capitals, such as Ashteroth and Jazer.

The appendage of the name of the province came only after a much later political or administrative system took effect. The term "Lebo-hamath" may be understood therefore as Lebo in the Land of Hamath. A reasonable *terminus a quo* for the addition of the name "Hamath" to the ancient name of Lebo is the establishment of the kingdom of Hamath as an independent political entity during the 11th or, at the earliest, 12th century B.C.E., when Greater Hamath replaced Kedesh as the important Hittite provincial capital in south and central Syria.[72]

68 Num 13:45. See *Enc. Miq.* 2, s.v. "Dibon".

69 Which is Muḫarašti: EA 335:17.

70 See note 66 above, and Mazar, *Cities and Districts*, 187; concerning Gath-carmel, see *ibid.*, 220, n. 14

71 1 Chr 26:31. See also note 44 above on *aluḪamātu*, *aluṢubut*.

72 Of course, one could date the establishment of the Assyrian province of Hamath to the year 720 B.C.E., but this seems unlikely. It should be noted that in the list of nations in Gen 10, the Hamathites appear together with Sidon, Heth, the Jebusites, Amorites, Girgashites and the dwellers of northern Phoenicia, as one of Canaan's offspring (vv. 15–19). The author of this list, who probably lived in the 10th century B.C.E. [see W.F. Albright, *From the Stone Age to Christianity* (1940), 327, n. 74] locates the Hittite kingdom of Hamath within Canaan for genealogical reasons. Heth was after all the son of Canaan! This contradicts historical reality and the geo-ethnic conception that prevailed among the ancient people of Israel. It also deviates from the boundaries specified in Gen 10:19. Nevertheless, the author's ethnographic scheme dictated that he record the Hamathites under the genealogy of the sons of Canaan.

Beth-she῾arim, Gaba, and Harosheth of the Peoples

The identification of Beth-she῾arim with Sheikh Abreik — a hill situated in south-western Galilee overlooking the western part of the Jezreel Valley — was based on the references in talmudic literature and on the results of the exploration of its necropolis carried out in 1936/7;[1] Beth-she῾arim (Hebrew: בית שערים, Aramaic: בית שריי, בית̣ שריין) is frequently mentioned as a Jewish town in Lower Galilee in the Roman period, as the residence and burial place of Rabbi Judah Hannasi, and as a central Jewish necropolis in Eretz-Israel.[2] The identification became obvious after the third and fourth excavation seasons at Sheikh Abreik and its necropolis in 1939/40. In the north-eastern part of the mound public buildings of the town were uncovered, including scanty remains from the 1st century C.E., a large building of the second and the beginning of the third centuries, and a synagogue with its dependencies from the third and fourth centuries C.E. The writer was able to date the destruction of the Jewish town to the time of the revolt put down by Gallus Caesar in 351 C.E.[3]

In the necropolis, eleven catacombs and a mausoleum were discovered. Four extensive catacombs, on the western slope of the mound, are of a public character; the decorations on the walls reveal to us a wide variety of motifs characteristic of the popular Jewish art of the Roman period. The necropolis yielded more than 200 inscriptions, mostly in Greek,[4] and a few

* This study is a revised version of the article which appeared in *HUCA* 24 (1952–1953), 75–84.

1 B. Maisler (Mazar), *Yediot* 5 (1937), 63f. (Hebrew); *idem, JPOS* 18 (1938), 41f.

2 For references, see B. Mazar, *Beth She῾arim* 1 (1973), 3ff.

3 *Ibid.*, 6.

4 M. Schwabe, *Yediot* 5 (1938), 77ff. (Hebrew); M. Schwabe and B. Lipschitz, *Beth-she῾arim* 2 (1974).

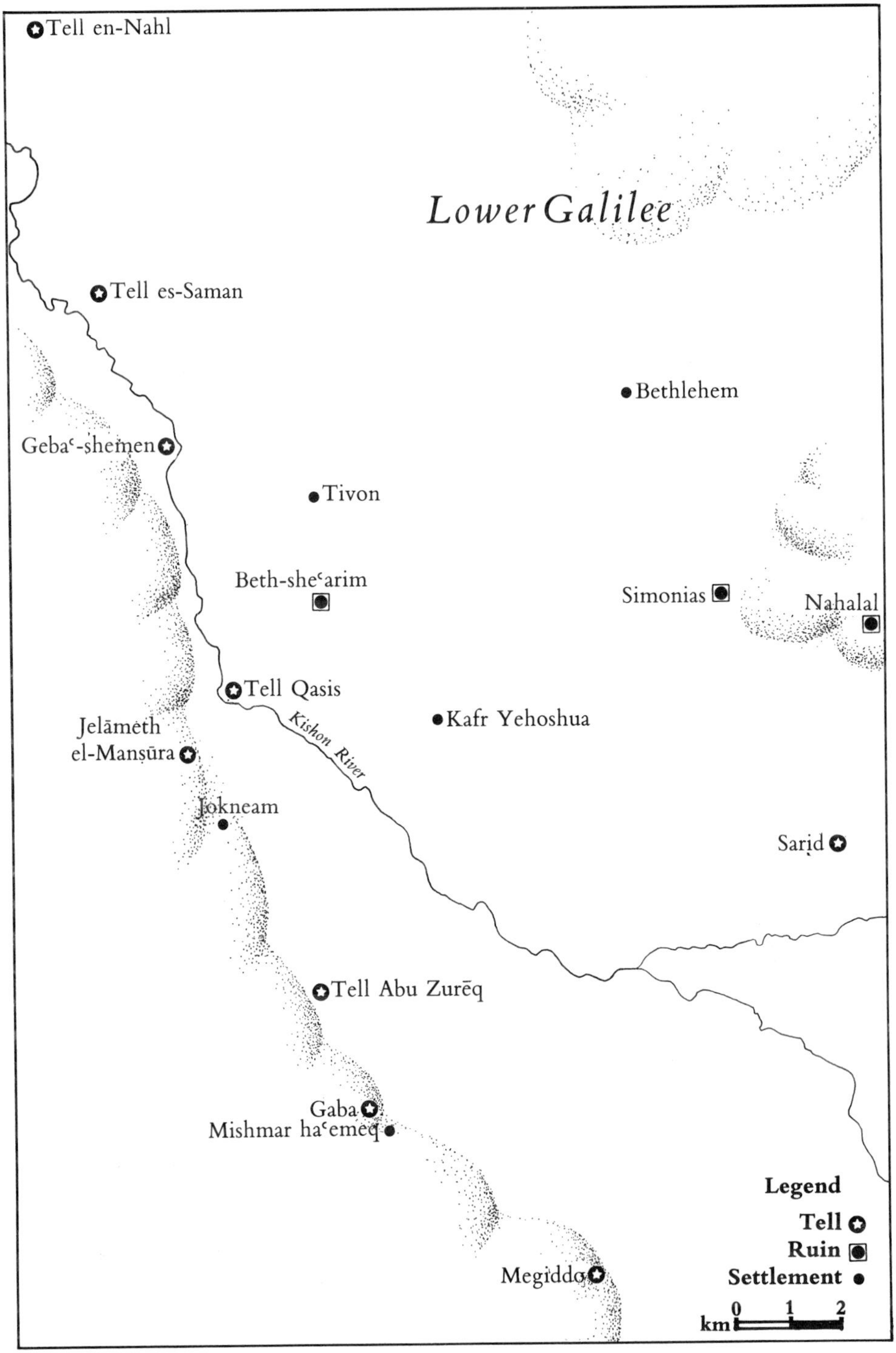

The Jezreel Valley and western Lower Galilee

in Hebrew, Aramaic, and Palmyrene,[5] and this abundant material provided definite evidence that the necropolis served as a central burial place for the Jews of the East during the 3rd–4th centuries C.E.

A most interesting Greek epigram written on a marble slab, which was found in the debris of the mausoleum, confirmed the fact that modern Sheikh Abreik occupies the site of Beth-sheʿarim. Prof. M. Schwabe's translation of the first passage of this epigram reads: "I, Justus, the Leontide, son of Sappho, am lying dead, after having picked [e.g. the fruits] of all wisdom; I relinquished the light, the unhappy parents who will mourn constantly, and the brothers, woe, in my Besara".[6] The spelling of Beth-sheʿarim in this inscription is Βεσαρα (ἐν [οἷς Β]εσάρ[οις]), the *t* being assimilated by the following *š*.

A similar spelling, Βησάρα, occurs in the *Vita* (118–119) of Josephus Flavius.[7] This historical source contains detailed information about Beth-sheʿarim-Besara, the centre of the estates which Queen Berenice, daughter of Agrippa I, owned in the Great Valley, and about Gaba of the Cavalry (Γαβα[α] πόλις ἱππέων), the neighbouring gentile settlement of the veteran cavalrymen of King Herod. Gaba, the seat of the decurion Aebutius (the Roman commander in charge of the Great Valley at the time of the Jewish Revolt in 66 C.E.), was located, according to Josephus, sixty stades (about 11 km) from Simonias (Khirbet Semūnīyye, now Shimron, near Nahalal) and twenty stades (about 3.7 km) from Besara, on the border of the territory of Acre. Aebutius attacked Josephus, who was encamped in Simonias, and when his offensive was broken by the Jews, he returned to Gaba, being followed by Josephus as far as the city of Besara. It thus appears that Gaba is west of Simonias, and Besara is located in between.

Josephus also relates that during his stay in Besara he appointed guards to watch the passes with great care, in order to prevent the Romans from suddenly descending upon the Jews who were gathering grain in Besara. From this it may be deduced that the area between Gaba and Besara was hilly and abounded in roads and paths, offering the enemy easy and protected access.

We obtain valuable additional information about Gaba from the description of Galilee in *Bellum Jud*. III, 3, 1, §36; according to this passage the location of Gaba is in the neighbourhood of Mount Carmel, which fits the details given in the *Vita*. More details are to be found in the *Antiquities* (XV, 8, 5, §294), according to which Herod fortified Gaba in Galilee and also established a military camp in the Great Valley. It is quite clear that

5 Mazar, *Beth Sheʿarim* (see note 2), 132ff.

6 M. Schwabe, *A Graeco-Jewish Epigram from Beth Sheʿarim* (1940).

7 Cf. also the tomb-inscription from Khirbet Qubeibe, near Lod: Ἄννας θυγατ[ρὸς] Μαθιθία Βισαρηνή [M. Schwabe and M. Avi-Yonah, *Yediot* 9 (1942), 31 (Hebrew)].

Josephus carefully distinguishes between Gaba in Galilee and the camp in the Valley; and it would therefore be a mistake to attempt to locate Gaba in the Jezreel Valley.[8] In another source containing the list of the gentile cities which were attacked by the Jews during the Revolt in 66/7 C.E. (*Bell* II, 18, I, §459), Gaba is mentioned between Acre and Caesarea.

The data of Josephus are also important for the history of Gaba prior to the time of Herod. One of the cities which Gabinius built in the time of Pompey is mentioned in the corrupted forms Γαμαλα or Γαβαλα (*Bell* I, 8, 4, §166) and Γαζα (*Ant* XIV, 5, 3, §88). Alt is of the opinion that the references in both sources are to Gaba; if this opinion is correct, then his assumption that the coins with the legend Γαβηνών on the reverse side, whose dating begins with 60–61 B.C.E., were minted in this city from the days of Titus until the 3rd century C.E., is also probable.[9] As we know that it was Pompey's policy to support the Hellenistic cities, it may perhaps be inferred that Gaba was already a gentile town and an important strategic point in south-western Galilee at the end of the Hasmonean period.[10] This would fit in well with the information of Georgios Synkellos concerning the gentile cities which were conquered by Alexander Jannai; among these is mentioned Gaba together with Mount Tabor, which is on the other side of the Jezreel Valley.[11]

The Byzantine monk Eusebius in his *Onomasticon* curiously mentions Γαβε as being situated "sixteen miles" from Caesarea, and identifies it with biblical Gibbethon.[12] It is improbable that Eusebius actually means Gaba Hippeon, because the short distance from Caesarea does not permit us to locate this site in Galilee or the Great Valley. Abel identifies this Gaba with Jebaʿ in the Plain of Sharon, about 24 km south of Haifa.[13] The latest Byzantine sources (from the 6th and 7th century) mention Gaba as a town in Palaestina Secunda, namely, in Galilee.[14]

8 Cf. M. Avi-Yonah, *Map of Roman Palestine* (2d ed, 1940), 38, n. 1; Mazar, *Beth Sheʿarim* (see note 2), 11, n. 54.

9 A. Alt, *ZDPV* 62 (1939), 8; cf. A.H.M. Jones, *The Cities of the Eastern Roman Provinces* (1937), 455, n. 42. For the period of Herod, cf. A. Alt, *PJb* 36 (1940), 86f.

10 There is, however, no basis for the assumption that Gaba is already mentioned in Judith, ch. 3 [cf. A. Alt, *ZDPV* 62 (1939), 5ff.; F. Stummer, *Geographie des Buches Judith* (1947), 5f.]. According to this story, Holofernes camped between Γαιβαν and Scythopolis; it is preferable to accept the reading Γαιβαν (Cod. Alex.) and to identify this site with ʿEin Ṭābūn, now Kefar Yeḥezq'el. This site is probably talmudic Ṭūbīnā or Ṭūbnīyā (*Tos. Shebiʿith* 7, 14, etc.; the vocalization is uncertain); cf. S. Klein, *MGWJ* 54 (1910), 21; Avi-Yonah, *Roman Palestine* (see note 8), 30, and Fons Tubania of the Crusaders (cf. Abel, *GP* 1, 445f.).

11 *Synkellos, Chronographie* (ed., Dindorf), 559:3.

12 *The Onomasticon of Eusebius* (ed., Klostermann), 70:8.

13 Abel, *GP* 2, 323.

14 A. Alt, *ZDPV* 62 (1939), 8ff. Gaba is mentioned as a seat of a bishop in a document from 536 C.E.; cf. *idem*, *PJb* 56 (1933), 77.

We may conclude from these various sources that Gaba was already a Hellenistic town in the second century B.C.E., and that it existed at least until the Arabic period. The information provided by Josephus makes it possible for us to establish its location in Lower Galilee, at the edge of the territory of Acre, near Mount Carmel, and in the vicinity of Besara, which was 3.7 km distant. It occupied an important strategic position and certainly commanded a key point of communication, from which it was easy to control the Great Valley and the hill country of south-western Galilee. The identification with Sheikh Abreik, as suggested by Gurein,[15] having been disproved, various attempts have since been made to identify it with other sites.[16] Worthy of attention is that of Alt, who locates Gaba at Jelāmet el-Manṣūra, about 1.5 km north of Tell Qeimūn (biblical Jokneam) and 4 km south-west of Beth-sheʿarim (Sheikh Abreik).[17] Unfortunately, Alt did not examine this insignificant site, nor did he pay attention to the fact that Jelāmet el-Manṣūra is located neither in Galilee nor near Mount Carmel, but on the slopes of Mount Carmel itself. Even less plausible is his second suggestion, according to which it is possible to identify Gaba with Qīra, which is south of Tell Qeimūn.[18] For this site is outside the territories of Galilee, far removed from the main roads, without strategic importance and nearly 7 km from Beth-sheʿarim.

During the second season of the excavations at Sheikh Abreik, the archaeological expedition of the Israel Exploration Society studied the area west of Sheikh Abreik in order to discover the location of Gaba. Special attention was paid to el-Ḥārithiyye, where Kibbutz Shaʿar Haʿamaqim was then being established; it soon became evident that the upper layers at this spot were Arabic and that the lower ones were Byzantine and Roman. To the Roman-Byzantine period belong stone structures and characteristic sherds; a long wall of small ashlars, discovered in the south of the mound, is apparently the outer wall of a Roman building, and the earliest pottery dates from the Herodian period. It is, of course, quite possible that a more precise survey or excavation will unearth even earlier sherds; but it should be pointed out that nowhere in the whole area of the mound were Iron Age sherds to be found, nor does the site itself lead one to believe that there existed here a pre-Hellenistic settlement.

There can be no question of the strategic importance of this site: the area of ruins is spread over the entire mound as far as the Haifa-Nazareth road

15 V. Guerin, *Galilee* 1 (1868), 395ff.

16 Abel (*GP* 2, Map IX) located Gaba south-east of Beth-sheʿarim, but he gives no explanation; cf. *ibid*., 21, 321–322.

17 A. Alt, *ZDPV* 62 (1939), 16ff.

18 *Ibid*., 17f.; *idem*, *PJb* 36 (1940), 80f.

running south, and even extends to the other side of the road; the site itself is located on the slopes of the hill country of Lower Galilee, beside the key point at the entrance from the Plain of Acre to the narrow pass leading to the Great Valley through which the River Kishon makes its way. Here, there is indeed an important road junction; besides the bridge (Jisr el-Ḥārithiyye) which is situated to the west of the mound, the road from the coast bifurcates to lead to Megiddo–Jenin and to Nahalal, Nazareth and ʿAfula. A garrison stationed in el-Ḥārithiyye could easily command the vital communication lines in this area. Furthermore, el-Ḥārithiyye lies 3 km from Beth-sheʿarim, and approximately 11 km from Simonias.

The above facts as well as the description given generally in the *Vita* of Josephus favour the identification of Gaba with el-Ḥārithiyye.[19] As for the fortified camp of Herod in the Great Valley (mentioned by Josephus),[20] it may perhaps be identified with the remains of the Roman camp at the foot of Mount Carmel, near Jelāmet el-Manṣūra, overlooking the western part of the Valley.[21]

The location of Gaba of the Cavalry raises another topographical problem. In Pharaoh Tuthmosis III's list of localities in Eretz-Israel,[22] there are mentioned, among the various city-states in the Jezreel Valley and the Plain of Acre, two cities with the name of Gebaʿ (Egyptian *Kbʿ*). One of them (no. 114) appears together with *ʿnqnʿm*, biblical Jokneam. The other one (no. 41), designated as *Kbʿ smn* — the predicative *smn* being perhaps a transcription of a Canaanite-Hebrew word for olive oil[23] — is mentioned together with *Mšr*, biblical Mishal, and *ʾksp*, biblical Achshaph, in the Plain of Acre (cf. Josh 19:25), which I considered to be located at Tell en-Naḥl and Tell Harbaj (near Kefar Ḥasidim) respectively.[24]

I had previously identified Gaba of the Cavalry with Gebaʿ, no. 114, of the Tuthmosis list;[25] but this seems less likely than the proposal by Yeivin,[26] who equates it with Gebaʿ-shemen. It is noteworthy that in the stele of Amenḥotep II (the son and successor of Tuthmosis III), which contains detailed information about his military campaigns to the East,[27]

19 This identification has been accepted by Avi-Yonah, *Roman Palestine* (see note 8), 38.

20 *Ant*. XV, 8, 5, §294.

21 Investigated by G. Schumacher, *ZDPV* 31 (1908), 125.

22 J. Simons, *Handbook for the Study of the Egyptian Topographical Lists* (1937), 111ff.; M. Noth, *ZDPV* 61 (1938), 60ff.; S. Yeivin, *JEA* 36 (1950), 51ff.

23 J. Müller, *MVAG* 12 (1907), 16. But A.F. Rainey [*JARCE* 10 (1973), 74–75] proposed interpreting *swmn* as *šʿmōneh*, "eight", and locating Gebaʿ-šʿmōneh at the small mound of Tell es-Samn, 800 m south-south-west of Tell Harbaj; cf. Abel, *GP* 2, 13.

24 B. Maisler (Mazar), *Yediot* 6 (1939), 158 (Hebrew); *idem*, *RHJE* 1 (1947), 49.

25 *Idem*, *Yediot* 11/3–4 (1944/5), 38 (Hebrew).

26 S. Yeivin, *JEA* 36 (1950), 57.

27 A. Badawy, *ASAE* 42, 1ff.; J. Wilson in *ANET*, 245ff.

Gebaᶜ-shemen is mentioned as the last station on his campaign in the Jezreel Valley, coming immediately after Anaharath (cf. Josh 19:19; perhaps Tell el-Mukharkhash south-east of Mount Tabor[28]) and *hw mkt*, the vicinity of Megiddo. It therefore becomes quite clear that Amenḥotep returned to Egypt via the Plain of Acre and the coast, and that Gebaᶜ-shemen was an important stronghold defending the entrance from the Jezreel Valley to the coastal plain.

It can be established that this Gebaᶜ, which is mentioned in the Egyptian documents of the 15th century B.C.E., is located in the same area in which there later stood a Hellenistic city of the same name. El-Ḥārithiyye is not a tell and gives no evidence of having been a Canaanite city in the Late Bronze Age; but about a kilometre south-west of el-Ḥārithiyye, near Jisr el-Ḥārithiyye and the spring, Tell ʿAmr is located. The small excavation carried out in this mound by Garstang[29] brought to light Arab sherds in the topmost layer, and, beneath this, pottery from the Late Bronze and the early Iron Age, and even some Hellenistic sherds. It is therefore apparent that this site was occupied from the Late Bronze (16th–13th centuries B.C.E.) to the Hellenistic period (perhaps with a gap in Iron Age II–III). As in many other cases, the settlement was moved from the small mound in the plain, on the bank of the Kishon River, to the more suitable site of el-Ḥārithiyye; and this probably took place during the Hellenistic period.[30]

By establishing the location of Gebaᶜ-Gaba at Tell ʿAmr and el-Ḥārithiyye, we can throw new light on the problem of Harosheth of the Peoples (חרשת הגוים), the presumed "seat" of Sisera which is mentioned several times in Judg 4. The supposed similarity between the names Haroseth and el-Ḥārithiyye (a genuine Arabic name) had led scholars of the last century to draw a parallel between the two; and when it became clear that el-Ḥārithiyye could not be considered for various reasons, most scholars were then led to agree with Albright's opinion, namely, that the location of Harosheth of the Peoples must be placed at the neighbouring Tell ʿAmr.[31] The identification of Canaanite Gebaᶜ with Tell ʿAmr, however, rules out this assumption; furthermore, we may well ask whether a town named *Ḥarōšet haggōyim* ever existed, for, with the exception of the refer-

28 And not Tell el-ʿAjjul; cf. Y. Aharoni, *The Land of the Bible* (1979), 168, 188 n. 86.

29 *Bulletin of the British School of Archaeology in Jerusalem* 2 (1922), 14ff.

30 It is not surprising that Geba is not mentioned in the biblical sources, for information about this area is sparse, and it is also doubtful whether this site was occupied during the period of the Israelite Monarchy.

31 W.F. Albright, *JPOS* 2 (1922), 284ff.; *idem*, *BASOR* 11 (1923), 11; 12 (1923), 18 ("almost certainly"); A. Alt, *PJb* 21 (1925), 42ff.; *idem*, in *Festschrift G. Beer* (1935), 8; Abel, *GP* 2, 343ff.; B. Maisler (Mazar), *Israel in Biblical Times* (1943), Map 7.

ences in Judg 4, we have no knowledge of this place. The name is compounded of two elements, the first of which is peculiar, and the second of which means, perhaps, a conglomeration of various ethnic groups living in one area, or at least represents an ancient term for an ethnically and socially indefinite population (hordes, tribes) in contrast to the permanent and politically organized inhabitants of a country or a region (cf. Tidal, King of Goyim, in Gen 14). Significant from this point of view is the name *Gᵉlîl haggōyim* (only in Isa 8:23), "The District of the Peoples", applied to a large area in northern Eretz-Israel. מלך גוים לגלגל (Josh 12:23) must be corrected according to the Septuagint B, which reads מלך גוים לגליל; thus the name was understood in the Hellenistic period, i.e., Γαλιλάια των ἐθνῶν (the Septuagint rendering of Isa 8:23) or Γαλιλαία ἀλλοφύλων (2 Macc 5:15).[32]

גליל הגוים recalls the designations גלילות הפלשתים (Josh 13:2), גלילות פלשת (Joel 4:4) and גלילות הירדן (Josh 22:10–11)— all clearly limited districts of a certain region or country.[33] הגליל (with the article) or ארץ הגליל (1 Kgs 9:11) was known as a distinctively demarcated district, including the regions north of the Jezreel Valley, from Kedesh (Josh 20:7) in the north-east to Cabul (1 Kgs 9:13) in the west.[34]

These considerations lead us to a new solution of the problem of Harosheth of the Peoples. It is apparently the name of an entire region or district closely related to Galilee of the Peoples, and not of a particular town in south-western Galilee (el-Ḥārithiyye or Tell ʿAmr). Jabin appears in Judg 4 as "the king of Canaan who ruled in Hazor" (4:2, 23–24). Hazor had already risen to prominence in the period of Amarna,[35] and after the settlement of the Israelite tribes in the hill country, it became the chief Canaanite city-state in northern Eretz-Israel, "for Hazor was the head of all those kingdoms" (Josh 11:10). Therefore the title "king of Canaan" fits Jabin correctly, for it means "head of the kings of Canaan" (cf. Judg 5:19).

Sisera, the chief of Jabin's army, "dwelt in Harosheth of the Peoples", and he had nine hundred chariots under his command (Judg 4:2–3, 13). According to the biblical narrative, he oppressed the Israelites twenty years (half a generation), apparently as the viceroy of Jabin in Harosheth; and here the reference is to the northern tribes Naphtali, Zebulun, and Issachar, as attested in the narrative and in the Song of Deborah. It becomes apparent that Harosheth is nothing else but the hill country of northern Eretz-Israel,

32 Cf. A. Alt, *PJb 33* (1937), 52ff.; 35 (1939), 72f.

33 Cf. N. Glueck, *AASOR* 25–28 (1945–1949), 299.

34 Similarly, other regions and districts in western Eretz-Israel are known as העמק or ארץ העמק (Josh 17:16), הנגב or ארץ הנגב, הככר, etc., and even חבל הים (Zeph 2:5–7). They all refer to clearly demarcated areas.

35 Cf. J. Garstang, *Joshua-Judges* (1931), 381ff.; W.F. Albright, *BASOR* 78 (1940), 8f.

the entire region occupied by the Israelite tribes, surrounded by the Canaanite city-states in the coastal plain, the Jezreel Valley and the Jordan Valley, and in some areas in Lower Galilee. This region was occupied by Sisera and his army,[36] and it was Sisera's responsibility to impose control over the semi-nomadic tribes. Barak, the charismatic leader of the tribes of Naphtali and Zebulun, "drew" Sisera to the Kishon River in anticipation of the arrival of an auxiliary Israelite army from central Eretz-Israel. Actually, Barak inflicted a severe defeat upon the Canaanites at the Waters of Megiddo (Wādi Lejjūn) with the help of the Josephite tribes (Judg 5:14, 18–19). This victory resulted in the liberation of the Israelite regions in the northern part of the country from Canaanite domination.

The aftermath of these events is to be found in Josh 11. The historical background of this narrative, loosely associated with Joshua, is apparently the new attempt of Jabin to reoccupy the hill country, perhaps with the purpose of renewing the Canaanite control over the vital roads leading from Hazor and the Jordan Valley to the Phoenician coast; but after the second defeat of Jabin and his allies in the battle by the Waters of Merom (Jebel Mārūn on the Israeli-Lebanese border),[37] Hazor was captured and destroyed by the Israelites.

The proposed determination of Harosheth of the Peoples as parallel to Galilee of the Peoples enables us to suggest that חרשת was originally an appellative referring to the hill country. It appears that this term is closely associated with חֹרֶשׁ, "wooded mountain",[38] Ugaritic *ḫršn*,[39] Akkadian *ḫuršānu*, "mountain".[40] It is remarkable that the Septuagint translation of חרשת הגוים in Judg 4 is Ἀρείσωθ τῶν ἐθνῶν, and it is quite difficult to indicate with certainty what was the older vocalization. Both the collective form חרשת or the plural form are possible.[41] In any case, it is apparently an early Canaanite designation of the hilly and wooded regions of northern Eretz-Israel, in contrast to the coastal plain and the valleys. This designation, also used in early Israel, was of course completely superseded by the term *Galil*.

The problem of Gebaᶜ, Gebaᶜ-shemen and "Gaba of the Cavalry" should be reconsidered. New archaeological finds show that "Gaba of the Cavalry"

36 For וישב in Judg 4:2, cf. 1 Kgs 11:16; Mesha inscription, 1. 8.

37 Cf. Aharoni, *The Land of the Bible* (note 28), 225–226.

38 Cf. 2 Chr 27:4 (the plural form חרשים) and also 1 Sam 23:15; Ezek 31:3. In Palestinian Aramaic חורשא means "forest", and even in Palestinian Arabic *ḫurš* appears as a loanword in the same meaning.

39 C.H. Gordon, *Ugaritic Textbook* (1965), 405.

40 *CAD*, Vol. *Ḫ*, 253–254; W. von Soden, *Akkadisches Handwörterbuch* 1 (1965), 360. The relationship between them is of course obscure. There are several parallels for the change of the ending, such as biblical ᶜAlmōn-ᶜAlemeth (ᶜAāmōt), modern ᶜAlmīt.

41 Cf. כנרת (Egyptian: *Knnrt*), כִּנֲרוֹת, כִּנְרוֹת.

should be located at Tell Abū Shūsha near Mishmar Haemeq. This identification is supported by several finds: a) a lead weight from the Roman period inscribed with the name of Gaba (Γαβη) and found on the slopes of the tell; b) coins of Gaba found on the tell and in its vicinity; and c) graves from the Roman period.[42] In a recent study Aḥituv has demonstrated that "Gaba of the Cavalry" should not be equated with the Gaba mentioned by Josephus in connection with Beth-sheʿarim (*Vita* 115–116). Likewise, Gebaʿ and Gebaʿ-shemen of the Egyptian documents do not refer to the same place. Gebaʿ-shemen may be reliably located at Tell ʿAmr. It is the forerunner of Gaba near Beth-sheʿarim where the Roman decurion Aebutius resided (el-Ḥārithiyye). On the other hand, Gebaʿ in the topographical list of Tuthmosis III is the forerunner of "Gaba of the Cavalry," Tell Abū Shūsha.[43]

As for Gaba of Eusebius (cf. above, p. 206), it should be identified with the deserted village of Jabaʿ on the western slopes of Mount Carmel.[44]

42 Cf. R. Giveon, *Göttinger Miszellen* 49 (1981), 33–36.
43 S. Aḥituv, *Canaanite Toponyms in Ancient Egyptian Documents* (1984), 99–100.
44 *Ibid*., 99, n. 209.

The Phoenicians in the Levant

The first century C.E. historian Pomponius Mela (I:12) wrote: "The Phoenicians were a wise people who excelled both in war and in peace, in seafaring, and in the administration of a kingdom". About 750 years earlier, the prophet Isaiah had described the greatness of "traders of Sidon! You were filled with men who crossed the sea", who "made kingdoms quake", and the might of "crown-wearing Tyre, whose merchants were nobles, whose traders (Hebrew: כנענים) the world honored", whose greatness is of "former times".[1] In Ezekiel's lament over the destruction of Tyre, he quotes an ancient Phoenician source in which Tyre is addressed: "...you who were peopled from the seas, O renowned city! Mighty on the sea.... O you who dwell at the gateway of the sea, Who trade with the peoples on many coastlands".[2]

A wealth of literature, both prose and poetry preserved in the Bible and in Greek and Latin sources,[3] exalts the splendour, greatness, and wealth of Phoenicia's ancient cities, and lauds the Phoenicians-Sidonians as outstanding seamen and craftsmen, and as enterprising merchants and settlers whose achievements also extended to the sphere of the mind in the form of rich literary and artistic creation and the invention of the alphabet. A similar picture emerges from the archaeological evidence,[4] in particular from Akkadian, Egyptian, and Phoenician epigraphic material: a culture profuse in

1 Isa 23. The traditional belief about Tyre's early origins (v. 7; cf. Ezek 26:17) was widely held in antiquity. It is instructive that Herodotos (II:44) heard from the priests of Melkart (Heracles) in Tyre that their city and temple had been founded 2300 years earlier.

2 Ezek 26–28. The fragments of Phoenician poetry incorporated into Ezekiel's lament over the destruction of Tyre probably date from its flourishing in the 10th and 9th centuries B.C.E. See in this volume, "The Philistines and the Rise of Israel and Tyre", pp 63–82.

3 See S. Gsell, *Histoire ancienne d'Afrique du Nord* (1921), vol. 2 in particular.

4 See D. Harden, *The Phoenicians* (2nd ed, 1971).

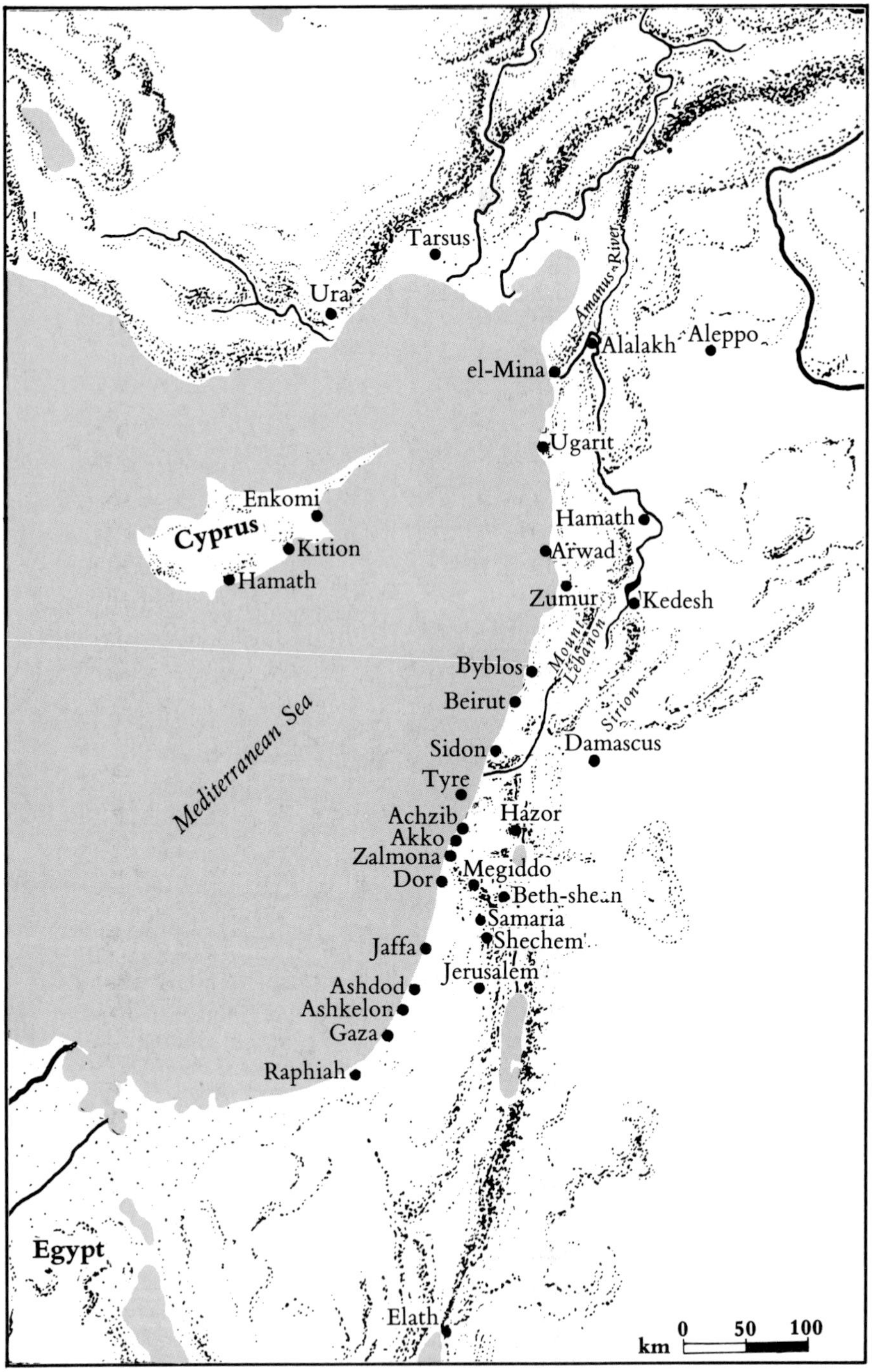

The Levantine coast: the birthplace of the Phoenician civilization

both material and intellectual achievements, enduring over a long period and which was a blessing to civilization.

The birthplace of Phoenician civilization was the long and narrow eastern coast of the Mediterranean from the Bay of Haifa north to the Cilician Gates. The coast here differs markedly from the southern coast, from the Carmel promontory to the Egyptian border. That coastline is straight, exposed and lacking any inlets. The Phoenician coast, on the other hand, is characterized by numerous inlets which make for good anchorage, and by a system of narrow coastal valleys lying between the mountain spurs which lead down to the sea from the east. Here, on the shores of the inlets, fortified settlements were established at sites chosen for strategic and navigational purposes. In some places, such as Tyre and Arwad (Aradus), the settlements were built on islands. The topographic conditions of this coastline suited a people that derived its livelihood from the sea. The valleys, with their abundant water sources, could at first supply the coastal towns with their agricultural needs. The larger the towns grew, however, the greater was the need to seek produce from further inland. The mountains touching the sea, especially Mount Lebanon, were forested and provided choice timber for shipbuilding, for local industry and export of this important commodity, mainly to Egypt, and to a lesser degree, to Mesopotamia.[5] The *Murex* snails were also exploited on a vast scale for one of Phoenicia's primary industries: purple and blue dyes.[6] Fishing[7] must also have had some importance in the life of the population. However, the mainstay of the economy of the coastal cities was seafaring, with Phoenicians serving primarily as middlemen for trade on the sea routes along the coast as far as Anatolia, the Aegean Islands, and Cyprus, which was one of the major centres of copper production.

The conflict with the Mesopotamian kingdoms of Sumer and Akkad, which had always had a major political and economic interest in gaining access to the ports of the "Upper Sea" (the Mediterranean), figured significantly in Phoenician life. In all periods, conquering armies and merchant caravans reached the coast from the lands of the Tigris and the Euphrates by way of the three access routes: via Aleppo in northern Syria through the Orontes Valley; via Qaṭna, or Kedesh, to the Eleutores (i.e. Nahr el-Kebir) Valley; and via Damascus to the Valley of Acre and southern Phoenicia. The location of the Phoenician coastal cities contributed to their growth as international trade centres and focal points in the political and bilateral cultural relations of peoples and civilizations.

5 See W. Helck, *Die Beziehungen Aegyptens zu Vorderasien im 3. und 2. Jahrt. v. Chr.* (1962), 28ff., 395ff.
6 See L.B. Jensen, *JNES* 22 (1963), 104ff.
7 See M. Nun, *Ancient Jewish Fishery* (1964), 68ff. (Hebrew).

One may well wonder how, despite the fact that the Phoenician coast was geographically splintered into small areas, in each of which evolved an urban centre which served as an international meeting place, the Phoenicians retained their ethnic, religious, and cultural uniqueness over a long period. They effectively assimilated foreign influence, utilizing eclectic elements in the arts and crafts, and adapting them for their own needs. Throughout their history, the inhabitants of the coast preserved their character and their West Semitic dialect, which is commonly known as "Canaanite", and which is very close to biblical Hebrew. The names of Phoenicia's ancient cities — Ugarit, Zumur, Arkat, Gebal (Byblos), Beeroth (Beirut), Sidon, Tyre, Achzib and ʿAkko (Acre) — are, for the most part, West Semitic. The same holds true for the Lebanon and Zaphon mountain ranges.[8] And the onomasticon of the rulers of the coastal towns mentioned from the time of the Egyptian Middle Kingdom onwards, likewise bears a typically West Semitic stamp.[9]

This situation continued until the assimilation of the Phoenicians into the Hellenistic *koine*-culture was in an advanced stage. Similarly, the religion of Phoenicia and its colonies endured almost unaltered for millennia, despite changing times and conditions. The names El, Baal, Reshef, Shemesh, Asherah, and Ashtoreth were retained by the Phoenicians. Only as a result of outside influence and internal developments did their mythology and rituals, as well as their socio-political organization, gradually undergo change. One should also emphasize that throughout all historical periods, the population of the Phoenician coast remained predominantly urban. The extent of Phoenician urbanization, with the flourishing of its institutions and economy, was in complete contrast to the lifestyle of the agricultural population of the surrounding areas.

The strong economic and, at times, political ties that linked Phoenicia's port cities to Egypt are of particular interest. These connections, by both land and sea, were of vital importance to the development of the coastal areas. We have evidence (including documents discovered at Byblos) that the close relations between Egypt and Byblos started during the Egyptian 2nd Dynasty (28th century B.C.E.) and gained momentum during the subsequent dynasties of the Old Kingdom. From Byblos, Lebanese wood was sent in exchange for goods representing the wealth of Egypt, and for gifts

8 See W.F. Albright, *The Bible and the Ancient Near East* (henceforth *BANE*) (1961), 332, 352.

9 Kings of Byblos in the 19th and 18th centuries B.C.E. include Abi-šemu, Yapi-šemu-abi, Yakin-ilu, and Yantin [identified by W.F. Albright, *BASOR* 99 (1945), 9ff. as Yantin-ʿammu, King of Byblos mentioned in the Mari documents]. An earlier king of Byblos was Ib-dadi, from the time of the 3rd Dynasty of Ur [W.F. Albright, *BASOR* 163 (1961), 45]. Mentioned in the Execration Texts are Ilumḳehat and Ammiḥur(?), Kings of Arkat; Tarʿammu, King of ʿAkko, and others.

from the Pharaohs to the temple of Baalat Gebal ("the Lady of Byblos"). It was not by chance that, as of the 6th Dynasty, the Egyptians called large ships which could sail for long distances, *kbnt,* "Byblian".[10]

These ties continued through the following periods, during which Egyptian influence largely determined the character of Byblos. It also seems that the repeated efforts of the people of Byblos, from the beginning of the second millennium B.C.E., to develop their own syllabic system of writing were inspired by Egyptian hieroglyphs.[11] The affinity to Egypt was also expressed in the use of Egyptian papyrus for writing. This was probably the reason why the Greeks called both papyrus, and books, by the name of Byblos: Βύβλος, hence Βύβλινος, a term that first appears in Homer.[12]

Starting from the 12th Egyptian Dynasty (the first quarter of the second millennium B.C.E.), when Egyptian influence in Canaan and Syria was at its zenith, we hear of multi-dimensional developments along the Phoenician coast, called in Egyptian sources *Fnḫw*, "the Land of the Tree-Fellers".[13] Two groups of Egyptian Execration Texts from the 19th and 18th centuries B.C.E. list numerous towns along the coast that served as political centres with close ties to Egypt. Among these towns are Ulaza, Arkat, Yarimuta, Byblos, Tyre, and ʿAkko, all important ports.[14] In confirmation, we note Egyptian finds from the same period, including statues and stelae of Pharaohs and their officials discovered at Ugarit, Byblos, Beirut, and other sites as far away as Crete and Cilicia.[15] On the other hand, the treasure discovered under the foundations of the temple of eṭ-Ṭod, and probably originating in one of the Phoenician cities, gives witness to Phoenician exports to Egypt.[16]

Additional discoveries in Byblos, including rich finds from the tombs of the kings of the city which date to the period of the Middle Kingdom in Egypt, also indicate that the material culture of the coastal cities was then

10 See S.H. Horn, *Andrews University Seminary Studies* 1 (1963), 52ff. The main reports on the excavations at Byblos are: P. Montet, *Byblos et l'Égypte* (1928) and M. Dunand, *Fouilles de Byblos* 1 (1939); 2/1 (1950); 2/2 (1958). See also W.F. Albright, *Enc. Miq.* 2, 404ff. with bibliography; and E.J. Wein and R. Opificius, *7000 Jahre Byblos* (1963).

11 The documents were published by M. Dunand, *Byblia Grammata* (1945), but so far efforts to decipher them have been unsuccessful. Most of them are written in syllabic script, which has over 100 symbols, and presumably represent the Byblian West Semitic dialect.

12 See W.F. Albright, *AJA* 54 (1950), 162ff.; G.J. Thierry, *VT* 1 (1951), 130f.

13 See Helck, *Die Beziehungen Aegyptens* (note 5), 277ff.

14 See Mazar, *Canaan and Israel*, 11ff.

15 See Helck, *Die Beziehungen Aegyptens* (note 5), 69ff. On the connections between Byblos and the Anatolian coast, one may perhaps learn from the Egyptian inscription from Byblos which mentions a Lycian; see W.F. Albright, *BASOR* 155 (1959), 31ff.

16 From the days of Amenḥotep II (1450–1428 B.C.E.), see F. Bisson de la Rocke, *Tôd* (1937), 113ff.; *idem*, *Le Trésor de Tôd* (1953).

at its height.[17] Cuneiform sources, in particular the 18th century B.C.E. documents from Mari on the middle Euphrates, frequently refer to Mesopotamia's relations with the coast, and to the caravans which arrived at Byblos and Tyre. From the Mari documents we learn that among the goods brought from the west were timber, fabrics, fine metal ware, oil, wine, and honey.[18] No less instructive is the fact that already at that time active trade was carried out between the Middle Minoan civilization of Crete, and Egypt and Western Asia, with towns such as Ugarit serving as intermediaries. It is no mere coincidence that *Kaptara*, i.e. Crete, appears in the mythology of Ugarit as the home of Kothar-and-Ḫasis, god of art and architecture, and that at Mari "Kaptaran" was the term used for certain highly valuable goods.[19]

The momentous developments that occurred during the first phase of MB II (Middle Kingdom in Egypt; 20th and 19th centuries B.C.E.) and even more so during the second phase (18th and 17th centuries B.C.E.) may be explained in the light of the following facts:
1) During the first phase, Egypt achieved great economic and political prosperity. This enabled it to extend its influence to Canaan and Syria, and along the coast as far as Ugarit. All of this activity boosted the barter trade with Egypt.
2) Following the rise of the Amorite kingdoms in Mesopotamia and Syria, caravan trade developed and expanded, due to their initiative and under their protection, reaching its zenith in the Mari period, during the reign of Ḫammurapi. These new conditions encompassed the whole of the ancient Near East and were favourable to international trade and diplomacy. The *lingua franca* of the region during that period was Akkadian, and major cities such as Ugarit, Aleppo, Qaṭna, Hazor, and Byblos cultivated close ties with the Mesopotamian centres.[20]
3) The flourishing of Minoan civilization in Crete was a major contributing factor to the development of international relations.[21]

These conditions were altered in the following period. The 17th century B.C.E. saw an upheaval in the political and ethnic constellations of the region.[22] Syria and Canaan were overrun by invaders, among them Hurrians

17 It should be noted that Byblos is already mentioned in Sumerian documents dating from the 3rd Dynasty of Ur (ca. 2000 B.C.E.); see E. Sollberger, *AfO* 19 (1959/60), 120ff.
18 See A. Malamat, *Enc. Miq.* 4, 567–568.
19 See B. Mazar, *Enc. Miq.* 4, 236–238.
20 See A. Malamat, *Isaac Beer Volume* (1961), 1ff. (Hebrew).
21 On the subject in general, see H. Kantor, in R. Ehrich, *Relative Chronologies in Old World Archaeology* (1954), 10ff.; and P. Äström, *Heraklion* (1963).
22 Without elaborating on the subject of the Hyksos in Egypt and historical events occurring during the 17th and 16th centuries B.C.E., one should note that scarabs of the "Hyksos" ruler Ḫyān

and Indo-Iranians, who lent to the population its mixed character and quasi-feudal system. Egypt fell under foreign rule and suffered an economic decline, and Mesopotamia ultimately fell under the domination of foreign kingdoms: the Kassites in the south, and Mitanni in the north. It is unclear how these events influenced the Phoenician coast, but it does appear that the Plain of Acre suffered the same fate as the rest of Canaan: already in the 14th century B.C.E., rulers bearing foreign names appear in towns such as ʿAkko and Achshaph. In southern Phoenicia, i.e. at ʿAkko, Achzib, and Kabri, we encounter fortresses fortified with the beaten-earth glacis characteristic of MB II construction in Canaan and Syria. The finds from the temple in Nahariya (and at Byblos) indicate that foreign influence became entrenched during that period.[23] Even Ugarit, far to the north, absorbed considerable, mainly Hurrian, foreign elements; nevertheless, its population, as a whole, retained its ancient West Semitic character, as evidenced by the language spoken and the religion practiced.

The northern Phoenician towns from Tyre to Arwad, on the other hand, appear to have been saved from drastic socio-political change and from the penetration of foreign ethnic elements who could have affected their demography. This is indicated by the "Canaanite"-speaking population that inhabited the coastal region at the end of the Middle Bronze Age, and about whom we learn from the 18th Dynasty Pharaonic military expeditions to the west of the Fertile Crescent. The population differed very little from that of the region during the period of the Middle Kingdom. It seems that the Phoenician coast suffered less than the other areas of Canaan and Syria from the invading armies of Egypt, when Tuthmosis III (ca. 1504–1450 B.C.E.) and his son Amenḥotep II (ca. 1450–1428 B.C.E.) mounted their campaigns in order to gain control of these areas, and to establish colonial rule.[24] It may be that the port cities saw a political and economic advantage in Egyptian colonial rule, whereas for their part, the Egyptians benefited from the economic exploitation of the coastal area, with its cedar forests, orchards, advanced industries, and ports which were vital as bases for its fleet.

discovered in Israel, and various objects bearing his name found in Egypt, in Knossos (an alabaster cover), at Boghazköy (an obsidian fragment), and in Byblos (a lion figurine), seem to indicate the existence of international relations in his time. See M. Stock, *MDOG* 94 (1963), 73ff. Additional findings are required for a full understanding of this elusive chapter in history.

23 See M. Dothan, *EI* 5 (1956), 41ff. (Hebrew); also *idem*, in *Western Galilee and the Coast of Galilee* (1965), 63ff. (Hebrew).

24 The list of Canaanite towns, which probably embraces only those which were part of the alliance defeated at Megiddo [see the summary by Y. Aharoni, *The Land of the Bible* (rev ed, 1979), 220ff.], does not include the Phoenician coastal cities. These towns were not affected by the early wars of Tuthmosis. They acknowledged his rule, and paid him heavy taxes.

The end to belligerency came during the rule of Amenḥotep II, when favourable conditions were created in the Egyptian provinces of Canaan and Syria — in particular, security was established along the land and sea routes, and with stable political and commercial conditions, the resumption of active international trade was facilitated. And in fact, under Tuthmosis IV (ca. 1425–1417 B.C.E.) and Amenḥotep III (ca. 1417–1379 B.C.E.), when Egypt was at its peak, and its Asian provinces had become an integral part of the powerful Egyptian kingdom, the time was ripe for the Phoenician port cities to develop extensive trade and shipping, as well as industry and specific crafts. This period may be termed "Pax Aegyptiaca", when Egypt established strong ties with its near and distant neighbours, including Mitanni and Cyprus (probably Elishah).

At about the same time, the term "Canaan" appears in one of the following three ways:

1) *knʿ* (in the Nuzi Documents: *Kinaḫḫu*), referring to the purple dye (ΠορΠύρα) produced from the *Murex*. It provided the basis for the main industry of the coastal cities producing the dyed fabrics renowned throughout the ancient world. This would explain the semantic evolution of the Greek word φοῖνιξ, "red purple", to Φοινίκη, "Phoenicia" or Φοινίκες, "Phoenicians", serving as a synonym for "Canaan";[25]

2) *Knʿnw*, "Canaanites", mentioned as early as the reign of Amenḥotep II, and referring to a respectable class and to the mercantile profession as a whole, in a sense similar to that known in the Bible.[26] The original meaning seems to have been "manufacturers and merchants of purple cloth";

3) Canaan in the sense of the Land of Canaan, the Phoenician coast south of Ugarit, as in its earliest mention in the inscription of Idrimi, King of Alalakh (15th century B.C.E.), and in two Ugaritic inscriptions.[27] Later, it came to signify part of the Egyptian province in Asia, as in the El-Amarna Letters dating from the second quarter of the 14th century B.C.E. Finally, both in 19th Dynasty Egyptian sources and in the Bible, it was used in reference to the entire Egyptian province in western Asia, which is "the land of Canaan with its various boundaries".[28] The term "Canaan" continued to be applied to the Phoenician coast, and the Phoenicians called themselves Canaanites until the Roman period. "Canaan begot Sidon, his

25 See E. A. Speiser, *Language* 12 (1936), 121ff.

26 See B. Mazar, *BASOR* 102 (1946), 7ff.; Albright, *BANE* (note 8), 356, n. 50.

27 The inscription of Idrimi, King of Alalakh, was published by S. Smith, *The Statue of Idrimi* (1949), see p. 14. On "Canaanite" and "Canaan" in the inscriptions at Ugarit, see A.F. Rainey, *IEJ* 13 (1963), 43ff.; J. Nougayrol, *Iraq* 25 (1963), 123. It has been made known that the earliest mention of the term "Canaan" is in the Mari documents; see G. Dossin, *Syria* 50 (1973), 277ff.

28 See W.F. Albright, *Enc. Miq.* 4, s.v. "Canaan"; also see in this volume, "Lebo-hamath and the Northern Border of Canaan", pp. 189–202.

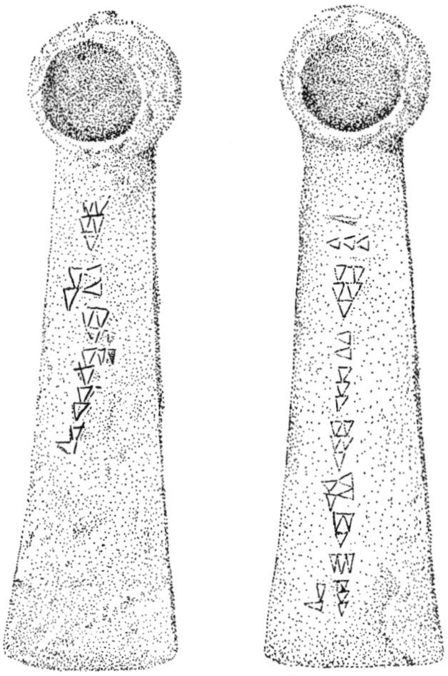

Bronze ceremonial adzeheads inscribed in the cuneiform alphabet of Ugarit from Ras Shamra (14th century B.C.E.) (*Enc. Miq.*)

firstborn" (Gen 10:15), and the Canaanites were not only traditionally listed among the peoples of the Land of Israel, but also as the inhabitants of the northern Phoenician cities: Arkatites, Zemarites, Arwadites, and Sinites.

It is only by inference that we can determine the common basis of the above three connotations of the term. Most probably, the term "Canaan" was used to designate the Phoenician coast because of the purple dye which was its main product. Only later was the term extended to encompass the entire Egyptian province in Asia. In Greek we find a similar semantic development: φοῖνιξ-Φοινίκη. Of course, it is possible that the reverse process occurred, i.e. the all important product, the purple dye, was named after the land of its origin.

The prosperity described above lasted throughout the El-Amarna period, which began towards the end of Amenḥotep III's rule and continued through the monarchy of Amenḥotep IV-Akhenaton (ca. 1379–1362 B.C.E.). During Akhenaton's reign, the Hittites captured northern Syria, including Ugarit[29] which, nonetheless, did not cease to be a centre of trade, fine craftsmanship, and industry. It remained an active part of a vast international constellation encompassing Egypt, Syria, Mesopotamia, Anatolia, the Aegean, and Cyprus.[30] Particularly noteworthy are the documents from Ugarit

29 On this period, see K.A. Kitchen, *Supiluliuma and the Amarna Pharaohs* (1962).

30 Cf. A.F. Rainey, *IEJ* 13 (1963), 313ff. Ura on the Cilician coast played an important role in the trade relations between Ugarit, the Hittite kingdom, and the Aegean Islands. C.H. Gordon has gone

which bear witness to its active trade relations by way of the sea with other sea ports on the eastern Mediterranean coast, among which were ʿAkko, Ashdod, and Ashkelon.[31] In addition to its autochthonous, West Semitic stratum which determined its character, the population of Ugarit also included Hurrians descended from the immigrants of the previous period, and vendors and artisans from diverse countries.[32] Alongside enormous material wealth and achievements in the arts and fine crafts, we find considerable intellectual activity. This is reflected in religious literature, particularly in epic and mythological works written in the Ugaritic, West Semitic language inscribed in the Ugaritic alphabet. There is no agreement as to what extent the Ugaritic language differed from the contemporary "Canaanite" of southern Phoenicia and Eretz-Israel. No less fascinating are the letters, lists of guilds, and administrative and economic records found at Ugarit dealing with the political order, social structure, economy, and religion not only of Ugarit, but of the coastal towns in general.[33]

Another significant feature of this period was the rise of the Mycenean civilization, and the establishment of Mycenean colonies in the Mediterranean Basin, especially on the island of Cyprus. Under the peaceful conditions of the early 14th century B.C.E., Mycenean trade reached the eastern coast of the Mediterranean and as far as the interior of the Land of Canaan.[34] From the beginning of the 14th century B.C.E. onward (the beginning of LB II), fine Mycenean ceramic ware of the Late Helladic IIIA type together with choice Cypriot products, and the examples of Mycenean craftsmanship, were widely distributed throughout the entire area, extending from Cilicia in the north to Egypt in the south.[35] It is possible that already at this time, merchants, artisans, seamen, and mercenaries from the

so far as to suggest that Ura should be identified with Ur (of the Chaldeans) mentioned in the Book of Genesis [*JNES* 17 (1958), 30f.]. These trade connections continued until the end of the 13th century B.C.E.

31 See *Ugaritica* IV (1962), 140ff.

32 It appears that these foreigners had their own commercial quarter in Ugarit, called the *karu* in one of the Akkadian Ugaritic documents [J. Nougayrol, *Le Palais royal d'Ugarit* IV (1956), 219]. It was similar in function to the חוצות in the days of the Israelite Monarchy (2 Sam 1:20; 1 Kgs 20:34).

33 On the archaeological material, see C.F. Schaeffer, *Les Fouilles de Ras-Shamra-Ugarit* (1929 and onwards); the final reports appear in the *Ugaritica* volumes. The epigraphic material was compiled by C.H. Gordon, *Ugaritic Textbook* (1965). See also A.F. Rainey, *The Social Structure of Ugarit* (1967) (Hebrew); M. Liverani, *Storia di Ugarit* (1962).

34 See, in particular, V. Vercoutter, *L'Égypte et le monde Egéen Préhellénique* (1956); H.L. Kantor, *The Aegean and the Orient in the Second Millennium B.C.* (1947), 56ff.; A. Furumark, *Opusc. Arch.* 4 (1950), 203ff.; F. Schachermeyer, *Die minoische Kultur des alten Kreta* (1964), 109ff.

35 See especially F. A. Furumark, *The Mycenean Pottery* (1941). See also F.M. Stubbings, *Mycenean Pottery from the Levant* (1951); H.L. Kantor, *The Aegean and the Orient in the Second Millennium B.C.* (1947), 33ff.

Mycenean area arrived at the shores of Canaan as alien residents. We have knowledge of Lycian, Sherden, and Danunite pirates and mercenaries in Canaan during the 14th century B.C.E. It may well be that the new city established on the estuary of the Kishon in the Bay of Haifa, Zalmona (Tell Abu Hawam), was actually a small port founded by Aegean or Cypriot seamen. The predominance of Mycenean material in the earliest stratum of Zalmona bears witness to this.[36] There is no doubt that the foundation of this town around 1400 B.C.E. was not an isolated instance, and that developments beginning in this period led to the foundation of new cities along the coast and to the expansion of shipping and trade. Another city probably founded in the period under discussion, was Dor, which later played an important role in the history of the Land of Israel. At this time Ashdod was also expanding into an important port, which developed very close ties with Ugarit.[37]

From the El-Amarna documents and some other Egyptian sources we learn of a long chain of ports on the coast of Canaan, some of which later gained political and economic importance. Among them were Arwad, Zumur, Ulaza, Ammia, Bathrouna, Byblos, Sidon, Tyre, and ʿAkko. The vigorous development of the coast was coupled with events in the interior, particularly along the main roads. The Egyptian fortress at Beth-shean (level IX) was erected at this time, and important cities such as Hazor (level XIV on the acropolis, level B1 in the lower city), Megiddo (level VIII), Gezer, Ashdod, Lachish (the second phase of the temple) and Gaza flourished. The tombs rich in Cyprian and Mycenean ceramics that were discovered in Jerusalem also date from this period.[38]

One should also take note of data concerning the bilateral relations operative between the Phoenician coast and Egypt. In addition to archaeological evidence indicating an uninterrupted flow of manufactured goods and fine crafts from Egypt to Canaan, and of Canaanite products shipped to Egypt, the sources speak of Canaanite merchants arriving on their ships at the Delta ports, and of Canaanite seamen in the service of the Pharaohs and Egyptian temples.[39] The bilateral relations between the two countries are increasingly felt in literature, religion, and art. It is not surprising that

36 See R.M. Hamilton, *QDAP* 4 (1935), 11ff.; also E. Anati, *ʿAtiqot* 2 (1959), 80ff. (Hebrew). Three phases were discerned in the Late Bronze Age strata (V and IVA) at Tell Abu Hawam, the earliest of which dates to the beginning of the 14th century B.C.E., and the latest ending with the destruction of the city by the Sea Peoples at the close of the 13th century B.C.E.

37 See bibliography in M. Dothan and D.N. Freedman, *Ashdod* 1 (1967), 8.

38 See R. Amiran, *EI* 6 (1961), 25ff. (Hebrew).

39 See Helck, *Die Beziehungen Aegyptens* (note 5), 462f.; on Egyptian navigation in general, see J. Säve-Söderbergh, *The Navy of the Eighteenth Egyptian Dynasty* (1946).

Phoenician poetry, such as the myth of the war between Baal and Yam, known from the Ugaritic documents, was translated into Egyptian.[40] Canaanite gods, such as Baal (especially Baal Zaphon, the patron of seamen), Reshef, Horon, Ashtoreth, Anath, etc. penetrated the Egyptian pantheon, and were eventually fully assimilated. We also have evidence of close ties between 1) Canaan (its coastal towns in particular); 2) the centres of the Kassite and Mitanni kingdoms in Mesopotamia, Cyprus; and 3) the Hittite monarchy in Anatolia and northern Syria. It should be noted that during this period the *lingua franca* of diplomacy and trade in Canaan and in the neighbouring states continued to be Akkadian.

These developments, characteristic of the early 14th century B.C.E., can be understood against the background of the following observations:

1) This was a high point in the history of the Egyptian kingdom, that included Canaan. The Egyptian fleet was at full strength, and peace and security reigned in the Levant.

2) This was also the beginning of the Helladic IIIA period, during which the Mycenean marine "empire" grew and achieved successes in seamanship, fine crafts, and barter.

3) The Phoenician ports could rely on Egypt for their security, and thus the time was opportune to expand the sphere of their trade, and to strengthen their merchant fleets. They could exploit the advantages of their central location in an area where several civilizations thrived: Egypt to the south, the Mycenean world to the west, Anatolia to the north, and Syria and Mesopotamia to the east.

It was only at the end of the reign of Amenḥotep III, and especially during that of Amenḥotep IV — the El-Amarna period — that this harmonious constellation started to came apart and the culture of Egypt's Asian province began to crumble. This deterioration, which affected all spheres of life, was the cumulative outcome of the weakening of Egyptian rule, the struggle between the Hittites and Egypt over the control of Syria, and the increasing penetration of nomadic tribes into Canaan. The decline reached its nadir at the end of the 13th century B.C.E. Throughout this long period of instability, insecurity, economic hardship, and revolts in which they took part, the coastal cities generally retained their strength. They did so in spite of the war between Egypt and the Hittites, the unrelenting pressure of the Amurru kingdom from the rear, the competition among themselves, and the constant danger from the hosts of *Ḫabiru* and nomadic tribes who were attracted by their wealth.[41]

40 Helck, *Die Beziehungen Aegyptens* (note 5), 539; G. Posener, *Annuaire de l'Institut de Philologie et d'Histoire Orientales et Slaves* 13 (1953), 461ff.

41 It should be noted that the Papyrus Anastasi I, from the days of the 19th Dynasty (*ANET*, 476ff.),

The endurance of the Phoenicians in the face of adversity, and their initiative and flexibility in adapting to changing conditions are well demonstrated during the following period, namely the period of transition from the Bronze Age to the Iron Age. That era saw a sharp decline in the power of Egypt in Canaan, the destruction of the Hittite kingdom, and extreme changes in the life and demography of Canaan. These changes resulted from the rise of the Tribes of Israel and the massive assault on its shores by the Sea Peoples, among them the Philistines. It is noteworthy that, while the political and ethnic scene of the ancient Near East, particularly of Canaan, was altered so drastically, the cities of Phoenicia from Arwad to ʿAkko escaped foreign conquest and the influx of immigrants. True, Ugarit, the large metropolis of the north, and the southern port of Tell Abu Hawam were completely destroyed,[42] and Tyre went into decline. But other major coastal cities such as Arwad, Byblos, and Sidon, upon gaining their freedom from Egyptian rule, became metropolitan city-states. They withstood both the Tribes of Israel then already in the north of Eretz-Israel, and the Sea Peoples who conquered the coast from Egypt to the Carmel.[43]

The Phoenicians now competed against the Sea Peoples for the control of the Levant and for the monopoly over sea trade. Byblos in the centre of Phoenicia, and the Land of the Sidonians to its south constituted, together with the Philistine districts, "the territory that remains" (הארץ הנשארת), i.e. those parts of Canaan not conquered by the Israelites (Josh 13:2–6; Judg 3:3).[44] From the few extant sources, one may conclude that Sidon was of particularly great importance, and that its influence extended as far as Laish in eastern Upper Galilee (Judg 18:28). Tyre, in contrast, was then under the yoke of Sidon. It is not coincidental that in Homer, and even in the Bible, the term "Sidonians" is synonymous with "Canaanites-Phoenicians".

mentions a long chain of coastal cities in the province of Canaan from Zumur to Raphiah, among which are Byblos, Beeroth (Beirut), Sidon, Zarphat (Sarepta), Usu, Tyre, Jaffa and Gaza. It appears that all of them engaged in both land and sea trade, and some served as Egyptian bases.

42 On the events leading to the disintegration of the Hittite kingdom and the destruction of Ugarit, see H. Otten, *MDOG* 94 (1962), 1ff. It appears that the prosperous port city of Ugarit was destroyed by the Sea Peoples after they had conquered Cyprus. They invaded by land and sea, and attacked the Hittite kingdom and its satellites in Syria at the beginning of the reign of Ramesses III, i.e. before the war launched by this Pharaoh against the Sea Peoples in the fifth and eighth years of his reign. [On the war, see W.F. Edgerton and J.A.W. Wilson, *Historical Records of Ramses III* (1936).]

43 One should note that Tiglath-Pileser I (1116–1078 B.C.E.) controlled the three Phoenician metropoles of Arwad, Byblos, and Sidon, and sailed from Arwad to Zumur (see A.L. Oppenheim, in *ANET*, 275). This is an important addition to the report of Wen-Amon and to the biblical sources. According to them, Byblos and Sidon were the major centres along the Phoenician coast in the 12th and 11th centuries B.C.E., whereas Tyre was merely one of the Sidonian towns. In this regard, see in this volume, "The Philistines and the Rise of Israel and Tyre", pp. 63–82; also A. Malamat, in *Western Galilee* (see note 23), 89ff.

44 See Aharoni, *The Land of the Bible* (note 24), 236ff.

Let us now turn our attention to an authoritative document dating to the first half of the 11th century B.C.E.: the report of the Egyptian priest Wen-Amon, describing his journey to Byblos in order to obtain Lebanese wood for the ritual ship of Amon in Thebes.[45] He used the term *ḥbr* (*ḥubur*) twice in reference to powerful guilds in different ports. These trade unions were headed by the king and included the mercantile aristocracy, the "Canaanites" who were the masters of the sea, the shipbuilders and outfitters, and the owners of warehouses and workshops. This again brings to mind the words of Isaiah: "... crown-wearing Tyre, whose merchants were nobles, whose traders the world honored". This organization of trade characterized relations between Tyre and the United Monarchy of Israel during the 10th and 9th centuries B.C.E. This is expressed in 2 Chr 20:35–36 by the use of the root *ḥbr* in this sense, and through parallel usage of the terms *ḥabbārīm* and "Canaanites", meaning "merchants", in Job 40:30.[46] From the report of Wen-Amon it emerges that Byblos was associated through *ḥubur* with the rulers of the Delta in Egypt. Sidon was in league with one of the Philistine cities on the coast, namely Ashkelon, which enjoyed great power during this period.[47]

The great change in the balance of power along the coast and the renewed impetus of sea trade occurred simultaneously with the aggrandizement of the Israelite Monarchy under David. He broke the might of the Philistines, captured the coastal plain from the Yarkon to the Carmel, and expanded the borders of the Land of Israel into the area of Phoenicia as well. It is even possible that Sidon was included within David's kingdom as suggested in some biblical depictions relating to boundaries (Josh 19:28–30; 2 Sam 24:6–7). Israel's expansion into Phoenicia was at its peak at this time; thereafter its hold gradually diminished. One may also attribute to the period of David certain poetic passages in the Bible which relate that the families of Israel settled in the hinterland of the Phoenician cities. A conspicuous example is the Blessing of Jacob: "Zebulun shall dwell by the seashore; He shall be a haven for ships. And his flank shall rest on Sidon" (Gen 49:13). Tyre, which had been subjugated by Sidon, seized the opportunity provided by this situation to become independent and to establish itself once again as an important port, showing much initiative in shipping and trade, while cultivating friendly ties with Israel.

There is no doubt that there was a causal relationship between the decline of Philistia and Sidon and the rise of Israel and Tyre. It was probably Abibaal, father of Hiram, who founded a new dynasty in Tyre and made it the metrop-

45 See the new edition of the text with detailed commentary in M. A. Коростовцев, *Путешествие Ун-Амуна в Библ* (1960).

46 See B. Mazar, *BASOR* 102 (1946), 9ff.; Albright, *BANE* (note 8), 389.

47 See in this volume, "The Philistines and the Rise of Israel and Tyre", pp. 63–82.

olis of the Land of the Sidonians. This he did with the support of Israel and probably also in alliance with it. It seems that the establishment of Tyrian trading posts such as Kition in Cyprus (near Larnaka of today), and Zalmona (Tell Abu Hawam) on the ruins of the ancient city destroyed by the Sea Peoples, already started during Abibaal's reign.[48] It was at this time most probably that Tyre stimulated the development of new ports as coastal trading stations, such as Hosa, Maḥlib, Zarphat (Sarepta), and Achzib.

An aerial photograph of Tyre from 1917 (*Enc. Miq.*)

The reign of Hiram, son of Abibaal, was a time of prosperity for Tyre. Ties between Tyre and the kingdom of Israel were strengthened during the reign of Solomon. This, together with a hiatus in Greek shipping which began after the Mycenean period and the absence of organized competition in the region, enabled Tyre to launch a new phase in international commerce, of which it was the focus. Trade was no longer confined to neighbouring countries, but extended far into the Mediterranean. Tyrian colonies were founded at Nora in Sardinia, Utica in North Africa, and Gāder (Cadiz) in Spain beyond Gibral-

48 See B. Mazar, *BASOR* 124 (1951), 21ff.; G.W. van Beek, *BASOR* 138 (1958), 38. One should also date to this period two tombs with rich funerary objects, discovered by W.M. Prausnitz at Achzib [*IEJ* 9 (1959), 271; 10 (1960), 260–261].

tar.[49] In the Red Sea, Israelite-Phoenician mercantile ventures opened a route to East Africa and to South Arabia.

It is no mere coincidence that Israelite historiography frequently refers to "the ships of Tarshish" of Hiram and Solomon, which sailed from Ezion-Geber to Ophir, and describes the visit of the Queen of Sheba to Jerusalem. A psalm (Ps 72) attributed to Solomon, and possibly dating from his days as heir apparent during David's lifetime (v. 1), expresses the wish "Let kings of Tarshish and the islands pay tribute, kings of Sheba and Seba offer gifts" (v. 10). The kingdom of Israel enjoyed a unique opportunity to serve as a bridge between the Mediterranean and the Red Sea. There was security along the roads, and there were peaceful relations with Egypt and the Hittite kingdoms of northern Syria. The initiative and imagination of the King's merchants and seamen that led to the development of industry and an abundance of finished products opened the way for considerable achievements in architecture, craftsmanship and shipbuilding, and for the refining and processing of metals, especially iron.[50] Merchants would sail to the western limits of the Mediterranean and beyond to exchange their industrial products for raw materials. The passage in Ezekiel (27:12) "Tarshish traded with you because of your wealth of all kinds of goods; they bartered silver, iron, tin, and lead for your wares" very likely alludes to metal imported by the Tyrians from mines in Sardinia and north-western Spain.

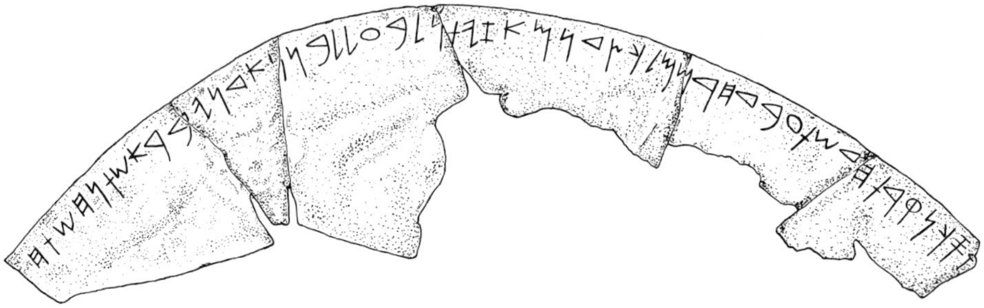

A bronze bowl with a dedication to Baal Lebanon which was found at Limassol in Cyprus: "Governor of *Krtḥdšt*, servant of Hiram, King of the Sidonians" (*Enc. Miq.*)

49 Strong arguments have been raised against the attempt [particularly by R. Carpenter, *AJA* 62 (1958), 38ff.] to assign a later date to Phoenician colonization in the west; see Albright, *BANE* (note 8), 34, 343ff. On this subject in general, see Harden, *The Phoenicians* (note 4), 52ff. There is reason to believe that the Phoenicians already began to exploit the rich mines of north-western Spain during the reign of Hiram, son of Abibaal. From there, they reached the port of Gāder (Cadiz). See my remarks as quoted by Albright, *BANE* (note 8), 347. The "Phoenician" findings in Spain are mainly from the area of Cadiz, Jerez, Cremona [G. Bonsor, *Early Engraved Ivories* (1928)], and Caceres ("The Treasure of Alisada"). See also R. Blanco, *Archivo Espanol de Arqueologia* (1956), 11ff. and a detailed survey by Schiffman [И.Ш. Шифман, *Возникновение Карфагенской Державы* (1963)].

50 On the introduction of iron into Eretz-Israel and its distribution throughout the ancient Near East, see in this volume, "The Philistines and the Rise of Israel and Tyre", p. 69, n. 4.

A bronze band from the palace of Shalmaneser III, King of Assyria (858–824 B.C.E.), at Balāwat (British Museum)

A cosmopolitan culture emerged — a form of Phoenician *koine* — combining eclectic elements from the various cultures with whom the Tyrians were in contact. The Phoenician alphabet, consisting of twenty-two distinct consonants, spread and was adopted throughout the Levant. As a result of the settlements and commercial activities of the Phoenicians,[51] this alphabet was, in time, even adopted by the Phrygians and the Greeks. Tyrian influence was felt in all spheres of Israelite life and became a cornerstone of its culture.[52] It is no wonder, therefore, that both in historical tradition and in poetic literature, Tyre is so freqently portrayed as the mighty metropolis of the Sidonians-Phoenicians, the wealthy centre of world trade, and the mother of colonies beyond the sea. This also adds meaning to the ancient poetry incorporated in Ezekiel's prophecy on the destruction of Tyre: "perfect in beauty, on the high seas were your frontiers, your builders perfected your beauty" (27:3–4), and

51 The Phoenician inscriptions from Sardinia (particularly from Nora), dating from the 9th century B.C.E., merit particular attention; see W.F. Albright, *BASOR* 83 (1941), 11ff.; and in this volume, "The Philistines and the Rise of Israel and Tyre", p. 77, n. 24; D. Diringer, *Writing* (1962), 132, P1. 40; F.M. Cross, *BASOR* 208 (1972), 13–19.

52 The influence of the Sidonian kingdom on its neighbouring states, including Israel and Judah, as clearly discernible in their economy, in their crafts and in their rituals, was also expressed in biblical literature. Illuminating information concerning the Aramean kingdom is provided by the stele found near Aleppo, which includes a dedication to Melkart, the god of Tyre, by Bar-hadad (Ben-hadad), King of Damascus [M. Dunand, *BMB* 3 (1939), 65ff.]. On the spread of the worship of Baal Šamêm, see in this volume, "The Philistines and the Rise of Israel and Tyre", pp. 63–82. Evidence concerning the penetration of Phoenician trade into the Aegean and in particular to Crete and Rhodes is quite conclusive [Harden, *The Phoenicians* (note 4), 61]. Homeric literature mentions Phoenician merchants and seamen and the fabrics and fine silver for which they were acclaimed [see F.H. Stubbings, *A Companion to Homer* (1962), 542f.]. On oriental influence in Greek culture, starting in the 9th century B.C.E., also see R.D. Barnett, *The Aegean and the Near East* (1965), 212ff.; J.R. Brook, *Fortetsa* (1957), 218f.

"with your great wealth and merchandise you enriched the kings of the earth" (v. 33). One of the "kings of the earth" was the King of Israel, a close neighbour and ally of Tyre. For about 150 years, from the reign of David to the end of the dynasty of Omri in northern Israel, the two neighbouring kingdoms cultivated close ties, "a covenant of brotherhood", in the (much later) words of Amos (1:9).[53]

53 Of the more recent literature on the Phoenicians one should mention S. Moscati, *The World of the Phoenicians* (1968); H.J. Katzenstein, *The History of Tyre* (1973).

The Phoenician Inscriptions from Byblos and the Evolution of the Phoenician-Hebrew Alphabet

The French archaeological excavations at Byblos, one of the oldest and most important Phoenician coastal cities, have yielded documents of great value for the study of writing in Bronze Age Canaan, and especially for the history of the Phoenician-Hebrew script. The French expedition laboured at Byblos for twenty-five years, first under the direction of Pierre Montet and later under Maurice Dunand. Dunand has since published a comprehensive work in which he compiled a considerable number of hitherto unknown inscriptions from Byblos among which are some in pseudo-hieroglyphic script on stone stelae and bronze blades, and two in the regular Phoenician-Hebrew alphabet. All are accompanied by a detailed commentary, and a review of the nature of the script and the evolution of the letters of the alphabet from their earliest beginnings.[1] I will not dwell here upon Dunand's illuminating assemblage of Bronze Age epigraphic material. I wish merely to point out that there is little warrant for assuming that the twenty-two letter Phoenician-Hebrew alphabet developed from an earlier script used in Phoenicia or elsewhere in the Land of Canaan, such as the pseudo-hieroglyphic script from Byblos.[2]

In his publication, Dunand arrives at far-reaching conclusions concerning the antiquity of the Phoenician-Hebrew alphabet. He bases himself chiefly

* The author wishes to mention those with whom he discussed problems concerning this article, especially the late Prof. N.H. Tur-Sinai, the late Prof. S. Yeivin, and Prof. N. Avigad, who also drew the figures.

1 M. Dunand, *Byblia Grammata* [*Études et Documents d'Archéologie* 2 (1945)].

2 Dunand devotes the fourth chapter of his book to the pseudo-hieroglyphic inscriptions; see pp. 135ff. On the attempts made to decipher the inscriptions before the year 1939, see S. Yeivin, *History of the Jewish Script* (1939), 57ff. (Hebrew), and my article in *JPOS* 8 (1938), 278ff.

upon two new Phoenician inscriptions from Byblos, to which he devotes a whole chapter.[3] These are dated by him to the Middle Bronze Age (17th century B.C.E.), and he concludes that the Phoenician-Hebrew alphabet should be dated much earlier than any scholar has hitherto proposed. In Dunand's opinion, this script with its twenty-two letters was created in the period of the Egyptian Middle Kingdom, and the people of Byblos used it simultaneously with earlier scripts, which have not yet been deciphered. This presupposition necessitates a thorough and searching examination of the two documents themselves. One is a dedication by Shiptibaal, King of Byblos, to the tutelary goddess of Byblos (Baalat Gebal), and the other, on a sherd, is short and truncated.

The Shiptibaal inscription was incised on a limestone stele which was uncovered in the cemetery of Byblos close to the seashore. Since the stele was not found in a clearly defined stratum but in debris outside the site, the text can be dated on palaeographic and linguistic grounds only. It consists of five lines, and as is common in Phoenician inscriptions from Byblos, the separation between the words is marked by a small divider. The letters are excellently formed, bearing all the signs of a long literary tradition. Almost all of them are clear, but in some cases we have been obliged to depart from Dunand's copy.[4] Together with my friend and colleague, N. Avigad, I examined the excellent photographs published in the book.[5] On the basis of our examination we propose the copy in Fig. 1, as in the following text and translation:

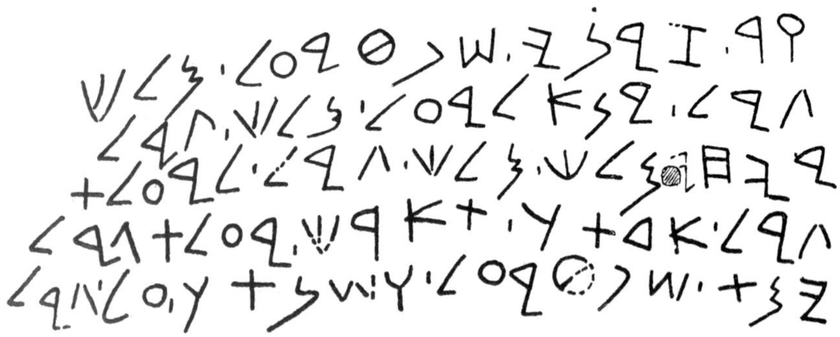

Fig. 1: The Shiptibaal inscription [B. Mazar, *Lešonenu* 14 (1946), 167]

3 Dunand, *Byblia* (see note 1), chapter 5.
4 *Ibid*., 146ff. and Fig. 49.
5 *Ibid.*, Pls. XVb and XVI.

1. [The] wall built by Shiptibaal, King of	1. קר ׀ ז בני ׀ שפטבעל ׀ מלך
2. Byblos son of Elibaal, King of Byblos	2. גבל ׀ בנאלבעל ׀ מלך ׀ גבל
3. son of Yehimelek, King of Byblos for Baalat	3. ביחימלך ׀ מלך ׀ גבל ׀ לבעלת
4. Gebal his Lady, [so that] Baalat Gebal will prolong	4. גבל ׀ אדתו ׀ תארך ׀ בעלת גבל
5. the days of Shiptibaal and his years over Byblos.	5. ימת ׀ שפטבעל ׀ ושנתו ׀ על ׀ גבל

The second inscription was engraved on the broad rim of a vessel, in fact between it and a cylindrical perforated, tube-like strip which was affixed under the rim in horizontal position. From the photograph and the facsimile published by Dunand,[6] it is very difficult to determine the nature of the vessel and its date. What we can say with certainty is that it is absolutely impossible to accept Dunand's view that this is a very large, round vessel of the typical Middle Bronze Age type, especially since there is no resemblance whatsoever between this sherd and the vessels from Tell Beit Mirsim and the other locales that he cites for purposes of comparison.[7] Certainly the unburnished red glaze is not indicative of the period. It is more likely that the sherd came from an oval vessel, not a round one. If so, Avigad is probably correct in comparing this vessel to the pyxis found in an Israelite shaft tomb at Samaria,[8] except that the former has the addition of the prominent perforated strip whose purpose is unknown. This feature has no parallel in excavations in Israel.[9] The inscription is truncated; parts of it are missing at the beginning and end. It reads as follows:

ʿAbda [or "Of ʿAbda"] son of Kalbiya the ...	ע]בדא ׀ בכלב ׀ ה[

Half of the left side of the curve of the ע in the name "ʿAbda" is missing, and there may possibly have been some letters, or at least one other letter preceding it. In my opinion it should be read לע]בדא, "To ʿAbda". On the edge of the break after the ה, only the sharp angle of a letter can be discerned. It could be one of the following letters: ג, ד, ר or even י. Dunand correctly explains the ה as the definite article, but his restoration is unacceptable. He proposes that the word should be read ה[יצר], "the potter", on the assumption that ʿAbda ben Kalbiya was the potter who made the vessel. It is far more likely that the name of its owner was recorded. This

6 *Ibid.*, 152ff. and Pl. XVa.

7 It can be stated with certainty that the sherd is not from the Middle Bronze Age.

8 See G.M. Crowfoot, *PEF Qst* 1932, 197ff. Fragments of another pyxis were also found at Samaria; see E.L. Sukenik, *Qedem* 2 (1944), 45 (Hebrew).

9 The help in seeking comparative material which I received from Prof. Ruth Amiran and the late Dr. I. Ben-Dor was much appreciated.

allows us to assume that the inscription began with the ל of possession, i.e., "[of ʿA]bda son of Kalbiya the...."[10] The last word may of course be restored in various ways, but since the vessel is unique it is permissible to suggest the restoration [ה[גלב, "the [barber]" or [ה[רפא, "the [physician]", professional titles which appear in Phoenician inscriptions.[11]

Palaeographically, we agree with Dunand that the two inscriptions date from the same period, in view of the great similarity in the forms of the characters. Only the ד is an exception. On the Shiptibaal stele it appears in the form of a triangle as in the classical inscriptions from Byblos (Ethbaal, Yehimelek, Elibaal), in the Gezer Calendar and in the stele of Mesha, King of Moab. On the ʿAbda vessel, however, the right arm of the ד is prolonged downwards. This gives it the appearance of a ר, as is the case in the Phoenician, Hebrew and Aramaic inscriptions of the 8th–7th centuries B.C.E. (see Table on p. 177).

A thorough examination of both the Shiptibaal and ʿAbda writings must involve their comparison with the following previously published alphabetic inscriptions from Byblos: 1) that ordered by Ethbaal, King of Byblos, for the sarcophagus of his father, Aḥiram;[12] 2) the graffito on the wall of the deep shaft leading from the surface to the burial chamber in which Aḥiram's sarcophagus was found;[13] 3) the ʿAzarbaal inscription;[14] 4) the dedication of Abibaal, King of Byblos;[15] 5) the stele of Yehimelek, King of Byblos;[16] and 6) the votive writing of Elibaal, King of Byblos.[17]

It should be borne in mind that we have a *terminus a quo* for only two of the above — Abibaal's dedication was engraved on a statue of Pharaoh Shishak I (second half of the 10th century B.C.E.), and that of Elibaal on a fragment of an Egyptian statue bearing the name of Pharaoh Osorkon I (end of the 10th century and beginning of the 9th century B.C.E.). To facilitate comparison, we have compiled the Table shown on p. 177. It clearly

10 On the ל of possession in the Phoenician and Hebrew inscriptions, see S. Yeivin, *Qedem* 2 (1944), 34 (Hebrew); Y. Yadin, *IEJ* 9 (1959), 184ff.; 12 (1962), 64–66; Y. Aharoni, *IEJ* 12 (1962); A.F. Rainey, *IEJ* 12 (1962), 62–63; *idem*, *PEQ* 1967, 32–41.

11 See Z. Harris, *A Grammar of the Phoenician Language* (1936), 94, 147: N. Slouschz, *Thesaurus of Phoenician Inscriptions* (1942), 359, 375 (Hebrew).

12 R. Dussaud, *Syria* 5 (1924), 135ff.; P. Montet, *Byblos et l'Égypte* (1928), 236ff. and Pls. CXXXI–CXLI; S. Yeivin, *Qedem* 2 (1944), 116ff. (Hebrew).

13 See L.H. Vincent's photograph and copy in *RB* 34 (1925), Pl. VIII.

14 M. Dunand, *BMB* 2 (1938), 99ff.; *idem*, *Fouilles de Byblos 1, Atlas* (1937), Pl. XXXII, W.F. Albright, *BASOR* 90 (1943), 35ff.

15 Ch. Clermont-Ganneau, *Recueil d'archéologie orientale* 6 (1905), 74ff.; Montet, *Byblos et l'Égypte* (see note 12), 54ff.

16 M. Dunand, *RB* 39 (1930), 321ff.; *idem*, *Fouilles de Byblos* 1 (1939), 30 and *Atlas*, Pl. XXXI, 2.

17 See Montet, *Byblos et l'Égypte* (see note 12), 49ff., Pls. XXVIII–XXXVI; another fragment of this document was published by Dunand, *Fouilles* (see note 16), 18.

Fig. 2: A stele of Pharaoh Osorkon I on which an inscription of Elibaal, King of Byblos, was inscribed (Louvre)

illustrates that in all the inscriptions included, a considerable number of letters are of the same nature and form. This similarity is conspicuous in the letters א, ז, ח, י, כ, ל, נ, ע, and ת.

The ג in the Shiptibaal inscription appears in two forms: one recumbent with its left arm longer than the right, as in the Abibaal dedication; the other more upright, with the right arm longer than the left, as in the Yehimelek and Elibaal scripts. Shiptibaal's ו also has two forms: one consists of a bar with a recumbent semi-circle at its head, as in the other Byblos inscriptions and in the Mesha Stele, while the other is a bar with a rounded hook added at the left of the head, as in the Gezer Calendar, in the ancient Cypriot text[18] (see Table on p. 177 and below), in Aramaic inscriptions from Syria, etc. The פ in the Shiptibaal and ʿAzarbaal inscriptions is similar but is differentiated by its sharp angle from the rounded פ of the other Byblian inscriptions, the Cyprus text and the Gezer Calendar. The ר of Shiptibaal was written in two forms: one with a sharp angle like that of Elibaal's script, the Cyprus text, the Gezer Calendar and the Mesha Stele; the other in the form of a bar with a semi-circle added at the left of the head, like the ר of the 9th and 8th centuries B.C.E. inscriptions from Syria and Eretz-Israel. Alongside the regular ש of Byblos we also find an apparently later form.[19] In summary, a review of the letters discussed suggests that the Shiptibaal and ʿAbda scripts represent an intermediate stage between the traditional, classical Byblian al-

18 Published by A.M. Honeyman, *Iraq* 6 (1939), 106–108. See also, W.F. Albright, *BASOR* 83 (1941), 15ff.

19 This form of the ש is unique and will require a separate study.

phabet, and that used in Syria and Eretz-Israel in the 9th and 8th centuries B.C.E.

Only three other letters in the Shiptibaal inscription have a special shape: ב, ט and ק. Dunand, on the mere assumption that these letters seem to have parallels in the pseudo-hieroglyphic scripts,[20] pushes back the date of the Shiptibaal inscription together with that of ʿAbda to about the 17th century B.C.E., hundreds of years earlier than the other Byblian documents with Phoenician-Hebrew alphabetic characters. His hypothesis is utterly groundless. To begin with, we have no proof that the early scripts of Byblos were alphabetic. Furthermore, we see no resemblance between the pseudo-hieroglyphic characters and the above-mentioned letters in the Shiptibaal inscription.[21] On the contrary, it can be shown that at least two of the three letters in question, namely ט and ק, are of the type found in written Hebrew of the 8th and 7th centuries B.C.E., and apparently even as early as the 9th century B.C.E.

In the Shiptibaal inscription the ט is written in the form of a circle within which runs a diagonal line, instead of the classical X, beginning with the Ethbaal inscription (and also in the Mesha Stele, the Lachish Ostraca, etc.). But it is precisely this ט with one diagonal line which we find on Hebrew seals[22] and on ostraca mainly from the 8th and 7th centuries B.C.E.[23] As for the ק in the Shiptibaal text, it appears in the form of a circle with a bar descending from it, instead of crossing it as in the classical form (the Aḥiram inscription, the Gezer Calendar, the Mesha Stele, etc.). This kind of ק is characteristic on weights and pottery of the 8th and 7th centuries B.C.E. in Eretz-Israel.[24] It seems clear, therefore, that these letters also antedate the classical Byblian script.[25] The one solitary letter in the Shiptibaal and ʿAbda inscriptions that has no parallel in the regular Phoenician-Hebrew writing is the letter ב, in which the bottom horizontal line is inclined to the right instead of to the left. But it is obvious that this is a local phenomenon adopted by Byblian scribes during a certain post-classical period.

20 See Dunand, *Fouilles* (note 16), chapter 8.

21 For example, the letter thought by Dunand to be the prototype of the ט in the Phoenician-Hebrew alphabet is explained by other scholars as ב. Incidentally, this sign does not resemble the ט of the Shiptibaal inscription. The only similar parallel in any of the ancient scripts is the ט on a sherd from Beth-shemesh dating from ca. 1200 B.C.E. [line 4; see Yeivin, *Jewish Script* (note 2), 109, Fig. 22]. However, the attempts to decipher the inscription are very tenuous and cannot serve as evidence.

22 The ט appears on the seals of Shephatyahu and Patisi, both apparently from the 8th century B.C.E.; see I. Ben-Dor, *QDAP* 12 (1946), 77ff.

23 D. Diringer, *Le iscrizioni antico-ebraiche palestinesi* (1934), Pl. XXIX.

24 *Ibid.*, Pl. XXIX.

25 It is worth recalling what was said above about the ד in the ʿAbda inscription

Palaeographic examination alone compels us to set the date of the inscriptions later, namely the 8th century B.C.E., or at the very earliest in the 9th century B.C.E. At all events, they definitely cannot predate that of Elibaal, King of Byblos, whose *terminus a quo* is the beginning of the 9th century B.C.E.

Our palaeographic evidence relating to the Shiptibaal and ʿAbda inscriptions is validated by their late language and script. In that of ʿAbda we note particularly the use of the definite article ה, first encountered in the Yehimelek inscription, line 2: מפלת הבתם, "the ruins of the temples".[26] It should also be noted that the abbreviated theophoric title ʿAbda (terminating in א) is of the type found in relatively late Phoenician and Hebrew names.[27] As regards the Shiptibaal wording, the essential evidence is that the third person masculine pronominal suffix is ו [אדתו] as in the Elibaal dedication. This is also the regular form in the Hebrew Bible and in the Siloam Inscription. On Ethbaal's father's sarcophagus, in the Mesha Stele and even in the late Lachish Ostraca this suffix is represented by ה.[28] Secondly, the name Yehimelek was written with a י after the ה, indicating a *plene* spelling when compared with the inscription of Yehimelek, King of Byblos, where the name was transcribed defectively, without a י. Dunand, however, did not copy this letter, assuming that in the space between the ה and the מ a letter had been omitted by the scribe; yet remnants of the letter י can be easily seen in the photographs, as detected by Avigad and myself on careful examination (see Fig. 1). As to the archaic form זבני (בני instead of בנא as in the late Phoenician inscriptions, or בנה as in Hebrew and Moabite), it has parallels not only in the Ethbaal and Yehimelek texts (בת | זבני | יחמלך), but in the inscriptions from Samʾal (Zenjirli).[29]

In both the Ethbaal and Shiptibaal inscriptions, the spelling of the word בן is interesting. It is noteworthy that in Ethbaal's texts the divider is already missing between the word בן and the proper name following it (אתבעל|בנ אחרם in line 1). The same is true for Shiptibaal (בנאלבעל in line 2). On the other hand, the scribe here omitted the נ in the word בן before the name Yehimelek and wrote ביחימלך (line 3). Dunand thought that this omission was a mistake on the part of the scribe. This is highly unlikely, since we find the same phenomenon in the ʿAbda inscription: בכלבי (= בן כלבי). It seems, therefore, that the word בן was shortened, the נ being dropped in both the above-mentioned case and in ביחימלך, while the lack

26 On ה as the definite article, see Harris, *Phoenician Language* (note 11), 55ff.

27 *Ibid*., 128.

28 See N.H. Tur-Sinai (Torczyner), *The Lachish Ostraca* (1940), 35–38 (Hebrew).

29 See Harris, *Phoenician Language* (note 11), 45.

of a divider in both of the other cases (בנאלבעל, בנאחרם) perhaps indicates that the letter was written before the א, but was not pronounced. That these are not isolated instances we learn from the Ugaritic document published by S. Yeivin.[30] It reads: לצ.[?]בעל בפלצבעל, "To Ṣ[.?]baʿal son of Plṣbaʿal". Yeivin also considered the possibility that the ב before the proper name פלצבעל was a contraction of the word בן. But "in view of the fact that there are no known examples of this kind of abbreviation and assimilation of the word בן", he decided to explain it as the Ugaritic preposition *b*, and to understand Plṣbaʿal as a place name.[31]

In the light of the facts presented here, there is, of course, no further room for doubt about the assimilation of the letter נ in בן, into the following word. I suggest that the same phenomenon is to be found in the Hebrew Bible: The name בדקר (2 Kgs 9:25) can only be explained in my opinion as בן־דקר (1 Kgs 4:9; in cuneiform *Bindiqiri*). Likewise, the word בענה (2 Sam 4:2, etc.) or בענא (1 Kgs 4:12, etc.) can only be explained as בן־ענה or בן־ענא, a name appearing in the El-Amarna Letters (as *Bin-A-Na*), in the Ugaritic documents as בנען, and elsewhere.[32] It also seems very probable that the name בדד (Hadad ben-bedad) in Gen 36:35 is really Ben-hadad or Ben-adad (for the alternative spellings: הדד/אדד, see 1 Kgs 11:14, 17, and 19ff; and there are many other examples.)

The above-proposed solution of the problem permits us to bridge the gap between the Elibaal dedication, which is incised on a fragment of an Egyptian statue bearing the name of Pharaoh Osorkon I (see above), and the Shiptibaal inscription. It also enables us to restore Elibaal's missing text. The preserved part is quite clear, and reads as follows:[33]

1. מש | ז פעל | אלבעל | מלך גבל | ביח[
2.]עלת גבל | אדתו | תארך [
3.]לבעל | ושנתו | על [

Scholars have attempted various restorations of the word ביח in line 1. Dussaud and Montet suggested ביח[רם] in the sense of "en consecration".[34] Aimé-Giron restored the missing part as ביח[לי], and understood it as referring to the place יחלי, *Waḫlia*, mentioned in one of the El-Amarna letters.[35] All of these attempts may now be discarded in the light of the Shiptibaal inscription. In my opinion, this word should undoubtedly be

30 See S. Yeivin, *Qedem* 2 (1944), 32ff.
31 *Ibid.*, 36.
32 See B. Mazar (Maisler), *JPOS* 16 (1936), 151–153.
33 Montet, *Byblos et l'Égypte* (see note 12), 25, Fig. 16 and Pls. XXXVI–XXXVIII.
34 See *ibid.*, 52, and Slouschz, *Thesaurus* (note 11), 8–9.
35 N. Aimé-Giron, *ASAE* 42 (1943), 328ff.

completed as [ביח]ימלך or [ביח]מלך, "son of Yehimelek". The great similarity between the Shiptibaal and Elibaal documents suggests that the Shiptibaal inscription dates only slightly later than that of Elibaal. There is no reason why we should *not* assume that Shiptibaal son of Elibaal son of Yehimelek in one inscription is the son of Elibaal son of Yehimelek in the other. For the sake of comparison we will reproduce both side by side, restoring the Elibaal text in accordance with the new data:[36]

1. קר | זבני | שפטבעל | מלך
2. גבל | בנאלבעל | מלך | גבל
3. ביחמלך | מלך | גבל | לבעלת
4. גבל | אדתו | תארך | בעלת גבל
5. ימת | שפטבעל | ושנתו | על | גבל

1. מש | זפעל | אלבעל | מלך | גבל |
ביח[ימלך | מלך | גבל]
2. לב]עלת גבל | אדתו | תארך [|בעלת | גבל]
3. ימת | א]לבעל | ושנתו | על [|גבל]

The following two observations regarding the Elibaal dedication must be made: (a) In line 2, I favour the restoration **בעלת גבל**, while at the beginning of line 3 there still remains enough room for the word ימת; (b) The reading of line 3 (על instead of עלי) follows Dussaud.[37]

From all that has been said thus far the following conclusions emerge:
1) Elibaal son of Yehimelek in one inscription is the father of Shiptibaal son of Elibaal son of Yehimelek in the other.
2) Both texts were written in the same style, and cannot be far apart in time.
3) The letters in the Elibaal dedication are almost identical to those of the Yehimelek inscription, and only slightly different from the Abibaal forms (or even from those of Ethbaal son of Aḥiram). The Shiptibaal inscription, however, shows noticeable signs of transition from the traditional classical Byblian form to a later form influenced by the script which had taken root in Syria and Eretz-Israel in the 9th and 8th centuries B.C.E. Nonetheless, concerning the two most characteristic letters, כ and ל, no change in the Shiptibaal script can be discerned, as the scribe employed the classical forms.
4) Linguistic evidence makes it necessary to lower the date of the two inscriptions to the time of Ethbaal. In matters of orthography the Shiptibaal inscription must be attributed to the time of that of Yehimelek.

In considering the date of the two inscriptions, we must not forget that the Elibaal text was engraved on a fragment of an Egyptian statue bearing the cartouche of Osorkon I son of Shishak I. Some scholars hold that Osorkon raised this statue at Byblos during his Phoenician campaign at the beginning

36 Our proposed restoration fits exactly into the gaps, as will be obvious to anyone who studies Montet's photograph and copy. The restorations proposed by Montet and others are impossible from this point of view.

37 See R. Dussaud, *Syria* 5 (1924), 145; for purposes of comparison, I here present Montet's attempted restoration [*Byblos et l'Égypte* (see note 12), 52].

of the 9th century B.C.E. The matter is still veiled in obscurity due to our uncertain knowledge of the campaign and its date, for the chronology of the 22nd Dynasty in Egypt has not been satisfactorily established.[38] What is clear is that Elibaal, King of Byblos, commanded the votive inscription to be carved on the statue (in the form of a semi-circle in the empty space around the cartouche) some time — perhaps even quite a long time — after the statue with its cartouche had been erected.

It is the inscription of Abibaal, King of Byblos, which is more problematic. This dedication, only part of which is preserved, was engraved on the statue of Shishak I, the very Pharaoh Shishak who ruled at the end of Solomon's reign and during the days of Rehoboam. The statue seems to have been raised at Byblos at the time of Shishak's campaign to Eretz-Israel, which is dated by Albright to 918 B.C.E., the fifth year of Rehoboam, King of Judah.[39] Before pursuing the question of the date of the inscription, let us first determine its content. Of the entire text only the two lines — both of them defective — to the left of the two cartouches with Shishak's name survive, along with the words על גבל which end it at the right of the cartouches. The following are the words in the two lines which can be discerned in the photographs published by Clermont-Ganneau:[40]

1.]א | אבבעל | מלך[
2.]גבל | ב... רם | לבעל[

Between the ב and the ר in line 2, there is an unrecognizable letter or possibly two merged letters. Clermont-Ganneau hypothesized, here reading צ,[41] and in copying, he inserted a question mark. Montet[42] removed the question mark and proposed the following restoration:

1. מש | ז נש]א אבבעל | מלך [| גבל
2. שכן | גבל | במצרם | לבעל]ת גבל | תארך | ים | אבבעל ושנתו] על גבל[43]

38 In a private conversation, the late B. Grdseloff surmised that the statue is actually of Shishak I, on which the cartouche with the name Osorkon I was later engraved. It is a fact that no Egyptian statue has ever been found with a cartouche engraved on the chest of the depicted figure.

39 See W.F. Albright, *BASOR* 100 (1945), 16ff., and also the chronology of E.R. Thiele, *JNES* 3 (1944), 137ff. According to my chronology, presented in the Atlas, *Israel in Biblical Times* (1941), the date is 926 B.C.E., but see H. Tadmor, *Enc. Miq.* 4, s.v. "Chronology".

40 Ch. Clermont-Ganneau, *Recueil d'archéologie orientale* 4 (1903), 74 and Pl. II.

41 In Clermont-Ganneau's words (*ibid.*, 77): "... le tsade ait quelque peu souffert et soit difficile a discerner".

42 R. Dussaud, *Syria* 5 (1924), 11–18; Montet, *Byblos et l'Égypte* (see note 12), 54ff. In Montet's copy (p. 53, Fig. 17), we find a צ resembling the one in the Mesha Stele, except that the upright line to the left is longer.

43 Montet translates as follows: "[Statue qu'a offerte] Abibaʿal, roi de Gobel, [*soken*] de Gobel en Égypte..."; Slouschz [*Thesaurus* (note 11), 7] as: [פסל אשר העמיד] אביבעל מלך גבל וסוכן גבל ממצרים. R. Dussaud, *Syria* 5 (1924), reads: [נגש] גבל מצרים.

This restoration is impossible. We have just seen that the reading במצרם is purely hypothetical, as is the content in general. The title שכן (=סכן) גבל במצרם, "governor of Byblos from Egypt" has no other parallel at Byblos. I propose the following restoration (taking the spaces into consideration), based on analysis of the two inscriptions discussed above, those of Elibaal and Shiptibaal:

1. מש | ז נש?]א אבבעל | מלך | [גבל | בנ... (son of ...)
2. מלך]] גבל | במ.רם | לבעל[ת גבל | תארך | בעלת גבל | ימת | אבבעל ושנתו]] על גבל

In line 2 במ... רם can be understood as בן מ... רם, just as ביחימלך is בן יחימלך, yet I cannot suggest a name to complete the restoration, as not only the צ is hypothetical but the מ is also not certain.[44] Perhaps a study of the original or of a new photograph may prove enlightening. In all events, this is definitely not the same Aḥiram, the father of Ethbaal, King of Byblos.

My suggested restoration of the Abibaal text — if it is correct — further complicates problems regarding the chronology of the kings of Byblos. From the inscriptions of Elibaal and Shiptibaal, one could draw the conclusion that Yehimelek was the founder of the dynasty at Byblos. He was succeeded by his son Elibaal and after Elibaal, his son Shiptibaal reigned. There is support for this conclusion in the monumental Yehimelek inscription commemorating the building of the "house" (the temple) of בעל שמם (Baʿal Šamêm) and Baalat Gebal (the female deity of Byblos). It reads as follows:[45]

1. The temple which Yehimelek, King of Byblos, built.	1. בת | ז בני | יחמלך | מלך גבל
2. He restored all the ruins of these temples.	2. האת | חוי | כל | מפלת | הבתם
3. May Baʿal Šamêm and Baalat	3. אלו | יארך | בעל שמם | ובעלת
4. Gebal and the assembly of the holy gods of Byblos prolong	4. גבל | ומפחרת | אל גבל
5. the days and years of Yehimelek	5. קדשם | ימת | יחמלך | ושנתו
6. over Byblos. For he is a legitimate and rightful king	6. על גבל | כמלך | צדק | ומלך
7. in the eyes of the holy gods of Byblos.	7. ישר | לפן | אל גבל | קדשם [|הא]

Now if Yehimelek was not the founder of a dynasty, the inscription would mention his father who reigned before him, which it does not. Abibaal, an earlier monarch, was evidently from another dynasty. Unfortunately the name

44 It is impossible to interpret this as a צ. On the right there is a superfluous stroke, and generally the letter is more rounded. What seems to be a small line above the left line is probably only a crack in the stone. As to the מ at the end of the line, it is very different from the previous מ and from that in line 1.

45 For the inscription, see Dunand, *Fouilles* (note 16), 30; *Atlas* (1937), Pl. XXXI, 2.

of Abibaal's father is not preserved in the Abibaal inscription, but his father's father bore the name מ... רם, which is still unexplained. It appears that the dynasty to which Abibaal belonged ruled over Byblos after Ethbaal son of Aḥiram and before Yehimelek. We can, therefore, deduce the following sequence of kings for the three dynasties in Byblos:

Dynasty I	(?) Aḥiram Ethbaal (?)
Dynasty II	M... rm (?) X (?) Abibaal
Dynasty III	Yehimelek Elibaal Shiptibaal

This table does not tell us anything about the length of time that elapsed between Abibaal and Yehimelek, so we do not know whether Abibaal was the last of his line. But palaeographic evidence compels us to conclude that the Abibaal dedication was written not very long before that on the stele of Yehimelek. It is a fact that the Abibaal letters are astonishingly similar to those of Elibaal and Yehimelek. The ג of the Abibaal script is different from that character in the Yehimelek and Elibaal texts, but both types appear afterwards in the Shiptibaal inscription (see the Table on p. 177).

Furthermore, there is no doubt whatever that the ʿAzarbaal inscription and that on the bronze arrowhead(?) found in a tomb near Ruweissa in southern Lebanon,[46] are earlier than the Ethbaal son of Aḥiram writing. Palaeographically, we must pay attention to the distinctly archaic forms of the Ethbaal script, especially the א but also the ג, ו, and ר (see the Table on p. 177). Linguistically, as we have shown, the evidence also compels us to push back the date of the Ethbaal text to the group of inscriptions discussed above. A further piece of evidence for assuming a considerable lapse of time between Ethbaal and Abibaal is to be found, as we have said, in the Abibaal dedication, from which we learn that between Ethbaal and Abibaal, *at least* two kings reigned (see the dynastic table above).[47]

46 See S. Ronzevalle, *Mélanges de l'Université St. Joseph* 7 (1926); R. Dussaud, *Syria* 8 (1927), 185; Yeivin, *Jewish Script* (note 2), 118 and Pl. V, 2.

47 We should recall that Ethbaal ordered the inscription to be engraved on Aḥiram's sarcophagus immediately after his father's death, at the beginning of his own reign.

Archaeological evidence prompted Montet to attribute the sarcophagus of Aḥiram and the graffito on the wall of the shaft leading to his burial chamber to the 13th century B.C.E. This date was upheld by Dussaud, Dunand, Hans Bauer and Harris.[48] Montet's chronological determination is based upon the discovery of a fragment of an alabaster vessel with the name of Ramesses II (1304–1237 B.C.E.) found in the burial chamber, which contained two unadorned sarcophagi in addition to Aḥiram's. The date is also based on the discovery of another alabaster vessel bearing the name of Ramesses II discovered in the above-mentioned shaft.[49] The pottery from this tomb (Tomb V at Byblos) belongs to the end of the Late Bronze Age or to the Iron Age.[50] It is evident that Tomb V at Byblos was in use for a long time, and the finds of alabaster fragments and sherds cannot attest to the date of Aḥiram's sarcophagus. We are not able to date the other two sarcophagi either. It is worth noting that at least some of the vessels published by Montet are of a kind characteristic of the 11th–10th centuries B.C.E.[51] It was not without reason, therefore, that various scholars decided to assign a later date to the sarcophagus and the inscriptions, in the 11th or the beginning of the 10th century B.C.E. regardless of the alabaster fragments.[52] Important evidence, particularly a detailed study of the artistic style of the reliefs on Aḥiram's sarcophagus and its lid (as well as of the ivory tablets found in the tomb), led Aimé-Giron to attribute the sarcophagus and the inscriptions to the 10th century B.C.E.[53] We also find this date totally acceptable.

The Ethbaal inscription is the earliest document from Byblos in the regular Phoenician-Hebrew alphabet. Several hundred years separate it from the pseudo-hieroglyphic and linear writings of the Middle(?) and Late Bronze Ages. Its letters are cursive and bear witness to a tradition of literacy. Hence, we may assume the Ethbaal script represents the end of a long process of development of the alphabetic script; but we know nothing at present of the stages of this evolution.

If the 10th century B.C.E. date for the Ethbaal inscription is correct, that of Abibaal must be later in time, since, as we have seen, the genealogy of Abibaal,

48 See especially, Dunand, *Byblia* (note 1), 139ff.

49 Montet, *Byblos et l'Égypte* (see note 12), 225ff.

50 The discovery of the two kinds of vessels was reported by R. Dussaud, *Syria* 5 (1924), 143; 11 (1940), 179ff. He attributes the Iron Age vessels to the 8th century B.C.E.

51 See in particular Montet, *Byblos et l'Égypte* (note 12), Pl. CXLIII, no. 856. The vessel is decorated with horizontal bands and concentric circles; cf. the similar vessel from Tell Abu Hawam, Level III in R.W. Hamilton, *ADAP* 4 (1934), 6, Fig. 8. The vessels in Fig. 99 (218) of Montet's book also belong to the early Iron Age.

52 See W.F. Albright, *Studies in the History of Culture* (1942), 34ff.; *idem*, *BASOR* 92 (1943), 9 in which the Ethbaal inscription is dated to the 11th century B.C.E., and at the latest to the year 975 B.C.E.

53 N. Aimé-Giron, *ASAE* 42 (1943), 284ff.

supported by palaeographic and linguistic evidence, necessitates a considerable lapse of time between the two documents. The most probable date is in the 9th century B.C.E. The fact that the King of Byblos engraved a dedication to Baalat Gebal on the statue of Pharaoh Shishak I gives us only a *terminus a quo*, i.e. that it cannot be earlier than the last quarter of the 10th century B.C.E. It is, however, very likely that Abibaal made use of the statue several generations after the campaign of Shishak. The same applies to Elibaal, who was separated from Abibaal by at least a generation, that of Yehimelek. For Elibaal's writing also we have only a *terminus a quo* — the time of Pharaoh Osorkon I, on the upper part of whose statue it was engraved. But nothing prevents us from attributing the inscriptions of Elibaal and his son Shiptibaal to a later period.

A *terminus ad quem* for the Shiptibaal dedication can, in my opinion, be set in the middle of the 8th century B.C.E. This is possible if we identify Shiptibaal with *Si-pi-iṭ-ṭi-bi-il-li*,[54] King of Byblos, who is mentioned in documents of Tiglath-Pileser III dating from 743–738 B.C.E. In one text he is referred to together with Jehoahaz (Ahaz), King of Judah; Panmuwa, King of Samʾal; Mittinti, King of Ashkelon and others. In another document he is mentioned with Rezin, King of Damascus; Menahem, King of Israel; Hiram, King of Tyre; Panmuwa, King of Samʾal and others — all of whom paid tribute to the King of Assyria.[55] This proposed identification suggests the following chronological determination for the inscriptions from Byblos: (1) Shiptibaal — the mid-8th century B.C.E.; (2) Yehimelek and Elibaal — the first half of the 8th century B.C.E.; (3) Abibaal — the second half of the 10th century B.C.E.

Historically and palaeographically, the proposal to date the Byblos texts in the 10th–8th centuries B.C.E. has *prima facie* validity. That of Shiptibaal includes a number of characters that are transitional in form between the classic Byblian alphabetic script and the later shapes. Some of them are later than the letters in the Mesha Stele of the second half of the 9th century B.C.E. This is true of one of the two forms of the ו and the ר, and especially of the ט and the ק, as it is of the ד on the ʿAbda vessel. On the other hand, it is undeniable that in all of the Byblian inscriptions we have discussed, the כ, מ and נ appear only in their archaic form, dating even earlier than the Mesha Stele, the Samʾal documents, and the dedication to Baal-Lebanon from the days of Hiram, King of the Sidonians (Tyre), who apparently was a contemporary of Tiglath-

54 The name should definitely be rendered as *Si-pi-iṭ-ṭi-bi-il-li* and not *Si-bi-iṭ-ṭi-bi-il-li* as was already recognized by K.L. Talqvist, *Assyrian Personal Names* (1914), 195b. For the rendering of *š* as *s* in Assyrian, compare for example *Samerina* — *Shomeron* — *Šamerain*. For the orthography, compare the name *Ši-ip-ti/e-baʿlu* in the El-Amarna Letters, where the West Semitic *s* = the Akkadian *š*.

55 Luckenbill, *AR* I, 276, §772; 287, §801. On the chronological problem, see especially E.R. Thiele, *JNES* 3 (1944), 155ff.

Pileser III.[56] They are likewise earlier than the Hebrew scripts from the 9th and 8th centuries B.C.E.

In the light of these observations, two possibilities can be raised:
1) The date of the Shiptibaal writing must be lowered to the middle of the 8th century B.C.E., and Shiptibaal is to be identified with *Si-pi-iṭ-ṭi-bi-il-li*, King of Byblos in the time of Tiglath-Pileser III. If this hypothesis is correct, archaic forms of certain characters were retained in the Byblian script until the 8th century B.C.E., whereas the shape of other characters changed in the course of time.
2) The Shiptibaal inscription must be dated earlier, in the 9th century B.C.E. If so, we must assume that this Shiptibaal preceded by several generations the Shiptibaal, King of Byblos, known to us from the documents of Tiglath-Pileser III. This theory has a palaeographic advantage, and better fits the evolution of the alphabet in the neighbouring countries, especially as regards the letters כ and מ. Consequently, bearing in mind the above comments on the *terminus a quo* of the inscriptions from Byblos and the suggested sequence of the kings of Byblos, we must date them as follows: (1) Ethbaal — 10th century B.C.E.; (2) Abibaal — end of 10th century to beginning of 9th century B.C.E.; (3) Yehimelek, Elibaal and Shiptibaal — 9th century B.C.E.

Finally, let me further review the principal comparative material from outside Byblos which has a chronological bearing on the dating of the Byblos inscriptions. We find the Byblian כ on a sherd discovered in the excavations at Tell Beit Mirsim, and apparently it should be attributed to the 10th century B.C.E.[57] In the Gezer Calendar, all the letters with the exception of ו are very similar to those of ʿAzarbaal, Yehimelek and Elibaal (see Table on p. 177). Unfortunately we lack the data necessary to date the Gezer Calendar. Archaeological considerations led Albright to date it around the second half of the 10th century B.C.E. He relied on the fact that Macalister did not find any middle Iron Age vessels in the Gezer excavations, and he therefore supposed that the city was destroyed at the end of the 10th century B.C.E., apparently at the time of Shishak's campaign.[58] It should be noted, however, that we have no decisive proof of the destruction of Gezer by Shishak. The date of the Calendar can be lowered to the time of Israel's wars against the Philistines prior to the reign of Omri (1 Kgs 15:27; 16:15). On the other hand, the agricultural calendar does not necessarily have to be related to a permanent settlement at Gezer. It

56 Yeivin, *Jewish Script* (see note 2), 121–122, attributes to the 9th century B.C.E. the votive inscription on a bowl found in Cyprus and dedicated to Baal Lebanon by סכן קרת חדשת עבד חרם מלך צדנם. On palaeographic and historical grounds this dating seems to me improbable. W.F. Albright, *BASOR* 83 (1941), 16, attributes the inscription to the 8th century B.C.E.

57 W.F. Albright, *AASOR* 12 (1932), 74 and Fig. 11. Albright claims that the sherd most probably belongs to Level B3 at Tell Beit Mirsim, i.e. to the 8th century B.C.E.

58 W.F. Albright, *AASOR* 12 (1932), 16ff.

is possible that it belonged to the owner of one of the local estates after the decline of the city,[59] and should be dated to the 9th century B.C.E.[60]

From the palaeographic point of view the inscription found by Honeyman in Cyprus[61] merits special attention. Its letters are similar for the most part to the classical scripts from Byblos, but there are certain distinctive features, such as the rounded א, the bar-shaped ו with round hook added at the left (compare the Shiptibaal form and the Gezer Calendar), and the ל rounded at the bottom as in the Mesha Stele. The Cypriot text also seems to belong to the 9th century B.C.E. In all events — like the Gezer Calendar — it must be pushed back to the time of Shiptibaal on palaeographic grounds.[62] Sardinian documents[63] provide us with a unique intermediate script. On the whole, the Sardinian letters resemble the classical forms from Byblos, but there are some in the Sardinian script which are lacking in the latter; the vertical line of the כ is extended on the right and its two other branches form an open angle on the left. The form of the ו resembles that of the Gezer Calendar, and in the ט there are two lines crossing each other, as in the Ethbaal inscription. There is a definite similarity between the Sardinian and the Samʾal documents, especially the Kilamuwa inscription from the end of the 9th century B.C.E. These writings provide additional support for our view that in the 10th to 8th centuries B.C.E., the consistency in the evolution of the Phoenician-Hebrew alphabet was not absolute, and outside influence and local features were adopted in various combinations in different areas. This helps us to understand the fact that in the Mesha Stele and in the Samʾal documents we find relatively archaic forms (like the ד, ו, ק and ר in the Mesha Stele) alongside novel forms.

In conclusion, I will mention the votive stele of Ben-hadad from the vicinity of Aleppo, published by Dunand[64] and studied by Albright,[65] and in which they hoped to find a date that could serve as an important landmark for palaeography. Albright explained the inscription on the stele as a dedication to בר הׄדד בר טבׄרׄ[מן ב]רׄ חׄזׄי[ן] מלך ארם, "Bar-hadad son of Tabrimmon son of Hezion, King of Aram" (cf. 1 Kgs 15:18). I have, however, examined the

59 The 7th century B.C.E. Assyrian contracts found at Gezer relate of an Israelite estate owner by the name of Netanyahu residing there; see B. Mazar (Maisler), *Tarbiz* 12 (1941), 120 (Hebrew); K. Galling, *PJb* 31 (1935), 81ff. If there were Israelite estate owners at Gezer in the 7th century B.C.E., probably they were also there in the 9th century B.C.E.

60 Palaeographically it certainly must be dated later, to the same time as the Ethbaal inscription. S. Birnbaum in *PEQ* 1942, 104ff. also attributes the Gezer Calendar to the middle of the 9th century B.C.E.

61 See A.M. Honeyman, *Iraq* 6 (1939), 106–108.

62 On this inscription, see also W.F. Albright, *BASOR* 82 (1941), 15ff. and Fig. 1.

63 *Ibid*., 17ff. and Figs. 2–3.

64 M. Dunand, *BMB* 3 (1939), 65ff.

65 W.F. Albright, *BASOR* 87 (1943), 23ff.

photographs,[66] together with my friend Avigad, and we can state categorically that Albright's proposed restorations are unacceptable. Even the letters read by Dunand as "Bar-hadad" must be restored in a different combination. After ב and ר, there are at least two and possibly three other letters, while line 2 begins with the דד. A well-supported date for this Ben-hadad inscription, therefore, cannot be determined, and it is impossible to draw from it the historical and palaeographical conclusions ventured by Albright and Dunand.

It is to be hoped that further discoveries will shed new light on the evolution of the Phoenician-Hebrew alphabet. At present, the material at our disposal is not sufficient to enable us to draw iron-clad conclusions about the various stages of development of the alphabetic script in the first third of the first millennium B.C.E., and still less about the beginnings of the Phoenician-Hebrew alphabet.

66 For further discussion of the Byblos inscriptions, see in particular W.F. Albright, *JAOS* 67 (1947), 153ff.; H. Donner and W. Röllig, *Kanaanäische und Aramäische Inschriften* (1964), nos. 1–8; J.C.L. Gibson, *Phoenician Inscriptions* (1982), 9ff.

Abbreviations

AASOR	*Annual of the American Schools of Oriental Research*
ADAJ	*Annual of the Department of Antiquities of Jordan*
AfO	*Archiv für Orientforschung*
AJA	*American Journal of Archaeology*
AJSL	*American Journal of Semitic Languages and Literatures*
ANET	*Ancient Near Eastern Texts Relating to the Old Testament,* ed. J.B. Pritchard (1969)
Antiq.	Josephus Flavius, *Antiquities*
AOAT	*Alter Orient und Atles Testament*
ASAE	*Annales du Service des Antiquités de l'Égypte*
BA	*Biblical Archaeologist*
BASOR	*Bulletin of the American Schools of Oriental Research*
BCH	*Bulletin de Correspondance Hellénique*
BIFAO	*Bulletin de l'Institut français d'archéologie orientale*
Bell.	Josephus Flavius, *Bellum Judicum*
BMB	*Bulletin de Musée de Beyrouth*
CAH	*The Cambridge Ancient History* 1–3 (3d ed, 1970–1977)
CdE	*Chronique d'Égypte*
CRAIBL	*Comptes Rendus de l'Academie des Inscriptions et Belles Lettres*
EA	J.A. Knudtzon, *Die el-Amarna Tafeln* 1–2 (1915)
EAEHL	*Encyclopedia of Archaeological Excavations in the Holy Land* (1975–1978)
EI	*Eretz-Israel: Archaeological, Historical and Geographical Studies* (Hebrew)
Enc. Miq.	*Encyclopaedia Biblica* (1950–1982) (Hebrew)
HTS	*Harvard Theological Studies*
HUCA	*Hebrew Union College Annual*
IEJ	*Israel Exploration Journal*
JAOS	*Journal of the American Oriental Society*
JARCE	*Journal of the American Research Center in Egypt*
JBL	*Journal of Biblical Literature*
JCS	*Journal of Cuneiform Studies*
JEA	*Journal of Egyptian Archaeology*
JEOL	*Jaarbericht van het Vooraziatisch-Egyptisch Genootschap "Ex Oriente Lux"*
JHS	*Journal of Hellenic Studies*
JKF	*Jahrbuch für Kleinasiatische Forschung*

JNES	*Journal of Near Eastern Studies*
JPOS	*Journal of the Palestine Oriental Society*
JSS	*Journal of Semitic Studies*
JSSEA	*The Journal of the Society for the Study of Egyptian Antiquities*
JThS	*Journal of Theological Studies*
KBo	*Keilschrifttexte aus Boghazköi* (1916–)
LdA	*Lexikon der Ägyptologie*
MDAIK	*Mitteilungen des Deutschen Archäologischen Instituts, Abteilung Kairo*
MDOG	*Mitteilungen der Deutschen Orient-Gesellschaft*
MGWJ	*Monatschrift für Geschichte und Wissenschaft des Judentums*
MVAG	*Mitteilungen der Vorderasiatisch-Ägyptischen Gesellschaft*
OLZ	*Orientalistische Literaturzeitung*
PEF QSt	*Quarterly Statement of the Palestine Exploration Fund*
PEFA	*Palestine Exploration Fund Annual*
PEQ	*Palestine Exploration Quarterly*
PJb	*Palästinajahrbuch des Deutschen Evangelischen Instituts für Altertumswissenschaft des Heiligen Landes zu Jerusalem*
QDAP	*Quarterly of the Department of Antiquities of Palestine*
RA	*Revue d'Assyriologie et d'Archéologie*
RB	*Revue biblique*
RdE	*Revue d'Égyptologie*
RE	*Real-Encyclopadie der Classichen Altertumswissenschaft*
RHA	*Revue Hittite et Asianique*
RHJE	*Revue de l'Histoire Juive en Égypte*
RHR	*Revue de l'Histoire des Religions*
Rla	*Reallexikon der Assyriologie*
RSO	*Revista degli Studi Orientali*
RT	*Recueil de travaux relatifs à la philologie et à l'archéologie égyptiennes et assyriennes*
VT	*Vetus Testamentum*
VT Supp.	*Vetus Testamentum Supplement*
WZKM	*Wiener Zeitschrift für die Kunde der Morgenlandes*
ZA	*Zeitschrift für Assyriologie und Vorderasiatische Archäologie*
ZAS	*Zeitschrift für Ägyptische Sprache und Altertumskunde*
ZAW	*Zeitschrift für die Alttestamentliche Wissenschaft*
ZDMG	*Zeitschrift der Deutschen Morgenlandischen Gesellschaft*
ZDPV	*Zeitschrift des Deutschen Palästina-Vereins*
ZthK	*Zeitschrift für Theologie und Kirche*

Abel, *GP*
F.M. Abel, *Géographie de la Palestine* 1–2 (1933–1938)

Luckenbill, *AR*
D.D. Luckenbill, *Ancient Records of Assyria and Babylonia* 1–2 (1925–1927)

Mazar, *Canaan and Israel*
B. Mazar, *Canaan and Israel, Historical Essays* (1974)

Mazar, *Cities and Districts*
B. Mazar, *Cities and Districts in Eretz-Israel* (1975) (Hebrew)

Septuagint Lag.
The Septuagint (Editio Lagardiana)

Am	Amos	Judg	Judges
Chr	Chronicles	Kgs	Kings
Deut	Deuteronomy	Macc	Maccabees
Ex	Exodus	Neh	Nehemiah
Ezek	Ezekiel	Num	Numbers
Gen	Genesis	Prov	Proverbs
Hos	Hosea	Ps	Psalms
Isa	Isaiah	Sam	Samuel
Jer	Jeremiah	Song	Song of Songs
Josh	Joshua	Zech	Zechariah
Jub	Jubilees	Zeph	Zephaniah

Indexes

*Biblical References**

Amos
1:3 167; 1:4 158; 1:5 160; 1:9 230; 1:9 76
3:9 186
6:2 196; 6:14 197

1 Chronicles
2:12–13 135; 2:13 91; 2:17 86, 130; 2:23 121, 158; 2:25ff. 149; 2:31f. 96; 2:33 149; 2:43 89; 2:43–45 86; 2:44 149; 2:47 94; 2:48 95; 2:49 135; 2:51 89; 2:53 96, 108, 129; 2:55 132
3:2 120; 3:5 95; 3:21 137; 3:23 137
4:2 108; 4:3 86; 4:4 94; 4:9–10 132; 4:11 148; 4:19 95; 4:20 149; 4:25 87; 4:39f. 54
5 57; 5:1–2 62; 5:3ff. 102; 5:9 191; 5:10 96, 102; 5:17 102; 5:18–19 102; 5:18–22 96
6 109; 6:56 122
7:21 38; 7:28 108; 7:31–40 46; 7:36–37 46
8:4 94; 8:13 38, 46; 8:33 135; 8:40 74
9:39 135
11:6 100; 11:8 44; 11:10 83; 11:10–47 90–96; 11:11 88; 11:23 91; 11:25 93, 101; 11:26 99; 11:27 93; 11:29 87; 11:35ff. 129; 11:42 101, 102, 127; 11:43–47 102
12 87, 89; 12:2 44, 74, 89; 12:4 89; 12:5 89; 12:7 91; 12:8 89; 12:9f. 96; 12:9–15 89; 12:17–19 87; 12:30 89; 12:38 102
13:5 195
14:7 48, 94, 135
16:39 89
18:8 195; 18:9–11 156; 18:10 130; 18:16 133; 18:17 133
19:6 125; 19:7 120, 125, 156; 19:10 155
20:5 93
21:15, 18 137
26:4 95; 26:30–32 109; 26:31 202
27:2 91; 27:4 91; 27:6 89, 93, 100, 103; 27:7 100; 27:10 94; 27:11 94; 27:15 94; 27:16 95; 27:30 86; 27:30–31 130; 27:31 96; 27:32 91, 131
29:29 86

2 Chronicles
1:3 89
3:1 51, 137
7:8 195, 196
8:3 198; 8:3–4 195; 8:3–6 157;

* The Books of the Bible are listed in alphabetical order.

References to Classical Literature

Ethnic Groups, Persons and Deities

Geographical Names